DEBATING U.S.–CUBAN RELATIONS

Two decades ago affairs between the United States and Cuba had seen little improvement from the Cold War era. Today, U.S.–Cuban relations are in many respects still in poor shape, yet some cooperative elements have begun to take hold and offer promise for future developments. Illustrated by the ongoing migration agreement, professional military-to-military relations at the perimeter of the U.S. base near Guantánamo, and professional Coast Guard–Guardafrontera cooperation across the Straits of Florida, the two governments are actively exploring whether and how to change the pattern of interactions.

The differences that divide the two nations are real, not the result of misperception, and this volume does not aspire to solve all points of disagreement. Drawing on perspectives from within Cuba as well as those in the United States, Canada, and Europe, these authors set out to analyze contemporary policies, reflect on current circumstances, and consider possible alternatives for improved U.S.–Cuban relations. The resulting collection is permeated with both disagreements and agreements from leading thinkers on the spectrum of issues the two countries face—matters of security, the role of Europe and Latin America, economic issues, migration, and cultural and scientific exchanges in relations between Cuba and the United States. Each topic is represented by perspectives from both Cuban and non-Cuban scholars, leading to a resource rich in insight and a model of transnational dialogue.

Jorge I. Domínguez is the Antonio Madero Professor for the study of Mexico and Economics and Vice Provost for International Affairs at Harvard University. He is a past president of the Latin American Studies Association.

Rafael Hernández is the Editor of Revista *Temas*, Cuba's leading magazine in the social sciences. He has been professor and researcher at the University of Havana and the High Institute of International Relations; Director of U.S. studies at the Centro de Estudios sobre América; and a Senior Research Fellow at the Instituto Cubano de Investigación Cultural "Juan Marinello," in Havana.

Lorena G. Barberia is a Program Associate at the David Rockefeller Center for Latin American Studies at Harvard University.

Debating U.S.–Cuban Relations

Shall We Play Ball?

Edited by Jorge I. Domínguez,
Rafael Hernández and
Lorena G. Barberia

Routledge
Taylor & Francis Group

NEW YORK AND LONDON

First published 2012
by Routledge
711 Third Avenue, New York, NY 10017

Simultaneously published in the UK
by Routledge
2 Park Square, Milton Park, Abingdon, Oxon OX14 4RN

Routledge is an imprint of the Taylor & Francis Group, an informa business

Library of Congress Cataloging in Publication Data
Debating U.S.-Cuban relations : shall we play ball? / edited by Jorge
I. Domínguez, Rafael Hernández and Lorena Barberia.
        p. cm.
   1. United States—Foreign relations—Cuba.
   2. Cuba—Foreign relations—United States.
   I. Domínguez, Jorge I., 1945- II. Hernández, Rafael.
   III. Barberia, Lorena, 1971-
   IV. Title: Debating United States-Cuban relations.
JZ1480.A57C8 2011
327.7307291—dc23   2011024005

ISBN: 978-0-415-89322-0 (hbk)
ISBN: 978-0-415-89323-7 (pbk)
ISBN: 978-0-203-80570-1 (ebk)

Typeset in Bembo
by HWA Text and Data Management, London

Printed and bound in the United States of America on acid-free
paper by Walsworth Publishing Company, Marceline, MO

We dedicate this book to our beloved *cuate*,

Carlos Rico (1950–2010),

pioneer Mexican scholar on U.S. policies toward Latin America,
teacher, ambassador,
exemplary as an intellectual and for his human integrity,
friend to so many whom he so generously helped in
Cuba, the United States, Mexico, and throughout Latin America

CONTENTS

TABLES

CONTRIBUTORS

Antonio Aja Díaz is a Professor, Researcher, and Director at the University of Havana's Centro de Estudios Demográficos and the Director of the Program on the Study of Latinos in the United States at Casa de las Américas. His teaching includes graduate courses on the sociology of migration, American society, race, and ethnicity. He has been a visiting scholar and professor at universities in Canada, France, Mexico, Puerto Rico, the United States and Venezuela. He has published books and articles in Cuba and other countries regarding Cuban migration to the United States and Venezuela, as well as on the factors, motivations, patterns and labor market configuration of these migratory flows. With Enrique Sosa, he is co-author of *Cuba y Cayo Hueso: Una Historia Compartida* (Editoral de Ciencias Sociales, 2006) and author of *Al Cruzar las Fronteras* (Centro de Estudios Demográficos and United Nations Population Fund, 2009).

Carlos Alzugaray Treto is a Professor and Senior Researcher at the University of Havana's Centro de Estudios Hemisféricos y de Estados Unidos and a member of the Cuban Academy of Sciences. He is a former Cuban ambassador to the European Union and to Belgium and Luxembourg and a former Cuban Minister to Ethiopia. He has been a visiting scholar at universities in the United States, Mexico, and Europe, and visiting professor at Beloit College, the University of the Basque Country, and the University of Winnipeg. He has published *De Eisenhower a Reagan: La política de Estados Unidos contra la Revolución Cubana* (Instituto Superior de Relaciones Internacionales, 1987), *De la Fruta Madura a la Ley Helms Burton* (Editorial Universitaria, 1997) and *Crónica de un Fracaso Imperial* (Editorial de Ciencias Sociales, 2000) and was one of the authors in *U.S.–Cuban Relations in the 1990s* (Westview Press, 1989). He has published widely on Cuban international relations, U.S.–Cuban relations, and varied international topics in Argentina, Brazil, Chile, Cuba, and Luxembourg.

Lorena G. Barberia is a Program Associate at the David Rockefeller Center for Latin American Studies at Harvard University. Since joining the Center in 2000, she has directed the Center's efforts to strengthen academic exchanges and deepen collaboration between Cuba and Harvard. With Jorge I. Domínguez and Omar Everleny Pérez Villanueva, she co-edited *The Cuban Economy at the Start of the Twenty-First Century* (Harvard University Press and David Rockefeller Center for Latin American Studies, 2004). Previously, she worked in Ecuador and Panama as a junior economist and on research projects at the Harvard Institute for International Development that focused on developing and transition economies.

Jorge I. Domínguez is the Antonio Madero Professor for the Study of Mexico and Vice Provost for International Affairs at Harvard University. He is the author of *Cuba: Order and Revolution* (1978) and *To Make a World Safe for Revolution* (1989), both from Harvard University Press; and, from Editorial Colibrí, *Cuba hoy: Analizando su pasado, imaginando su futuro* (2006), and *La política exterior de Cuba (1962–2009)* (2009). With Rafael Hernández, he co-edited *U.S.–Cuban Relations in the 1990s* (Westview Press, 1989). With Omar Everleny Pérez Villanueva and Lorena Barberia, he co-edited *The Cuban Economy at the Start of the Twenty-First Century* (Harvard University Press and David Rockefeller Center for Latin American Studies, 2004). He is a past president of the Latin American Studies Association. He co-edits the Routledge series of books on U.S. relations with Latin American countries.

Susanne Gratius is Senior Researcher at the Fundación para las Relaciones Internacionales y el Diálogo Exterior (FRIDE) in Madrid, Spain. She had worked as a Researcher at the Department of the Americas at the German Institute for International and Security Affairs (SWP) in Berlin and at the Iberoamerican Studies Institute (IIK, today GIGA) in Hamburg. Until 1999, she was Coordinator at the European–Latin American Relations Institute (IRELA) in Madrid. Her publications include "Why does Spain not have a Policy for Latin America?" *FRIDE Policy Brief 29* (with Thomas Legler), "Latin America is Different: Transatlantic Discord on how to Promote Democracy in 'Problematic Countries'" in *Promoting Democracy and the Rule of Law: American and European Strategies* (Magen, Risse and McFaul, editors, Palgrave Macmillan, 2009) and "Cuba, EE UU y Europa: perspectivas de cambio" in *Política Exterior*.

Rafael Hernández is the Editor of Revista *Temas*, Cuba's leading magazine in the social sciences. He has been professor and researcher at the University of Havana and the Instituto Superior de Relaciones Internacionales (ISRI); Director of U.S. studies at the Centro de Estudios sobre América for 18 years; and a Senior Research Fellow at the Instituto Cubano de Investigación Cultural "Juan Marinello" in Havana (1996–2008). He has taught as a visiting professor at various U.S. and Mexican universities and served as visiting scholar at U.S. and Latin American academic institutions. He has published widely on Cuban and U.S. policies, inter-American relations, international security, migration, and Cuban culture, civil society, and politics. He was founding editor of *Cuadernos de Nuestra América*, and coordinator of the Cuba exchange program with the Latin American Studies Association. With Jorge Domínguez, he co-edited *U.S.–Cuban Relations in the 1990s* (Westview Press, 1989) and with John H. Coatsworth, he co-edited *Culturas Encontradas: Cuba y los Estados Unidos* (Harvard University Press and David Rockefeller Center for Latin American Studies, 2001). He edited *Sin urna de cristal: Pensamiento y cultura en Cuba contemporánea* (Instituto Cubano de Investigación Cultural Juan Marinello, 2003) and wrote, with Dick Cluster, *The History of Havana* (Palgrave Macmillan, 2006).

Hal Klepak is a Professor Emeritus of History and Strategy at the Royal Military College of Canada and a Principal Adviser to the Minister of National Defense for the VIII Conference of Defense Ministers of the Americas. His research is in the fields of Latin American diplomatic and security issues, Canadian foreign and defense policy and conventional strategy. He has also directed the security program for the Canadian Foundation for the Americas (FOCAL). He has published *Cuba's Military 1990–2005: Revolutionary Soldiers during Counter-revolutionary Times* (Palgrave MacMillan, 2005) and *Confidence Building Sidestepped: The Peru–Ecuador War of 1995* (York University Centre for International and Strategic Studies, 1998), among other works.

Peter Kornbluh is a Senior Analyst at the National Security Archive, where he directs the Cuba Documentation Projects. From 1990 to 1999, he taught at Columbia University, as an adjunct assistant professor of international and public affairs. He is the author/editor/co-editor of a number of Archive books, including the Archive's first two documents readers: *The Cuban Missile Crisis, 1962* and *The Iran–Contra Scandal: The Declassified History*, both published by the New Press. He also edited *Bay of Pigs Declassified: The Secret CIA Report on the Invasion of Cuba* (The New Press, 1998). He is co-author (with William LeoGrande) of the forthcoming book: *Talking with Castro: The Untold History of Dialogue between the United States and Cuba*, from which his chapter on the 1973 Anti-Hijacking Accord is adapted.

Sheryl Lutjens is a Professor and the Director of Women's Studies at California State University, San Marcos. She is a coordinating editor of *Latin American Perspectives* and a member of the editorial boards of *Cuban Studies* and the *International Journal of Cuban Studies*. With Jennifer Abbassi, she is the editor of *Rereading Women in Latin America and the Caribbean: The Political Economy of Gender* (Rowman & Littlefield, 2002) and author of *The State, Bureaucracy, and the Cuban Schools: Power and Participation*

(Westview Press, 1996). Her current research interests include women, family, and gender relations in Cuba, Cuban educational policy, children and/in international relations, and questions of theory and methodology in the study of Cuba.

Milagros Martínez Reinosa is a Senior Advisor to the University of Havana's Vice Rector of International Relations and executive secretary of the university's Department of Caribbean Studies. Her research interests are focused on Cuban foreign policy and Cuba's relations with the Caribbean and the United States, in particular the history of academic exchanges between Cuba and the United States as well as Cuban migration. She has lectured at City University of New York, Florida International University, University of South Florida, Tampa, University of Florida, Gainesville, University of Pittsburgh, St. Thomas University (Minnesota), Carnegie-Mellon University, the National Autonomous University of Mexico, the Monterrey Institute of Technology and Higher Education in Mexico, the National University of Colombia, the Javeriana University of Colombia, and the Complutense University of Madrid, Spain.

Eduardo Perera Gómez is a Researcher at the Centro de Investigaciones de Política Internacional—CIPI in Havana, Cuba, which is a Havana-based think-tank that promotes research on global politics. He is a former member of Cuba's diplomatic corps and served as political advisor to the Cuban Ambassador to the European Union, Belgium, and Luxembourg from 2006 to 2009. His research focuses on European integration, Europe's relations with Latin America, and EU–Cuba relations. He is a faculty affiliate of the History Department at the University of Havana and the Instituto Superior de Relaciones Internacionales (ISRI) and teaches at both institutions.

Archibald R. M. Ritter is a Distinguished Research Professor Emeritus in the Department of Economics and the Norman Paterson School of International Affairs at Carleton University in Ottawa, Canada. He has also worked at the United Nations Economic Commission for Latin America and the Caribbean in Santiago, Chile, the Department of Energy, Mines and Resources, Government of Canada, and the Long-Range Planning Unit, Ministry of Planning and National Development, Nairobi, Kenya. He was Chair of the Economics Department at Carleton (2001–2004). He works on the international dimensions of development and on Latin American development generally, with a special emphasis on Cuba and Chile. He has published *The Economic Development of Revolutionary Cuba: Strategy and Performance* (Praeger, 1974); (editor, with J. Kirk) *Cuba in the International System: Integration and Normalization* (Macmillan, 1995); and *The Cuban Economy* (University of Pittsburgh Press, 2004).

Jorge Mario Sánchez Egozcue is a Researcher and Professor at the University of Havana's Centro de Estudios de la Economía Cubana (CEEC). He has presented his work at conferences, leading universities and research institutions in Belgium, Canada, France, Mexico, Trinidad-Tobago, and the United States. He focuses on international trade, macroeconomics, social and economic development, and the application of econometric models to monetary, exchange rate, and trade policies. He has been a visiting professor at the Institut des Hautes Etudes de l'Amérique Latine (IHEAL) at the Université Sorbonne Nouvelle and a visiting scholar at the David Rockefeller Center for Latin American Studies at Harvard University. He has published in Cuban journals and edited collections. He is also an author in *The Cuban Economy at the Start of the Twenty-First Century* (Harvard University Press and David Rockefeller Center for Latin American Studies, 2004) and in *Redefining Cuba's Foreign Policy* (University Press of Florida, 2007).

ACKNOWLEDGMENTS

The U.S. sponsor of the project has been the Harvard University David Rockefeller Center for Latin American Studies, supported by funds from the Christopher Reynolds Foundation. This Foundation has established itself as the leading philanthropist focused on the U.S.–Cuban relationship. We salute its statesmanship and are grateful for its patience with us over the past five years since the original grant. The Cuban sponsor of the project has been the magazine *Temas*, supported by the Ministry of Culture and the Cuban Film Institute (ICAIC), which published all of these papers in Spanish in Cuba in its special issue, volumes 62–63 (April–September 2010). Of course, many other institutions have supported or facilitated our individual work, and this time especially the ability to hold our workshop in Havana, attended by nearly all of the authors. Domínguez and Hernández are especially grateful to our co-editor, Lorena Barberia, the "worker bee" who has sustained this and other projects all along and to Kathleen Hoover who has helped put the book together. We are grateful to Dick Cluster for his superb work as translator, building on a distinguished career, informed also by his knowledge of Cuban history, culture, and politics. All of us have been honored by Vicente Bonachea, the artist who created the image for the special issue of *Temas* and the book. We recognize once again former U.S. Ambassador Richard Bloomfield, in the late 1980s president of the World Peace Foundation, for helping us launch and fund the 1989 book project. And we appreciate the support and patience of Michael Kerns, our Routledge Editor, for a project that took longer than he or we would have wanted.

A book of this type requires the work of many, and the good will of many more. We express our appreciation to all for making it possible for the project to reach a successful conclusion and the book to be published, and for enabling us to revisit this topic and our chosen approach to the topic two decades after our first undertaking. Thank you in particular, for allowing us to show again what two of the key actors in U.S.–Cuban relations, Barack Obama and Raúl Castro, have said in other contexts: Yes, we can[1] and Sí, se puede.[2]

Notes

1 "And where we are met with cynicism and doubts and those who tell us that we can't, we will respond with that timeless creed that sums up the spirit of a people: Yes, we can." Barack Obama, Victory Speech, Chicago, Illinois, 4 November 2008.
2 "Recordar como pudimos, a pesar de la confusión y desánimos iniciales, enfrentarnos a los duros primeros años del Período Especial a comienzos de la pasada década y salir adelante. Entonces lo dijimos y lo repetimos con más razón hoy: ¡Sí, se puede!" Raúl Castro, Camagüey, 26 July 2007.

ABBREVIATIONS AND ACRONYMS

AAAS	American Association for the Advancement of Science
AASCU	American Association of State Colleges and Universities
ACLS/SSRC	American Council of Learned Societies/Social Science Research Council
ACLU	American Civil Liberties Union
ACOREC	Agencia de Contratación a Representaciones Comerciales [Cuban Agency for Contracting Commercial Representations]
ACP	African, Caribbean and Pacific Group of States
ALBA	Alianza Bolivariana de los Pueblos de América [Bolivarian Alliance for the Americas]
ANEC	Asociación Nacional de Economistas de Cuba [National Association of Cuban Economists]
ASTA	American Society of Travel Agents
ATM	Automatic teller machine
BRIC	Brazil, Russia, India, and China
CAA	Cuban Adjustment Act
CAFTA	Central American Free Trade Agreement
CANF	Cuban–American National Foundation
CARICOM	The Caribbean Community
CBI	Caribbean Basin Initiative
CBTI	Caribbean Basin Trade Initiative
CDA	Cuban Democracy Act of 1992
CDC	U.S. Centers for Disease Control
CDI	Center for Defense Information
CEA	Centro de Estudios de las Américas

CEAP	Centro de Estudios de las Alternativas Políticas
CEEC	Centro de Estudios de la Economía Cubana
CESEU	Centro de Estudios de los Estados Unidos
CFSP	Common Foreign and Security Policy
CIA	U.S. Central Intelligence Agency
CIEI	Centro de Investigación de la Economía Internacional
CIPS	Centro para la Investigaciones Psicológicas y Sociológicas [Center for Psychology and Sociology Research]
CITMA	Ministerio de Ciencia, Tecnología y Medio Ambiente [Cuban Ministry of Science, Technology and the Environment]
CMEA	Council for Mutual Economic Assistance, also known as COMECON
COPA	Cooperative Programs for the Americas
CSA	Caribbean Studies Association
CUC	Cuban convertible peso
CUJAE	Instituto Superior Politécnico José Antonio Echeverría [Higher Polytechnic Institute José Antonio Echeverría]
CUNY	City University of New York
DEA	U.S. Drug Enforcement Administration
DG DEV	European Union's Directorate-Gerneral for Development
DG RELEX	European Union's Directorate-General for External Relations
DRCLAS	David Rockefeller Center for Latin American Studies
ECDET	Emergency Coalition to Defend Educational Travel
ELN	Ejército de Liberación Nacional [Colombian National Liberation Army]
ETA	Euskadi Ta Askatasuna [Basque Homeland and Freedom]
EU	European Union
FAR	Fuerzas Armadas Revolucionarias [Cuban Revolutionary Armed Forces]
FARC	Fuerzas Armadas Revolucionarias de Colombia—Ejército del Pueblo [Revolutionary Armed Forces of Colombia—People's Army]
FBI	U.S. Federal Bureau of Investigation
FDI	Foreign direct investment
FIU	Florida International University
FMLN	Frente Farabundo Martí para la Liberación Nacional [Farabundo Martí National Liberation Front]
GSP	Generalized System of Preferences
GTMO	U.S. base near Guantánamo, Cuba
IADB	Inter-American Development Bank
IATCD	International Agricultural Trade and Development Center
IFSA	Institute for Study Abroad

ILO	International Labor Organization
INS	U.S. Immigration and Naturalization Service
IPK	Instituto de Medicina Tropical "Pedro Kourí" [Tropical Medicine Institute Pedro Kourí]
ISRI	Instituto Superior de Relaciones Internacionales [Higher Institute for International Relations]
LASA	Latin American Studies Association
MIA	Missing in action
MN	Moneda nacional or Cuban peso
NGO	Non-governmental organization
NSC	U.S. National Security Council
OAS	Organization of American States
OCLC	Online Computer Library Center
ODA	Official development assistance
OFAC	Office of Foreign Assets Control
PAHO	Pan American Health Organization
PCC	Partido Comunista de Cuba [Cuban Communist Party]
POWs	Prisoners of war
PP	Partido Popular [People's Party in Spain]
PSOE	Partido Socialista Obrero Español [Spanish Socialist Workers' Party]
SMCEs	Small, medium and cooperative enterprises
TGF	Tropas Guarda Fronteras [Cuban Coast Guard]
UNEAC	Unión de Escritores y Artistas de Cuba [Cuban Writers' and Artists' Union]
USAID	United States Agency for International Development
USCG	U.S. Coast Guard
USCIS	U.S. Bureau of Citizenship and Immigration Services
USITC	U.S. International Trade Commission
USSR	Union of Soviet Socialist Republics
WTO	World Trade Organization

1

INTRODUCTION

*JORGE I. DOMÍNGUEZ AND
RAFAEL HERNÁNDEZ*

"The purpose of scholarship," we wrote in 1988 as our opening sentences for the book of which this is the sequel, "is to shed light on issues, not to settle disputes that lie properly in the domain of government officials. However, scholars can respond to moments when officials review issues to confirm existing policies or to change them."[1] At the time, we thought that the moment would be propitious for a re-examination of U.S.–Cuban relations. The Cold War was coming to an end in Europe. Cuba and the United States had been key players in the southern African settlement negotiations that would bring independence to Namibia, the end of apartheid to South Africa, and international security to Angola. The United States and Cuba had also reached a bilateral agreement on migration. Other small steps were being taken in the bilateral realm that might facilitate a change in the relations between the U.S. and Cuban governments. At the end of 1988, moreover, the United States would elect a new president. "Should the governments of the United States and Cuba choose to continue on the path of negotiations in the 1990s," we concluded, "they will be able to say that they are building on the policies that they agreed to launch during the closing eighteen months of Ronald Reagan's presidency."[2]

We were not wrong in thinking that the moment was propitious for substantial change in U.S.–Cuban relations. But we were wrong in our barely-concealed optimism that such change might happen in the 1990s. A colleague, Dr. Abraham Lowenthal, often urges others to distinguish "wishful thinking," which is rarely helpful, from "thoughtful wishing," which often can be. Then, as today, we believe that we are engaged in the latter. Today, as then, our goals are grounded in a reality that would benefit from change even as we proceed fully conscious that change remains difficult. Then we wrote, and today we reaffirm: "Our purpose in this book is to sketch where and why the United States and Cuba differ; to identify the issues where differences are likely to endure because they stem from the central values and interests of such different political and economic regimes; and to point to those other issues where skillful diplomacy might find joint interests to settle disputes in accord with these countries' respective national goals."

Nearly two decades apart, it is still the case that the differences that divide the countries and their governments are real, and not just matters of misperception or occasional ineptitude of some officials, although both of these factors have at times mattered. "Indeed, some of the differences in values and principles might not even be subjects for negotiation," we wrote in 1988.

Today the world is changing once again in ways that will open a new chapter in U.S.–Cuban relations. The worst financial crisis and economic recession since World War II broke out in 2008 and its consequences are still being felt. In addition, the U.S. role in the world changed considerably in the 2000s. The United States remains the one unrivalled superpower, yet its experiences in the wars in Afghanistan and Iraq have left it more reluctant to deploy massive military forces overseas, and the shock of the worldwide financial crisis may have rekindled its interest in international economic cooperation.

In February 2008, Raúl Castro became President of Cuba. In January 2009, Barack Obama became President of the United States. Former President Fidel Castro (born 1926) entered a hospital on 31 July 2006 and has been convalescing since then.

Today, as when we wrote in 1988, we believe that discussion is superior to shouting and that parties to a dispute ought to search for noncoercive alternatives to address the conflicts between them. Each side should pursue its interests effectively but also peacefully and honorably. Poor as U.S.–Cuban relations are in many respects, there are also cooperative elements in place—the continuing migration agreement, professional military-to-military relations at the perimeter of the U.S. base near Guantánamo, and professional Coast Guard–Guardafrontera cooperation across the Straits of Florida, among others. The United States has become Cuba's principal international supplier of food and important society-to-society initiatives are under way.

Therefore, in this book we are compelled to examine a process of U.S.–Cuban relations that has engendered internal contradictions. Some elements in U.S.–Cuban relations attract the two sides and induce cooperation between them, while other elements are rooted in conflicting interests, which repel one side from the other.

Debating U.S.–Cuban Relations: Perspectives and Structure

In this project as in its predecessor, we believed it valuable to ask two scholars to address the same general topic.[3] For each of the six topics, one author is a Cuban scholar and the other author is from outside Cuba. Each author brings a different perspective to the subject matter. Each chapter is written as a "thought piece," drawing on what is sometimes a lifetime of research on these topics. We think that it is especially valuable for authors to describe the "lenses" through which we seek individually to make sense of events.

The scholars who have joined our projects, this one and its predecessor, do not necessarily agree about the past, the present, or the future of U.S.–Cuban relations. Such disagreement is not a mistake on our part as project leaders. It was and remains a deliberate decision to represent a spectrum of at times diverging views, subject to the constraints of civil discourse. We believe that it would be misleading to create the illusion of agreement between scholars, if in fact they differ. Readers may gain more from a frank and transparent consideration of the issues. We celebrate the utility of differences to shed light on paths that could lead to eventual or partial agreement, without making such agreement a requirement for publication in this project. No one, therefore, should presume that any statement in this project is endorsed by anyone except the person making it. Quite the contrary, readers should presume the existence of disagreement. Out of those disagreements, readers should find light, not just heat.[4]

This book also arises from a willingness to engage in dialogue across academic disciplines regarding key problems at the heart of the conflict between the United States and Cuba. As with the book published in 1989, this joint work stems from a debate between political scientists, economists, historians, sociologists, and experts in international and strategic studies. Both times, we have incorporated parallel perspectives, each intellectually sound but also distinctive, which at times may oppose each other, in the belief that they would complement each other to give the reader a more accurate account not only of the "facts" but also of the state of thinking about these events and processes. We have not simply printed views that seek to undermine each other or to shout down everything that "the other" may have said but, rather, to present a joint approach built on multiple points of view to highlight the salience of, and impart depth to, the analysis of complexity in U.S.–Cuban relations.

The debate that informs this book took place almost twenty years after the collapse of the Soviet Union. We draw our authors from Cuba, the United States, Canada, and Europe. Many have known each other for years and have argued many of these points along the way. For this project, however, we also convened a workshop, held in Havana in February 2010, to debate their first drafts and enable the authors in their revisions to anticipate reasonable objections.

The authors were to think about the present, and what may have changed in the world and between these two countries, as well as within each of them, since the world-historic turning point between 1989 and 1991. The charge to the authors was to think critically about U.S.–Cuban relations, and look for gains, setbacks, or paralysis in the study of each topic, as its features may have changed in recent years. The chapters are mindful of the fundamental differences in values and interests that distinguish the political regimes in Cuba and the United States but also alert to the possibilities for cooperation between individuals or entities in both countries, as is already the case in aspects of their bilateral relations. Such incipient cooperation serves as a bridge between the two countries—albeit one still under construction. We urged the authors to think about bilateral relations in the context of change, not wedded to perspectives that may have been warranted in the past, and to roam beyond mere inter-governmental relations.

The purpose of the debate that gave birth to this book is to address, realistically and critically, the recent past and the present in U.S.–Cuban relations, in their full complexity and subtlety, to build a framework to assess the evolution of the conflict, as well as the examples of cooperation, evident in the accumulation of lessons learned by both sides in this relationship. These authors are not fantasizing about the future but grounding their thoughts about the future in actual experiences. Therefore, each chapter considers three key questions: what has happened, what is happening, and what if.

Each author was at liberty to define his or her own framework and evidence for the analysis but each chapter aims to do the following:

- At the start, identify the evolution of the main domestic and international factors and problems on the topic of each chapter, emphasizing the post-1990 years.
- Characterize the current state of relations, noting aspects of conflict, gains, setbacks, and prospects for change. Analyze policies on each side, both those in the bilateral realm as well as in the wider international realm that affect bilateral relations. Topics include the salience of foreign policy, internal or regional contexts, and the impact of domestic politics on foreign policy, including the role of governmental and private actors.
- Assess the future as it may be discerned from the prior analysis, envisaging both the persistence of present circumstances and the possibility of a wider change.
- Consider the prospects for cooperation if circumstances were to favor such a possibility. Could both countries build on the few areas of cooperation that already exist? In what ways would this serve the national interest? Are opportunities being missed or needlessly foreclosed? What lessons could be drawn from current instances of cooperation to think about how to better them or how to apply them to other areas? What dangers lurk and what obstacles may impede progress? In what way could accumulated knowledge be harnessed to build more productive relations?

We have selected six grand themes around which we have organized our joint inquiry. These are political, security, economic, and cultural issues and themes in U.S.–Cuban relations as well as the triangular relations that engage the United States and Cuba with the Cuban diaspora and with Europe, respectively. We have chosen authors whose work and seriousness of purpose we respect. We know them to be open to discussion with those who may disagree with them.

We believe that these are the more significant topics in contemporary U.S.–Cuban relations. We realize, of course, that others may miss some chapters. In contrast to the book published in 1989, this one has no chapters focused on the triangular relations that involve the United States, Cuba, and African countries, nor the first two with Latin American countries. Unlike the late 1980s, fortunately the United States and Cuba no longer harbor salient disagreements with regard to Africa, nor are such conflicts likely. There are also no salient regional conflicts in Latin America and the Caribbean that provoke clashes between the United States and Cuba, as was the case twenty years ago, even though both the United States and Cuba are quite active in the Americas. Nevertheless, the triangular relationship between the United States, Cuba, and Latin America deserves some attention, to which we turn in the next section.

The Triangle Between the United States, Cuba, and Latin America and the Caribbean

In the closing years of the Cold War, the United States and Cuba clashed over Central America (Nicaragua, El Salvador, and Guatemala) and south-west Africa (Angola, Namibia, and South Africa). Negotiations undertaken between 1988 and 1991—in the context of the collapse of Communist Europe including the Soviet Union—successfully removed the U.S.–Cuba dimensions from those wars as well as leading to major international and domestic changes in each of these two subregions. As a result of the Soviet collapse, Cuba had to redesign its foreign policy. Once regional conflicts were settled, Cuba repatriated its troops from Angola and Ethiopia. In the early 1990s, it would also withdraw its military missions the world over. Thus, in the early 1990s, Cuba had lost two key strategic assets: its privileged alliance with one of the world's two superpowers and its own military capacity to weigh in on conflicts in Africa and Central America. Cuba remained alone on the world stage—facing the United States.

Cuba had had bad diplomatic relations with all Central American governments except for Nicaragua's Sandinista government (1979–1990); with the defeat of the latter, the Cuban government was shut out from Central America in the 1990s. Moreover, Cuba had no diplomatic relations with Haiti or the Dominican Republic. And, although Cuba had relations with most Anglophone Caribbean countries, these had been chilled since 1983 when the United States and several Eastern Caribbean countries intervened in Grenada to overthrow its government and expel several hundred Cubans who had been assisting the fallen government.

In the face of uncertainty, Cuban leaders and their diplomats re-charted the course of Cuban foreign policy in the 1990s. Relations continued, albeit not in the military domain, with African countries, gradually rebuilding civilian cooperation especially in health care and education. Yet, the most noteworthy change was in the Caribbean Basin where Cuba established diplomatic relations and would in due course send its civilian cooperation to Guatemala, Belize, Honduras, and Haiti— all utterly unprecedented since 1959. Cuba's international civilian cooperation programs would also deploy personnel to Grenada and nearly all Anglophone Caribbean countries but also much further south, such as to Paraguay.

Cuba's diplomatic and economic engagement with Latin America took a sharp turn starting at the end of the 1990s, thanks to key domestic political changes in Venezuela, Bolivia, Nicaragua, and Ecuador, with the presidential elections, respectively, of Hugo Chávez in 1999, Evo Morales in 2005, Daniel Ortega in 2006, and Rafael Correa in 2007. All four became Cuba's allies after winning democratic elections from the opposition. On 14 December 2004, Cuba and Venezuela signed a far-reaching agreement to exchange Cuba's educational and health care personnel services for Venezuelan petroleum. This agreement became the foundation stone for the ALBA, the Bolivarian Alliance for the Peoples of Our America, subsequently joined by Bolivia, Nicaragua, and Ecuador as well as Dominica, St. Vincent and the Grenadines, and Antigua-Barbuda.[5] Moreover, during the course of the century's first decade, center-left politicians became the presidents of Argentina, Brazil, Chile, Panama, and Uruguay; diplomatic and trade relations and various forms of cooperation developed with these countries as well. Cuba closed the century's first decade with diplomatic relations with all governments in Latin America and the Caribbean, once Costa Rica and El Salvador established them. Cuba has diplomatic relations with 181 countries worldwide, in particular having rebuilt them with both Russia and China.[6]

These international changes, and in particular those within the Americas, produced a new framework for U.S.–Cuban relations. The U.S. government under the Bush administration aimed to isolate Cuba—that policy failed. Upon Barack Obama's election as President of the United States, the president *pro tempore* of the Caribbean Community (CARICOM), Baldwyn Spencer, also prime minister of Antigua-Barbuda, urged him to lift the U.S. trade embargo on Cuba.[7] At the summit of the Americas in April 2009, President Obama's first official trip to the region, the Cuba question reappeared. Cuba's was the only government in the Americas not invited to this summit yet its presence was felt from the start. President Obama announced what seemed like a change in U.S. policy toward Cuba:

> The United States seeks a new beginning with Cuba. I know there is a longer [applause], I know there is a longer journey that must be traveled to overcome decades of mistrust, but there are critical steps we can take toward a new day. I've already changed a Cuba policy that I believe has failed to advance liberty or opportunity for the Cuban people. We will now allow Cuban-Americans to visit the island … I'm prepared to have my administration engage with the Cuban government on a wide range of issues—from drugs, migration, and

economic issues, to human rights, free speech, and democratic reform ... I'm not interested in talking just for the sake of talking. But I do believe that we can move U.S.–Cuban relations in a new direction.[8]

As the following chapters will show, however, the changes that took place in U.S.–Cuban relations following this speech would turn out to be quite modest. One change that did occur after the summit of the Americas was the vote in June 2009 of the Organization of American States (OAS) to lift Cuba's formal exclusion from the OAS, which had been based on classic Cold War criteria, while retaining Cuba's suspension from membership because of the characteristics of its political regime. All along, however, the Cuban government had indicated that it had no interest in joining the OAS.

Cuba's principal foreign policy challenge is its relations with the United States, but this relationship also reverberates within and throughout the Americas. Thus the topic has become much more complex because of the multiplication of governments that think that the state of U.S.–Cuban relations affects them. This mixture of new domestic, regional, and global factors and actors that impinge upon the United States and Cuba came together especially in 2008 when the United States and Cuba each got a new president.

In the meantime, Cuba's boundary with the United States and with Latin America and the Caribbean became more porous. During the past half century, never had Cuba's social and political fabric been so exposed to the impact of the outside world. Well over two million tourists visited Cuba in 2010. They resembled in many ways those who flow throughout the Caribbean, providing significant economic resources but also posing serious challenges to the environment, public health, and the development and preservation of culture and society. Thus, in Cuba as elsewhere in the Caribbean, the permeability of borders uncovers arenas and passages that may lead to opportunities for cooperation.

Cuba, the Caribbean, and the United States share challenges that would be well addressed through cooperation at their borders. Think of hurricanes, and the opportunities to share meteorological information, cooperate to protect marine resources, and learn from these events about responses to other extreme events in the natural world. Also at their borders they could cooperate to enforce the rule of law, threatened by criminal networks, drug trafficking, and migrant smuggling rings. The potential for cooperation that the United States shares with the Caribbean island archipelago could, if implemented in practice, greatly advance the well being of millions of people.

Notes

1 Jorge I. Domínguez and Rafael Hernández, "Introduction," in *U.S.–Cuba Relations in the 1990s*, ed. Jorge I. Domínguez and Rafael Hernández (Boulder: Westview Press, 1989), 1.

2   Ibid., 2, is the source of this and the next two quotations.
3   We inserted Peter Kornbluh's chapter by itself, however, because it provided succinct and thoroughly documented information that supplements what is found in the other chapters.
4   This approach also explains some decisions regarding editorial style. We have left it to each author to choose the preferred word when referring to the Cuban "Revolution" or revolution, the U.S. "blockade" or "embargo," and Guantánamo, Guantanamo, or GTMO, among others. Most authors indicate their reasons for their word choices.
5   Honduras was a member of the ALBA in 2008–2009; a military coup in 2009 was followed by Honduras' withdrawal from the ALBA.
6   Cuba has an embassy in 120 of the 192 members of the United Nations; 103 governments have ambassadors accredited in Havana. See "La normalización de las relaciones Unión Europea–Cuba y las potencialidades de la cooperación al desarrollo," http://america. cubaminrex.cu/Actualidad/2008/Mayo/Intervencion.html.
7   *Prensa Latina*, November 6, 2008.
8   *Official Remarks of United States President Barack Obama at the Opening Ceremony of the Fifth Summit of the Americas*, 17–19 April 2009 (Port of Spain, Trinidad & Tobago, 17 April 2009).

2

INTIMATE ENEMIES

PARADOXES IN THE CONFLICT BETWEEN THE UNITED STATES AND CUBA

RAFAEL HERNÁNDEZ

It would be hard to find another area of international relations and political analysis that has suffered from such a curious burden of conventional wisdom and prejudgments as the relations between the United States and Cuba. In both political discourse and a good deal of interpretative analysis, the understanding of this conflict is constructed following a linear logic that reduces it to a mere bilateral interaction born out of the stubborn attitudes of one or the other actor and perpetuated in cyclical actions and reactions that continue *ad infinitum*.

This one-dimensional focus leads to circular reasoning, dead ends, and *reducto ad absurdum*, which in turn produce a fatal illogicality fed by two sources. One, the more general, stems from the perplexity of common sense when faced with politics. The second, however, stems from the arguments so easily accepted both by political reasoning and by many analyses thereof. Why is the U.S.–Cuba confrontation so stubborn and endless? Why do the two governments hold fast to confrontational courses that are, in many cases, counter-productive for both? This essay takes on aspects of the conflict, examining their "illogical" or paradoxical nodes. It attempts an alternative focus that goes beyond the "discord" between "two stubborn actors" trapped in their respective intransigencies. The essay seeks to understand the conflict in its greater political complexity.

Inverting the logic usually attributed to the conflict requires examining its other side, where actions or options of dialogue and convergence of interests can be found. Thus, I will try to explain both dimensions—*confrontation* and *cooperation*—not as incompatible phenomena or successive stages but as coexistent and, to some extent, mutually consistent. My hypothesis is that the same factors and issues that underlie tensions and confrontations also generate spaces of connection and understanding, though not necessarily of agreement. A corollary is that the equation of the conflict—

which involves not just two or three actors but many—operates in a contradictory way: although relations seem frozen still in the Cold War, currents of interchange now flow at various levels.

When we pierce the various "layers" of the conflict, at bottom we find a hard residue of distrust and ignorance, generated over the course of two centuries by hostility, hegemony, differences of scale, and insubordination. Yet this residue coexists with intense channels of communication between the two nations, which have emerged from their close geopolitical, cultural, and social proximity.

I will try to systematize some significant axes of these relations by way of seven paradoxes and to highlight briefly the basic elements giving rise to each.

What Are the Major Obstacles?[1]

In the immediate post-Cold War period (1991–2001), the two governments' objections and reactions to each other changed dramatically. Between 1959 and 1990, the United States accused Cuba of acting as a Soviet proxy[2] and exporting the Revolution to Latin America and Africa. The Cuban response was that neither its internationalism nor its alliances with governments or revolutionary movements were negotiable. With the demise of the socialist bloc in Eastern Europe (1989–91), the end of the conflict in southwest Africa (1988), and the cessation of the Central American wars (1988–90), Cuba was no longer an ally of Moscow (the USSR had disappeared), nor did it have troops in Africa or military advisors in the Sandinista army in Nicaragua or support the Farabundo Martí National Liberation Front in El Salvador in any way.

U.S. objections then shifted to focus on the system itself. Within this logic, Cuba needed to "create a market economy and democratize the political system"; this would lead to normalization. The Cuban reaction was "socialism or death." Within the Island's logic, Washington had to scrap its double standard and preconditions to deal with Cuba as it had with China and Viet Nam. How realistic were these alternatives?

In the first place, to what degree would internal economic and political changes in Cuba provoke a substantial change in the U.S. position? In the post-Cold War era, Cuba was no longer seen as a threat to U.S. national security. In the military-strategic realm, besides withdrawing its troops from abroad, Cuba had halved the size of its armed forces, maintaining only the minimum level of resources required for its self-defense.[3] In the economic realm, the state ceded important areas of agriculture, food supply, some domestic services and some small manufacturing to a non-state production sector and to markets where prices fluctuate freely. It undertook new policies, seeking foreign investment, expanding tourism, and opening the domestic market to the free use of hard currency. In the realm of political liberties, it broadened the public sphere and the spaces for expression of dissent, made migratory procedures more flexible, and allowed more space for NGOs. All this occurred during the so-called Special Period,[4] in spite of the impact of the crisis. None of these changes brought any relaxation of tensions from the U.S. side, nor even signals of desire for dialogue with the Island, but rather a reinforcement of the embargo (Torricelli Act, 1992). If we examine this dynamic over the course of the following twenty years, we find no indication that changes inside Cuba (short of a capitalist restoration) would lead to any progress in the two countries' relations.

Secondly, to what extent is there any historical and strategic basis for a projection of the changed U.S. policy toward China and Viet Nam onto the Cuban case? When the United States modified its relations with China in 1972, China was very far from the market socialism of today. Its main attraction for a politician like Nixon and a strategist like Kissinger was China's antagonism toward the USSR, marking a deep division within the socialist bloc and the international revolutionary movement. When the Clinton administration restored relations with Viet Nam in 1995, the most symbolic catalyst was not the country's economic liberalization but rather the opportunity to bring an end at last to the longstanding trauma of the U.S. prisoners of war (POWs) and missing in action (MIAs) whose remains had not been recovered.

Naturally, U.S. corporations were in favor of these diplomatic and commercial openings. But any comparison of these two cases with Cuba's must acknowledge the difference in scale between the geo-economic interests at play. If Cuba had a billion potential consumers or were located in a region with intense and dynamic financial and commercial galloping-growth such as that of the Asian "tigers," then U.S. policy would face utterly different challenges. But there are no Caribbean tigers, nor are Cubans tending to multiply (in fact, they are doing the opposite).

Finally, if one takes Washington's position toward the Island literally, the policy is not to demand mere economic reforms or some changes in the political system, but rather a fundamental break with its economic, social, and political order. Nothing indicates that the U.S. government would be content with a form of market socialism; it seeks nothing less that a capitalist restoration.

What Are the Main Forces Influencing U.S. Policies Toward Cuba?

During the Cold War, the supreme actor on the U.S. side was the national security establishment, that is, the organs of strategic command in foreign policy, all represented on the National Security Council. From their point of view, the entire political-economic framework of the Cuban state could be summarized by a single name: Fidel Castro. The post-Cold War period brought an unexpected change. According to U.S. officials and many analysts, Cuban policy thereafter would depend on the Cuban American National Foundation (CANF), which was thought to control the Florida vote and, therefore, had the power to maintain its hard line and block any move toward change by the executive branch or the Congress. Curiously, this idea found its mirror image in Cuba, which since that time has insisted that the "Cuban-American mafia" controls Washington's policy toward the Revolution.

In 2006 an unexpected change took place on the Cuban side when Raúl Castro took the reins of national policy. First as acting president, and then in full possession of the presidential post, he has offered "olive branches" to the North and expressed his willingness to talk about any subject as long as talks would be without preconditions or double standards.[5]

If we accept the portrayal of actors and forces in the above scenario, the hypothetical alternatives for solving the conflict would be: a) Cuba should negotiate with the Cuban American National Foundation; b) the Island's government should work toward promoting a new Cuban-American lobby that would overpower CANF; and c) the United States should recognize the significant change in Cuba's political situation.

a. It is quite surprising that two perspectives as different as those of Washington and Havana should find common ground in the idea that "the tail wags the dog" in their understanding of the equation involving CANF and the U.S. government. However, conceding such a determining weight to this lobby makes it hard to explain how the two governments could agree to negotiate a peace in Africa, sign migration accords (1984, 1995), and return the boy Elián González to Cuba, to mention only three very important negotiations that CANF radically opposed.[6]

b. For many years, a Cuban-American anti-lobby has been a potential alternative. Well-known Cuban-American individuals as well as Cuban-American associations, including some that are openly anti-Castro, oppose the embargo and favor dialogue with the current Cuban government. There are moderate figures with sufficient anti-communist credentials[7] for the U.S. government to accept them as legitimate "democratic voices requesting a new policy that would support the Cuban people's fight for freedom." What keeps them from competing with the right wing and CANF? More than any action by the Island's government, they would need to be recognized by the United States as a party with which to negotiate (as Reagan did with CANF in 1983).[8] A decision to deal with parties other than the extreme Cuban-American right—an option always available to the White House—would put moderate exiles front and center on the political stage and so legitimize a new chapter in Cuba policy.

c. If we accept as a fact that the main actor in Cuban politics has changed, then we are now experiencing the post-(Fidel) Castro transition, and the United States ought to be negotiating with Raúl Castro. Since that has not occurred, we must question the validity of the above hypothesis. Discussing those implications requires an understanding of other paradoxes that I will consider later in the essay.

What Political Circumstances Would Be Required, on the U.S. Side, for an Improvement in Relations?

Classically, at least three are usually cited: a) that Cuba must not be seen as a threat to national security; b) a Democratic president, because liberals are more given to negotiation than conservatives; and c) this president must be in his or her second term, no longer worried about winning the next election. I will examine each in turn.

a. As the post-Cold War period continued, the Pentagon and the intelligence community officially determined that the Island no longer represented a military threat.[9] For the same reason, new flashpoints of international attention—Central Asia, the Mideast, North Korea, China, Russia—took the Island's place on the primordial radar of the national security apparatus, which had directed Cuba policy for decades. Nonetheless, the policy did not change, precisely because presidents had their hands full with other grave national and international problems so the subject of Cuba rarely reached the Oval Office desk. The argument that there is no Cuban threat, paradoxically, now operates against any policy change.

b. A comparison of bilateral relations during the administrations of John F. Kennedy and Lyndon Johnson with those of Richard Nixon, Gerald Ford, and George H.W. Bush seems to show, on the contrary, that (with the lone exception of Jimmy Carter during his first two years, 1977–78) Democrats were no better at bilateral relations than the Republicans during the Cold War. The scarce evidence since the end of the Cold War simply shows that Clinton did not go to such extremes as George W. Bush. It is also likely that President Obama will be better than his predecessor, which, in general terms, is not saying much in favor of the Democrats. Naturally, for Cuba and for those who favor a change of policy, it is preferable to deal with a Jimmy Carter, Bill Clinton, or Barack Obama in the White House than with a Ronald Reagan or a George W. Bush. But no more than that. Over the course of half a century, the weight of this factor in terms of a change in relations has shown itself to be in practice secondary and insufficient.

c. The origin of the oft-repeated "second term" theory is an enigma. First, since 1959 and in the context of the Cold War, no Democrat managed to get re-elected so there has been little chance to test the hypothesis. Of the four presidents to win re-election, the only Democrat (now in the post-Cold War era) was Clinton. Unlike Reagan and G.W. Bush, Clinton did not threaten to use force against the Revolution but he did propose the document, "Support for a Democratic Transition in Cuba",[10] not exactly a step forward. Of the other three, Reagan's and G.W. Bush's second terms were hardly propitious for Cuba, but rather the reverse. In the case of Richard Nixon's second term, the relative détente of 1973–74 seems to have been Kissinger's work (as during the brief Gerald Ford interregnum), rather than the work of Nixon who was embroiled in Watergate.

If, notwithstanding, we were to accept the three axioms about necessary U.S. political circumstances as valid, we would have the following "logical" alternatives: 1) to wait for Cuban oil production to make the Island a net exporter, or for a Cuban–Russian joint venture to revive construction of the nuclear electric plant at Juraguá, or for some unexpected crisis to place Cuba higher on the list of the North's national security concerns; 2) to wait for a second Obama term in which he might be freer of current domestic and international political priorities.

With respect to the first, the Island's changing profile on the U.S. national security radar screen offers a perfect example of how a particular issue can be either a catalyst or an obstacle, a reinforcement or a threat to relations. It is likely that the Cuban government, nearly all the inhabitants of Cuba, and the oil companies would welcome growth in exploration and extraction of crude oil along the coast and in the area of Cuban mineral rights extending into the Gulf of Mexico. Washington lobbyists might join in such enthusiasm, including Big Oil, the most powerful interest group in U.S. politics, on a par with the military industries. But automatically, Cuba would also pop up on the radar screen of the Pentagon's preemptive war strategies. The same would occur in the case of any revival of the Juraguá project. On the other hand, in both cases environmental organizations and many citizens on both sides of the Florida Straits would fear the threat that such "advances" would pose to the natural environments of the southern United States and of the Island. As a result, any upward movement of Cuba on the list of national security priorities would usher in a contradictory situation, with potential costs and benefits, which would increase both opportunities and risks, uncertainty, and the volatility of the political climate.

With respect to the second alternative, even if the Cuban government joined the rest of the world in "voting" for Obama in the 2008 elections, it would not be advisable for it to plot a strategy based on the expectation of "a Democrat" who need no longer worry about winning "a second term" and who is willing to spend the political capital needed to change the fifty-year-old course of relations with Havana. There is no evidence to suggest that decisions postponed for "the right moment," "the best conditions," "step by step," etc., have been anything but wishful thinking. On the other hand, the Cuba issue's considerable "stickiness" to other internal and international affairs, such as possible crises in Central America and the Caribbean, the action of interest groups in local Florida and New Jersey politics, or media-manipulated and inflated concerns about particular events on the Island, confers a sizable stripe of unpredictability that would daunt the enthusiasm of any second-term-Democratic-president and his or her Cuba experts at the moment of choosing whether to take the plunge. For all these reasons, it is unlikely that any of these scenarios (whether or not they come to pass) could effectively lead to a process of real change.

What Political Circumstances Would Be Required, on the Cuban Side, for an Improvement in Relations?

From the U.S. point of view, at least three circumstances have been identified: a) Fidel Castro is out of the government; b) Cuba shows true political will to improve relations instead of sabotaging progress already made; c) Cuba makes the first move, offering concessions that constitute positive signals and responding to each favorable measure taken by the United States.

a.   Cuba has been governed by Raúl Castro since July 31, 2006, without any noticeable positive signal from the other side. Washington has not considered the change in presidents to be significant, and has even questioned whether Raúl is really in charge, rather than Fidel behind a screen.

b.   The examples cited as evidence that the Cuban government deliberately upsets any process of improvement in relations include such events as the opening of the port of Mariel to free emigration (April 1980) in the midst of a U.S. presidential campaign, and, especially, the downing of the small planes belonging to Brothers to the Rescue (February 24, 1996) when the approval or defeat of the Helms–Burton bill was being negotiated in the halls of Congress. According to this viewpoint, both in 1980 and in 1996 there was a process of rapprochement going on between the two countries, which the unexpected Cuban actions torpedoed. However, the fact is that in 1980, when the Cuban government opened the port of Mariel,[11] relations with the Carter administration had already cooled thanks to several Congressional incidents spurred by leading figures on the National Security Council and, above all, because of the change in the regional climate wrought in 1979 by the Sandinista revolution in Nicaragua and the New Jewel Movement government in Grenada.[12] In reference to the airplane incident, even before their downing and the approval of the Helms–Burton law, the president's discourse (and especially that of his Cuba advisors) failed to announce any alternative policies, but rather proposed a strategy of internal destabilization known as "Track II" (see discussion of Track II in chapter 3), which would complement the embargo.[13] According to the Cuban government, high officials of the U.S. administration were warned about the danger of a crisis in the run-up to both Mariel and the aircraft downing, and also about the need to take preventive actions, but these warnings fell on deaf ears. All the openings that unleashed migration crises (1965, 1980, and 1994) took place in the absence of any accords truly in effect; the Cuban measures, rather, have been ways of applying pressure to achieve such accords. As far as low-altitude violations of Cuban airspace are concerned, the

Cuban position has remained unchanged since the closing days of the Missile Crisis in November 1962.[14] To sum up: although in each of these cases one may view the Cuban response as very drastic, in none was it unpredictable. All the antecedents and historical patterns of behavior would have made it possible to calculate Havana's reaction, even the most extreme one.

c.   The most recent era offers new examples of *quid pro quo* as the logic required to build dialogue: "Cuba has not responded to the Obama administration's lifting of restrictions on travel and remittances by Cuban-Americans; the ball is in Cuba's court." "Cuba has to make [internal] changes to improve [bilateral] relations with the United States: free political prisoners, create a market economy, and compensate Cubans whose properties were affected by the laws of 1959 and 1960." The acceptance of that approach without debate is curious considering that the U.S. measures in question—to which Havana is supposed to respond—were based on presidential campaign promises made to South Florida voters, especially Cuban-Americans and their relatives on the Island, not to Raúl Castro's government.

If we hypothetically accept the U.S. logic regarding necessary political conditions on the Cuban side, we could imagine the following strategies and scenarios for Cuba: a) waiting for Raúl Castro's second term, in 2014, when sufficient time will have gone by for the United States to see his government as distinct from Fidel's; b) Cuba promising that none of Cuba's responses to U.S. policy would interrupt any real or potential dialogue or unleash any sort of crisis; c) Cuba responding to any U.S. measure with an equivalent one of its own, so as to encourage further policy change from the U.S. It is unlikely that any of these scenarios would prove realistic or effective in improving relations. In addition, the following may be added:

a.   Although for many Cubans Raúl Castro's administration has not done everything that needs to be done nor yet instituted the promised "structural changes," it would be difficult to demonstrate that his policies are simply more of the same. Muting the policy known as the "Battle of Ideas," which emphasized ideology and political mobilization along with reduced reliance on markets, providing state lands to private cooperatives, merging government departments and shrinking the state apparatus, replacing nearly all cabinet ministers and many other high officials (including practically the entire economic team), granting new licenses for self-employment, lifting restrictions on renting rooms and buying cell phone accounts in hard currency, ending compulsory attendance at residential rural high schools ("schools in the countryside"), and announcing impending reforms that imply a million layoffs, closing workplace cafeterias, and eliminating the ration book and other subsidized or free goods and services in order to balance the national budget—all of these reflect new policies and a different style of leadership. To analyze the present and future of these policies on the basis of the articles Fidel has been writing—most of them about international and historical topics—and to adopt the premise that he remains at the helm of Cuban policy reflects specious reasoning that is of little use to understanding these policies.

b.   Even recognizing the dangers that a crisis relationship with the United States implies for Cuba's national security, the balance has not always been negative. As a result of the Missile Crisis (1962), Washington committed itself to refrain from using its military forces to directly attack Cuba. Thanks to the migration crisis, the United States found itself forced to negotiate to reach significant agreements with Cuba and, in the last of these (1994), to change its immigration policy dramatically. It is true that in some cases involving military measures—like the downing of the aircraft in 1996—the decisions were very costly because of the danger of direct confrontation and their immediate political consequences. Nonetheless, since 1996 no air or sea craft coming from the United States has again violated Cuban airspace or Cuban waters. Thus, in real terms, even this controversial event reconfirmed the positions of both parties regarding violations that could unleash escalations that would endanger the national security of either side. In fact, the post-crisis forward steps affected both U.S. and Cuban policies. The outcome of the most recent migration crisis (1994) in the accords of 1995 led Cuba to commit itself to receive those who tried to leave illegally without applying any penalties, whether the individuals were intercepted by U.S. authorities or by the Cuban Coast Guard. The lesson of such experiences is not that Cuba should provoke the United States from time to time with a crisis, migratory or otherwise. Within its logic of avoiding an escalation of the conflict with the North, the Cuban government has maintained a severe stance toward the hijacking of ships, to the point of judging those responsible with the full brunt of the law and applying very drastic penalties. Nonetheless, the pattern of crisis-to-progress shows that Washington has sat down to negotiate with Havana only when obliged to do so by circumstances and in accordance with an issue of its national interest. This has occurred when a bilateral issue coincides with a larger global priority.

c.   This *quid pro quo* requirement contrasts with the rest of Cuban foreign relations, including those with European countries or the European Union, developed on the basis of international interests and not of preconditions that imply internal changes on the Island.[15] As that experience demonstrates, the closer the bilateral relations grow, the greater the chances that other countries' policies or experiences might be taken into account by Cuba.

Another construct unsupported by much evidence is the notion that a politics of *quid pro quo*—action and reaction in the face of measures by the other party— can lead to dialogue and normalization. Specific agreements about boat hijacking and migration,[16] *ad hoc* cooperation between the two countries' coast guard and meteorological services, licenses for academic exchange or the sale of food by U.S. companies, permission for overflights and dialogue between military officials at the Guantánamo base, opening and maintaining interests sections in the two capitals— all these have been significant individual measures. None, however, can be shown to have resulted from a policy of action–reaction, nor have they had the capacity to extend their effect to other areas of relations. With the exception of the emigration issue, which implies for the United States control of its southern flank and therefore a national security priority, no other issue has been resolved in any stable way by any multiplication of the isolated examples of cooperation, not even in such areas as drug trafficking, environmental protection, and prevention of natural disasters. Experience suggests that if some step-by-step policy process could work effectively, it may be a series of unilateral steps in which each party undertakes its own initiatives without tying them to the other party's response or seeing them contaminated or threatened by "lack of reciprocity."

How Feasible Is Any Mutual Agreement on the Democracy Issue?

If there is one issue that has occasioned deep disagreement not only between the two governments but between the two countries and political cultures, it is democracy. The U.S. idea that Cubans are unable to govern themselves and that the mission of the United States is to "save Cubans from themselves"[17] is much older than the Revolution. The Latin American viewpoint that "the United States seems destined by Providence to plague America with misery in the name of liberty" is at least as old as Simón Bolívar's famous phrase.[18]

Both during the Cold War and after, the respective positions on the two political systems have remained strictly symmetrical: Cuba is merely a totalitarian dictatorship, without a scintilla of democratic qualities; the United States is nothing but an imperialist superpower lacking in any democratic practice. Each side thinks that the institutions on which the other prizes itself do not function because they are anti-democratic and manipulated by a powerful elite. Each side thinks the other lacks a legitimate, fair, and truly popular electoral system and fails to elect the best officials. These perceptions can only lead to the following alternatives for solving the conflict: a) getting Cuba to change its opinion of democracy in the United States; and b) working toward a change in U.S. opinions about Cuban socialism. Apparently, then, these premises offer no glimpse of even the most minimal change in the two countries' relations, present or future. Still, let us examine them more closely.

a. Although Cuban anti-imperialism has been reinforced by fifty years of socialism, the attitude has been in existence since the colonial era. Although the U.S. system is not a model for the majority of Cubans, and they may find its imperial politics repugnant, still they believe that it is possible or at least desirable to coexist in peace with their powerful neighbor (even if it almost never proves itself to be a "good neighbor"). For the inhabitants of the Island, baseball, modern technology, the work ethic, business organization, and U.S. music and film have long been objects of admiration and cultural influence, in many cases for nearly a century and a half. These ties of singular intimacy, as President William McKinley put it, allow a Yankee to feel much more welcome and safer among the residents of Santa Clara, Bayamo, or Guanabacoa than in any city of the Middle East, Central Asia, or Africa, or even in most of the capitals of Latin America and the Caribbean.

b.   Even Cubans who criticize socialism find that the United States does not treat Cuba like other countries—China, Viet Nam, Libya, Saudi Arabia, and many more—that would not by U.S. standards qualify as democratic. Many are also surprised to see how accepting the majority of U.S. citizens are of their own version of democracy. Yet, it is improbable that the majority of Cuban socialists would take on the evangelizing mission of enlightening their Northern neighbors and converting them to the Cuban revolutionary ideology. Nor does it seem likely that average U.S. citizens would today take up the classic "white man's burden" in their stance toward Cuba and its problems.

If the question of democracy were so important to the United States in its relations with the Island, majority public opinion would not have come to favor normalization and the lifting of the embargo. This evolution does not imply that those in the North have stopped seeing Fidel, Raúl, and the Cuban system as totalitarian; rather, paradoxically, the existence of so foreign a political regime, maintained over half a century on the U.S. doorstep, has had more of a stimulating than a repelling effect. Many in the United States dream of visiting Cuba not only to enjoy its culture and society but also to "see Castro-style communism before it disappears," like those who might get excited about visiting some Jurassic Park to which they have been denied entry.

What Normalization?

For many, the formal break in U.S. diplomatic relations with Cuba in January 1961 and the legislative enactment of the economic embargo against the Island in February 1962 have embodied the "discord" between the two countries. In its current manifestation, this outlook may be summarized as follows: the lack of diplomatic relations between the United States and Cuba, along with the embargo, express the continuation of a conflict born out of the Cold War, whose *raison d'être* has disappeared. In terms of solving the conflict, this logic leads to the conclusion that normalization of relations and an end to the embargo would replace confrontation with peaceful dialogue, respect, mutual understanding, and non-interference in internal affairs.

The corollary of such a definition is that normalization of relations constitutes an end in itself. With the opening of embassies and the end of the trade and financial embargo, the two countries could begin to relate like any other two countries in the international system. Framed this way, the task is reduced to considering what political circumstances would allow for a process of dialogue–negotiation–diplomatic-normalization.

However, the issue of normalization is more complex than that of the conditions and desires which would lead to the negotiating table. The first question is: Have the United States and Cuba ever had *normal* relations "like any other two states in the international system"? Even before 1959, real U.S.–Cuban relations did not resemble others in the hemisphere. For the United States, the Cuba issue has always been closer to an internal affair than an international relationship. Both before and after the 1934 abolition of the U.S. Platt Amendment to the Cuban Constitution, relations with the United States determined a certain type of Cuban state, an economic and social order, a structure of power, and even a political culture.

If relations became *normal*, would they be like those that Washington maintains with Mexico, Canada, the United Kingdom, or Germany? Besides restoring the emblems that would identify the two embassy buildings and ending the embargo, what would distinguish these *normal* relations? It is not clear whether *normalization* would automatically imply abstention from interfering in affairs that the other party considers internal, or from political-ideological confrontation beyond "normal disagreements between any two states," or from the deployment of certain actors whom the other party perceives as destabilizing to its national security or sovereignty. The issue of normalization is more complex than it seems at first glance.

Recognizing its full significance, seeing it as something more than a technical juridical status, normalization would not be an end in itself but, rather, just a hope that certain problems of mutual concern could be subject to diplomatic dialogue.

What Real Role Does the Issue of Freedoms Play Between Cuba and the United States?

Historically, the government of the North has felt itself responsible for guarding the liberties of Cubans. The Cuban response, especially since 1898, has been seen by many in the United States as ungrateful. Regardless of their ideologies, part of the Cuban population is convinced that Cuba would be much better off if the United States would stop interfering in its internal affairs. The idea that this belief is associated with revolutionary ideology or socialism is only partly correct. Many on the Island, including non-communists, have understood their country's history as a repeatedly frustrated search for freedom, frustrated precisely by the U.S. presence in national life. These two clashing national visions could be expressed like this: a) "The U.S. commitment [is to] support the Cuban people against the tyranny of Fidel Castro's regime [through policies] that help them to bring the dictatorship to a speedy end;"[19] b) "No one who maintains an alliance or association with the United States, or receives its support, is a legitimate defender of Cuban freedom."

This irreconcilable polarity does not, however, imply that all Cubans reject any type of U.S. "freedoms," especially those associated with consumption, a variety of products, the comforts of domestic life, or the so-called entertainment industry from Disneyland to gambling, including the many incarnations of the "American Dream." This is the image of the North lodged in the minds of many Cubans who aspire to emigrate.

Now, if we consider the obverse of this polarity, we can see that, paradoxically, the search for freedom is also a powerful bridge connecting the two sides. Although the ideological poles repel each other, the social, cultural, and economic ones attract. In effect, *freedom to travel* and *freedom of commerce* today probably constitute the two greatest points of convergence between the two countries. In the long run, the notion of freedom could lead to unexpected routes of communication associated with deep historically knitted relations that persist parallel to the conflict, whose strength can be equal to that of the antagonism.

Areas for Cooperation

In the context of U.S. foreign policy, especially with regard to the Americas, the Cuban case stands out as a paradox *par excellence*. While Washington's Latin America policy is to promote free trade with many political and economic facets, the United States maintain a *total embargo* toward the Island, covering trade, finance, use of the dollar, banking ties, transport, goods of Cuban origin in third countries, purchases from U.S. subsidiaries in third countries, travel and temporary residence, monetary transfers to Cuban NGOs or others located in Cuba, and access by Cuban students to post-graduate programs in the United States. That is, the U.S. truly maintains a *blockade*.

An equally upside-down posture can be seen in the national security agenda, e.g., drug trafficking, illegal immigration, terrorism. In most Latin American cases this agenda is characterized by stagnation or antagonism, yet these particular areas are the ones in which there is the greatest degree of mutual understanding and cooperation with Cuba. As some observers have noted,[20] and as the Cuban government itself has recognized, U.S. military officials get along better with their Cuban counterparts and have more respect for them than they do with and for many others in the hemisphere, notwithstanding Cuba's inclusion in the U.S. list of terrorist countries.[21]

Paradoxically, although the "Cuban threat" lives on in U.S. political imagery as the heart of the conflict with the Revolution, there is no other state in the region with which the United States has achieved such a level of cooperation and substantial progress around these critical national security issues. On the basis of this concrete and specific experience, a layer of mutual trust is growing up, which sustained dialogue and negotiation could expand in the future on an opposite tack from that of negativity and strident rhetoric.

In a general sense, my point of departure is the conviction that both sides, Cuba and the United States, have a lot to learn from each other and a lot to gain from a process of rapprochement. I find curious the notion that, in a true revival of relations, it is Cuba that will reap all the benefits.

We should not underestimate the knowledge accumulated in specialized Cuban institutions, nor assume that the enterprising Cuban-Americans will descend on the Island to assume a tutelary role with their rustic cousins. Emigré professionals in countries that have active recruitment programs in Cuba (Canada, Australia), or in other countries such as Mexico, Chile, Finland, Spain, or the United States itself, do not behave as if their origin is a handicap. Many assert that their preparation in Cuba has been better than what is found in other latitudes.

Further, the fundamental context of the relations between the two sides is not limited to commerce and investment, even in a "strictly economic" sense. In the following paragraphs, I will sketch a group of concrete issues about which both countries have indicated interest and inclination to cooperate and have even sometimes achieved a degree of collaboration. The "two sides" in question are not limited to the high executive branches of the two governments; they include some official agencies, state governments, legislatures, companies, NGOs, civil society organizations, universities, cultural institutions, churches, and other entities.

Economy

Estimating the size of the Cuban market for U.S. trade or investment requires taking into account that the end of the embargo would create completely new conditions for economic and social development on the Island and would lead to change on a different basis than the current one. For example, it would offer new opportunities for non-traditional products and services (medical, educational, cultural, scientific, and sport) that, through cooperation arrangements like those already existing with Latin American and African countries, would be an alternative to the traditional view of Cuba as "the country of sugar, nickel, tobacco, and rum." On the other hand, understanding that process and estimating its significance for U.S. interests involves looking at the micro level, that is, at regional economies, various sizes of businesses, various market segments and niches, etc. where the linkages would really occur.[22]

Without an end to, or a progressive weakening of, the embargo, on the other hand, the fundamental circumstances will not change. Such a possible weakening of the embargo should not be confused with the licenses that have been granted on a case-by-case basis to certain U.S. corporations to sell quantities of food to Cuba through limited and restrictive authorizations and without bank financing or credits. The United States has not liberalized its policy toward Cuba. The embargo remains intact from the legal and practical point of view because it does not permit normal trade. Yet at the same time, these limited transactions suggest that, if the embargo were to end, a mutually beneficial economic exchange could unfold.

Among the areas for such cooperation are: research and development programs in a variety of sectors;[23] tropical, traditional, and "green" medicine; alternative production and sale of pharmaceuticals outside of transnational corporate control; public administration; institutional support for and development of cooperatives and small businesses; work organization; design of small and medium size firms; and more.

Public Health

As in most areas, bilateral relations in the health field are not starting from zero. In fact, the Pan American Health Organization (PAHO) has been one of the few hemispheric bodies in which Cuba and the United States have been able to sit down together. More than once, the Center for Disease Control (CDC) in Atlanta has cooperated with Cuban authorities in the response to epidemics of diseases such as hemorrhagic dengue and polyneuritis. Given that PAHO has identified the Cuban health care system as one of the best in the region, and given the importance of this issue in the domestic U.S. agenda (especially that of the current administration), existing ties could multiply. An example is helping victims of the Haitian earthquake. Despite suspicions about the presence of U.S. troops on Haitian territory, Cuba and the United States have held foreign-ministry level talks to coordinate assistance.[24]

Though with different connotations, the idea of the family doctor is in common use on both sides of the divide, as is the idea of preventive and community medicine. Mass education programs on the Island about HIV/AIDS and drug consumption, as well as the role of community and youth activists, are experiences of mutual interest.

Disaster Prevention, Environmental Controls, Civil–Military and Military–Military Cooperation

Cuba's installed capacity for confronting disasters constitutes infrastructure capital for international cooperation. The Cuban Civil Defense system includes the armed forces, scientific institutions, the mass media, and social organizations.[25] The base of this system is active participation by communities and social sectors directly affected, and by the population in general.

Although there is no bilateral treaty, the anti-drug-trafficking agencies of the two countries have collaborated on occasion. As has been reported,[26] Cuba cooperates in this sphere with European countries, which have supplied training and equipment to Cuba's Interior Ministry. Only White House policy is keeping the Drug Enforcement Administration (DEA), the Coast Guard, the Navy, the intelligence agencies, and the FBI from advancing their own work through an accord with Cuba like those they have with other Caribbean countries.[27]

In the area of armed forces relations, Cuba has promoted "agreements that offer all countries confidence in the use of the maritime and air spaces that surround them."[28] A preliminary list of specific plausible areas for bilateral and multilateral cooperation would include:[29] preventive protection against natural disaster; environmental monitoring especially of toxic substances in the Caribbean waters, nuclear materials, and epidemics; coastal protection; legal and community-based management of pollutants; protection of air and maritime security, saving the lives of illegal migrants, and prevention of piracy and hijacking; surveillance and interception of drug trafficking; military contacts to improve relations and mutual cooperation, trust-building measures in relation to military maneuvers, and information exchange; sports, historical, cultural, and academic encounters, and exchange of military delegations.

Public Sector Administration

In the current Cuban situation, movement from a highly centralized management system to one that is more participatory and less vertical has been recognized as a major axis in the "updating of the model"[30]—what some call the "path of reforms." Along this path to reorder the economy, free productive forces, and restore social development and the standard of living, the watchwords are decentralization, less bureaucracy, more participation and better control.[31] Such essentially political rather than purely "economic" priorities require that regional and local institutions must have greater control and decision-making power over their own resources.

Social Policy: Urban Problems and Social Development

A look at the agendas in this issue area reveals a long list of problems that would make fertile ground for exchanges of experience, such as: emphasis on social work and other forms of prevention and attention to the most disadvantaged communities; development of new mechanisms and participatory programs to confront poverty and marginality; policies for promoting blacks, women, and young people to responsible positions; treatment of the causes of human and citizen insecurity, and accessibility of public services and transport. In this field, Cuba now must seek and implement a new model of sustainable social development and it must move from a social policy of uniform benefits to everyone to one that is more decentralized, multi-focused, and sensitive to the actual needs of individuals.

Education

Cuba has accumulated vast experience not only in socializing education within its borders but also in international cooperation. This could be a basis for cooperation with the United States both at a basic level of social policy and in terms of educational quality (in comparison with the rest of Latin America), access to special education, etc. For its part, the Island could benefit in the areas of configuration of flexible curriculum, interactive pedagogy, making full use of information technology, etc. Some of the areas of exchange would be: literacy programs and mass basic education; curriculum design and educational administration; university-level education; training of teaching personnel; and distance education in technical fields and higher education.

Final Considerations

Cubans have become used to preparing for war with the United States, not preparing for dialogue and negotiation. High-level U.S. government officials have specialized in attacking the communist island, which has kept them from learning to understand it and to achieve their objectives by other means. Neither side is prepared to face an adversary rather than an enemy. Each side's success in a scenario of rapprochement depends on its ability to acquire such knowledge and turn it into real policy.

A change in relations should not be seen as a typical zero-sum game. Both sides can win substantial benefits and minimize their costs.[32] Following its own national interests, the goals of a new U.S. policy ought to be: neutralizing the neurosis that the Cuban Revolution has generated and continues to produce in the U.S. government; moderating current and future Cuban actions that may prejudice U.S. policies and goals; increasing U.S. ability to influence the politics of the Island in a general way; and obtaining greater benefits from specific areas of bilateral activity. None of those goals necessarily implies a friendly relationship with the Cuban regime, only a dialogue.

What does the United States have to lose and to gain in a dialogue-negotiation with Cuba? The costs could be: having to confront long-established resistance within the permanent bureaucracy, which continues across successive administrations, and from groups that carry out domestic politics around the Cuba issue, including the Cuban-American right wing; offering *de jure* recognition to the Cuban regime after half a century of non-recognition; submitting exchanges with Cuba to the terms of reciprocal agreements instead of the past unilateralism (for example, the launching of Radio and TV Martí, etc.).

The benefits would be: responding to a constituency of interest groups (agro-industrial, oil, biomedical, tourism-related) and freeing Cuban-American business people, previously hostages of established policies, to express themselves and organize in favor of tighter ties; lifting the embargo, paving the way for companies nationalized in 1960 to receive long-pending compensation under Cuban law; removing a point of contention with Latin America and with other industrialized countries threatened by the Helms–Burton Act, and easing the constant bilateral tension within international organizations; improving the flow of information between the two countries via legitimate exchange of radio and television programs, a fiber-optic cable connection, and improved mail, telephone, and internet service; consolidating the stability of migration agreements so as to avoid disorderly flows and crises; reaching formal agreements to cooperate in drug traffic interception, naval and air security, military and coast guard coordination, environmental protection, and other areas.

Pursuing its national interests, Cuba's goals can be defined as preservation of its independence, sovereignty, and national development model. With specific respect to the United States, they could be stated as "minimizing the level of hostility in effect since 1959." What can Cuba win and lose in a rapprochement with the North?

Among the benefits: winning recognition of the revolutionary regime, which favors Cuba's independence and self-determination; lessening the cost of security and defense, and the burden on economic development imposed by constant hostility and embargo; gaining access to U.S. markets and to U.S. capital flows, with a multiplier effect on all Cuba's foreign relations; improving relations with the émigré community; forming alliances or convergences of interest with various sectors of U.S. society; facilitating cooperation in areas related to geographic contiguity, such as those noted above; and acquiring a new platform on which to pursue the return of the Guantánamo naval base to Cuban sovereignty.

As far as costs are concerned, although many Cubans favor détente and appreciate its economic benefits, they also remain worried about its political and ideological effects. These could affect the national consensus in a period during which social and political cohesion is of strategic value. A wave of U.S. capital flooding a Cuban economy that has not completed its reform process could have some counter-productive effects. The U.S. government could try to steer the flow of capital to favor its political goals. Various groups—Cuban-American organizations, NGOs, other institutions, and the U.S. ideological apparatuses—would have more avenues to influence the Cuban domestic context.

Given the fundamental asymmetry of power between the two sides, once the words "let's play cards" are spoken, the "hands" will be quite unequal. If the United States were to reverse its policy and begin to "make concessions" in return for "equivalent Cuban responses," the government of the Island would find itself in an unprecedented tactical and strategic situation. This won't be one more round but, rather, a whole new rule book. In other words, with any increased chance of an alternative form of relations, the risk profile of *quid pro quo* increases. For Cuba, to take on this challenge could mean to adopt a conservative line and play defensively only; or it could mean to invent a new proactive strategy for the game. Within such a new approach, the ability to realign the available resources of political power would be decisive. Classically, the sources of political power in a situation of asymmetric confrontation lie in alliances and in consensus. This issue is complex both for Cuba and for the United States. Besides allied powers, affinities within the international system, and sympathetic ideological currents, the dynamic of rapprochement not only highlights and energizes the role of "rivals" or "opponents" but also that of "allies" within the "enemy's" own camp. The identities of such allies of the United States in the region, in Europe, and also on the Island are obvious. The allies of Cuba are also well known, paradoxically including novel ones such as many business executives and military officials who had classically been the "tips of the imperialist spear."

In a scenario of re-encounter between the United States and Cuba, both governments face the challenge of overcoming old dogmas, dealing with changes in the respective political consensus of each, trying to reshape those and restructure their alliances. The main weakness Cuba must overcome is not its lesser military or physical power but its siege mentality. That of the United States is not its ineptitude in dealing effectively with "communist regimes" but its sense of superpower omnipotence.

In the post-Cold War context, it is hard to maintain that the United States has the same bottom line as it did in the 1960s or 1980s, that is, to avoid at all costs the emergence of "other Cubas" in the region. (The current concern may be "other Venezuelas" or "other Bolivias.") Rather the new bottom line is to maintain a bilateral relationship with the Island that goes beyond the mere "damage control" of shedding an outmoded policy. The real bottom line of Cuban policy may be reduced to two principles: *no preconditions* and *no double standards.*

As to the game of *quid pro quo*: Cuban strategy in the past never accepted it, but in point of fact neither did U.S. strategy because so far the North has preferred negation to negotiation to a means to achieve its ends. If, however, bilateral rapprochement and diplomatic dialogue were to move forward, many new issues could appear on the table. The line Cuba would have to draw in such a scenario would be how to keep domestic political affairs within the area of dialogue rather than negotiation. The issues of structural transformation in the Cuban economic and political system, individual liberties of expression, movement, and association, the nature and role of the mass media, and other issues related to citizens' rights are not only "internal" affairs but they are also related to the "updating" of the socialist model. Therefore, to subject them to the dynamic of relations with the United States or any other foreign power could be politically counter-productive in terms of Cuban public opinion. A political will toward change, which would join the issues of this internal agenda to the conveniences of a more "harmonious" relationship with the neighbor, would lose legitimacy even in the eyes of those pushing for such changes within the Island. It would be something like subordinating the patterns of life within a family to agreements with the upstairs neighbor.

From the U.S. side, the course to follow would be dictated by the pragmatic character of its goals (damage control). Since the 1990s, liberal and conservative analysts have coincided as to the ineffectiveness of traditional U.S. policy toward the Island and on the advisability of excluding threats from the scenario of a change that might lead either to stability or crisis; that is, they have called for a *preventive* rather than *preemptive* strategy.

From the Cuban side, Cuban civil society from Communist party members to the Catholic church have reached a consensus that a U.S. policy of dialogue with

Cuba would contribute to depressurize the domestic atmosphere and facilitate the process of change, generational turnover in the leadership, and more decentralization of the system, and it would also contribute to empower the most constructive and valuable elements of both cultures and peoples. Even if we limit our focus only to members of the "socialist family" (those who prefer a transformed Cuban socialism, not a Caribbean or Latin American capitalism), they would be in a more favorable context to promote a more democratic model if some degree of détente with the North allowed the siege mentality to dissipate somewhat. If one listens to discussion of this subject as it is carried out in Cuba, one can tell that Cuban socialists aspire to a type of democracy different from that which predominates in Latin America and the Caribbean, which is defined as the end of military dictatorship and commitment to periodical elections within highly regulated multiparty systems.[33] The Cuban discussion points toward radical democratization of the society and system as a whole, including the production process, the community, schools, workplaces, economic management, and social and political organizations including the Cuban Communist Party.[34]

On the other hand, negotiating disagreements within a bilateral agenda does not mean an end to the networks of interests hostile to the Cuban Revolution. Normalization of relations does not imply de-activation of those sectors, nor does acceptance of a dialogue with the Cuban government require the United States to renounce its goal of restoring its influence within the Island. This issue will affect the future policies of both governments.

A closer relationship and a growing flow of communication between the two shores will cloud the "front lines" of the theater of conflict. Clear and distinct definitions of "inside" and "outside" will make less sense. The confrontation will shift to multiple spaces of the public sphere, linked in turn to the international arena, instantaneously reconfiguring the correlation of forces. For the Cuban government, the issue will no longer be how to keep the enemy from "penetrating" because in a certain sense it is already "inside," but how to reshape and promote the domestic consensus on a new basis. Beyond physical barricades or ideological trenches at specific points, the new situation places the issue of reactivating a political culture front and center, even if that culture was thought to be already established. This challenge cannot be reduced to one of mobilizing physical detachments at selected moments. It involves facilitating a mobilization of social consciousness that may get rid of established channels and old rituals that have lost their effectiveness.

How might the conflict change within the U.S. arena? Besides the "new allies" for Cuba mentioned above, a new Cuba–U.S. relationship would open up the unprecedented possibility of establishing other new relationships between Cuban-Americans (not only academics, but also members of organizations, institutions, and even businesses) and their counterparts on the Island. Would the Cuban-American elite keep paying its dues to the declining industry of anti-Castroism even as real business between the two shores prospers? Would its members hold onto their identities as ideologues rather than businesspersons or would they opt to behave like other historical emigrant groups (Vietnamese, Chinese)? This question makes little sense according to the conventional wisdom about the nature of this elite and its public self-presentation but a new relationship between the two countries would also bring a fundamental change in those circumstances.

Finally, to what degree can those hostile networks—the old jockeys of anti-communism and their Spanish-language editorialists—withstand the emergence of economic and strategic interests that, thanks to a political decision "from above," would broaden the terrain of contact between the two sides? To the extent that this new correlation of forces emerges and growing traffic across the Florida Straits displaces the volatility and fragility that characterized the previous political climate, it will become less likely that the old networks of hostility and the old bureaucracies can launch their classical torpedoes to destabilize the process of rapprochement. One defense against possible adverse contingencies and unpredictable threats can be, precisely, a multiplicity of ties. Beyond such contingencies, the conflict has already entered a transition phase. As often occurs between human beings and between their nations, when favorable circumstances arise, an apparently small step can unleash a march that exceeds all expectations. That unpredictable process has already begun.

Notes

1 I would like to thank the participants in the authors' workshop for this volume for their valuable comments.

2 U.S. Department of State and Department of Defense, *The Soviet–Cuban Connection in Central America and the Caribbean* (Washington DC: March 1985).

3 According to estimates by the Stockholm International Peace Research Institute, Cuban military spending dropped sharply from 4.2% of gross national product in 1989 to 1.6% in 1995, representing a 4.7-fold drop in absolute numbers. Armed forces personnel dropped from nearly 300,000 to barely 70,000. Stockholm International Peace Research Institute, *Cuba – Military Expenditures, Armed Force, GNP, Central Government Expenditure and Population, 1985–1995* (Stockholm: SIPRI, 1997).

4 "The changes provoked by Cuba's abrupt disconnection from the socialist bloc will have economic repercussions comparable only to those of a war, for which reason the scenario will be called a 'special period in time of peace.'" Translated from Colegio de Defensa Nacional (CODEN), *Defensa nacional. Unidad, independencia y soberanía* (Havana: Ediciones Verde Olivo, 1997), 83.

5 Raúl Castro, "Ningún enemigo podrá derrotarnos," interview in *Granma,* Havana, August 18, 2006, and "Discurso el 2 de diciembre de 2006," *Granma,* Havana, December 3, 2006; Agencia EFE, "Raúl Castro tiende un ramo de olivo al próximo presidente de Estados Unidos," July 26, 2007. On negotiating a prisoner exchange, see R. Castro's comment during the ALBA summit in Cumaná, Venezuela, April 16, 2009, available at http://cubadebate.superforo.net/politica-en-cuba-f1/discurso-de-raul-en-la-cumbre-del-alba-t1559.htm.

6 For a more detailed analysis, see the essays by Lorena G. Barberia and Antonio Aja Díaz in this volume.

7 Eloy Gutiérrez Menoyo, Alfredo Durán, María Cristina Herrera, Silvia Wilhelm, and Carlos Saladrigas, among others.

8   Raúl García, Lourdes Cervantes Vázquez, and Rafael Hernández, "La Fundación Nacional Cubano-Americana, y la conexión anticubana en los Estados Unidos" *Cuadernos de Nuestra América* 7, no. 1 (Jan.–July 1984): 145–173.

9   Defense Intelligence Agency, *Cuban Threat to U.S. National Security*, November 18, 1997.

10 William J. Clinton, *Apoyo para una transición democrática en Cuba*, Washington DC, 1997, available at www.state.gov.

11 Rafael Hernández and Redi Gómis, "Retrato del Mariel: el ángulo socioeconómico, *Cuadernos de Nuestra América* 3, no. 5 (Jan.–June 1986): 123–51.

12 See fuller discussion in Rafael Hernández, "La lógica de la frontera en las relaciones Estados Unidos–Cuba," *Cuadernos de Nuestra América* 4, no. 7 (1987).

13 Richard Nuccio, Cuban Affairs Advisor in the White House, summarizes the policy toward Cuba in two words: "pressure and contact … a similar strategy contributed to the collapse of communism in the former USSR." See "Nuccio defiende política de Clinton hacia Cuba," *El Nuevo Herald,* Miami, February 4, 1996.

14 See more extensive analysis in Rafael Hernández, "30 días. Las lecciones de la Crisis de octubre y las relaciones Estados Unidos–Cuba," in *Otra guerra. Ensayos cubanos sobre estrategia y seguridad internacional*, ed. Rafael Hernández (Havana: Editorial de Ciencias Sociales, 1999).

15 Cuba has embassies in 120 of the 192 United Nations member countries. Of these, 103 have accredited embassies in Havana. See "Intervención del embajador de Cuba" in the conference "La normalización de las relaciones Unión Europea–Cuba y las potencialidades de la cooperación al desarrollo," at http://america.cubaminrex.cu/Actualidad/2008/Mayo/Intervencion.html.

16 Press statement of the Cuban delegation to the February 19, 2010, round of migration talks with the United States, *Granma,* Feb. 20, 2010.

17 "We have given them the great gift of freedom and constitutional government, but we have never taught them how to use it. […] Our responsibility, therefore, does not end by giving to Cuba the forms and names of freedom. We have got to help keep Cuba libre by saving Cubans from themselves." George Marvin, "Keeping Cuba Libre" (World's Work, Sept. 1917, p. 67).

18 "Carta al Cor. Patricio Campbell," Guayaquil, August 5, 1829, at www.simon-bolivar.org.

19 Report to the President from the Commission for Assistance to a Free Cuba, May 6, 2004, http://state.gov/p/wha/rt/cuba/.

20 See essays in this volume by Jorge I. Domínguez and Hal Klepak.

21 U.S. Department of State, "Patterns of Global Terrorism" (Entry for Cuba), May 21, 2002, at http://www.state.gov/s/ct/rls/crt/2001/html/10249.htm.

22 The Center for Agricultural and Rural Development at Iowa State University stated: "Cuba has the potential to be *one of Iowa's top export markets in a number of key product categories.*" (www.card.iastate.edu). According to a representative of Louisiana: "If the strict trade sanctions were lifted […] the market size for U.S. rice could reach 800,000 MT, with Louisiana´s share totaling as much as 480,000 MT. *This is 14 times as much rice as Louisiana is currently selling."* Rodney Alexander, "Trip to Cuba Sheds Light on Untapped Market for Louisiana Producers," *Thoughts from Capitol Hill,* June 6, 2007, available at www.house.gov (emphasis RH).

23 David Cyranoski, "The Scientific Diplomat," *Nature* (January 20, 2010).

24 According to the Cuban Foreign Ministry, "Some actions of cooperation between Cuba and the United States have already taken place, in an effort to quickly confront the emergency provoked by the earthquake" and "It is expected that future interchanges of this sort will take place in that territory." See "EEUU y Cuba sostuvieron reunión de alto nivel en Nueva York sobre ayuda a Haití," *Escambray,* Sancti Spíritus, April 1, 2010.

25 See http://www.cubagob.cu/ingles/otras_info/minfar/defensa, y cor. José E. Betancourt Lavastida, "La prevención como estrategia en la reducción de desastres," *Defensa Civil de Cuba* (December 2007): 10.

26 See the article by Hal Klepak in this volume.

27 At various opportunities, Cuba has offered to collaborate with the United States government in this area, without achieving an agreement. See Fidel Castro, "Discurso en el Aniversario del 26 de julio," *Granma*, July 27, 1999.

28 CODEN, op. cit., 36.

29 Ibid, 45.

30 Raúl Castro Ruz, "Clausura de la Asamblea Nacional del Poder Popular," *Granma*, Havana, December 21, 2009.

31 Raúl has criticized "the tendency to apply the same recipe everywhere," and "those who think that resolution of every problem requires measures on a national scale." See "Conclusiones de la sesión constitutiva de la VII Legislatura de la Asamblea Nacional del Poder Popular," *Granma*, Havana, February 25, 2008.

32 Here I am returning to arguments put forward nearly two decades ago in Rafael Hernández, "Conflict Resolution between the U.S. and Cuba: Clarifications, Premises and Precautions," in *Cuba in the International System. Normalization and Integration*, ed. Archibald Ritter and John Kirk (London: Macmillan, 1995).

33 Public opinion and social movements in Latin America and the Caribbean have cast doubt on the party systems, the credibility of traditional political institutions, and the "partyocracy" itself.

34 In *Temas* magazine alone, the list includes Aurelio Alonso, "La institucionalidad civil y el debate sobre la legitimidad," no. 29 (2002): 36–45; Alfredo González, "Socialismo y mercado," no. 30 (2002): 18–29; Lilia Núñez, "Más allá del cuentapropismo en Cuba," no. 11 (1997): 41–50; Juan Valdés Paz, "Agricultura y gobierno local," no. 11 (1997): 63–75; Nelson Valdés, "El Estado y la transición en el socialismo: creando nuevos espacios en Cuba," no. 9 (1997): 101–111; Haroldo Dilla, "Pensando la alternativa desde la participación," no. 8 (1996): 102–109; Gilberto Valdés, "La alternativa socialista: reforma y estrategia de orden," no. 6 (1996): 101–112; Julio Carranza *et al.*, "Cuba: reestructuración económica, socialismo y mercado," no. 1 (1995): 27–35; Víctor Figueroa, "Los campesinos en el proyecto social cubano," no. 44 (2005): 13–25; Ariel Dacal, "¿Por qué fracasó el socialismo soviético?" no. 50–51 (2007): 4–15; Julio Díaz Vázquez, "Diez reflexiones sobre el socialismo," no. 53 (2008): 179–185; Julio A. Fernández and Julio C. Guanche, "Se acata pero … se cumple: Constitución, república y socialismo en Cuba," no. 55 (2008): 125–137; Hiram Hernández, syposium "Qué se para ti la Revolución: 50 años de Revolución: los jóvenes opinan," no. 56 (2008): 152–160; Mayra Espina, "Mirar a Cuba hoy: cuatro supuestos para la observación y seis problemas-nudos," no. 56 (2008): 132–141; Emilio Duharte, "Reformas y probables tendencias de desarrollo del sistema político cubano," no. 56 (2008): 121–131; René Márquez, "Meditaciones sobre la transición socialista cubana," no. 59 (2009): 147–156; Carlos Alzugaray, "Cuba cincuenta años después: continuidad y cambio político," no. 60 (2009): 37–47; the debates "¿Por qué cayó el socialismo en Europa Oriental?" no. 39–40 (2004): 92–111, and "Sociedad civil en los 90: el debate cubano," no. 16–17 (1999): 155–175; and the symposia "Miradas sobre el socialismo y el hombre: un simposio," no. 44 (2005): 93–121, and "Sobre la transición socialista en Cuba: un simposio," no. 50–51 (2007): 126–162.

3

RESHAPING THE RELATIONS BETWEEN THE UNITED STATES AND CUBA

JORGE I. DOMÍNGUEZ

- Cooperative and professional military-to-military relations at the land border.
- Cooperative and professional coast-guard-to-coast-guard relations at sea.
- Mutually beneficial market-conforming large-scale agricultural trade.
- Effective bilateral migration relations agreement between sovereign equals.
- Respective peoples value each other's music, art, and culture.
- Longest-lasting highly effective hurricane tracking professional relations.
- Large diplomatic missions posted at the respective capital cities.

Cuba and the United States are already, in some respects, exemplary neighbors. The list above is not social science fiction. It is accurate, even if most works on U.S.–Cuban relations do not start this way because they highlight the unrelenting hostility between the two governments.

When in the late 1980s I wrote my chapter for *U.S.–Cuban Relations in the 1990s*,[1] such a list could not have been written. Cooperative and professional bilateral military and coast-guard relations had yet to develop around the U.S. base near Guantánamo (hereafter GTMO)[2] and in the Straits of Florida. U.S. agricultural exports to Cuba, and Cuban payment in cash for them, seemed unthinkable. A bilateral migration agreement, signed in 1984, suspended, and then re-started in 1987, would be changed greatly in 1994–5. It was not difficult to imagine that bilateral academic and cultural relations might some day improve but that had yet to happen. Long-lived and successful relations between the Miami and Havana weather bureaus suggested the promise of increased bilateral cooperation on environmental and scientific issues but such wider prospects had yet to be realized. Only the diplomatic representation in each other's capital cities was in place. Nevertheless, the late 1980s and early 1990s was a significant turning point in the history of

U.S.–Cuban relations and in the relations between each country and the world. With the collapse of the Soviet Union and the end of the Cold War in Europe, the international system changed dramatically, also reshaping U.S.–Cuban bilateral relations more than the authors of *U.S.–Cuban Relations in the 1990s* imagined.

An extraterrestrial should be forgiven, therefore, for making a logically impeccable but empirically inaccurate inference. The extraterrestrial would have observed the change in the structure of the international system and in U.S.–Cuban relations in the late 1980s and early 1990s as well as the many concrete instances that followed in bilateral cooperation between the United States and Cuba, enduring even in the 2000s. The extraterrestrial would have inferred that the prior, broader international structural change caused the cooperative agreements. Wrong.

The cooperative bilateral relationships that developed between the United States and Cuba did not stem from a strategic reconsideration of bilateral relations; each was an *ad hoc* response to a particular problem. The two governments torpedoed new strategic grand designs, even though each built customized spaces for bilateral cooperation. The rhetoric of official relations was bellicose even as they reached concrete agreements.[3]

Why, then, was there a strategic failure but many tactical successes in relations between the U.S. and Cuban governments? Why did these governments fail to seize the opportunity presented by the changed international systemic context to build a different bilateral strategic relationship to foster cooperation over practical matters? Why did bilateral relations change so little during both the William Clinton and the George W. Bush presidencies? Will Barack Obama and Raúl Castro fail as well to seize the opportunity for a strategic change in their relations?

The International Strategic Window Opened Wide

The collapse of the USSR in 1991 had a major impact on the international system and on Cuba itself. By the early 1990s, one consequence was the resolution of the entire agenda of U.S. security concerns with regard to Cuba, as Gregory Treverton ably reported in *U.S.–Cuban Relations in the 1990s*,[4] to wit:

- Soviet offensive nuclear weapons based in Cuba.
- Cuba as a fortress for its own and Soviet military power.
- Cuban military deployments in Africa.
- Cuban military deployments in Latin America.

The disappearance of the Soviet Union cancelled U.S. concerns over the Soviet presence in Cuba. In part also as a result of this shift in the structure of the international system, Cuba repatriated its troops; such redeployments cancelled U.S. concerns over the remainder of Treverton's U.S. security agenda. *U.S.–Cuban Relations in the 1990s* analyzed the successful negotiations—in which Cuba and the

United States were key actors—toward the agreement to end the international wars in southern Africa and lead to South African troop withdrawal from Angola and Namibia's independence from South Africa. Those southern African negotiations were part of the process to end the Cold War between the United States and the Soviet Union.

Treverton accorded lower salience to a fifth U.S. security concern with regard to Cuba, namely, U.S.–Cuban disputes over revolutionary regimes and processes in Central America, even if other U.S. observers worried more over this issue area. Treverton, instead, noted the relative prudence that had come to characterize Cuban and Soviet policies in Central America by the late 1980s. Treverton wrote that "much will depend on the peace process and how both regimes and oppositions in Nicaragua and El Salvador fare in it." Writing in the same book, Juan Valdés Paz noted two features of Cuban policy toward Central America in the late 1980s, namely, "on the one hand, to give the greatest possible support for the people's movement against U.S. counterrevolutionary policies; on the other, to support a negotiated political solution to the conflict."[5]

The defeat of the Sandinista National Liberation Front in Nicaragua's election in 1990 and the peace agreements in El Salvador in 1992 and Guatemala in 1996 ended the Central American wars. The United States and Cuba played constructive roles in making and sustaining such agreements.

The agenda of U.S. security concerns with regard to Cuba disappeared—a propitious incentive for improved U.S.–Cuban relations. Both governments had shown vision and competence in working with each other to contribute to end wars in southern Africa and Central America.

Why, then, did these governments—creative, trustworthy, and capable at working with each other with regard to third-country areas—fail to build a new strategic bilateral relationship? The answer lies in discrete decisions, each of which at the time seemed rational to each side, although the result was adverse to a bilateral strategic settlement. Each government focused on the characteristics of the domestic political regime in Cuba. Each government responded to the other's foreign policy initiatives with suspicion; only the narrowest bilateral initiatives survived such scrutiny. Only twice since the early 1990s has either government sought to reshape bilateral relations comprehensively—the United States in 1995, Cuba in late 2001 and early 2002—but "the other" in each case was unprepared each time to respond. The U.S. and Cuban governments, for the most part, remained stuck within, respectively, "sanctions-alone" or "resistance-alone" policy frameworks.

The "Bush 41" Years: No Bilateral Strategic Window Opens

The George H. W. Bush administration refrained from building on its positive experience of negotiations with Cuba over peace in southern Africa (1989) and El Salvador (1992) in order to await the collapse of Cuba's political regime in the aftermath of the collapse of European communist regimes. In the bilateral realm vis-à-vis Cuba, this Bush administration, bold everywhere else in the world, chose to wait.[6] At that time, this decision seemed rational, even if it would prove inaccurate, because Washington expected that the Cuban regime would collapse once the Soviet Union disappeared.

The Cuban government had opposed most changes enacted in the late Soviet period under Mikhail Gorbachev. As European communist regimes tumbled, President Fidel Castro emphasized his government's commitment to the preservation of socialism as it had actually existed. The Cuban government had negotiated over southern Africa and Central America but it would not negotiate about its own political regime.

In the 1992 U.S. presidential election, Democratic Party candidate William Clinton outflanked the Bush administration on the political right in order to win Florida: he endorsed a bill whose main sponsor was U.S. Representative Robert Torricelli and whose main advocate was the Cuban-American National Foundation. The Bush administration had opposed this bill but, in the midst of his presidential re-election campaign, President Bush reversed course and endorsed the bill, which was enacted with bipartisan support as the Cuban Democracy Act of 1992 (CDA). The rational behavior of each candidate led to an outcome that neither would support as statesmen.

The CDA enacted tougher trade sanctions to prevent subsidiaries of U.S. firms located in third countries to trade with Cuba. It stopped Cuban agricultural imports from U.S. subsidiaries, which had amounted to 18 percent of Cuba's total trade in 1991.[7] The law enabled the Cuban government to claim that it was U.S. policy to starve Cubans.

The Clinton Years: A Bilateral Strategic Window Opens, Then Closes

Angry about these new sanctions, the Cuban government opposed with fury other provisions in the CDA, which came to be known as Track II and were implemented gradually in 1993–5. The CDA envisaged authorizing U.S. pharmaceutical or agricultural exports to Cuba, the donations of food and medicine to Cuban non-governmental organizations (NGOs), efficient telephone communications between the two countries, promoting academic and sports exchanges, easing Cuban-American travel to Cuba, opening news bureaus in both countries, and facilitating money remittances.

The Cuban government chose not to describe these U.S. measures as building blocks toward new bilateral relations and, instead, worried about their potential to destabilize its domestic political regime. It approached these new opportunities with caution and on a case-by-case basis, even though there was much for Cuba to gain. For example, by the mid-1990s Cuban-American remittances had become an engine for Cuba's economic reactivation, ranking with sugar exports and tourism among the top three sources of Cuban foreign exchange.

Cuba and the United States reached agreements regarding NGO donations and better telephone services. Cubans became participants in academic exchanges, especially with the U.S.-based Latin American Studies Association (LASA).The Cuban Academy of Sciences also worked with the Inter-American Dialogue to develop professional exchanges that could lay the groundwork for better cooperation over environmental and related sciences. The U.S. government responded to such Cuban initiatives with suspicion, at times discouraging U.S. participants from such events.[8]

Suddenly and unexpectedly, a bilateral strategic window opened. In the summer of 1994, a riot off Havana harbor—the first major disturbance since the early 1960s—led the Cuban government to permit unregulated emigration by boat or raft to the United States. By summer's end, the U.S. and Cuban governments negotiated a new bilateral agreement, expanded in May 1995. These agreements remain in force and have handled the lawful emigration of 300,000 Cubans to the United States.

Then, to avoid an accidental military conflict and enforce the respective migration laws in the Straits of Florida, the U.S. and Cuban governments negotiated *ad hoc* agreements to govern security cooperation between the Coast Guard and the Guardafronteras and between Cuba's Eastern Army and the military authorities at GTMO (during the 1994 rafters' crisis, many Cubans picked up by the U.S. Coast Guard were temporarily held at GTMO.) The Clinton administration refrained from publicizing these politically sensitive military agreements.[9]

The migration agreements and security cooperation along the Straits of Florida and the perimeter of GTMO came about because both governments took advantage of an accident—the 1994 migration crisis—to work together to open the bilateral strategic window. No one compelled them to respond constructively to a crisis that could have led to a worse outcome. Instead, the two governments framed their policies toward each other to foster cooperation.

In the United States, moreover, the political situation was propitious: the 1994–5 migration agreements were a setback for the Cuban-American National Foundation and its allies, temporarily freeing the Clinton administration from such entanglements. In October 1995, with bipartisan support, the Clinton administration defanged a bill sponsored by U.S. Senator Jesse Helms to tighten U.S. sanctions on Cuba; at the time, the U.S. Senate had a Republican majority.

The migration agreement, the security agreements, elements of the CDA's much-maligned Track II, and the propitious U.S. domestic politics could have been the cornerstones for a new strategic bilateral relationship. The U.S. government then launched a sustained effort to revamp its strategic approach, departing from a sanctions-alone policy; it would last until February 1996. This initiative would fail because its bedrock objective was to change Cuba's domestic political regime—the Cuban government's one non-negotiable item.

The architect of this short-lived albeit ambitious policy was Richard Nuccio, in May 1995 appointed special adviser to the president and the secretary of state for Cuba. Nuccio's Track II policies in fact had three tracks. Track II.1 sought to build support among Cuban-Americans to assist Cuban civil society to bring about change, weaning Cuban-Americans away from the sanctions-alone policy that their leaders had hitherto emphasized. Track II.2 re-oriented U.S. policy to help Cuban civil society. Track II.3 worked with Latin American and European governments to fashion a common policy toward Cuba, deliberately ceding leadership in the design of Cuba policy to the European Commission.[10]

Track II.3 succeeded most. In early February 1996, European Commission Vice President Miguel Marín met in Havana, separately, with President Fidel Castro and the leaders of Concilio Cubano, a newly formed Cuban human rights and opposition coalition. Marín requested the revision of laws criminalizing certain political speech-making and the authorization of small-sized businesses; he proposed expanded economic and political cooperation with the European Union. Marín had Nuccio's support and encouragement. No agreement was reached. Marín returned to Brussels empty handed. The Cuban government arrested the leaders of Concilio Cubano.

Then, on 24 February 1996, the Cuban Air Force shot down two unarmed civilian aircraft that had violated Cuban air space at times in the past, and at least one of them did so on that day; at the time of the shootdown, these airplanes were flying over international waters. The International Civil Aviation Association and the United Nations Security Council—with the votes of Russia and the People's Republic of China—criticized the shootdown. The U.S. government considered direct military retaliation against Cuba but, instead, enacted the Cuban Liberty and Democratic Solidarity Act of 1996, better known as the Helms–Burton Act. The executive branch also cancelled or made very difficult the collaborative endeavors of the preceding few years. For its part, the Cuban government imposed additional constraints even on its own think-tanks, impairing its own capacity to understand the world beyond Cuba. The bilateral strategic window shut.

Even so, both governments attempted conciliation. The White House backed away from enforcing Helms–Burton. Under the law, the President of the United States may waive the implementation of Title III, which would otherwise authorize extensive litigation over property claims in Cuba. Since July 1996, Presidents Clinton, George W. Bush, and Barack Obama have waived Title III without fail every six months. Thanks to negotiations with the European Union, the United States for the most part avoided applying Title IV, which would deny visas to executives of international businesses that "traffic" with Cuba. Moreover, on 16 May 1996, the United States unilaterally decided to deactivate the 14,000 mines around GTMO's perimeter; the process was completed by early 1999.[11] In January 1999, the U.S. government re-authorized most of the cooperative measures that it had permitted prior to February 1996, expanded this time to include organized cultural travel to Cuba to visit museums, works of art, etc., direct air flights, Cuban-American remittances, and academic exchanges.

Cuba also adopted cooperative policies. On 8 October 1996, Cuba and the United States cooperated in the capture of 1.7 tons of cocaine aboard the boat *Limerick*. In the late 1990s, Cuba proposed further cooperation with the United States to combat drug trafficking. In July 1999, the two governments agreed to facilitate coordination and authorize joint boarding and inspection of ships suspected of illegal activity.[12] But Cuban officials reacted angrily to the reappearance of Track II diplomacy, which the U.S. government now called "people to people" relations, although they welcomed the eased U.S. regulations regarding "cultural" tourism and other transactions.

In late 1999 and early 2000, the high-pitched emotional battle over the boy, Elián González, illustrates the importance of how U.S. and Cuban leaders "frame" their policies toward each other. The boy's mother took off with her son, Elián, to cross the Straits of Florida without either Cuban government authorization to depart or U.S. government authorization to enter. She died in the crossing; the boy's relatives in Miami claimed him. The father, still in Cuba, claimed the boy, to which he was entitled under the laws of Cuba and the United States, as both President Fidel Castro and President William Clinton agreed. The United States returned the boy to his father in Cuba.

The two governments could have celebrated the Elián incident as a breakthrough in bilateral relations, agreement between their presidents, and compliance with the rule of law. The Elián case could have opened the path to further cooperation (just as the 1994 rafter crisis did), not rhetorical thunderbolts. Instead, the incident generated intense emotional conflict. The bilateral strategic window remained shut.

The "Bush 43" Years: Cuba Reopens the Strategic Window, and Both Governments Close It

The Cuban government opened the bilateral strategic window in fall 2001, although the unfolding events had been unexpected by both governments. The window opened on 11 September 2001. President Fidel Castro's instincts were exactly right: In response to the terrorist attacks on New York and Washington, the Government of Cuba condemned such incidents and offered its sympathies to the United States. It also offered medical assistance and opened its air space and airports to U.S. or other aircraft in need of emergency diversion or landing.[13] In subsequent months, Cuba ratified all twelve United Nations conventions against terrorism.

That same fall, the Cuban government outmaneuvered the George W. Bush administration in negotiations over economic relations. In November 2001, the U.S. government proposed donations to Cuba in response to the devastation of Hurricane Michelle, issuing two statements: a respectful letter from the State Department, and an undiplomatic statement from the White House. Cuba deliberately ignored the second statement and responded only to the first, with comparably respectful language—an old diplomatic technique known as Trollope's ploy, the same ploy that the United States used in 1962 during the Missile Crisis in its negotiations with the Soviet Union. In 2001, Cuba proposed that it be allowed to buy food and medicine, paying in cash, making use of the U.S. Trade Sanctions Reform and Export Enhancement Act of 2000, enacted but not yet implemented. Cuba's proposal became the basis for agreement. By the end of Bush's first term in 2004, the United States accounted for 44 percent of Cuba's agricultural imports.[14]

On 11 January 2002, the Government of Cuba also reported that the U.S. Government had given it "ample and detailed information on the steps that would be taken" to house Afghan/Taliban prisoners at GTMO and "ensure that the security of our people is in no way jeopardized." Cuba vowed not to obstruct such deployments and refrained from increasing its troop presence around the base, even though more U.S. forces were sent there. Cuba pledged to "keep in contact with the personnel at the American naval base to adopt … measures … to avoid the risk of accidents." The Cuban statement emphasized that it would "make every effort to preserve the atmosphere of détente and mutual respect that has prevailed in the past few years," including additional medical and sanitation cooperation.[15]

On 19 January 2002, Cuban Armed Forces Minister, General of the Army Raúl Castro noted the climate of mutual respect and cooperation in relations between military officers along GTMO's perimeter evident for several years. He went on to say, "This minimal cooperation shows what might be in many other areas," adding "we are prepared to cooperate as far as possible."[16]

Cuba had been a valued participant in scientific and academic exchanges, a reliable partner in implementing the migration agreement, and a professional colleague over shared security issues. In the 1990s, it cooperated in instances of drug trafficking interdiction and proposed a wider framework for bilateral cooperation; the U.S. government demurred at the time. General Castro's remarks placed these other Cuban initiatives in a broader strategic context. Also in 2002, the Cuban government followed up on General Castro's remarks, making a comprehensive proposal to sign agreements with the United States over migration, terrorism, and drug trafficking.

U.S. officials did not take public note of Cuba's actions on 11 September or thereafter regarding terrorism, seemed embarrassed at being outmaneuvered into breaching the U.S. trade embargo, and acknowledged but otherwise dismissed Cuba's cooperation around GTMO or in the Straits of Florida. Nevertheless, there was some movement on the U.S. side.

In May 2002, former President Jimmy Carter traveled to Cuba. Undersecretary of State John Bolton sought to undercut Carter's visit by accusing Cuba of undertaking a limited offensive biological warfare research and development effort. U.S. Secretary of State Colin Powell undercut Bolton, stating that the only U.S.

evidence was that Cuba possessed advanced biotechnological research capabilities, not that it had undertaken a biological weapons program.[17]

On 20 May 2002, President Bush delivered the most conciliatory pair of speeches of his presidency regarding Cuba. By then, he had already waived implementation of Title III of Helms–Burton twice and had implemented its Title IV only lightly. In fall 2001, his administration had informed the Cuban government of its plans to send Afghan Taliban prisoners to GTMO. The two governments had agreed upon procedures for the export of U.S. agricultural products to Cuba. U.S. government rhetoric remained often insulting but its policies augured a possible "Nixon-to-China" scenario: a credibly anti-Castro U.S. president had greater freedom to settle with the Castro government.

The Bush speeches of 20 May 2002 were delivered in Miami and in the East Room of the White House. With many Cuban-American leaders in his Miami audience, the president emphasized that the future of Cuba would be in the hands of Cubans, which was why he proposed direct assistance to dissidents and civil society in Cuba. He stipulated steps for the Cuban government to undertake: free political prisoners, respect human rights and legal political contestation, permit independent civil society organizations and political parties, open a pathway to elections with international observers, and undertake additional market-oriented economic reforms. If the Cuban government were to adopt those policies, the president said that he would work with Congress to "ease the ban on trade and travel between our two countries."[18] And, in a paragraph included only in the East Room speech, the president affirmed, "Fidel Castro has a chance to escape this lonely and stagnant isolation. If he accepts our offer, he can bring help to his people and hope to our relations."[19]

The Cuban government dismissed the speech. President Bush's tone was harsh. The proposed U.S. funding for the domestic opposition signaled to Cuban leaders that Bush sought domestic regime change in Cuba—their non-negotiable position. Yet, Cuban leaders missed three elements in Bush's speech:

- He told Cuban-American leaders that they would not be the protagonists in Cuba's future.
- He spelled out his willingness to work with a government still headed by President Fidel Castro.
- He conditionally promised to accelerate the lifting of sanctions faster than the schedule spelled out in Helms–Burton.

Cuba could have ignored the offensive elements and, as in fall 2001 with regard to agricultural negotiations, employed Trollope's ploy. It could have taken up Bush's challenge, drawing from its own initiatives earlier in the same year while ignoring the harsh rhetoric. That was an opportunity foregone, a frame not chosen.

Cuban-American leaders understood why Bush's speech mattered. Their loud complaints quickly closed shut this policy alternative. They did not want to be subordinate to processes within Cuba. They knew that Helms–Burton excludes Fidel and Raúl Castro from a transition government (Section 205 (a) (7)) and that Helms–Burton restricts U.S. aid to Cuba during a transition government to very modest forms of food, medical, energy, and military demobilization assistance (Section 202 (b) (2) (A)). President Bush, instead, proposed to engage a Castro-led government, as if it could qualify for "transition government" status under Helms–Burton, to accelerate the lifting of U.S. sanctions on Cuba.

Between mid-2002 and March 2003, the bilateral strategic window shut tight. The U.S. government made clear in June 2002 that it was uninterested in Cuba's proposal for a broad agenda for bilateral negotiation.[20] And as the United States went to war in Iraq in March 2003, the Cuban government cracked down on the domestic opposition, imprisoning dozens of its leaders. The European Union imposed an array of mild sanctions on the Cuban government, to which the latter also responded in anger.[21]

In October 2003, President Bush created the Commission for Assistance to a Free Cuba. In May 2004, the Commission recommended, and the administration implemented, policies to impede society-to-society relations. Travel by U.S. citizens to Cuba became extraordinarily difficult. Cultural and academic exchanges became nearly impossible. Visas to most Cuban scholars were summarily denied; U.S. college study-abroad programs in Cuba nearly ground to a halt.[22] Cuban-Americans would be able to visit their family in Cuba only once every three years. The U.S. government dropped the word "peaceful" from its descriptions of U.S. policy toward a "democratic transition" in Cuba. The report dealt with Cuba's future in harsh, ungenerous, and ill-informed terms.[23] In July 2006, a differently constituted Commission issued a second report. It recommended some additional sanctions but it had some sensible statements. For example, the U.S. government "reassure[d] the Cuban people that the U.S. Government will not support any arbitrary effort to evict them from their homes."[24]

From mid-2002 onwards, neither Cuba nor the United States took positive initiatives toward each other. Nevertheless, the bilateral cooperation noted at the start of this chapter remained, waiting to serve as the cornerstone of a new relationship.

Raúl Castro and George Bush: U.S.–Cuban Relations Reassessed

In the moments that followed President Fidel Castro's transfer of power on 31 July 2006 to First Vice President Raúl Castro and a team of senior officials, the world was reminded about conflict scenarios for future U.S.–Cuban relations. Cuba mobilized its armed forces and called up its ready reserves. Some Cuban-American politicians in Miami called upon Cubans to rise up in arms. The U.S. government deployed Coast Guard cutters to prevent a massive emigration from

Cuba to the United States. In fact, nothing happened, but these events forewarn us that much could go wrong.

U.S. Secretary of State Condolezza Rice took a step on 6 August, stating: "But I want to lay one thing to rest. The notion that somehow the United States is going to invade Cuba because there are troubles in Cuba is simply far-fetched and it's simply not true … We are not going to do anything to stoke a sense of crisis or a sense of instability in Cuba."[25]

In his first public statement upon assuming Cuba's top job, printed on 17 August 2006, Raúl Castro reassured Cubans that all was well and proposed negotiations to the U.S. government to build better relations. He repeated the theme on 2 December, Cuba's armed forces day, the fiftieth anniversary of the *Granma* yacht's landing, and the delayed celebration of Fidel Castro's eightieth birthday. Not to be misunderstood, the acting president noted that Cuba would resist U.S. efforts to impose its preferences on Cuba.[26]

The Assistant Secretary of State for Western Hemisphere Affairs, Thomas Shannon, responded within the week of General Castro's first statement and within two weeks of the second. He resurrected President Bush's 20 May 2002 statements as the basis for U.S. policy toward Cuba, ignoring the two reports of the Commission for Assistance to a Free Cuba: "It is our view that Cuba's future has to be determined by the Cuban people, that ultimately no political solution can be imposed from the outside, neither from the United States nor any other country." Shannon reiterated Bush's expectations of domestic change in Cuba, noted that Cuba had not accepted them, but highlighted that "the offer's still on the table." Shannon went on to note, "what we're seeing [in Cuba] is a transfer of power to institutions and not to individuals," which corresponds to how Cuban leaders officially described the processes in Cuba.[27] On 13 December, Secretary Shannon returned to the description of U.S. policy as supportive of a *peaceful* democratic transition in Cuba. In words uncommon among U.S. officials, he commented on President Fidel Castro as possessing "a revolutionary legitimacy going back to the late '50s. He had a charisma, a political skill."[28]

Raúl Castro and Barack Obama

Barack Obama campaigned for U.S. president while saying little about Cuba. The United States was at war; its economy was in a tailspin—Cuba mattered less. He made three promises with regard to Cuban policy, however. First, he would facilitate relations between Cuban-Americans and Cubans, revoking the Bush administration policies that made Cuban-American travel and the sending of remittances exceedingly difficult. Second, as a worldwide policy, he would engage with any government to settle problems; he did not exclude Cuba from such a policy. Third, he would change little else in U.S. policy toward Cuba. By the end of his first year in office, he had fulfilled his first promise, taken some steps along the second, and tiptoed around the third.

On 13 April 2009, the U.S. government lifted restrictions (frequency, duration) on Cuban-American family visits to Cuba and on the frequency and amounts of remittances to relatives in Cuba. Also liberalized were rules regarding telecommunications links with Cuba and gift parcel regulations.[29] Four days later, at the opening of the Summit of the Americas, President Obama adopted a new frame: "To move forward, we cannot let ourselves be prisoners of past disagreements. I am very grateful that [Nicaragua's] President [Daniel] Ortega did not blame me for things that happened when I was three months old ... I didn't come here to debate the past—I came here to deal with the future." With regard to Cuba, he added, "I'm prepared to have my administration engage with the Cuban government on a wide range of issues—from drugs, migration, and economic issues, to human rights, free speech, and democratic reform."[30]

On 22 May the United States proposed and on 30 May Cuba accepted to resume the bilateral migration talks that President Bush had suspended in 2003. Both governments also agreed to discuss the resumption of direct mail service. Cuba proposed as well to hold bilateral talks on drug trafficking, fighting terrorism, and hurricane and disaster preparedness; the United States demurred. The first migration talks were held on 14 July 2009 and the first postal talks on 17 September 2009.[31]

President Raúl Castro at various times reiterated the views he had been expressing since August 2006 regarding his disposition to negotiate with the United States. His government would join the United States to resume discussions on migration and direct mail. On the eve of the Summit of the Americas meeting (from which Cuba was excluded), he broke new ground to affirm his willingness to discuss "any topic" with the United States, including freedom for those imprisoned in Cuba for actions against its government provided the United States would simultaneously free Cuba's so-called "Five Heroes"—Cuban agents whom the U.S. government imprisoned on the grounds of espionage.[32] U.S. Secretary of State Hillary Clinton welcomed President Castro's offer.[33] Days later, former President Fidel Castro, in his role as Op Ed columnist ("Reflexiones"), endorsed his brother's initiative, calling the willingness to discuss any topic an example of "courage and self-confidence in the principles of the Revolution." Fidel Castro compared Raúl Castro's offer to pardon those whom the two Castros called U.S. agents (otherwise known as dissidents), imprisoned in March 2003, to his own decision after the failed 1961 Bay of Pigs invasion to return the captured invaders to the United States.[34]

By the end of 2009, however, the two governments had rediscovered their skill at aborting opportunities for conflict resolution. As President Raúl Castro put it in his 20 December speech to the Cuban National Assembly, the U.S. government, which retained all the "instruments of its policy of aggression against Cuba, ... does not turn away from its effort to destroy the Revolution and generate a change in our social and economic regime." In late 2009, the president said, the United States had supported "subversion" in Cuba; he reported the arrest of a U.S. contractor (later identified as Alan Gross) operating in Cuba in support of civil society entities (Gross would be held in a Cuban prison without charges and for over a year). President Castro also denounced a "coordinated anti-Cuban campaign" to create the perception of increased repression in Cuba. He reiterated his pledge to resolve differences with the United States, still ready to discuss "any topic," but not if it were to imply changing Cuba's domestic regime. And he insisted that he was responding directly to Secretary Clinton's previous remarks.[35]

Consistent with Barack Obama's third promise during his presidential campaign, little else had changed in U.S. policy toward Cuba. The U.S. government remained committed to a change in Cuba's domestic regime. On 14 December 2009, in a broadranging speech on U.S. human rights policy, Secretary Clinton asserted that Cuba's government was "able but unwilling to make the changes their citizens deserve." She pledged to "vigorously press leaders" such as Cuba's "to end repression, while supporting those within societies who are working for change."[36] In November, President Obama had sent a statement for publication in Yoani Sánchez's dissident blog.[37]

The fundamentals of the U.S. policy of economic sanctions on Cuba had also not changed. Helms–Burton remained the law, though the president had waived Title III sanctions (as Bush and Clinton had). For example, in August 2009 the U.S. government fined the Australia & New Zealand Bank Group for helping Cuba and Sudan finance their international purchases. Later on, it compelled Credit Suisse to pay $536 million for processing payments for Iran, Cuba, and other countries under U.S. sanctions.[38] In October 2009, the U.S. Treasury denied a license to the U.S. Philharmonic Orchestra to take its donors to the concerts that it had hoped to perform in Havana; without the donors, the Philharmonic had to cancel the concerts.[39] Cuba remained on the list of states that support acts of terrorism; new U.S. antiterrorist measures announced early in 2010 failed to distinguish Cuba from other much more likely suspects.

Yet, an alternative reading of U.S.–Cuban relations was still possible as the century's second decade opened. Reread the list at the start of this chapter. All of it remained true and small steps were under way in both countries to strengthen means of cooperation. The Obama administration had quietly but systematically changed the policy on granting visas to Cuban academics, artists, and performers. The Bush administration had stopped nearly all of those visits; in 2009, U.S. visa processes returned to what had prevailed at the start of the decade. In January 2011, the Obama administration reversed most of the Bush administration decisions taken in 2004 that had stopped nearly all academic and cultural group travel from the United States to Cuba. The new rules would make it easier for such exchanges necessitating travel to take place.

In addition, the U.S. Treasury's Office of Foreign Assets Control had granted many specific licenses for trips to Cuba organized by sports, cultural, or academic entities, also matching the policy at the start of the decade. And in a decision brimming with symbolism, in April 2009 U.S. federal prosecutors added to the charges against Luis

Posada Carriles, who was in U.S. custody. Cuba holds Posada responsible for blowing up a Cuban civilian airplane and committing other acts of terrorism. The Cuban government took note of this decision.[40]

Moreover, U.S.–Cuban relations had become denser than they had been at the end of the Clinton administration. U.S. agricultural exports to Cuba were first authorized in 2001. In 2008, Cuba imported over $800 million from the United States; the United States had become Cuba's fourth most important import partner. And, although Cuba's tougher financial circumstances in 2009 led to a reduction of imports from many countries including the United States, Cuba still imported $85 million more from the United States in 2009 than it did in 2007 or than in any year when it had imported from the United States between 2001 and 2006.[41] By 2006, the United States supplied 96 percent of Cuba's rice imports and 70 percent of its poultry meat imports.[42]

The number of undocumented migrants interdicted remained fairly stable in the years since the 1995 bilateral migration agreement, though rising a bit from the late 1990s to the 2000s.[43]

Regarding narcotics, no government among the southern near-neighbors of the United States ever gets this much praise from the U.S. Department of State: "Cuba is neither a significant consumer nor a producer of illegal drugs … The U.S. Government does not have direct evidence of current narcotics-related corruption among senior Government of Cuba officials." The Obama administration noted some coordinated drug interdiction operations between Cuban security forces and the U.S. Coast Guard.[44] Indeed, the Cuban government, too, publicized its bilateral cooperation in drug interdiction with the United States.[45]

Barack Obama and Raúl Castro could work out many of their lesser differences but it was not likely that there would be a meeting of minds over the characteristics of the domestic regime in Cuba. They could use a cooperation frame, as they did during the first half of 2009, or a conflict frame, as they did during the second half of 2009.

Imagining Several Futures for U.S.–Cuban Relations

Scenario 0.

The prospects of Scenario 0 appeared in the hours that followed the transfer of powers in Cuba on 31 July 2006—military mobilizations in the United States and Cuba and a call to arms from zealots in the Miami Cuban-American community. Assume an accidental spark, and a conflagration ensues.

Scenario 1. "Clinton Plus."

U.S.–Cuban relations return to their level at the end of the Clinton administration. Some of this has happened already. There is already the cooperation noted at the start of this chapter. The two governments have re-started discussions on migration and begun them on direct mail. The U.S. government has begun to issue visas to Cuban artists and academics. In January 2011, the Obama administration reauthorized the "people to people" policies that permitted U.S. citizens to travel to Cuba for academic and cultural purposes (curriculum, undergraduate and graduate research, museums, monuments, musical concerts, and arts exhibits but not beach tourism) as well as exchanges of varying duration in the arts, sports, and related endeavors. Conceivable changes in this scenario include upgrading their exchanges regarding the GTMO perimeter and Coast Guard/Guardafronteras cooperation.

The "plus" in this scenario takes note that Bush administration authorization of U.S. agricultural product sales has continued, and that the Obama administration's liberalization of Cuban-American travel and remittances—already beyond the Clinton administration standards—would likely remain in force.

Cuba's domestic political and economic regimes change little. There would be no strategic re-thinking of bilateral relations. The U.S. government would retain sanctions on Cuba. The Cuban government would resist the United States.

This scenario would make it difficult for Cuba to develop its economy. Cuba's economic prosperity would remain tied to support from the Government of Venezuela under President Hugo Chávez. Yet, it hardly seems a winning long-term strategy for Cuba to hitch its star to highly volatile petroleum prices and to Venezuela, a country whose state has been, before Chávez and still under Chávez, far less competent than Cuba's—Venezuela must import tens of thousands of Cubans to deliver basic social services that the Venezuelan state cannot deliver otherwise. This scenario is compatible with the survival of a Cuban political regime headed by General Raúl Castro or his successors but not with Cuban prosperity.

Scenario 2. Bilateral Tactical Cooperation.

The two governments stop preventing each other's diplomats from performing their normal tasks in the respective capital cities and shift to vitriol-free official rhetoric to express disagreement. They enhance and institutionalize their cooperation to interdict drug traffic. They design an approach to collaborate against international terrorism. Cuba has proposed such cooperation in the past but the U.S. government believes that Cuba's initiatives "have not been offered with forthright or actionable proposals as to what the U.S. government should expect from future Cuban cooperation"[46]—a difficulty that active diplomatic negotiation may remedy. The United States would drop Cuba from its list of state sponsors of terrorism. (In January 2010, as part of its tightening of counter-terrorism measures, the Obama administration confirmed Cuba's inclusion on this list.)[47] Both governments expand academic and cultural exchanges much further, extending fellowship support to citizens of the other country for study at each country's institutions. They develop environmental and scientific exchanges, first by permitting nongovernmental organizations to take the lead, and then by undertaking inter-governmental cooperation. They start on topics of shared interest such as migratory species, hurricane tracking, oil and other spills in the Straits of Florida, and research on biodiversity. But that's all.

Scenario 2 differs from Scenario 1 because in Scenario 2 each government takes modest initiatives to which the other reciprocates.

Scenario 3. Obama Takes the Lead.

The Obama administration takes cognizance that, under Helms–Burton, the president may use his regulatory authority to permit exceptions to nearly every aspect of U.S. sanctions policy on Cuba except the authorization of free U.S. citizen travel to Cuba.[48] The administration would accept a proposal of Cuba's Foreign Minister Bruno Rodríguez:[49] the U.S. government would unilaterally and unconditionally lift all U.S. restrictions that prevent the free flow of information between the two countries, including facilitating Cuban access to information technology and the Internet. The U.S. government would authorize trade as well as donations in such products. The president would similarly license trade in medical products, thereby permitting some Cuban exports to the United States.

The U.S. government motivation would be to foster the conditions for domestic change in Cuba. The Cuban government would react with self-confidence, not outrage or panic, expecting to gain more from economic growth. Time would tell who is right.

Scenario 4. Raúl Castro Takes the Lead.

The Cuban government emulates the economic strategy successfully followed in China and Vietnam, leading to a market re-orientation of the Cuban economy. China would support it. Canada and the European Union would encourage it. Such a strategy would make it much more difficult for the Obama administration not to shift its Cuba policies and to do so much more quickly.

In September 2010, the Cuban government announced an array of potentially significant economic policy changes designed to reduce the number of government employees, expand self-employment, further facilitate the employment of contract labor by agricultural cooperatives, and other economic policy measures. The Communist Party of Cuba convened its Sixth Party Congress for April 2010 to discuss, widen, and deepen the scope of economic policy changes. These changes and proposals matter more as forecasts for a possible future than for their actual content in 2010 and 2011, however. The changed economic policies remain cumbersome and restrictive, a far cry from the economic policy framework prevalent in China and Vietnam. Even the rhetoric employed in the Communist Party's economic program (*Lineamientos*) for the Sixth Party Congress is noteworthy for its timidity. For example, it generally refers to "non-state" entities and activities and to processes of economic "updating," fearful of embracing unchaste words such as "private sector" or "market reforms."

Scenario 5. Regime Change.

Suppose Cuban citizens decide that multi-party contestation and competitive multi-party elections, the free expression of different and often opposed ideas, independent civil society organizations pursuing their own goals, deregulation of much social and economic life, mass media independent of the state, a market economy, and reduction of the right of the state to shape much of daily life constitute an appropriate political framework for Cuba. This would open the prospects for qualitatively different relations with the United States, Canada, the European Union, the majority of Latin American countries, and Japan.

Cautions, Speculations, and Conclusion

It is not just right-wing zealots in the United States who care about a transition to a different political regime in Cuba. There is a wide consensus in the United States and throughout much of the Americas about the value of liberal democratic politics, institutionalized in the Inter-American Democratic Charter. The European Union is also self-consciously a union of democratic countries. The debate within the United States, and between its government and other governments, has been about the means to foster open competitive multi-party politics in Cuba, respectful and supportive of a vibrant and independent civil society, *not* about these objectives. The quality of Cuba's future relations with the governments of democratic countries will depend, therefore, on the characteristics of Cuba's domestic political regime. The quality of Cuba's future relations with any government of the United States certainly will.

It is not just gerontocratic officials who care about Cuba's socialist heritage and its accomplishments. Large numbers of Cubans care as well. Indeed, Cuba's key assets for any version of its future are what its government calls the "achievements of the Revolution." Cuba's investment in health and education prepare its people to compete in the world. Cuba's economic hardships since 1990 also lowered its costs of production by worldwide standards. The combination of high-quality and inexpensive human capital, with effective market incentives not unlike those that prevail in China and Vietnam, should make Cuba a vibrant competitor in world markets for quality products and services, powering its economy to prosperity.

Cuba today needs the United States to remove its sanctions regime. Cuba tomorrow needs more. Cuba is ready for many potential responses to the removal of U.S. sanctions. With regard to trade, Cuba does not have protectionist tariff and non-tariff barriers to impede its engagement in international markets. With regard to intellectual property protection for Cuban patents and trademarks, Cuba would reap significant gains especially in U.S. markets from its biotechnology products, rum brands, or music.

Long-term U.S.–Cuban migration relations should be easier to manage than U.S. migration relations with Mexico, the Dominican Republic, or Central American countries because Cuba has been below the demographic replacement level since 1978. Cuba's aging demographic structure most likely renders the long-term migration flow modest.

Cuba's key asset is the creativity of its people. Its "human capital" generates culture as a source of value for its people's enjoyment and enlightenment, the affirmation of its identity, and the export of an array of services. Cuba's dynamic presence in a world economy can emulate Taiwan—another small former-sugar-producing country, long governed by a single party run on Leninist principles, existing for decades on the edge of a hostile huge northern neighbor, which made a partnership with its diaspora to become one of the world's economic powerhouses.

Cuba's diplomatic corps may serve the Cuba of the future with distinction, as it long has. Cuba's armed forces could serve as peace-makers and peace-keepers in United Nations missions, drawing on their substantial experience and expertise working in African countries and elsewhere. Cuba's public assets—the human capital embedded in its most successful state institutions—can safeguard and enhance its sovereignty in the future as they have in the past.

The governments of Cuba and the United States today can think afresh and big or, as they repeatedly have, they can miss yet one more opportunity to re-shape their relations. The good news is that both countries have avoided war. The bad news is that both countries have lost the peace. And Cubans have suffered grievously from direct and opportunity costs. Cubans should not fear the future. They are already prepared for it in many ways thanks to the work of so many for so long. The future can be better if citizens and public officials in both countries take risks and build the basis for a shared success.

Notes

1 Jorge I. Domínguez, "The Obstacles and Prospects for Improved U.S.–Cuban Relations: A U.S. Perspective," in *U.S.–Cuban Relations in the 1990s*, ed. Jorge I. Domínguez and Rafael Hernández (Boulder, CO: Westview Press, 1989), chapter 1.

2 Following Jana K. Lipman, *Guantánamo: A Working-Class History between Empire and Revolution* (Berkeley: University of California Press, 2009), I will call the Cuban city Guantánamo and the U.S. base near that city, GTMO, as many who work there do.

3 For a general account of U.S.–Cuban relations, see Daniel P. Erikson, *The Cuba Wars: Fidel Castro, the United States, and the Next Revolution* (New York: Bloomsbury Press, 2008).

4 Gregory F. Treverton, "Cuba in U.S. Security Perspective," in *U.S.–Cuban Relations in the 1990s*. For Cuba's policies, see Carlos Alzugaray Treto, "Cuban Foreign Policy during the 'Special Period': Interests, Aims, Outcomes," and Soraya Castro Marino, "Cuban–U.S. Relations: A View from Havana, 1989–2002," both in *Redefining Cuban Foreign Policy*, ed. H. Michael Erisman and John. M. Kirk (Gainesville: University Press of Florida, 2006).

5 Treverton, "Cuba in U.S. Security Perspective," 75. Juan Valdés Paz, "Cuba's Foreign Policy toward Latin America and the Caribbean in the 1980s," in *U.S.–Cuban Relations in the 1990s*, 198.

6 The Bush administration also enacted nuisance provisions such as a $100 per day limitation on what authorized U.S. travelers could spend in Cuba, a restriction on flight arrival and departure times for charter operators between Miami and Havana airports, a reduction of the amount that Cuban-Americans could send to their relatives in Cuba every quarter from $500 to $300, etc.

7 Donna Rich Kaplowitz, *Anatomy of a Failed Embargo: U.S. Sanctions against Cuba* (Boulder, CO: Lynne Rienner, 1998), 152.

8 I have personal knowledge of many of these exchanges. U.S. officials were unhappy about Cuban participation in LASA international congresses. The Inter-American Dialogue's exchange with the Cuban Academy of Sciences was my project. Some U.S. officials were supportive; others eventually made the continued participation of U.S. scientists impossible after the enactment of the Helms–Burton Act in 1996.

9 See Hal Klepak, *Cuba's Military 1990–2005* (New York: Palgrave, 2005), chapter 5.

10 These paragraphs draw from Richard A. Nuccio, "Cuba: A U.S. Perspective," paper prepared for the Brookings Institution Conference on "Transatlantic Tensions: The Challenge of Difficult Countries," 9–10 March 1998, Washington DC.

11 U.S. Department of Defense, DefenseLink News, 16 May 1996, 11 December 1997, 15 January 1998, 20 January 1998, and 29 July 1999, http://www.defenselink.mil/news/.

12 Interviews, Miami, 4 February 1998. See also Peter Kornbluh, "Cuba, Counternarcotics, and Collaboration: A Security Issue in U.S.–Cuban Relations", *Cuba Briefing Paper Series*, no. 24 (Washington DC: Georgetown University, 2000), 810.

13 *Granma*, 7 January 2010, for the Cuban Foreign Ministry's use of that previous step to explain Cuba's policy toward the United States.

14 U.S. Department of Agriculture, http://www.fas.usda.gov/itp/cuba/cuba-faq.html.

15 "Statement by the Government of Cuba to the National and International Public Opinion," 11 January 2002, courtesy of the Cuban Interests Section, Washington DC.

16 Raúl Castro Ruz, "Comparecencia televisiva," *Noticiero dominical*, NTV, Cuba, 20 January 2002.

17 http://www.state.gov/secretary/rm/2002/10113.htm.

18 The Miami speech version is shorter, "ease economic sanctions."

19 For the East Room speech, http://www.whitehouse.gov/news/releases/2002/05/print/20020520-1.html. For the Miami speech, http://www.whitehouse.gov/news/releases/2002/05/print/20020520-6.html.

20 http://www.cubaminrex.cu/politicaregional/amenorte3.htm.

21 For European Union policies, see Joaquín Roy, "Cuba and the European Union: Chronicle of a Dead Agreement Foretold," in *Redefining Cuban Foreign Policy*, ed. H. Michael Erisman and John M. Kirk (Gainesville: University Press of Florida, 2006).

22 Harvard College's program for its undergraduates to study at the University of Havana has operated under the laws of both countries and it has never been interrupted.

23 See U.S. Department of State, Commission for Assistance to a Free Cuba, "Report to the President," May 2004, especially 32–33, 171–172, 193, 223, 227, 419.

24 U.S. Department of State, Commission for Assistance to a Free Cuba, "Report to the President," July 2006, 39–42, 48, 69, 70, 73, 84, 86.

25 http://www.state.gov/secretary/rm/2006/70014.htm.

26 *Granma*, 18 August 2006 and 2 December 2006.

27 http://www.state.gov/p/wha/rls/rm/2006/71070.htm.

28 http://www.state.gov/p/wha/rls/rm/2006/q4/77864.htm.

29 http://www.thewhitehouse.gov/the_press_office/Fact-Sheet-Reaching-out-to-the-Cuban-people/.

30 http://www.whitehouse.gov/the_press_office/Remarks-by-the-President-at-the-Summit-of-the-Americas/.

31 *Granma*, 15 July 2009 and 18 September 2009; U.S. Department of State, "Cuba–U.S. Postal Talks," 18 September 2009, http://www.state.gov/r/pa/prs/ps/sept/129358. htm; U.S. Department of State, "Cuba Migration Talks," 14 July 2009, http://www.state. gov/r/pa/prs/ps/2009/july/126041.htm.

32 *Granma*, 17 April 2009.

33 http://www.america.gov/st/texttrans-English/2009/April/.

34 *Granma*, 22 April 2009.

35 *Granma*, 21 December 2009.

36 Hillary Rodham Clinton, "Remarks on the Human Rights Agenda for the 21st Century," http://www.state.gov/secretary/rm/2009a/12/133544.htm.

37 http://www.desdecuba.com/generationy/?=1179.

38 *Granma*, 27 August 2009; http://www.miamiherald.com/banking/story/1385652. html.

39 *Granma*, 2 October 2009.

40 *Granma*, 9 April 2009.

41 For the respective Cuban and U.S. statistics, see Cuba, Oficina Nacional de Estadísticas, *Anuario estadístico de Cuba, 2008*, Table 15.3, and also http://tse.export.gov/ accessed 21 February 2010.

42 http://www.fas.usda/gov/itp/cuba/cuba-faq.html; http://tse.export.gov/ accessed 21 February 2010.

43 U.S. Department of Homeland Security, United States Coast Guard, "Alien Migrant Interdiction," http://www.uscg.mil/hq/cg5/cg531/AMIO/FlowStats/FY.asp.

44 U.S. Department of State, Bureau of International Narcotics and Law Enforcement Affairs, *2009 International Narcotics Control Strategy Report. Vol. 1: Drug and Chemical Control. Cuba* (27 February 2009), http://www.state.gov/pinl/rls/nrcrpt/2009/vol1/116521.htm.

45 *Granma*, 12 February 2009.

46 U.S. Department of State, Bureau of International Narcotics and Law Enforcement Affairs, *2009 International Narcotics Control Strategy Report, Vol. 1: Drug and Chemical Control. Cuba*. 27 February 2009, http://www.state.gov/p/inl/rls/nrcrpt/2009/vol1/116521.htm.

47 U.S. Department of State Daily Press Briefing, Assistant Secretary Philip Crowley, 5 January 2010, http://www.state.gov/r/pa/prs/dpb/2010/01/134720.htm.

48 See Vicki Huddleston and Carlos Pascual, *Learning to Salsa: New Steps in U.S.–Cuban Relations* (Washington DC: Brookings Institution Press, 2010), chapter 2.

49 See text of his remarks at the United Nations General Assembly in *Granma*, 29 October 2009.

4

CUBA'S NATIONAL SECURITY VIS-À-VIS THE UNITED STATES

CONFLICT OR COOPERATION?

CARLOS ALZUGARAY TRETO

During the Cold War, the conflict between Cuba and the United States was marked by a series of confrontations in the national security arena that, in some cases, raised international tensions to a frightening level. The 1962 October Crisis was one such event, bringing the world to the brink of nuclear war. But the threat of armed confrontation was not limited to that crisis alone. Significantly, in the United States that event is generally referred to as the Missile Crisis, and in the Soviet Union as the Caribbean Crisis, but in Cuba we name it as above, by the date it took place because this was not the only time we faced the threat of invasion by the armed forces of the United States. There was danger of an armed attack on at least four other occasions: in 1961, during the battle of Playa Girón or the Bay of Pigs; in 1965, when President Lyndon B. Johnson ordered the invasion of the Dominican Republic; in the early 1980s, when the United States accused Cuba of being behind the conflicts in Central America; and in 1983 when U.S. troops attacked the sites of Cuban construction workers during the invasion of Grenada.

Nor has there been any lack of other tense situations related to security issues. Even between 1977 and 1981, the only period since 1959 when the two governments drew closer and began active cooperation in pursuit of normalization of relations, on more than one occasion deterioration or a step backward was caused by events that one or both sides perceived as threats to their national security interests. Such a series of events within a short interval is paradoxical given that, at the same time, many reciprocal gestures demonstrated that both Havana and Washington were inclined toward taking measures to build mutual trust, avoid tension, and advance cooperation.[1]

The hypothesis behind this essay is that, on bilateral Cuba–U.S. security issues, a number of factors make advancement extremely difficult. Thus, the future development of ties will require a great deal of patience and political willpower on the part of the two governments and also on that of other social subjects who can contribute to normalization. This does not necessarily mean a disappearance of areas of sharp conflict.[2]

To the majority of Cubans, the fundamental cause of the current confrontation between the two countries lies in Washington's policy toward the Island, about which I wrote in 2005:

> Many U.S. administrations—now totaling ten—have sought to provoke "regime change" through the creation of a viable opposition, subordinated to Washington's interests, which would be able to replace the revolutionary authorities in Havana and restore a regime that would conform to the logic of domination that prevailed in Cuba until 1958. However, the main contradiction within this policy has always been the same—how to achieve it when the Cuban government has always enjoyed broad popular support thanks to two important factors: 1) its defense of the country's sovereignty and its autonomous and internationalist foreign policy, which brings pride to the majority of Cubans; and 2) its putting into practice social justice policies that resolve the country's main dilemmas and place Cuba in a position very different from that of the rest of Latin America and the Caribbean, where poverty and inequality prevail. To deal with this contradiction, Washington tried to advance a multifaceted and complex policy along tracks that have ranged from training paramilitary groups to carry out hostile and/or terrorist actions on Cuban soil (including even organized military groups such as the so-called Brigade 2506, which suffered defeat at Playa Girón or the Bay of Pigs) to imposing an implacable economic, commercial, and financial blockade. Other variants have included financing minority groups of Cuban citizens prepared to betray[3] their country by collaborating with an enemy government, and putting into practice all sorts of psychological warfare operations designed to tarnish Cuba's image abroad and to politically and ideologically subvert the Cuban system.[4]

Starting Points

The factors that heighten tension in every area of Cuba–U.S. relations are not all historical ones. They can be summarized as follows:

1. The first and most important is the physical-geographical factor, which has a determinant effect on two constant elements:
    a) Proximity. Without being contiguous, the two countries share an important sea border, and a land border at the Guantánamo naval base. Although the latter is not as permanent as the former, it has existed for more than a century.

b)   Asymmetry. Cuba and the United States are two nations whose "hard power" resources are not symmetrical. This unequal relationship leads to "characteristic patterns of structural misperception and their amplification," even between countries with the same sociopolitical system, as Brantly Womack has demonstrated for cases in another continent and context.[5]

2.   The second is of a geopolitical nature, having to do with Cuba's strategic position in the hemispheric and world contexts, in U.S.–Caribbean relations, and in U.S.–Latin American relations in their broadest conceptualization. For the security concerns of both Cuba and for the United States, this factor has been a significant one both before and after the Cold War.[6]

3.   The third factor is a historical-political one having to do with the inevitability of a simultaneously intimate yet conflictual relationship.

a)   It is intimate from both sides, since neither nation can ignore the presence of the other and the existence of two poles of attraction. Rarely does anything happen on U.S. soil without repercussions in Cuba and—only slightly less so—rarely does anything happen in Cuba that does not interest the United States.

b)   It is conflictual because U.S. governing elites have seen Cuba as a country whose control is important to their own national security and that vision has had a substantial impact on how a large number of Americans view Cuba; while a majority of social, economic, and political sectors in Cuban society have felt that the maintenance of mutually beneficial ties should not and cannot be determined by a relationship of subordination, as was the case between 1902 and 1959. In support of this statement, one might cite speeches by Fidel Castro and other leaders and/or works by Cuban academics, but probably the best description comes from Louis A. Pérez, Jr., a U.S. academic of Cuban ancestry, one of the best-known specialists on the subject of relations across the Florida Straits:

> Cuba occupies a special place in the history of American imperialism. It has served as something of a laboratory for the development of the methods by which the United States has pursued the creation of a global empire. In the aggregate, the means used by the United States in Cuba constitute a microcosm of the American imperial experience: armed intervention and military occupation; nation building and constitution writing; capital penetration and cultural saturation; the installation of puppet regimes, the formation of clientele political classes, and the organization of proxy armies; the imposition of binding treaties; the establishment of a permanent military base; economic assistance— or not—and diplomatic recognition—or not—as circumstances warranted. And after 1959, trade sanctions, political isolation, covert operations, and economic embargo. All that is American imperialism has been practiced in Cuba.[7]

4.   The fourth factor is of an economic nature. Especially from the Cuban side, it has to do with the Island's vulnerability because of its lack of natural resources, which prevents an autarchic socio-economic development path and requires a search for economic allies and partners if Cuba is to pursue its goals. The ideal economic-commercial partner for Cuba, by virtue of its nearby location and its technological development, has been the United States. At a certain time, the Island also was relatively economically significant from Washington's point of view. However, it must be noted that, even recognizing the economic importance of a normal relationship with the northern neighbor, the history of past relations, which were never normal, would advise a degree of apprehension from the Cuban side with respect to possible U.S. aspirations for commercial and financial relations to carry the onerous price of political dependence.

A last starting point for discussing the two nations' ties in the security sphere has to do with a recent debate over this term in the field of international relations. Three well-known scholars of the subject, Barry Buzan, Ole Waever, and Jaap de Wilde, have described this debate as follows: "As a consequence, two views of security studies are now on the table, the new one of the wideners[8] and the old military and state-centered view of the traditionalists."[9]

The events of 11 September 2001 and the greater importance conceded to the subject of terrorism have given renewed pre-eminence to the issue of global and regional political-military security. The paradoxical result has been not only to heighten the traditionalist vision but also to emphasize socio-economic matters. In fact, this is nothing unexpected. Since the 1960s, '70s, and early '80s, the majority of academics and practitioners (military and security officers, politicians, and national and international officials) have recognized that economic development and security are intrinsically linked.[10]

In this context, a new term has emerged: "multidimensional security," which is intended to reflect the whole diversity of new individual, national, regional, and global or international realities and, at the same time, military, political, economic, social, cultural, and environmental ones. Who can deny that for some Caribbean islands individual and national security includes the issue of climate change (which is destroying their coastlines and their means of subsistence), or that the homogenizing tendency of the neoliberal globalization project represents a danger to the survival of the identities of some social groups?

It is equally paradoxical that criticism of the concept of multidimensional security has emerged from two distinct groups that seldom agree on anything else: traditional specialists in the field (who generally adhere to the school of political realism and neorealism within the discipline of international relations) and activists from the progressive sector of civil society. However, the reasoning behind their criticisms differs. The traditionalists think that extending the security agenda to the above-mentioned subjects overly broadens the field of study and clouds the definition of the pure and simple essence of security which pertains exclusively to the state and its survival. The civil society activists who are involved in oppositional or progressive organizations think that including the economic, social, cultural, and environmental spheres in security studies, or giving them such a connotation, serves to "securitize" the social agenda and thus leads to more bellicose solutions. In their opinion, such a tendency favors the most militarily powerful capitalist states and, especially, the United States—with evident dangers.

Nonetheless, it is worth arguing that accepting that a given issue affects the security of a nation or a social group does not necessarily lead to a military solution. It is merely a matter of establishing that the given issue is of such gravity that ignoring it would represent a danger to survival, even if the solution is an economic, social, or political one.[11]

In the case of the Cuba–U.S. relationship, it can be asked whether there is any doubt that Washington's actions against Havana, as part of a persistent policy directed at regime change at all costs, constitute a constant danger to the Cuban nation's security. Although in this essay I will try to balance the traditional and the "widener" perspectives, I have no doubt that Cuban society must take a broad and sweeping concept of security very much into account if it is to remain free of external impositions.[12]

Security Relations After the End of the Cold War

As the end of the Cold War unfolded in the late 1980s and early '90s, many of the main concerns of the United States' Cuba policy disappeared.[13] The supposed threat to U.S. national interests represented by Havana's alliance with Moscow no longer figured in the agenda because the Soviet Union ceased to exist. Cuba simply did not have a major military and political ally. The Cuban government not only negotiated and signed the southwest African peace accords, which, among other things, ended the presence of Cuban troops in Angola, but it was also slowly but surely withdrawing its military contingent from Ethiopia. In that period, Cuban diplomacy contributed to the negotiation and pacification process in Central America, eliminating another frequently mentioned sticking point in Washington's conflict with Cuba.[14]

Thus a new era in the two countries' relations opened, auguring greater cooperation. But this did not occur. The George H. W. Bush administration was committed to the creation of a "new world order," which had no room for showing tolerance toward a socialist Cuba 90 miles away. Secretary of State James Baker made the U.S. position clear, in response to suggestions that the successful negotiation of the 1988 southwest Africa peace accords during the Ronald Reagan presidency showed that other areas, too, could be negotiated with Havana.

On 28 March 1989, wire services revealed the existence of a leaked memorandum by the new secretary of state, addressed to all U.S. diplomatic representatives in Latin America and the Caribbean, rejecting any possibility of improving relations with Cuba. The so-called Baker Memorandum, as the document was known in the media, specified that under Bush the United States would not negotiate any normalization of relations, even a partial one, and that the only conversations with Havana would be those affecting U.S. national security, if and only if they offered no benefit to Cuba and did not legitimate its authorities.[15] Furthermore, the president's own memoirs, jointly written with his national security adviser General Brent Scowcroft, demonstrate to what degree pressure on the USSR to end economic and military aid to Cuba figured among the priorities in discussions with Moscow.[16]

The pressures generated by Washington's diplomacy in Moscow could not be seen in Havana as anything other than a clear attempt to damage Cuba's national security. This became particularly clear in 1991 when Soviet President Mikhail Gorbachev announced the unilateral withdrawal of all Soviet military personnel from the Island without previous discussions with the Cuban government.[17]

Besides invasion of Panama in December 1989, interpreted in Havana as an indirect threat to Cuban security, the Bush administration carried out a series of actions that can hardly be seen as likely to create a climate of mutual trust. Certainly they were not "prudent," a term much used by the U.S. side in diplomatic exchanges with Cuba to emphasize the type of Cuban behavior they hoped to see on the world scene.[18] British-American researcher Gillian Gunn reviewed these actions in 1993:

1990

January: U.S. Coast Guard vessels fired on and attempted to board a Cuban-chartered freighter in international waters, alleging suspicions of drug trafficking, which were disproved when Mexican authorities inspected the ship.

February: When questioned repeatedly during a visit to the Soviet parliament in Moscow, Secretary Baker himself refused to rule out the possibility of an invasion of Cuba by U.S. armed forces.

March: In open defiance of international laws and regulations, the Bush administration created Television Martí. Vice-President Dan Quayle publicly mentioned the possibility of creating an underground resistance group in Cuba similar to the Nicaraguan "contras."

May: U.S. armed forces held military maneuvers in the Caribbean, including a simulated invasion of the Puerto Rican coast, which appeared to be rehearsals for an eventual attack on Cuba. (The goal of the exercise was to "free" an Island under the power of a dictator named Ortsac.)

1991

May: New military maneuvers in the Caribbean, along with an increase in the number of military personnel at the Guantánamo base because of the influx of Haitian refugees.

Mid-year: High Pentagon officials publicly suggested the possibility of drawing up contingency plans for "humanitarian intervention" in Cuba.

December: Cuba discovered a commando group of terrorists with arms and explosives who had come from the United States and were attempting to infiltrate the country.[19]

The Cuban response to what it perceived as growing threats consisted of reinforcing defensive measures by way of military maneuvers under the code name "Cuban Shield," carried out at the end of 1991. In a different realm, the government took extraordinary action against a group of military officers who were discovered attempting to create a drug trafficking operation between Colombia and the United States by way of Cuba. These activities were prosecuted in Case Number 1 of 1989, which resulted in the execution of several high-ranking officers including a division general and a colonel. The Cuban leadership justly judged that such activity constituted a threat to Cuban national security because it offered the *casus belli* that certain sectors in the United States would have used to push for an invasion, similar to what did indeed happen that same year in Panama.

Alongside traditional threats to Cuba's national security, the years of the Bush Sr. administration coincided with the most challenging economic period faced by Cuban society since the triumph of the revolution. The hardships suffered by the Cuban people were comparable only to the hard years of the 1960s when the John F. Kennedy administration first imposed a full economic, commercial, and financial blockade and these began to take their toll on an economy previously completely subordinated to that of the United States. In this post–Cold War context, pressures on the USSR to end its preferential economic treatment of Cuba assumed their true significance.

This led Cuban authorities to take the extraordinary measures, which have been called the "special period in time of peace" in allusion to contingency plans adopted before 1989 to confront war-time situations. According to the logic of Buzan, Waever, and de Wilde in relation to the use of the concept of security, Cuba in 1989–95 confronted a situation of "existential threat" that led it to take "extraordinary measures."[20] The last significant act of the George H. W. Bush administration with respect to Cuba, signing the Torricelli Act in 1992, constituted a new menace to the country's security because it blocked commerce between Cuba and U.S. corporate subsidiaries in third countries and imposed a punitive measure against navigation of the seas by introducing a six-month prohibition of access into U.S. ports leveled on any ship that had entered a Cuban harbor.

In addition, the Torricelli Act included so-called measures for increasing contact with the Cuban people. Under the presumptuous label of "Track II," these provisions put into practice a *modus operandum* already well-known in U.S. policy toward Cuba: combining economic pressure on the government (the stick) with apparent benefits for the society (the carrot) with the goal of fomenting subversion and/or destabilization of the political system. This approach implies an irresolvable contradiction: convincing the Cuban people of the advisability of overthrowing their current government in order to obtain the benefits of normal relations with the United States.

In these same circumstances but under the administration of Bill Clinton, a new series of events between 1994 and 1996 further heightened tensions in security relations to the point where they might have provoked a military conflict. I refer to the so-called "rafter crisis" in the summer of 1994 and the downing of two small aircraft of the Miami-based counter-revolutionary organization Brothers to the Rescue in February 1996.

As Lorena Barberia and Antonio Aja point out in their respective essays elsewhere in this book, there are complex causes for the historical emigration of Cubans to the United States, notwithstanding the specific conditions that hamper or facilitate it at any given moment. In 1994, the economic crisis increased the structural conditions favorable to the ignition of a new migratory explosion. Certainly, one of the major conditions was the continued application of the Cuban Adjustment Act of 1966, which allows all Cuban citizens who enter the United States, even illegally, to be admitted on their own recognizance for a period of one year, after which they automatically receive permanent resident status—an exclusive privilege not granted to any other alien citizen. That this policy has promoted and continues to promote illegal emigration is beyond doubt. This law was at the root of the Mariel migration crisis of 1980.

In the critical circumstances of 1994, the Cuban government faced an extremely complex dilemma: if it prevented illegal departures, which were becoming ever more numerous, it would be criticized; if it did not, this could provoke an uncontrollable situation, which could possibly lead to an armed conflict. Circumstances became particularly difficult that summer, and the government decided to open the ports and to refrain from interfering with illegal departures.[21]

Facing an equally difficult situation and in the midst of another migration crisis related to the departure of thousands of Haitian citizens who did not enjoy the benefits of an Adjustment Act, but felt forced to leave by the military coup against the government of Jean-Paul Aristide, the Clinton administration, not without some reluctance,[22] opted to negotiate a series of migration agreements with Cuba. These were the first important accords signed since 1959 between the two countries and had several effects:

1. They favored cooperation between the coast and border guard services of the two countries.[23] Both security corps had cooperated before but now their relations moved from the informal sphere to the institutional one to guarantee that illegal migrants intercepted on the high seas by the U.S. Coast Guard would be formally turned over to their Cuban counterpart, the Tropas Guardafronteras. Thus began the so-called "wet-foot, dry-foot" policy.
2. Given that during the crisis, up until the moment of signing the accords, the Clinton administration had decided to send some migrants to the naval base

at Guantánamo where it had established a refugee camp, it was necessary to establish some cooperation between the military authorities on both sides of the demarcation line. That collaboration, begun in 1994, has continued to develop into a full-blown confidence-building regime.

3. The migration agreements formalized the holding of semi-annual meetings between high-ranking diplomatic officials from both sides for the purpose of monitoring fulfillment. That, in turn, allowed for the maintenance of a channel of communication, which often transcended migration issues, until George W. Bush canceled the meetings in 2006.

The other incident that proved revealing was the downing of the two small planes flown by the counter-revolutionary organization Brothers to the Rescue on 24 February 1996. This unfortunate event had its origins in the provocative maneuvers of the organization's pilots, led by José Basulto, a Cuban-American who had served as a Central Intelligence Agency operative in the 1960s.

As the rafter crisis was intensifying, Brothers to the Rescue planes began flying over the Florida Straits for the alleged purpose of offering humanitarian aid to those riding on makeshift craft. However, with the signing of the migration accords the number of illegal emigrants braving the sea to take advantage of the Cuban Adjustment Act began to drop. Basulto and his followers then began illegally to penetrate Cuban airspace and carry out provocations such as dropping leaflets over the city of Havana. Such actions, in violation of international and Cuban law, also meant breaching the regulations of the U.S. Federal Aviation Administration because they involved the falsification of flight plans to obtain takeoff permission.

As has been confirmed by various sources, including Richard Nuccio, President Clinton's special national security adviser on Cuba, this affair had been discussed via diplomatic channels by both governments, and the Cuban government repeatedly said that the flights must be stopped or, if that did not happen, Cuba would take measures in accord with existing regulations and with its power to maintain international flight security. President Fidel Castro explained this exchange when he personally accused President Clinton of having failed to act:

> And we warned him, we informed him in peaceful terms, really, in reasonable terms, that, please, he should do whatever was possible to prevent those flights, and he promised to prevent the flights. He didn't want to or couldn't fulfill that promise. He knows the story of those aircraft quite well and of the efforts we made to prevent an incident, all the more so in the midst of an electoral campaign when anything might serve as raw material for introducing Cuba into his political campaign.[24]

Recently, Fidel Castro referred again to the downing of the Brothers to the Rescue aircraft in 1996. In one of his *Reflexiones*, published in the *Cubadebate* website on 10

August 2010, he mentioned the incident and said that shortly before 24 February 1996, Bill Richardson, the Secretary of Energy in the Clinton administration, had visited Cuba as an emissary for the president to assure him that the flights would be stopped and "with that I decided not to worry any more about the problem."[25] Contrary to his habit of defending in detail any major national security decision taken, the former president has been reticent to talk about this and explain exactly what happened that day, thereby reinforcing the hypothesis that he told the Air Force commanders, who with great frustration had been restraining themselves and their pilots in the face of very extreme provocations produced by Basulto and his men, to take any proper action, convinced that nothing would happen. Although provoked in many ways by Brothers to the Rescue, the action taken by the Cuban Air Force cannot but be qualified as a tragic mistake. Other options could have been explored before acting in such a forceful manner, producing the death of four persons and damaging the image of Cuba.

Jorge I. Domínguez has recalled how close Cuba and the United States came to military conflict as a result of this event, brought about by the provocative irresponsibility of non-state actors who carried out quasi-terrorist actions and by the negligent complacency of the U.S. government apparatus.

> For the first time since the missile crisis of 1962, a United States president considered giving orders to U.S. armed forces to initiate a military action against Cuba (confidential interviews in Washington DC, 1996). There were several military options implying various forms of retribution. The president decided against all of them but, in their place, agreed to accept the Helms–Burton Act.[26]

The Helms–Burton Act, by its nature and content, is a codification of most of the elements of the "regime change" policy that the United States has deployed against Cuba since the beginning of the revolution.

Among the positive points of the Clinton period must be mentioned a joint anti-drug-trafficking operation organized by police forces of both countries; the positive declarations by Gen. Barry McCaffrey, head of the White House office of drug control, about the need to cooperate with Cuba; expanded collaboration between the coast guards of the two countries to prevent new violent incidents on the sea borders; and widened contact and coordination between the military commands in the area of Guantánamo.[27]

Nonetheless, before Clinton handed the presidential chair to his successor George W. Bush, several incidents related to terrorism muddied mutual security relations and continue to hold the potential for further complicating them unless both parties seek a solution, whether unilaterally or through negotiations. Cuba and the United States share a common interest in eliminating terrorism, but their different approaches to the question constitute the "elephant in the room" in any normalization process.

In 1997–99, there was evidence of increased terrorist activity carried out against Cuba from United States territory. In 1997 a series of terrorist acts took place in Cuba aimed at hotels in the growing tourist industry; an Italian tourist was killed in one such attack. Recent revelations from a man arrested in Caracas on a warrant from Interpol and extradited to Cuba by the Venezuelan authorities strongly confirmed that these acts were instigated and organized from El Salvador by Luis Posada Carriles, who had been prosecuted and sentenced in Venezuela in the 1970s for the bombing of a Cubana Airlines regular flight from Barbados to Cuba, on 6 October 1976, which resulted in the death of its 73 passengers and crew.[28] In 1999, Posada Carriles, who had escaped from a Venezuelan prison, reappeared in Panama during the Iberoamerican Summit. After a public accusation made by President Fidel Castro, the local police arrested him and several Cuban-American terrorist suspects who, it was alleged, traveled to Panama to carry out an assassination attempt against the Cuban leader during the meeting. Posada Carriles had a long history of serving U.S. intelligence agencies, including his participation in the activities known as "Iran–Contra" and in the "dirty war" against Nicaragua.

One year earlier, in September 1998, five young Cubans were detained by Federal Bureau of Investigation agents in Miami and accused of acts of espionage against the United States and in favor of the government in Havana. They were held for 33 months without bail and, finally, in 2001 they were charged and tried in the very city with the largest concentration of citizens of Cuban origin in the United States. As was demonstrated in their trials, the accused parties neither sought nor obtained information that would be prejudicial to U.S. national security, though they admitted working for the Cuban government with the mission of seeking information that would allow the neutralization of future terrorist acts against Cuba. However, the prevalent hostile climate in Miami led them to be sentenced to long prison terms, with life sentences in two of the cases.[29]

The trial and sentencing of the five Cubans—known in their country as the "Five Heroes" and in the United States as the "Miami 5" or "Cuban 5"—took place under the administration of George W. Bush, as did several appeals by the defendants. The appeals at first seemed to bear fruit when a panel of judges of the U.S. Court of Appeals, 11th Circuit, in Atlanta overturned the sentences and ordered a new trial. This action was later modified by the full court, however, and in the summer of 2009 the Supreme Court refused to hear the case, which has remained in limbo after minor reductions in the sentences.[30]

Things were further complicated by the pardon of Luis Posada Carriles and his accomplices issued by the president of Panama in 2005, whereupon they were sent to an unknown location in Central America from which, Posada has confessed, he illegally entered the United States. Today he enjoys conditional liberty in Miami where he is supported by the ultra-right of Cuban-American émigrés. The United States government has been slow at best in bringing him to trial or revealing its evidence against him, and it has not extradited him to Venezuela where he is wanted by the courts because of his notorious escape. The Obama administration seems more interested in doing something but, as seen from the point of view of Havana, it is still far too little and very late.

In terms of traditional security issues, only in 2003 was there a true threat under the Bush administration. The initial victory of U.S. armed forces in Iraq that spring could only have negative repercussions for Cuba. Miami was the only city in the world where demonstrations in support of Washington's course of action were held, and the suggestion was made that, after Saddam Hussein, it was Castro's turn next. This idea clearly entered the minds of the president and his associates, as seems to be confirmed by Bob Woodward, the star reporter of the *Washington Post*, in the third part of his chronicle of the war. According to this account, the president himself told General Jay Garner that after Iraq he could aspire to another similar role: head of the military occupation government of Cuba when that moment should arrive.[31]

Another initiative of the Bush administration, which pointed toward a possible armed conflict although much less urgently, was the creation of a Commission for Assistance to a Free Cuba, which released two voluminous reports, one in 2004 and another in 2006. These went beyond the traditional threats and, in their ambitious scope, reinforced the perception that the U.S. government remained implacably committed to a policy of changing the political system in Cuba no matter what. Concomitantly, the administration created a State Department position for a Cuban transition coordinator who was given funds to pursue "regime change" on the Island.

Nonetheless, the measures to build mutual trust at Guantánamo and in the Florida Straits continued to be consolidated. Cooperation between the two coast guard forces in fulfillment of the migration accords also continued, although the monitoring talks were called off.

From the Cuban side, several signals indicated an opening in security matters even under George W. Bush. In September 2001, Cuba offered medical aid and opened its airports to U.S. planes. In 2005, it offered public health assistance to contribute to mitigating the damage caused by Hurricane Katrina. Another significant gesture also took place in 2002, when Cuba raised no objection to the transport to the Guantánamo naval base of suspected terrorists captured by the United States in Afghanistan, and offered its collaboration in case of need, as Jorge Domínguez points out in his chapter in the present volume.

Current Situation

Traditional Security

Hostility, asymmetry, and geographic proximity require Cuba to develop and maintain a deterrent strategy, developed over the years, and an armed force that is small but well trained. The United States has the capacity to attack Cuba with very little warning and occupy part of the country. The Cuban response has been to proclaim and openly promise that such an action would have an unsustainable cost over the long run even if it were to achieve some initial successes. What happened in Iraq confirms the validity of the Cuban strategy of a "war of the whole people." At the same time, the Cuban government has carried out a program of confidence-building measures in all the sectors of possible conflict. This policy has borne fruit.

Guantánamo. While repeating on numerous occasions that it considers the treaty establishing a U.S. naval base in Guantánamo to be illegal, Cuba has also steadily sought the return of this territory by means of broader diplomatic negotiations. Therefore, Havana has not cashed the checks that the United States government issues to "pay" the rent on the land. In recent debates over the status of the detainees on the base, in the context of the global war on terrorism, Washington has recognized that Cuba holds true sovereign power over the territory. Both countries have created measures of mutual trust in the area surrounding the base and have even carried out joint training exercises for cases of natural disaster such as fires, hurricanes, and pandemics.

Migration

This is one of the most conflictual security issues in the two countries' relations. Cuba has traditionally been a source of emigration toward the United States. After the triumph of the revolution, Washington made use of the migration issue as one more instrument of its destabilization policy aimed at a "change of government." Migration crises occurred in 1965, 1980, and 1994. Their fundamental cause was the U.S. policy of stimulating illegal emigration from Cuba, a policy consolidated by the passage of the Cuban Adjustment Act in 1966. After various failed attempts, the two countries finally signed mutual migration accords in 1994 and 1995, establishing the annual issuance of 20,000 permanent immigration visas to Cuban citizens. The goal is to allow a regular, legal migration flow controlled by the two governments. This agreement stipulates cooperation between Cuban border guards and their counterparts in the U.S. Coast Guard, which has contributed to safe and secure navigation in the Florida Straits. However, Washington's refusal to suspend or repudiate the Cuban Adjustment Act has been an obstacle to effective implementation of the accords.

Terrorism

Cuba has been the target of terrorist organizations, which in the past had close ties to the U.S. government or, as a minimum, have enjoyed a great degree of tolerance from U.S. law enforcement agencies, owing, no doubt, to the years in which the CIA carried out covert actions against the Island, some of them bordering on terrorism, if not terrorist on their own terms. The most recent acts were bombs placed in Havana hotels in 1997, four years before the attacks on the Twin Towers and the Pentagon.

The man behind those bombs is Luis Posada Carriles. This well-known terrorist, who has still not been tried in the United States for his crimes, represents a thorny problem for security relations because his situation undermines the credibility of any U.S. measure to deal with the scourge of terrorism.

Cuba has tried to deter such actions and has sent agents to penetrate terrorist groups in U.S. territory, as no doubt the United States has done to defend itself. Although U.S. law enforcement authorities were aware of these activities and apparently let them continue for several years, given that some of the agents cooperated with them, the agents were then arrested and sentenced to long prison terms. Inexplicably, the United States continues to place Cuba on the list of countries promoting terrorism, although nearly every specialist in that area has concluded there is no evidence at all to support this accusation.[32]

Drug Trafficking

There is cooperation in practice in this area but no formal institutionalization in spite of Cuba's having presented several proposals. It is known that U.S. law enforcement agencies and authorities have argued that a formal agreement would be much more effective. There have been attempts in the past to accuse the Island of links with the drug trade but all have been discredited. Most specialists judge that Cuba has efficient mechanisms to combat drug trafficking. There are signals that the Obama administration might be inclined to sign a formal agreement with the Cuban side.

Environment and Natural Disasters

Some limited and insufficient collaboration between meteorological authorities of the two countries does exist. The blockade and the lack of normal relations are obstacles to seeking and establishing new areas of collaboration. The recent humanitarian crisis in Haiti demonstrates the potential for cooperation as well as the difficulties in achieving it. Although there has as yet been no public confirmation, both parties have established a cooperation regime based on the abilities and strengths of the Cuban health mission in Port-au-Prince and the U.S. capacity to mobilize material and financial resources.

Hemispheric Security

Up until now, Cuba has not participated in the existing hemispheric security mechanisms. It has allied itself with the countries that criticize the United States for the restoration of its Fourth Fleet, the agreement with Colombia to locate seven military facilities in that country's territory, the coup d'état in Honduras, and the presence of thousands of U.S. troops in Haiti.

Politico-Economic Stability and Security

For years, the United States has carried out a policy replete with elements of subversion and destabilization directed against Cuba: economic sanctions to produce "hunger, desperation, and the overthrow of the government"; financing and training of the opposition; media campaigns by way of stations such as Radio Martí, TV Martí; etc. The policy has not succeeded in toppling the government or destabilizing the country. But it undoubtedly creates a "siege mentality" and reinforces the perception that a normalization of relations with the United States in any sphere, but specifically on security issues, is impossible.

Cuba's stability—something that ought to be of interest to a neighbor as powerful as the United States—has been preserved thanks to the policies that have been carried out. But the Island's authorities have recognized that the revolution could possibly be destroyed from within. This introduces an important element into Cuban national security policy and opens up some questions for Washington. The Cuban government is in the midst of a process of updating its economic model, which will inevitably have political consequences. Like it or not, all of this will affect Cuba's capacity to maintain its social stability and cohesion, which is to say, it will affect the country's national security policy. This will also be important for the United States, which cannot block the process but can make it either harder or easier.

In mid-2010, the Raúl Castro government and the Obama administration seemed ready or were actually working to advance on three security issues described in these pages. First, both governments have been conducting very discreet conversations and are actually cooperating in Haiti, where Cuba has deployed one of its very effective health missions and the United States has contributed with material resources given an obvious security concern. Disaster relief cooperation is a security issue on which both countries complement each other.

Second, the liberation of several prisoners jailed in 2003, for cooperating with the U.S. Interest Section in Havana, after a process of negotiations in which the Cuban Catholic Church (with the participation of the Spanish government) played a key role, has opened the way to a possible elimination of restrictions to travel to Cuba and, maybe, an exchange of prisoners between both countries. Cuba is interested in getting back its "Five Heroes." The United States, on the other hand, has insisted on the liberation and return of Alan Gross, a USAID contractor detained while carrying out illegal activities in the Island (distribution of cell phones and laptops among opposition groups) at the behest of the U.S. government. In this context, Cardinal Jaime Ortega, the key Church negotiator for the prisoner release visited Washington in July and August 2010, on the second occasion meeting with General James Jones, the President's National Security Adviser.[33]

Third, both governments have started to talk about possible cooperation on the issue of oil spills in the Gulf of Mexico after the disaster caused by the sinking of the Deepwater Horizon. This is a particularly important security issue because Cuba is attempting to develop its deepwater oil and gas reserves, a strategic necessity given its economic vulnerability. A recent Brookings Institution policy brief strongly recommends a series of initiatives.[34] The Cuban government has given ample signals that it is ready and considers cooperation in this area fruitful for its national security interests.

Conclusion and Future Scenarios

In the historical period preceding the one analyzed here, two opposite visions took shape. To the governmental leaders and the majority of the Cuban people, the United States has been a permanent and powerful threat to national security. To the government leaders and elites and a good part of the population of the United States, Cuba has been a small country capable of endangering legitimate U.S. interests, through its alliance with extra-continental powers (case in point, the Soviet Union), its example and attraction (soft power) in the eyes of other Latin American countries, and the internationalist policies that led it to actively support liberation movements in Africa from Algeria to South Africa.

The Cold War's legacy is a security relationship that is complex and, in general, conflictual and potentially explosive. This agenda has continued into the succeeding period, which has been marked by the continuation of multi-tracked Washington policies designed to produce "regime change" in Cuba and to limit Cuba's role as an example for the region. It has been marked as well by a logical Cuban response of emphasizing stubborn but realistic resistance and a disposition to seek any possibility of normalization that respects Cuba's sovereignty and self-determination. This has opened up opportunities for limited cooperation in certain security spheres, which is one of the most interesting and enduring traits of the relationship after the end of the Cold War.

The potential for armed conflict springs from the existence of two borders between countries that have been mutually hostile for the past fifty years. The sea frontier runs throughout the Florida Straits with a separation of as little as 145 kilometers, a distance that jet aircraft can cover in a few minutes. The land border separates a Cuban defensive perimeter from U.S. troops stationed at the Guantánamo naval base, which is situated on land occupied by the United States for more than a century under the provisions of a treaty that Cuba, with merit, views as lacking legitimacy.

The most important fact is that the two nations are close enough to each other to share security issues such as borders, terrorism, migration, environment, natural disasters, and drug trafficking, but the hostile U.S. attitude toward an independent Cuba, when joined with the asymmetry in the countries' hard power resources, imposes significant obstacles for advance and requires Havana to act cautiously with respect to all of these issues. Nonetheless, in normal conditions there would be broad opportunities for cooperation.

In terms of traditional security threats, there are obvious signs that both parties prefer the present stable environment and see possibilities for more cooperation and confidence-building measures. These have been adopted on both the maritime and land borders, facilitating some forms of cooperation between the two countries' armed forces, including the Cuban border guards and the U.S. Coast Guard.

The border agreement signed during the Carter administration was strengthened by the migration accord of 1995, which has been respected and implemented by both governments. The United States has prevented Miami groups hostile to Cuba from mounting provocations in the border area, especially since the downing of the Brothers to the Rescue airplanes in 1996.

Nonetheless, a structural contradiction exists insofar as security is concerned. This contradiction is between, on the one hand, the confidence-building measures in the areas of potential armed conflict and the pragmatism shown by both sides in such sensitive areas as migration, and, on the other hand, the manifest U.S. hostility toward the social, economic, and political regime which has prevailed in Cuba over the last fifty years. Although it is possible to widen cooperation in areas such as the struggle against drug trafficking, the structural contradiction constitutes an obstacle to any greater forward motion, especially on issues such as the struggle against terrorism. The influence of some non-governmental actors such as Cuban-American conservative political figures is a clear demonstration that there are constraints to what can be done. The mutual accusations of terrorism, which carry a lot of weight in the Cuban case, are the "elephant in the room," especially because Washington applies the hard sanction of putting Cuba on the list of "states that sponsor terrorism," when there has not been any concrete and proven accusation of Cuban participation or stimulus to terrorist actors that have damaged the United States or any other country.

The asymmetric nature of the close relationship makes it difficult to overcome those obstacles unless bolder measures are taken. For the United States, seeking broader cooperation with Cuba on security issues is not a high-priority matter. Nor does it seem to be a priority to take the necessary steps to change the current state of relations, reduce conflict, and move forward in cooperation. Although this perspective might be evolving with the Obama administration, which seems more prone to take positive action to increase contacts and cooperation, the fact remains that Cuba is not a high-priority issue.

However, that is not the case for Cuba. The relationship with the United States is of high priority. Normalizing that relationship is an attainable strategic goal.

Just as Cuba made a decision to pursue military invulnerability and has achieved that goal under extremely difficult conditions, the central goal of all future Cuban policy involves guaranteeing its economic and political invulnerability in the context of a generational transition of elites and leaders. Thus, achieving a degree of normalization in relations with the United States, albeit not free of conflicts, is a desirable end rather than an impossible goal. Given the argument that Cuba is not a priority for Washington, Havana must take the initiative, exploiting any opening that might appear. The release of 52 political prisoners, which began in the summer of 2010 and will continue over the next few months is one such action. It creates an opening for that sector of the Washington foreign policy elite that prefers a more cooperative relationship, as is the case with the Brookings Institution, for example.[35]

Having survived the worst moments for such ties with the departure of the Bush administration from the scene, a new strategic window of opportunity is opening, which could allow for the entrance of new, more peaceful and cooperative breezes.

Notes

1   This was, of course, during Jimmy Carter's presidency in the United States. Readers might consult the following: Luis Mesa del Monte, "La Administración Carter (1976–1980)," in *De Eisenhower a Reagan: la política de los Estados Unidos contra la Revolución cubana*, ed. Instituto Superior de Relaciones Internacionales (Havana: Editorial de Ciencias Sociales, 1987), 237–90, and Lars Schoultz, *That Infernal Little Cuban Republic: the United States and the Cuban Revolution* (Chapel Hill: University of North Carolina Press, 2009), 291–361.

2   Rafael Hernández, "El problema de la 'solución del conflicto' entre los Estados Unidos y Cuba," in *Otra guerra. Ensayos cubanos sobre estrategia y seguridad internacional*, ed. Rafael Hernández (Havana: Editorial de Ciencias Sociales, 1999), 122–48. I have also speculated on this issue in "Is Normalization Possible in Cuban–U.S. Relations after 100 Years of History?," paper presented at the International Studies Association annual convention, Washington, February 16–20, 1999, and in a seminar at the Robert Schuman center of the European University Institute in Florence, March 7, 2000 [unpublished] and in 'Cuba y Estados Unidos en los umbrales del siglo XXI: perspectivas de la cooperación,' *Cuadernos de Nuestra América*, 15, no. 29, January–June 2002, Havana, Centro de Estudios sobre América, pp. 49–76.

3   Jorge Domínguez has pointed out that my use of the word "betray" is too strong and should be reconsidered since the Cuban government itself accepted to change the term "mercenary" to "invader" to designate those Cuban nationals who were recruited by the CIA to attack their country in the Bay of Pigs, during a conference that took place in Havana in 2001. He further suggested that the problem is complex and defies a sharp definition like the one I used in 2005. I recognize that he might be right, but I cannot change what I wrote in 2005. If I were to write the same paragraph today, I would probably use another more nuanced word. But it must be emphasized that, in my own view, it is personally unethical, politically immoral and legally unacceptable to serve as instrument of the policies of a foreign power, which is attempting to illegally undermine or subvert one's own country and institutions. That, I am afraid, is the case of the United States with Cuba.

4   Carlos Alzugaray, "La política de los Estados Unidos hacia Cuba durante la segunda administración Bush: continuidad y cambio," in *Estados Unidos-América Latina. Los nuevos desafíos: ¿Unión o desunión?*, ed. Víctor López Villafañe and Soraya Castro Mariño (Mexico City: Joralé Editores and Orfila, 2007), 189–90.

5   Brantly Womack, "Asymmetry and Systemic Misperception: China, Vietnam and Cambodia during the 1970s," *Journal of Strategic Studies* 26, no. 2 (June 2003): 116.

6   Rafael Hernández, "Cuba y la seguridad en el Caribe," in *Otra guerra*, 70–97.

7   Louis A. Pérez, Jr., *Cuba in the American Imagination: Metaphor and the Imperial Ethos* (Chapel Hill: University of North Carolina Press, 2009), 1.

8 For these authors, the "wideners" broaden security studies to include topics that come from the economic, environmental, and social spheres. For the purposes of this essay, that concept allows for extending practical cooperation to areas such as hurricanes, climate change, or an oil spill in the Gulf of Mexico, which would be important to close neighbors such as Cuba and the United States.

9 Barry Buzan, Ole Waever and Jaap de Wilde, *Security: A New Framework for Analysis* (Boulder: Lynne Rienner, 1998), 1.

10 See also my texts: "La seguridad nacional de Cuba y el diferendo con los Estados Unidos," *Estudios e Investigaciones del ISRI* 18 (1988), and its English translation, "Problems of National Security in the Cuba–U.S. Historic Breach," in *U.S.–Cuban Relations in the 1990s*, ed. Jorge I. Domínguez and Rafael Hernández (Boulder, CO: Westview Press, 1989); "Dinámica de la seguridad nacional y regional en la Cuenca del Caribe," in *Sistemas políticos: poder y sociedad (estudios de casos en América Latina)*, a collection of papers from the 18th Congress of the Asociación Latinoamericana de Sociología (Caracas: Nueva Sociedad, 1992); and "Cuban Security in the Post-Cold War World: Old and New Challenges and Opportunities," in *Cuba in the International System: Normalization and Integration*, ed. Archibald R.M. Ritter and John M. Kirk (London: Macmillan, 1995).

11 Barry Buzan, Ole Waever and Jaap de Wilde, *Security*, 21.

12 That was precisely the gist of my argument, in the debate with Gregory Treverton, in my 1989 essay in the book co-edited by Domínguez and Hernández cited above, note 11, supra. See also 14, infra.

13 For a description and analysis of what the United States viewed as the main threats emanating from Cuba toward the end of the Cold War, see Gregory F. Treverton, "Cuba in U.S. Security Perspective," in Jorge I. Domínguez and Rafael Hernández, *U.S.–Cuban Relations in the 1990s*, 63–84.

14 See Juan Valdés Paz, "Cuba's Foreign Policy Toward Latin America and the Caribbean in the 1980s", in Domínguez and Hernández, *U.S.–Cuban Relations in the 1990s*, 198.

15 René Mujica Cantelar (then Deputy Chief of Mission at the Cuban Interests Section in Washington), "El futuro de las relaciones Cuba-Estados Unidos: una visión cubana sobre la perspectiva de Washington," *Cuadernos de Nuestra América* 7, no. 15 (July–December 1990), 214–15, and a version in English, "The Future of Cuban–US Relations: A Cuban View," in *Cuban Foreign Policy Confronts a New International Order*, ed. H. Michael Erisman and John M. Kirk (Boulder: Lynne Rienner, 1991), 68.

16 George Bush and Brent Scowcroft, *A World Transformed* (New York: Vintage, 1989), 134–5, 155, 163, 165, 223, 273, 287, 507, 509, 530, 533 and 547.

17 The speed with which Mikhail Gorbachev acceded to James Baker's requests is recounted in Lars Schoultz, *That Infernal Little Cuban Republic*, 429.

18 Personal memories of the author, at that time Deputy Director, North America Division, Cuban Ministry of Foreign Affairs (MINREX).

19 Gillian Gunn, *Cuba in Transition: Options for U.S. Policy* (New York: Twentieth Century Fund, 1993), 19–20.

20 Barry Buzan, Ole Waever and Jaap de Wilde, *Security*, 21.

21 For a very interesting alternative interpretation, see Jorge I. Domínguez, "¿Cooperando con el enemigo? Las políticas de inmigración de los Estados Unidos hacia Cuba," in *La política exterior de Cuba (1962–2009)* (Madrid: Editorial Colibrí, 2009), 491–566.

22 Lars Schoultz, *That Infernal Little Cuban Republic*, 469 ff.

23 The counterpart of the U.S. Coast Guard in Cuba is the Dirección de Tropas Guardafronteras (Directorate of Border Guard Troops) of the Ministry of the Interior.

24 Fidel Castro Ruz, "Discurso en la clausura del Congreso Pedagogía 97 (Teatro Carlos Marx, 7 de febrero de 1997)," available at www.cuba.cu.

25 Castro, Fidel, "El gigante de las siete leguas (Parte 2), Reflexiones de Fidel," *Cubadebate*, 13 August 2010: http://www.cubadebate.cu/reflexiones-fidel/2010/08/13/el-gigante-de-las-siete-leguas-parte-2/?subscribe=active#subscribe2.

26 Jorge I. Domínguez, "Las relaciones cubano-norteamericanas: de la Guerra fría a la guerra más fría," in *La política exterior*, 448–9.

27 See Jorge I. Domínguez, "La política de los Estados Unidos hacia Cuba durante la segunda presidencia Clinton," in *La política exterior*, 459–86.

28 See the report by Cuban journalists Deisy Francis Mexidor and Marina Menéndez Quintero published in the Cubadebate website and based on the testimony of Salvadorian terrorist Francisco Chávez Abarca: "Cuba's Reasons: Continuation of Terrorist Plans from the US," http://razonesdecuba.cubadebate.cu/capitulo/bajo-el-signo-del-terror/, downloaded in PDF format on September 24, 2010.

29 One of them, Gerardo Hernández Nordelo, was sentenced to two consecutive life terms.

30 The case has been widely reported in the domestic and international press.

31 Bob Woodward, *State of Denial: Bush at War, Part III* (New York: Simon & Schuster, 2006) 224.

32 See Wayne Smith and Anya Landau, "Keeping Things in Perspective: Cuba and the Question of International Terrorism" (Washington: Center for International Policy, 2001) available at http://www.ciponline.org/cuba/cubaandterrorism/keepingthingsinperspective.pdf.

33 See Fernando Ravsberg, BBC correspondent in Havana, "Algo se cuece" ("Something is cooking"), in *Cartas desde Cuba*, 12 August 2010, http://www.bbc.co.uk/blogs/mundo/cartas_desde_cuba/2010/08/algo_se_cuece.html.

34 Jorge R. Piñon and Robert L. Muse, "Coping with the Next Oil Spill: Why U.S.–Cuba Environmental Cooperation is Critical, U.S.–Cuba relations at Brookings," *Issue Brief* Nº 2, Washington DC, The Brookings Institution, May 2010, http://www.brookings.edu/papers/2010/0518_oil_spill_cuba_pinon.aspx#.

35 See *CUBA: A New Policy of Critical and Constructive Engagement, Report of the Brookings Project on U.S. Policy Toward a Cuba in Transition*, Washington DC: Brookings Institution, April 2009, http://www.brookings.edu/reports/2009/04_cuba.aspx.

5

CUBA–U.S. COOPERATION IN THE DEFENSE AND SECURITY FIELDS

WHERE ARE WE? WHERE MIGHT WE BE ABLE TO GO?

HAL KLEPAK

- What has been the evolution of U.S.–Cuban collaboration in security and defense since 1989?
- What is the actual context today of such collaboration?
- What are we likely to see in this field if the current diplomatic situation persists?
- What might trigger better relations?
- What cooperation might there be in these areas if relations were to improve?

The Historical Context

In 1959–60, the revolutionary government broke entirely the 60-year dependent relationship that the Cuban military had had with the armed forces of the United States. The Cuban Army and Rural Guard had been set up by the United States directly in the several years of military occupation that the country repeatedly endured between 1898 and the 1930s, until the Roosevelt government dropped the Platt Amendment limiting Cuba's independence at the beginning of the period known as the Good Neighbor Policy (1934–54).[1]

The United States was the model for all three Cuban armed services, and it provided the vast majority of their weapons, tactics, ships, vehicles, aircraft, external training opportunities, and doctrine. The expansion and improvement of the Rural Guard into the three traditional armed services occurred mainly in response to United States needs in the two world wars and the Cold War as well as of course to domestic Cuban needs for internal security and the protection of property, itself largely U.S., in the countryside. The Cuban armed forces essentially had no roles other than those of support for the national objectives writ large of the United States in the security area.[2]

This situation, underscored by the presence of a U.S. naval station at Guantánamo, the Mutual Assistance Pact signed during the Korean War giving the United States special access to Cuban strategic resources in case of conflict, and the presence of large U.S. air, naval and army missions with the Cuban forces, underwent immediate and drastic change with the arrival of Fidel Castro's government.[3] Fidel, while anxious to buy arms in the early days from the United States or its allies, soon realized that his reform program was going to elicit such a negative reaction from Washington that such a goal would be unattainable. He would then search for alternative sources, ignoring and then reducing the traditional influence of the United States on the Cuban military within his own *Fuerzas Armadas Revolucionarias* (FAR) as they were to be called as of September 1959.[4]

The bilateral defense connection, massively strong for 60 years, was simply gone within a few short months. And soon the Soviet Union would replace the United States as model and source for most of what Cuba needed to maintain its defenses. At the same time those defenses, in the face of increased attempts by the United States to unseat the revolution, became much stronger and the FAR were simply transformed into a large and powerful deterrent force such as the Island, and arguably Latin America had never seen.

The ensuing "alliance" with the Soviet Union, while in fact never any such thing except for a very few months in 1962, troubled Washington greatly though perhaps not as much as some think. The Pentagon tended to see Cuba not so much as a threat in the larger sense but rather more as a potential nuisance for U.S. shipping bound for Europe or via the Panama Canal or from the Gulf of Mexico through the Florida Straits or the Caribbean. While the U.S. was certain that it could easily neutralize Cuban military efforts if Havana were unwise enough to come into a wider war between the two great alliance systems, the FAR could nonetheless add one more negative factor to concerns about lines of communication to Europe.[5]

With the end of diplomatic relations in 1961, the military situation continued, of course, to deteriorate with the U.S. military expecting until rather the last minute to have some role in supporting the Bay of Pigs invasion, and the next year taking Cuba very seriously indeed during the October Missile Crisis when the Island was quarantined and the possibility of a real invasion actively planned for. Later the growth of the Soviet connection kept the Pentagon's attention but only sparked it seriously when the prospects for an actual troop, missile, or naval deployment seemed real. Otherwise the threat, while present, was not considered massive and just as much attention was placed on what the United States saw as Havana's "adventurism" in support of subversion and insurgency in South and Central America and in Africa and the Middle East as there was on the supposed danger from Cuba in a strictly military sense.

On the other side, Cuba permanently worried about the possibility, sometimes remote, sometimes close, of a U.S. invasion. It was also troubled by U.S. policies of turning a blind eye to, although admitting the illegality of, the use of U.S. territory by extremist Cuban-Americans to launch terror attacks on the Island. While never engaged in a formal alliance with Moscow, Havana did feel nervous about any U.S.– Soviet tensions even though for much of this period it urged on the USSR a still more forward policy in standing up to Washington.

Cuba's military stance was, however, not an offensive one but rather one grounded firmly in armed deterrence. A large regular force, based on conscription and supplemented by a vast national militia, all of it supported with massive supplies of Soviet equipment was established in the years after the Missile Crisis. And the strategy chosen was to ensure that any U.S. attack would be so expensive in casualty terms for that country that no possible political objective that Washington could have could make the game worth the candle. In Raúl Castro's own terms, for Cuba, "to avoid war means to win it."[6]

Even during these years of the deep Cold War, however, relations around the base at Guantánamo were generally fairly good. While there were incidents on occasion, and in 1989 to 1994 even some serious ones, humanitarian issues were handled if not routinely at least correctly when they occurred and no incident was allowed to get out of control.[7]

The Period 1989 to Today

In the early 1990s, the crippling blows dealt to Cuba by the so-called "special period" that followed the collapse of the Soviet Union and the end of its support for Cuba brought some calls in the United States for magnanimity when dealing with the Island. But other approaches prevailed; soon the U.S. was "closing in for the kill," first with the Torricelli and then the Helms–Burton legislation of 1992 and 1996 respectively. Something had happened, however, in the strictly defense area, which was not mirrored in any sense in what was going on in Congress. In 1986, President Reagan, reacting doubtless to the warming up of relations with Gorbachev's Soviet Union, declared that the United States No. 1 security threat was no longer the Soviet Union and was now the illegal importation of drugs.

At the same time the collapse of the Soviet bloc and the "peace dividend" meant that it was possible to expect the U.S. forces to become involved in less conventional tasks. These "non-traditional" concerns were many and expanded the "threat" to other areas such as illegal migration, epidemics that cross frontiers and kill, natural disasters, and even climate. It appeared that everything would be put into the security basket despite Latin American warnings that this was what had recently most threatened regional democracy, with the armed forces being responsible for all security matters in a context where this merely exacerbated their overwhelming role in the state.

In the United States, there was increasing input from the armed forces not only in countering the international illegal narcotics trade, a role the U.S. military were given offshore as of the late 1980s, but also in dealing with illegal migration and natural disasters (a longstanding role but now a growing one). An initially reluctant U.S. military establishment, used to the "high policy" issues of traditional national defense and the Cold War, was wary of having such roles increase unduly and threaten historic prestige and importance. But budgetary conditions being what they were, the military soon changed their minds and took to the new roles with at least some degree of keenness.

This, alongside the collapse of any prospect of Cuban military cooperation with Russia, was the key element to a context that was to allow Cuba–U.S. security cooperation to begin and grow. With these new roles as their responsibility, and therefore with increasing cooperation with other U.S. agencies such as the United States Coast Guard (USCG), the Drug Enforcement Agency (DEA) and others also involved in anti-drugs and anti-illegal migration activities, the Department of Defense found its perception of Cuba changing quickly.

Key Washington security and defense circles came to the view that Cuba no longer constituted any threat to the United States except in the rather vague sense that too rapid and violent an end to the regime there might entail vast migration northwards to the United States and this was to be avoided for all manner of domestic political reasons. This view was confirmed dramatically when Cuban-American and other conservative Members of Congress in 1997 obliged the Pentagon through the Graham Amendment to answer the direct question as to whether Cuba was still a threat to the United States.

The Pentagon, even when its report was sent back for review after it received greatly critical reaction from "Miami," stuck to its guns. The FAR were declared to have no offensive capability outside Cuba, no programs for the development of weapons of mass destruction of any kind, and little interest in subversion and thus to be no such threat. In response to criticisms U.S. senior officers defended the report and suggested, in what was also becoming something of a trend albeit a less powerful one, that the United States should be finding ways to cooperate with its southern neighbor and not to confront it.[8]

This of course was based on the new assessment of Cuba, now found to be an interesting partner for the United States because of shared strategic analysis of certain central threats to both. Havana and Washington, each for its own reasons, feared the growth of the illegal narcotics phenomenon. Fidel had enjoyed a superb record in this field having outlawed marijuana growing in the areas of "Cuba Libre" that he had freed during the fighting in the Sierra Maestra in 1956–9. In addition, he had taken Havana from being one of the main centers for drug use and distribution under the mafia rule of the 1940s and 50s and made it virtually drug-free in the anti-corruption campaign of 1959–61.[9]

This positive record changed somewhat, however, as a result of the involvement of some Cuban senior officials in drug dealings related to the Colombian insurgency in the 1980s. In 1989, in the famous trial of Division General Arnaldo Ochoa and his collaborators from the FAR and the Ministry of the Interior (MININT) for engaging in drug deals with Colombian *narcotraficantes*, Fidel and Raúl thus had even more reason to show zero tolerance on the issue. Despite his fame as a hero from the fighting in Angola, Ochoa was shot as were two other senior officers. In the context of attempts by some in the United States to link the FAR, the Cuban state, and Raúl himself to the illegal drug trade and use it as a pretext for firm action against the regime (as it was being used against President Noriega in Panama at the same time), Ochoa's crime was seen as treasonous and not just about drug trafficking.[10]

The DEA, Coast Guard and Pentagon could hardly fail to be impressed by the seriousness with which Cuba was addressing the drugs issue, a situation heightened as the special period, the great effort at belt tightening declared by Fidel in the summer of 1990, began to take effect. For now, tourism would explode with many visitors bringing drugs to the Island almost as a matter of course.[11] Fidel was determined that Cuban society would not be undermined, as so much of the rest of the world was then being, by this scourge. Cooperation with the United States for this, and other foreign policy reasons more linked to *raisons d'état*, appeared ever more crucial.

The special period underscored such a need, soon adding the migration issue in the starkest of terms in the years to come. The massive suffering of the Cuban people caused by the collapse of the Soviet connection and the hardening of the U.S. "blockade" meant that the demand to leave the Island grew apace over the first half of the 1990s. In 1994, the launching of boats, rafts, tire inner tubes and almost any other floating device from Cuban shores had become a constant of national life. The USCG and even the U.S. Navy found themselves deeply involved in saving such craft and their passengers; an immigration crisis of major proportions ensued with the bulk of those found sent for very long periods to the U.S. base at Guantánamo and not allowed into the United States automatically as had been the practice before.

Cuba did not on this occasion attempt to put a stop to the flood and thus forced the United States to enter negotiations on how to handle the crisis. The migration talks gave rise to two new accords that finally brought an end to the worst of the problem for the United States. The accords among other matters called for regular meetings to be held between the authorities of both countries to review progress on the issue and for direct cooperation between their two national security services in dealing with illegal migration and its effects.[12] Here again, on a non-traditional threat concern for both countries, cooperation flourished and allowed a major security question to be addressed. And, by then, the 1991 Cuban withdrawal from Angola and the 1990 defeat of the Sandinista government in Nicaragua, combined with Cuba's financial disaster at home, sealed the end for the "adventurist" foreign policy with which the United States found such fault.[13]

In this context, there developed even closer links between the U.S. naval authorities at Guantánamo and Cuba's *Tropas Guarda Fronteras* (TGF) formation on the other side of the "border." Monthly routines could be complemented by those called by either side for whatever purpose they felt useful. In addition, facilities for easier communications links in case of emergency were set up on both sides. When new types of U.S. naval aircraft came into service that required more Cuban sea and airspace in order to land safely, Havana gave permission with alacrity for such space to be used when needed.[14] And when U.S. aircraft, using Guantánamo or not, needed overflight permission to pass through Cuban airspace on their way to natural disasters or other relief missions to the south, that permission was easily obtained without the strains of earlier periods.

The U.S. Interests Section in Havana, in perhaps the most visible change, received as part of the migration accords a permanent U.S. Coast Guard officer at lieutenant-commander rank to oversee the agreements that had been put in place and act generally as liaison officer between the USCG and relevant security forces in Cuba. He was given a degree of access to TGF and other defense and security operations and installations of the Cuban state that is often the envy of other countries' defense attachés in the country, even those closely linked to Cuba by ideological or other ties.[15]

Today

This evolution in thinking on both sides has allowed for a relatively stable connection between the two nations' security forces, which is low-key and mutually beneficial, does not draw great unwanted public attention, and has set the stage for an expansion of the linkages if both sides wished to move in that direction. If it is difficult for the Pentagon, DEA, Coast Guard and other security agencies to speak loudly about their cooperation with Cuba as a result of the powerful Cuban-American lobby in Congress and their exceptional influence on the press, it is also difficult for the FAR to trumpet a close connection with a country that is after all referred to constantly in Cuba as "the enemy." Cooperation continues regularly, however.

Direct cooperation remains centered around Guantánamo and the anti-illegal migration activities set in motion by the bilateral accords of the mid-1990s. The latter is a daily affair involving the rather tragic interception of boats moving north with illegal migrants towards the United States that are stopped and seized by patrol vessels from either or even both nations' coast guards and on occasion navies.[16] The passengers are returned to the Island through cooperation between the two security forces' networks while the crews can be arrested for illegal trafficking in human beings.

The Guantánamo cooperation continues as it has for decades and has merely become more visible because of the opening of the terrorist interrogation centers there. Indeed, Cuba was quick to offer the United States assistance in the fight against international terrorism and not only gave Washington a guarantee that Cuban air, sea and land spaces would not be used by terrorists against the United States but also assured the United States that, if it had further needs in Guantánamo linked to the issue, Cuba would try to assist.

The cooperation on narcotics interception is more subtle but hardly less real. The FAR have important roles assigned to each of the three services in the anti-drugs role. The Navy assists the TGF in finding and intercepting suspicious craft that come into Cuban national air space or waters or even that behave suspiciously outside them. The Air Force does the same with flights over suspicious craft, pinpointing their movements, as well as with checking on potential "*bombardeos*" of drugs into the sea around the Island.[17] The Army has the task of mounting sometimes very large-scale sweeps of areas of beach or swamp where there is some suspicion a "*bombardeo*" has occurred. This is usually done with reservists since it is very manpower intensive.

Since 1994, the United Kingdom has a relatively large program of training and equipment provision to MININT in the anti-drugs role. Not only is sophisticated equipment provided to Havana but Cuban officials are given the most up-to-date training in the field, both on the ground in Cuba and in the United Kingdom itself. The British have expressed in no uncertain terms their admiration for the Cuban role and have continued the program even when political pressure has forced the closing down of others.[18] The United States has made no public statements on this program but its officials are more than clear that they are simply delighted that this cooperation is carrying on.[19]

In this context, Cuban intelligence about the movement of suspicious aircraft or boats is freely available to the British as well as to the Royal Bahamian Defence Force, with which Cuba has close ties. And the Cubans know very well that it turns up as quickly as possible in U.S. hands as well, which is the main reason the information is passed on in any case.[20] The problem, as usual, is that of having the information at hand in a timely fashion and passing it on in this indirect way is obviously far from ideal. On a great many more pressing occasions the Cubans have found other, more direct, methods to pass the information on to USCG officers so that it can be acted upon quickly.[21]

At the time of writing it is not clear to just what degree there has been cooperation in the aftermath of the Haiti earthquake of early 2010 but a number of the many Cuban doctors there are of course reserve officers. And while the extent of such cooperation is not yet clear, there have been public statements on both sides that such cooperation is taking place and at least some real discussion of expanding it. The same is to some extent true of cooperation on the weather, especially in the key area of natural disaster preparation. This is frequently mentioned as a logical area of working together and in the wake of Hurricane Katrina the U.S. military has been given greater roles in this field.[22] But to date there have been no official announcements about what cooperation there might be, or how it is conducted.

Cuban foreign policy has had a clear objective since at least the end of the 1980s to build confidence with the United States, or at least with certain key sectors within the security apparatus of that country, through clearly useful cooperation efforts in line with U.S. objectives in the wider security field. A particularly poignant example is that, in the desperate conditions of the special period, the navy has not laid down or bought any ships since the 1980s except for the construction of three fast patrol craft recently brought into service for the anti-illegal migration and anti-narcotics roles. This is not an accident, and Cuba has clearly in this case "put its money where its mouth is."

The evident opposition of the Pentagon to any provocative move on the part of the United States in the potentially tense situation provoked on 31 July 2006 with the illness of Fidel has also reassured the FAR that its efforts to build bridges to key U.S. security sectors have been at least partially successful. The FAR know very well that they cannot at this stage expect those sectors to be pro-Cuban but they also know that there has been something like confidence building going on for some time with those agencies and that at times like the summer of 2006 those connections prove their worth.[23]

And If Relations Remain Bad?

There is not much more room for improvement in the cooperation between the two countries in defense and security if there are no overall better relations than those that exist today. Defense and security cooperation is based on common views of central issues regarding that area of concern, and these certainly exist in this case. But currently it has been possible to maintain the level of cooperation by being relatively away from the public eye; its importance has ensured that extremists on both sides of the Florida Straits think twice before tackling it in a very critical way. Despite efforts to torpedo the Pentagon's response to the Graham Amendment, for example, U.S. extremists knew that taking on the Department of Defense, an agency difficult to accuse of being "soft on communism" or uninterested in issues of national security, was likely to be counter-productive. However, this has not always been the case with those on the extremist edge.[24]

Almost any further developments would probably catch the public eye in southern Florida in ways that would be difficult to control. The way the inclusion of Cuba in the repetition of the list of states sponsoring terrorism occurred in the winter of 2009/10, despite the amazement of U.S. allies and opponents alike, would suggest that the battle is far from won for further cooperation in defense and security. Despite any number of positive opinions stated by Homeland Security and related officials in the United States since 2001, the influence of domestic politics on even a central plank of U.S. security policy like the "war on drugs" is still clear.

It is vital that relations actually improve for there to be an environment where the commonality of views mentioned can give rise to more extensive and publicly acknowledged cooperation. Even on matters as vital to the United States as drugs, and with virtually the entire anti-narcotics establishment of the U.S. government keen to cooperate with Cuba, there has been no stomach in Washington to respond favorably to Havana's repeated calls for a formal accord between the two countries to work against the scourge. The frustration in the FAR and MININT on the issue is more than reflected in the corridors of the Pentagon, Coast Guard and especially the DEA.[25]

While there is little doubt that the Defense Department, the USCG, the DEA, and almost certainly natural disaster, immigration, anti-terrorist and other U.S. agencies are quite ready to turn the page and start to cooperate more with Cuba, there is little opportunity for them to do more without a lead from higher up the political chain. And so far there is little such lead, to say the least. The thaw in the bilateral relationship is seemingly still far away despite President Obama's election campaign talk of opening dialogues with adversaries rather than making war on them. And Cuba, while not unwilling to talk about cooperation in any or all of these fields, shows little hurry and understands the U.S. political dynamic very well after all these years; there is now little optimism after so much time has passed under the Obama presidency and so little has happened vis-à-vis Cuba or even Latin America in U.S. foreign policy.

Thus we might expect to see anti-illegal migration operations continue as they do today, under the accords in place but with no further deepening of linkages. Likewise, without a formal accord, we would see anti-drugs cooperation continue indirectly and not at the level of efficiency that U.S. and Cuban security services would hope for. And in Guantánamo we would likely see no further progress of importance, except perhaps for some small steps, e.g. improving security arrangements via joint fire brigade exercises. Only perhaps in the climate field could one imagine slightly larger steps being taken without attracting public ire in the United States. Certainly, in the key area of anti-terrorist cooperation there would continue to be total deadlock while the official policy of Washington remains treating Cuba as a sponsoring state and a pariah while the unofficial statements of many U.S. officials continue to see it as a potential partner.[26]

Possible Triggers for Change?

What might trigger such a change in the relationship? I undertake this speculative endeavor quite reluctantly and only because the book's editors have requested it. Thus in the realm of conjecture, the first triggering change might be in Miami itself. The nature of the Cuban-American community has evolved with much more room for political debate there on issues related to how to deal with Cuba, a less certain electoral pattern of behavior than in the past, and the older generation of extremists seeming to be fading from the scene. If this trend continues, U.S. presidents or security agencies might be willing to face the lessened political and electoral risk then posed to those who wished to change the relationship, and could be willing to engage in a real dialogue with the Island. That dialogue would almost certainly make public and clear the degree to which Cuban and U.S. views on regional security mesh in a number of ways.

The emergence of a truly moderate leader in the Cuban-American community might be a further catalyst for change and might be able to sway that community towards a more rapid change in approach to Cuba and to U.S. policy towards the Island. The old leadership of the Cuban-American National Foundation is gone and the new leaders, especially since the fiasco of extremist views dominating the Elián González case and the death of Jorge Más Canosa, have also shown more moderation in recent years. A leader who could play both to the moderate wing of the old guard of exiles and to the new immigrants who are not viscerally anti-Castro, and who could offer unity to the community for the future, might be able to become popular enough to undo the efforts of the extremists who have dominated that community for so long. And even if it is true, as many have argued that it is not so much southern Florida's votes as the "old" Cuban-American community's financial contributions to politicians that makes U.S. policy remain so firmly anti-Castro, that political lobby would doubtless be greatly weakened by a visibly more moderate "Miami."

Another possible trigger might be the death of Fidel, Raúl or both. The name "Castro" elicits such emotion that the physical disappearance of Fidel or both brothers might have such an impact on U.S., and especially southern Florida public opinion, that the way would be open for quicker "normalization" of relations. As we have seen, there are powerful forces at work in U.S. security affairs, as well as of course in trade, investment and tourism sectors, hoping for progress on the Cuba file sooner rather than later. They would be in a position to move with force if such events occurred, particularly in light of the freeing of the president's hands via the end of provisions of the Helms–Burton Act of 1996, for his negotiating with a Cuban government not led by one of the Castros.

Cubans are often well aware that the Cuban Adjustment Act of 1966, whereby Cubans "fleeing" the Island are allowed guaranteed access to the United States once they touch land as well as a privileged position there once arrived, may well not long survive the end of the Castro government. It is not impossible either that the deaths of such persons would be accompanied by some disorder in Cuba. In any case, there might well be a major movement of people northwards when such deaths take place. Under these circumstances, there would be a strong desire on the part of the U.S. Coast Guard, immigration services, and probably the Pentagon, and of course on the part of many politicians opposed to yet another massive dose of immigrant arrivals, to gain quick control of the situation and halt the migration. Assuming that the revolution does not end with the death of the Castros and that any disorder is kept under such control that U.S. intervention is unnecessary, one could imagine negotiations sooner rather than later to ensure a smooth and peaceful change in the quality of the relationship and to make certain that calm on both sides of the Florida Straits is maintained.

A third situation that might trigger moves for better relations could be the continuation or intensification of the spate of natural disasters that have hit the Americas, and indeed the world, in recent years. As "Katrina" and Haiti 2010 have shown, the impacts of such events can be local or widespread and there seems no reason to expect that the hemisphere is not to be hit at least as much in future years as in the recent past by such phenomena.

Cuba is a long and thin island lying across a large part of the direct passage from the south and east towards the United States. Hurricanes that hit the Island often turn northwards towards Florida or northwestward towards the Gulf States. Cuban weather tracking is an important potential asset for the United States in the case of hurricanes and, as mentioned in the cited Inter-American Dialogue report, there is much room for cooperation in this area. It is also noteworthy that many experts believe that Cuba has much to teach even the most developed of countries on preparing for hurricanes and public relief afterwards.

The discovery of truly important and exploitable petroleum resources in Cuban waters of the Gulf of Mexico might also act as a catalyst for change. To date, as is well known, the economic exploitation of those deposits has not been interesting because of the costs involved compared with the prices obtainable in today's market for the quality of product found. But there are many who feel that this is likely to change with time. If that were to occur, the pressures in the United States to have a part of the action, especially in such a secure and contiguous zone to U.S. territory as the Cuban zone of the Gulf, might prove irresistible for U.S. policy makers. In such a context, cooperation would be essential to set the stage for direct working together on what would likely prove such a huge project.

A further possibility for a trigger is reform of Cuba's economy of such a nature that there is true international access to the Island, stimulating a race to exploit its potential in all or nearly all sectors. In such a situation, U.S. investors and exporters might put such pressure on the U.S. government that it agreed to a real effort to improve relations. Given the advantages of defense and security cooperation to the United States, under such circumstances it is difficult to imagine Washington would not attempt to profit from the improved general context by pushing for greater cooperation in this area as well.

If in the United States pressures in Congress, or more generally by activists on the right to travel, won their case and tourism from the United States exploded, those seeking greater security cooperation with Cuba could argue more forcefully that U.S. citizens needed proper security when on the Island and therefore a closer bilateral relationship in that field was required.

Finally, in this list of conjectures, there is the possibility that a pandemic, one of the many common in recent years, might strike the region with such force that both countries would be desperate to control its spread. Only Cuba, in the whole Third World and perhaps in the First as well, is in a position to mount a massive medical campaign off its shores. In the context of "new" or "non-traditional" threats with which the armed forces and other security services of the United States have been involved in recent years, this might well lead to closer cooperation between the two countries in this area of concern.

And If Things Actually Got Better?

Whatever the stimulus for an improvement in relations, there is ample reason to see such a change as leading to significantly greater cooperation in the defense and security field. This is because the two nations see many elements of the current strategic picture in similar ways, although there are many limits to a shared overall vision.

Perhaps most importantly both Havana and Washington view instability in Mexico as a cause for alarm. Cuba has been deeply affected by Mexican events since colonial times when the Island and the mainland shared much. The Mexican independence movement had enormous impact on the Island and many royalists fled the new republic for Cuba in the 1820s where they were joined by whites from the Yucatán fleeing the Mayan rebellion three decades later. And the Mexican Revolution had an enormous impact on no less a figure than Fidel Castro who chose Mexico for the organization of the expedition that eventually toppled the Batista dictatorship.[27]

This fear of Mexican instability is of course linked to the shared view of the importance of dealing with the international illegal drug threat in a major way. While Cuba has denounced at times what it views as the "militarization" of the international effort against the trade, it has always agreed that the problem should be addressed with energy and originality of approach, combining a strong element of repression with an equally strong effort in education and medical support. Cuba's neighbors without exception are feeling the scourge's effects more than the Island itself but Cuban authorities are in no way complacent and argue for more and more efficient joint effort for the future and not less.

This is certainly a view shared by Washington and the security situation in Mexico, especially in the northern border regions, has the United States troubled indeed. The corruption, poor training, inadequate intelligence services, poor pay and other living conditions, mediocre leadership, and insufficient equipment of the many and varied Mexican police forces do not make for much chance of success in the fight to control the drug lords. And bringing in the army proved necessary but hardly enough to bring order out of the chaos.

Cuba's excellent police force, combined with its generally good intelligence services and high morale, might allow for eventual cooperation among the three countries in what is a shared vision of threat. This might be extended to anti-drugs cooperation that includes the armed forces as well since Mexico's military has had a massive anti-drugs role since at least the 1970s and knows the problem well, while the FAR have a record second to none in dealing with the special challenges of this fight.

Bilaterally, there is much room for greater cooperation in this field as well. Cuba badly needs more patrol vessels and aircraft to ensure that its coverage of its long Island, hundreds of smaller islands and cays, and vast maritime zone is as efficient as possible. The United States could easily assist in this and do so at a level much greater than can the United Kingdom, helpful as that country has been to Cuba to date. Training and access to new technologies would be equally important for Cuba to do an even better job of interdiction and follow-up passage of information.

It must also be said that whatever the views of some in the United States, in most of Latin America and the Caribbean, Cuba represents legitimacy and a proper interest in the well-being of local peoples and has proven its devotion to those ideals over the long haul. Cuban involvement in an inter-American but especially a Caribbean-wide effort in the area of the control of narcotics is a legitimizing element not easily acquired elsewhere, which the United States lacks at the moment. In the context of joint task forces such as the one currently operating out of Key West, and of other regional initiatives, a Cuban presence could be invaluable.

The three specific countries that have shores on the Gulf also share a great deal in their vision of illegal migration. Mexico is of course engulfed in this problem as well, having not only its own massive problem to address but also having to deal with illegal migrants from Central and South America, and more recently even with some Asians and others who use Mexican land or sea spaces to move north. A Cuban dimension to a trilateral approach would give a legitimacy to U.S. efforts that they do not currently enjoy and might allow the matter—one on which there are not as yet common approaches in the region—to be addressed in a more humane and efficient way.

While this point is being made in connection with the mutual interest in seeing a stable Mexico shared by both Havana and Washington, it is illustrative of a common view about trafficking in persons and illegal migration in general which both capitals have, even though there is a need for nuance in such an assertion since they do not necessarily see the root causes of the problem in anything like the same way. But this has not restricted bilateral cooperation in this dramatic area of actually achieved mutual support. And there is no reason to think that this could not be expanded to a more fluid cooperation, and extended more widely, than merely the bilateral sphere where again Cuban legitimacy is of enormous potential utility for inter-American and pan-Caribbean cooperation.

Both countries likewise wish to see a stable and prosperous Caribbean Basin for the development of tourism, mutual cooperation efforts of all kinds but including the security field, and perhaps most dramatically natural disaster preparation and relief. In the context of better bilateral relations between the United States and Cuba, there is surely no reason to delay the expansion of efforts to make the region a more secure place across the board. While Cuba initially criticized sharply the U.S. military "takeover" of Haiti in the wake of the earthquake of 2010, it did not do so about the actual assistance given and, as discussed, there is ample if not entirely complete evidence of cooperation on the ground between Cubans and U.S. assistance agencies.[28] Both Cuba and the United States likewise agree that the stability of Haiti has an important role in wider good relations especially because of its constant immigration dimension for its neighbors.

Both capitals also view the terrorist threat as a serious one, whatever the declaratory policy of the United States might be. As we have seen in the Pentagon and McCaffery statements cited above and visible in innumerable public statements from Homeland Security officials and others, the U.S. security services are perfectly aware that Cuba is neither a security threat nor a sponsor of terrorism. While Cuba certainly had a period when the "export of revolution" formed part of its national defense strategy, it has long abandoned such an approach to bringing about major change in Latin America and the world. In addition, Fidel's personal distaste for actual terrorist methods is evident from the days of the insurgency in the Sierra where his reaction to the attempted use of such approaches to revolution was swift and firm.[29]

Cuba's geo-strategic situation is such that in the long run cooperation with it against international terrorism can easily be invaluable. When the 11 September attacks took place, it was not only Canada which, despite the potential dangers for itself, immediately offered to take in aircraft bound for the United States that could no longer land there. Cuba also made that offer, although in its case politics prevailed again and the offer was not taken up. Given Cuba's prestige with many revolutionary movements worldwide, it has proven a useful outlet for countries that wish to give some of their terrorists a place to go (especially after an incident) but who likewise wish them to be controlled there and not allowed to continue acting against their target states. Spain's ETA and Colombia's ELN are two cases in point. But it is vital to keep in mind that these arrangements are not made against the wishes of the states in question but rather with their active compliance with the approach taken.

Both Spain and Colombia, for example, are grateful to Cuba and are certain that Havana keeps a close watch on the individuals involved. Far from being pro-terrorist, Cuba has shown itself to be exactly the opposite. This does not mean it has no sympathy at all for the cause for which the terrorists act. Cuba differs from the United States in that it feels that the only way to address most terrorism effectively is by attacking its root causes of injustice, foreign domination, and inequality. But Havana recognizes the requirement to deal firmly with terrorists as well, although it does not feel that widespread international military campaigns do much more than create even more terrorists. Hence its slogan has been "against terrorism and against war," something with which Washington is obviously not in agreement. In day-to-day affairs, however, Cuba is clearly a potential collaborator in helping to ensure U.S. security in this field, as it has frequently offered to be since 2001. And once again, its unrivaled legitimacy as a state that understands the root causes of terrorism and the need to deal with them if one hopes to rid the world of this other scourge means that it is able often to speak with authority to both sides. This does not escape many U.S. strategic analysts even if they do not necessarily speak of it often.[30]

The Cuban Customs and Immigration services are efficient, form a direct part of the Ministry of the Interior, and are keenly aware that Cuba must never be seen by the United States as a real problem in the terrorism sphere. The rest of MININT is perhaps even better aware of the potential dangers for Cuban survival of a perception in Washington that Cuba harbors or supports in any way terrorist movements, and intelligence services take the matter extremely seriously. It would be an easy matter for the two countries to have their equivalent security services active in this field to begin to work together whatever their ideological differences might be. The profit would clearly be shared through increased national security for both.

In the case of further developments in the petroleum exploration in the Gulf of Mexico, there would also be every reason and great potential for bilateral (or even trilateral) cooperation in ensuring the security of oil rigs and other elements deployed in the zone in question. This security would be not only against potential terrorist attack but also against the danger of natural disasters and would, given both U.S. and Cuban requirements in the era of terrorism, contribute to dealing with a mutually troubling phenomenon. Obviously before any progress at all can be made on such a front, there would have to be an end to the assertion that Cuba is somehow—so far undefined by the U.S. State Department—a sponsor of international terrorism.

Thus in the general and the specific senses, an improved bilateral relationship could find itself spawning quite significant defense and security cooperation between the two countries. How odd then that the pull towards closer relations is not stronger. Or is it really odd at all?

The Limits to Cooperation in Defense and Security

Despite all that has been said above, the reality is still that Cuba and the United States differ on a vast range of major subjects at the present time and are unlikely to be able to change that situation in a major way without a different way of looking at the world in Havana, Washington, or both. Those different approaches to the world reflect a great deal, but most especially they are the product of the historical experience of each country, both generally and in terms of the bilateral relationship between them.

Cuba is a revolutionary socialist state and the United States is a conservative capitalist one. Indeed, in many senses Cuba is the *porte-étendard* of socialism today in the world just as the United States is that of more or less unbridled capitalism. Cuba is immensely proud of this status if more than a little worried about it as well, and the United States, while shaken deeply by the economic crisis, remains proudly capitalist and free-market oriented. At the same time, Cuba practices a popular democracy that has little time for what it sees as bourgeois competitive elections and, at least while the U.S. blockade/embargo and economic war continue, human rights as individual ones in competition with those of the collectivity. The United States meanwhile practices traditional electoral democracy with great emphasis on individual human rights.

In line with this overall divergence, Cuba follows a foreign policy that eschews direct military support for revolution within the Third World but that nonetheless shows solidarity with what are termed progressive movements in many of those countries, even when often their credentials for such a distinction are slight. The United States, on the other hand, sides generally with very conservative regimes and normally stands for stability and the status quo, even when the governments that benefit from that status are repressive in the extreme. While this is not so much the case in Latin America since the end of the Cold War, it remains the case in an enormous part of the world. This distance between the two nations can be closed only with great difficulty.

Cuba is against the current vogue for the redefinition of sovereignty to limit its scope and impact since it feels that, in the real conditions of what in many ways is a unipolar world, the only country to benefit from this limitation is the hegemonic power itself, and thus smaller countries must perforce suffer. The United States, while not willing to give up much sovereignty in its own case, does believe that others should. Here again the gap between the two positions, especially on the right to military intervention in the domestic affairs of states, is wide indeed.

Havana does not see instability in many countries as necessarily a bad thing if it leads to deep reform of what Cuba sees as corrupt or reactionary regimes. The United States, on the other hand, tends to see any instability as a problem. The United States has vast investment around the world and particularly in Latin America; it feels that the changes Cuba believes are necessary to improve world conditions threaten those investments and give priority to collective needs rather than corporate or individual profit. Havana still calls for a new world economic order based on need and not merely on profit, something the world's greatest economic power, and principal beneficiary of the present way of doing things, is unlikely to see in a favorable light at any time soon.

The FAR themselves are the armed servant of a revolutionary project that sets out to transform society while the U.S. armed forces see themselves as helping to maintain a status quo whose effects are overwhelmingly positive for the United States. They tend to be extremely conservative, although this is a nuanced generalization, as has been shown in this short chapter.

It is difficult to imagine the United States abandoning entirely its *droit de regard* on Cuban affairs, even the most internal ones. The relationship has never been a "normal" one in this sense, a point made by more than one author in this book. The two countries have different and in many ways contradictory projects not only for the hemisphere and the world, but also for the future of Cuba. Havana's includes entire freedom of choice for the Cuban state as to its path, while Washington's insists that whatever end-state Cuba moves toward should in essence be to the liking of the United States.[31]

Without an end to the U.S. blockade/embargo, it is unthinkable that Cuba would accept to re-integrate into the inter-American system. Indeed, its diplomacy, like that of several other members of ALBA, the leftist inter-state alternative project for the Americas, is to establish a new Latin American system in which the United

States does not have the overwhelming position that made Argentine thinker Manuel Ugarte refer to its predecessor organisation, the Pan American Union, as the U.S. "ministry of colonies" and as a "congress of mice presided over by a cat."[32] Since in these new bodies the United States will not even be present, the best Washington can hope for is to have like-minded Latin American states that are members to carry its concerns to the group.

Cuba is extremely unlikely to sign (again) the Rio Treaty (the Inter-American Treaty of Reciprocal Assistance), the accord under whose umbrella most inter-American security arrangements have been made. (Cuba is still formally, however, in the view of some international jurists, a signatory of that collective security agreement and hence, at least *de jure*, an ally of the United States.) Nor is it likely to integrate into other hemispheric security bodies, although it is surely not too much to imagine that, if things were better bilaterally, it might attend the Conference of Defense Ministers of the Americas and possibly that of the Public Security Ministers if that assembly becomes more permanent.

What Cuba would almost certainly accept would be a non-aggression pact with the United States, which would be a guarantee that both sides would abide by generally non-provocative behavior norms in their relations with the other party. Whether the United States would be willing to sign such an accord, given its own view of its historic rights to a *droit de regard* on Cuba, is another question. But without progress in the bilateral relationship, any moves in this direction are out of the question at the moment.

Conclusion

The evolution of the defense and security elements of the Cuba–U.S. relationship, such as it is, is fascinating on many levels. While before the end of the Cold War, security and defense, at least in public discourse, were the most prickly elements making any friendly relationship possible, since the end of that era this same field has been one of the most positive ones for the maintenance of at least vaguely favorable linkages in certain key sectors.

With the U.S. and Cuba seeing eye to eye on many security and defense matters, especially illegal migration and the drugs trade but also to some degree terrorism, natural disaster and some other issues, there has developed a largely informal set of arrangements that serve the interests of both countries and do not elicit much negative public reaction. Formal agreements on migration combine with informal procedures and approaches on drugs interdiction, safety and confidence building in Guantánamo, natural disaster cooperation, and to some degree climate to produce a picture of two countries that do talk to one another. Daily cooperation between the countries in these areas has made more than one officer in both countries' security services remark on not only how good cooperation is at the moment but how easily it might be improved to the benefit of both capitals.

The United States has immense capacity to assist Cuba in doing an even better job in the areas of greatest concern to U.S. security agencies, and Cuba has enormous human resources to assist with those worries. If the United States has the technology, military power, money, weapons and equipment, strategic lift, command and control capabilities, and so much else to offer to a wider cooperative effort in this field, Cuba has the medical staff, experience, inter-American and wider international legitimacy, geographic position, and political will to make the most of those resources. Given better relations at the bilateral level, it is hard to imagine that the already extant connections between the two countries' armed forces and other security services cannot flourish, once given the chance. But all discussion of such advances must take into account that the two countries see the world and react to events in quite different ways. The building of further defense and security cooperation, that field so given to misunderstandings and exaggeration in any case, would have to be undertaken with due caution but also with hope that it might help generate, as well as be the product of, greater cooperation across the board and a more healthy relationship for both parties.

Notes

1   For the earlier period, see Marilú Uralde Cancio, "La Guardia Rural: un instrumento de dominación neocolonial," in *La Sociedad cubana en los albores de la República*, ed. Mildred de la Torre (Havana, Editorial Ciencias Sociales, 2002), 25–282; and for the later, see Rafael Fermoselle, *The Evolution of the Cuban Military 1492–1986* (Miami, Ediciones Universal, 1987); and Louis Pérez, *Army Politics in Cuba 1898–1958* (Pittsburgh, University of Pittsburgh Press, 1976).

2   See the Cuban national chapter in Adrian English, *The Armed Forces of Latin America* (London, Jane's, 1984).

3   For the period up to the fall of Batista, see Servando Valdés Sánchez, *Cuba y Estados Unidos: relaciones militares* (Havana, Editora Política, 2005), especially 51–92.

4   The abolition of the old armed services, and their formal replacement by the three "revolutionary" forces that make up the FAR today, occurred with Laws 599 and 600 of September 1959, the same that named Raúl Castro as Minister and gave him the new rank of Army General (*General del Ejército*). See Luis Buch Rodríguez and Reinaldo Suárez Suárez, *Otros pasos del gobierno revolucionario cubano* (Havana: Editorial Ciencias Sociales, 2002), 90–92.

5   See the best work on the bilateral connection in Yuri Pavlov, *The Soviet–Cuban Alliance 1959–1991* (New Brunswick, NJ, Transaction, 1993) and for U.S. analysis see the superb Lars Schoultz, *National Security and United States Policy toward Latin America* (Princeton, Princeton University Press, 1987).

6   Raúl Castro, "XXX Aniversario del Desembarco del Granma," in *La Revista Militar* (2 December 1986), 288–291.

7   Interview with Brigadier-General José Solar Fernández, former commander of the Frontier Brigade of the FAR at Guantánamo, quoted in Luis Báez, *Secretos de Generales* (Barcelona, Lozada, 1997), 277–278.

8   Anthony Boadle, "Cuba's Military No Threat, Turns to Farming," *The Miami Herald*, 31 March 1998; and Christopher Marquis, "Cuba Still No Threat, Pentagon Insists but Defense Chief Tempers Report," *The Miami Herald*, 7 May 1998.

9   Francisco Arias Fernández, *Cuba contra el narcotráfico: de víctimas a centinelas* (Havana, Editora Política, 2001).

10   President Reagan had said in 1983 that "there is strong evidence that Castro officials are involved in the drug trade, peddling drugs like criminals, profiting on the misery of the addicted." See Jay Mallin, *History of the Cuban Armed Forces: from Colony to Castro* (Reston, VA: Ancient Mariners Press, 2000), 350. For more on the accusations, see Armando Ferrer Castro, *Conexión en Cuba: la historia de la poderosa red de funcionarios cubanos con el narcotráfico internacional* (Mexico, Planeta, 1990). Raúl's views are in his later interview, *El Sol de México*, "Somos los más antidroga del mundo," 23 April 1991, 20. For Fidel's retrospective views on the Ochoa Affair, see Ignacio Ramonet, *Cien horas con Fidel* (Havana: Consejo de Estado, 2006), 419–435.

11   "Politics–Cuba: Worried about Drugs," *International Press Service*, 5 October 1998.

12   See Joint Communiqué between the United States and Cuba concerning Normalizing Migration Procedures, *U.S. State Department Consolidated Treaties and International Agreements* (Washington: 1994), 301–304.

13   See the series of pieces on this subject in *Cuba's Foreign Relations in a Post-Soviet World*, ed. H.M. Erisman and John Kirk (Gainesville, University Press of Florida, 2000).

14   Conversations with FAR and Foreign Ministry officials in Havana, 1996–2003.

15   Conversations with USCG officers in Havana and Washington as well as the defense attachés of seven countries in Cuba during the period 1998–2006.

16   In the Cuban case, the independence of the TGF patrol system is limited by the close links between it and the Navy. The chain of command goes through the FAR in any case, and there is much shared repair, training, communications, doctrine, tactics, and manning. There is little in the open literature on this but much can be gleaned from works such as Cuba, Ministerio del Interior, *Las Reglas del juego: 30 años de seguridad del Estado* (Havana, Editorial Capitán San Luis, 1992); and Fernández Arias, *Cuba contra el narcotráfico*, 92–105.

17   A *bombardeo* is the dropping from aircraft or from boats of drug packages, which will then be picked up by smaller and less visible boats coming in to do so from the U.S., Haiti or the Bahamas. Many of them drift onto Cuban beaches and even more into Cuban waters.

18   "Entrega Reino Unido Donativo a Cuba," *Granma Internacional*, 21 February, 1997, quoted in Fernández Arias, *Cuba contra el narcotráfico*, 178–179.

19   The chief of Interpol, a United States citizen, heaped praise on Cuba's anti-drug role in 2002. See "Chief of Interpol Praises Cuba for its Fight against Drug Traffic," *Prensa Latina*, 17 January 2002.

20   This is not always the case. The Royal Navy maintains an anti-drugs escort vessel permanently in the Caribbean and Cuban intelligence has led to some quite amazing narcotics seizures by the British as well. Fernández Arias, *Cuba contra el narcotráfico*, 167–168 and the author's interviews with Foreign and Commonwealth Office staff, London, April 2000.

21   These are really more than just rumors. See Francisco Fernández Arias, *Drogas y mentiras: dos agresiones contra Cuba* (Havana, Editorial Capitán San Luis, 2008), 104.

22   See for example Inter-American Dialogue, *The Environment in U.S.–Cuban Relations: Recommendations of Cooperation* (Washington, Inter-American Dialogue, 1997).

23   The author develops further some of these ideas in his *Confidence Building and the Cuba–United States Confrontation* (Ottawa, Department of External Affairs and International Trade, International Security Research Paper, March 2000).

24   Miami Republican Representative Ileana Ros-Lehtinen made the quite extraordinary comment about the U.S. Defense Department's assessment of Cuba, "These Pentagon types are very politicized. They get their instructions very directly from the White House." See Christopher Marquis, "Pentagon Wants U.S. Military to Work with

Cuba," *The Miami Herald*, 21 February 1998. In January 2011, Representative Ros-Lehtinen became the chair of the Committee on Foreign Affairs of the U.S. House of Representatives.

25 See on these issues the excellent work of Jorge Rodríguez Beruff and Gerardo Cordero, *El Caribe: la 'tercera frontera' contra las drogas* (Buenos Aires, Biblos, 2005).

26 Many senior retired military and security services personnel have echoed these assessments. General Barry McCaffery, U.S. drug "tsar", as he was styled when he headed the DEA, not only said that Cuba was "an Island of resistance to the drug threat" but added on terrorism that Cuba would be "supportive of any attempt to solve the problem by peaceful means," saying also that the Cubans "… certainly are not a terrorist threat and I do not believe they are harbouring terrorist organizations." On Cuban–American terrorist attacks against Cuban civilian targets, McCaffery said "the United States should make sure it does not happen anymore." Marc Frank, "Former U.S. Drug Tsar Meets Castro in Cuba," Reuters, 3 March 2002.

27 See Otto Hernández Garcini et al., *Huellas del exilio: Fidel en México 1955–1956* (Havana: Casa Editora Abril, 2004); and for Fidel's view Ramonet, *Cien horas con Fidel*, 206 and 589.

28 "Reitera Cuba disposición de cooperar con todos," *Juventud Rebelde*, 19 January 2010.

29 Tad Szulc discusses this point in his *Fidel: a Critical Portrait* (New York, Avon, 1986), 342.

30 On Cuba and terrorism see Anya Landau and Wayne Smith, "Keeping Things in Perspective: Cuba and the Question of International Terrorism" (Washington: Center for International Policy, 20 November 2001), in http://www.ciponline.org/cuba/ipr/keeepingthingsinperspective.pdf.

31 The *Report to the President* of the Commission for Assistance to a Free Cuba, submitted to and praised by President Bush in 2004, has not been rejected by the Obama administration. For a Cuban view of it, see Nicanor León Cotayo, *El Plan Bush: Made in USA* (Havana: Editorial Unicornio, 2006).

32 Manuel Ugarte, *La Patria Grande y otros textos* (Buenos Aires, Theoria, 1996).

6

TERRORISM AND THE ANTI-HIJACKING ACCORD IN CUBA'S RELATIONS WITH THE UNITED STATES

PETER KORNBLUH

On March 25, 2010, the infamous figure of Luis Posada Carriles appeared publicly on the streets of Miami during a protest march against Cuba. Openly participating in the demonstration, and speaking with reporters, Posada's much publicized presence reminded the international community that the United States has given sanctuary to one of most renowned international terrorists of his era—a fugitive sought by Interpol, an admitted bomber of hotels and discothèques in Havana, and a man whom the U.S. intelligence community has identified as responsible for the mid-air destruction of Cubana flight 455 in October 1976, in which 73 men, women and children perished.

Posada's public presence in the United States undercuts the credibility of the U.S. State Department's list of "State Sponsors of Terrorism" published annually by the U.S. government. The list includes such rogue nations as Syria, the Sudan, and Iran. And since 1982, when the Reagan administration decided to equate support for revolution with support for terrorism and punish the Castro government for backing the Sandinistas in Nicaragua and the FMLN in El Salvador, the list has included Cuba. "Cuba remains on the list," the State Department advised members of Congress in a letter on December 28, 2009, "because the Cuban Government continues to harbor members of foreign terrorist organizations within its territory," a reference to militants from the Basque ETA, and the Colombian ELN and FARC who are living in Cuba.[1] Left unstated is that the Spanish government requested—and indeed signed an agreement with Cuba—to accept the ETA members in 1984, and President Armando Uribe has accepted the presence of the Colombians in Cuba and asked Cuba to assist in mediating the ongoing guerilla conflict.

The U.S. government has also accused Cuba of being "opposed to U.S. counterterrorism policy." But the historical record demonstrates that the Castro government has made an effort going back to the early 1960s, when the very first issue of terrorism in the skies became a part of Cuba's relations with Washington, to support, indeed, to sponsor measures that would discourage terrorist activities. This history has long been forgotten in the debate in the United States over Cuba and terrorism. It is history that should be recalled as common ground for fighting terrorism as well as advancing toward better relations.

First Discussion: Che Guevara and Airplane Hijackings

The middle-of-the-night meeting between Ernesto (Che) Guevara and Kennedy White House aide, Richard Goodwin, in Montevideo, Uruguay on August 17, 1961, will go down in history as the first major discussion between a high U.S. official and a Cuban Government representative on how to improve relations between Havana and Washington. After thanking Goodwin for the Giron invasion, which Guevara said "had been a great political victory for [the Cubans], enabled them to consolidate, and transformed them from an aggrieved little country to an equal," *Commandante* (*sic*) Che proposed an effort to arrive at a "*modus vivendi*" between the two nations. It was in this context that Cuba first raised the troubling issue of airplane hijackings from the United States to Cuba. Goodwin reported to Kennedy on what Che said:

> Guevara touched on the matter of plane thefts. He said he didn't know if I knew but they had not been responsible for any hijackings. The first plane was taken by a young fellow who was a good boy but a little wild and who is now in jail. They suspected that the last plane was taken by a provocateur (a CIA agent). He is afraid that if these thefts keep up it will be very dangerous.[2]

Guevara suggested that the United States and Cuba negotiate an agreement, which would address the issue of hijackings from both countries and put an end to this "dangerous" practice. Since he understood that finding "a practical formula for such a *modus vivendi*" would be difficult, he recommended beginning with "subordinate issues." Che suggested "discussion of the airplane issue" as a starting point for talks between the United States and Cuba on peaceful coexistence.[3]

Cuba certainly had its own security interests in wanting to create a deterrent to air and ocean hijackings. Indeed, the Castro government wanted Washington to repatriate exiles who had used violence to hijack planes and boats to escape the island. Cuba took the first step: in a 1961 diplomatic note, the Castro government proposed a mutual accord to return all hijackers to their country of origin. But the Kennedy administration ignored this proposal.

At the time, as Goodwin would recall in 2001 at the 40th anniversary conference on Playa Giron held in Havana, the Kennedy administration was not interested in discussing better relations, or even efforts to counter the budding issue of skyjackings, an early manifestation of terror in the air. Instead, the White House instigated

Operation Mongoose, which led to the 1962 October Crisis. In the aftermath of that crisis, Castro and Kennedy did engage in a series of messages attempting to return to the idea of peaceful coexistence. Indeed, on November 22, 1963, Kennedy was assassinated at the very moment that an emissary of his, a French journalist named Jean Daniel, was meeting with Fidel to convey a "message of peace" from the United States.

Castro, Nixon, and the Anti-Hijacking Accord

The issue of pursuing better relations between the United States and Cuba was set aside for years to come but airplane piracy emerged as a significant, and escalating, terrorist phenomenon that neither country could afford to ignore. Between 1961 and 1967, 17 planes were hijacked to Cuba; 17 more were diverted in 1968 out of 35 skyjackings around the globe. Between 1969 and 1972, the number of plane hijackings worldwide escalated to 280. The majority of them were diverted to Cuba.[4]

Richard Nixon was an inveterate Castro-hater; he "disliked Castro intensely," his national security adviser, Henry Kissinger would recall.[5] As Vice-President in April 1959, Nixon became—and he remains—the highest level U.S. official to hold a meeting with Fidel Castro. (There is even a photograph of them shaking hands outside of Nixon's office.) Although Nixon's report to President Eisenhower made clear that he was quite impressed by Fidel's charisma and leadership qualities, Nixon would later write in his memoirs that he emerged from that meeting as a leading advocate of overthrowing Cuba's revolutionary regime.

But, with a dozen hijackings to Cuba in the first two months of 1969 alone, the new Nixon administration secretly entered into talks with Castro about returning the perpetrators of the hijackings to the United States. Using the Swiss Embassy as an intermediary in Havana, the State Department approached Castro to negotiate a deterrent. Quietly, Cuba began to expel some hijackers to third countries, and encourage others to leave. But, as the virtual epidemic of hijacked planes continued to put Cuba in the international spotlight as a destination for plane pirates, Castro issued a public message to Washington: on September 19, 1969, he announced a new Cuban law on dealing with hijackers. The law stated that Cuba would now prosecute or extradite all foreign hijackers. Extradition, however, would only take place with countries that had negotiated a bilateral anti-hijacking accord with Cuba.

"The decree calls for reciprocal agreements and also covers persons diverting ships," the Department of State reported to Nixon. "The *quid pro quo* which Castro presumably intends to exact is not clear and may give us trouble," the memo noted referring to Cuba's position that reciprocity meant the United States would have to treat Cuban exiles who had hijacked planes and boats as terrorists and return them to the island. "However, we believe the Cuban decree could represent a significant step and are considering how best to respond to it." The highly publicized law "now appears to be a major gambit by Cuba," National Security Council staffer Viron Vaky advised, "not only with respect to the hijacking situation but perhaps in terms of relations with us as well."[6]

Soon the Department of State was sending secret diplomatic notes through the Swiss Embassy trying to find a "neutral" solution to returning U.S. hijackers from Cuba. But for political reasons the Nixon administration refused to budge on what Kissinger termed the "troublesome reciprocal elements"—Castro's demand that the United States also return Cuban exiles who had committed hijacking crimes. The 1969 efforts to arrive at an official anti-hijacking accord ended without resolution.

In both word and deed, however, Cuba continued to signal its willingness to find a solution to airline hijackings. A secret memo from Kissinger's office on "sanctions against countries which are uncooperative on hijacking"—the predecessor to the current State Department list of state sponsors of terrorism—stated that Cuba was, in fact, cooperating. "Cuba has now become one of the best behaved of the hijacking states, since it immediately allows the planes and passengers to return and often jails the hijackers," the NSC reported. "It recently returned its first hijacker, and offered to return all hijackers provided we do the same (a commitment we cannot make because of the political asylum aspect)."[7] For fear of offending the exile community by repatriating Cubans who had hijacked boats and other forms of transportation, the Nixon administration significantly delayed formulation of an anti-hijacking accord.

After a particularly violent set of criminal skyjackings in October and November 1972, including one in which a guard was killed and the hijackers extorted $2 million from Southern Airways, Fidel Castro again took the diplomatic initiative to propose an official accord to halt this terrorist phenomenon. Radio Havana announced that the Cuban government was "ready to take such steps which might lead to the adoption of a broad agreement" to deter future hijackings, if the U.S. government "shows an equal willingness and interest." The government statement continued:

> We believe … that both countries are interested in taking steps to resolve this problem, which recurs systematically. The Government of Cuba states that it cannot be in its interests, nor does it in any way desire, for the territory of Cuba to be used as a refuge for persons who are responsible for criminal acts … Nor is the Cuban government in any manner interested in promoting hijackings of planes, seagoing vessels or illegal entries into or exits from the United States.[8]

In response, on November 16, Secretary of State William Rogers passed the following message to the Cubans: the U.S. government was "prepared to negotiate an arrangement regarding hijacking and other serious crimes which may be committed in the future." The Nixon administration would also "consider favorably any arrangement and location for such talks that would expedite agreement." The

Cubans reacted expeditiously; nine days later, Castro officials met with the Swiss ambassador and formally presented a draft treaty on hijackings. "On the basis of equality and strict reciprocity," it read, both governments would punish with 10 to 30 years of imprisonment any person who "seizes, takes control of, appropriates, or diverts" an aircraft or other vessel. In a clause on violent exile operations in the United States, the draft accord also obliged both countries to pursue and severely punish those persons who were using its territory to promote or plan "acts of violence or depredation against aircraft or vessels of any type."

Within a week, U.S. officials worked out a response for President Nixon to approve. "To facilitate agreement we have followed the Cuban text as closely as possible, but certain changes were necessary," Secretary Rogers reported to the president on December 2. The major differences in the U.S. counter-proposal were:

- to agree to give serious consideration to extraditing hijackers instead of prosecuting them in the country in which they land;
- to rule out retroactive action against acts of piracy thereby protecting Cuban émigrés in the United States;
- to stiffen the sentence for aircraft piracy; and
- to return any funds or property obtained illegally.

U.S. officials passed this draft to Swiss intermediaries in Washington a few days later. Over the next eight weeks the Swiss Embassy in Havana hosted Cuban officials to negotiate the accord along the lines of the U.S. proposal. By mid-February, the two countries had arrived at a formal agreement, and signed a "Memorandum of Understanding on Hijacking of Aircraft and Vessels and Other Offenses."

The February 15, 1973 accord states that all hijackers of aircraft or other vessels "shall be considered to have committed an offense" and would either be returned to their country of origin for prosecution or prosecuted in the country to which they had arrived. Both nations agreed to facilitate the rapid return of passengers and crew as well as the vessels and aircraft. Cuba won a concession from the United States that it would punish those exile groups using U.S. territory to plan sabotage against Cuban boats and planes. "Each party," the agreement stated, "shall try with a view to severe punishment … any person who, with its territory, hereafter conspires to promote, or promotes, or prepares, or directs, or forms part of an expedition which from its territory or any other place carries out acts of violence or depredation against aircraft or vessels of any kind …" [9]

For Fidel, signing the hijacking treaty with the Nixon administration represented an advance of multiple Cuban interests. The continuing and increasingly violent hijackings put Cuba in a negative international spotlight as a haven for terrorists. Forcing the United States to prosecute or return Cubans who hijacked boats or planes could serve as a deterrent for violent seizures of Cuban vessels on the island; moreover, counter-terrorism cooperation could address Cuba's leading national security concern: the violent U.S. based anti-Castro operations of the militant exile community. And, there was the possibility that the success of these negotiations could create a foundation for broader talks about a change in U.S. policy toward more normal relations. As Che Guevara had pointed out to Richard Goodwin in August 1961, an agreement on air piracy could be one of those "subordinate issues" that could pave the way for talks on a *modus vivendi* between Washington and Havana.

From the start of the talks, however, Nixon had feared that an anti-hijacking accord would be interpreted as a change in Washington's overall posture of hostility toward Cuba. On February 13, 1973, as Secretary Rogers presented the president with the final language of the accord, Nixon's secret Oval Office taping system picked up his continuing anxiety about this issue:

> *Nixon:* Does it get into anything in terms of normalization of relations because that's the only thing that would concern me? If you could cover that because I don't want the Cuban community to go up in a, up in a …
> *Rogers:* … What I would say is that it doesn't change any policy as far as Cuba's concerned.[10]

Two days later, when Secretary Rogers announced the new accord, he went out of his way to state that cooperation on hijacking did not signal a thaw in the hostile U.S. approach to the Castro regime. The bilateral agreement, he explained to reporters, "does not foreshadow a change of policies as far as the United States is concerned."[11]

After the Accord

The 1973 hijacking accord lasted until October 1976, when it was derailed by the most harrowing act of airline terrorism in the Western Hemisphere until the Al Queda attack in New York and Washington on 9/11, 2001. The target was not the United States, but Cuba. On October 6, 1976, Cuban exile terrorists, working out of Caracas, Venezuela, placed a bomb aboard a Cubana DC 10 jetliner. The plane blew up off the coast of Barbados, crashing into the sea, and killing all 73 persons on board, including the Cuban Olympic Fencing team. FBI and CIA documents identified the intellectual authors of the terrorist attack as the two godfathers of anti-Castro violence, Orlando Bosch and veteran former CIA operative Luis Posada Carriles. "We are going to hit a Cuban airliner and Orlando has the details," one Top Secret CIA report quoted Posada as declaring only days before the jet exploded just after takeoff from the seaside airport in Barbados.[12]

After the telephone number and name of the FBI attaché was found in the notebook of one of the Venezuelans who placed the bomb on the plane, Fidel Castro angrily denounced what he believed was U.S. complicity with the terrorist attack. In retaliation he abrogated the hijacking accord, which now seemed inconsequential in deterring heinous acts of terror against the Cuban people.

During the Carter administration the Cubans agreed to observe the tenets of the accord, and it has endured ever since. Its history reflects the cooperation, and mutual interest, that Cuba has exercised for the past fifty years in addressing concerns that both countries have about terror, violence, and their impact on average citizens. It was Cuba, the historical record reveals, that initiated negotiations to address the early phenomenon of transportation-related terrorist actions, and Cuba that persisted, even as the U.S. government preferred to cater to the violent interests of some exile groups who operated, for the better part of five decades, from its shores. The accord stands as a rare successful example of Cuba–U.S. bilateral diplomacy.

It could be argued that the hijacking accord obligates the United States to bring "severe punishment" on Luis Posada Carriles and Orlando Bosch who, after all, conspired to carry out an act of extreme violence against a Cuban aircraft and its passengers. But in 2010, Posada and Bosch were living freely in Miami; Bosch had been there for 23 years. Posada faced only minimal charges of immigration fraud and lying about terrorist acts—rather than prosecution for committing them—and it was unclear if he would ever be fully prosecuted, let alone actually imprisoned, for terrorism-related crimes. His public presence on the streets of Miami is a living symbol of the hypocrisy of the United States putting Cuba on a list of states that harbor terrorists.

Notes

1 See U.S. Department of State letter to Congressman James McGovern, December 28, 2009. This letter was provided to the author by the Congressman's office.
2 Memorandum for the President, "Conversation with Commandante Ernesto Che Guevara of Cuba," August 22, 1961, 2. These memoranda can be accessed on the website of the National Security Archive, http://www.gwu.edu/~nsarchiv/bayofpigs/19610822.pdf.
3 Ibid. 4.
4 For statistics on skyjackings and Cuba, see Karen Feste, "Reducing International Terrorism, Negotiation Dynamics in the U.S.–Cuba Skyjack Crisis," a paper presented to the 19th annual conference of the Association for Conflict Management, Montreal, Canada, June 25–28, 2006.
5 Henry Kissinger, *Years of Renewal* (New York, Simon and Schuster, 1999), 771.
6 Vaky to Kissinger, "Cuba's New Anti-Hijacking Law–A Significant Development," September 23, 1969, reproduced in FRUS, 1969–1976, Vol. E-10, Documents on American Republics, 1969–1972, Doc. 208.
7 White House, Kissinger to Peter Flanigan, "Possible Actions Against Countries Which Are Uncooperative on Hijacking," October 31, 1970. National Archive, RG 59, Central Files, 1970–1973.
8 The Radio Havana announcement is cited in the *Washington Post,* "Havana Decries Hijacks," November 16, 1972.
9 The 1973 Memorandum of Understanding has been published in the *American Journal of International Law*, 67, no. 3, 619.

10   Nixon tapes, Feb. 13, conversation no. 43–66 (WH Telephone Jan 31–Feb 27, 1973).
11   Quoted in Lars Schoultz, *That Infernal Little Country* (Chapel Hill: University of North Carolina Press, 2009), 259.
12   CIA, Intelligence Information Cable, "Activities of Cuban Exile Leader Orlando Bosch during his Stay in Venezuela," October 14, 1976. This document and others relating to the case of Posada Carriles can be seen in various postings on the website of the National Security Archive, www.nsarchive.org.

7

THE EUROPEAN UNION AND ITS ROLE IN U.S.–CUBAN RELATIONS

EDUARDO PERERA GÓMEZ

Relations between the European Union (EU) and Cuba, though of recent vintage (1988), have been singularly intense. They have also been burdened by each actor's connection with the United States such that it more closely resembles a triangular relationship than a typical bilateral one, because the third party's effect has been proportionately greater than in other subsystems. In this non-equilateral triangle, the two short sides connect the EU and the United States (the deepest and most extensive bi-continental relationship in history)[1] and the United States and Cuba (for evident historical, geopolitical, and security reasons).

The EU lacks significant capacity to influence U.S.–Cuban relations largely because of the EU's structural and functional inability to shape a common foreign policy, exert pressure on Washington, and overcome its own permeability and susceptibility to U.S. pressure. The EU is neither monolithic nor homogeneous. Its hybrid structure is organized around two interconnected but distinct levels of sovereignty: supranational and intergovernmental. The so-called Common Foreign and Security Policy (CFSP) operates at the intergovernmental level, under rules requiring unanimous decision-making but with 27 separate national realities,[2] a situation reflected in the lack of global results.

Decisions on policy toward Cuba are taken in the EU Council on the basis of unanimity among member states,[3] even though their interest in the issue varies, as does the priority they assign it and their different roles in various issue areas that shape relations with the Island (human rights, democracy, anticommunism). Further, each country's political position varies over time according to changes in administration, factors related to their institutional organization, the state of each country's relations with the United States and of Cuba's relations with the United States, and what points are under discussion as part of the EU's common agenda.

It becomes extremely hard for European countries to establish a truly "common position" on Cuba (or on many other issues) beyond certain minimum agreements. Only in this context can we understand the 1996 Common Position on Cuba (hereafter referred to as the Common Position).[4] It remains the EU's main reference point on Cuba policy but member states have applied it at their discretion in consonance with their national interests.

It is, therefore, not at all strange that EU–Cuban relations have so far been dominated by bilateral dealings between member states and Cuba, which reflect the real issues involved, while Cuba–EU ties have been confined to an ideological-symbolic dimension, which cannot be ignored, however.

Since the 1958 Treaty of Rome created the European Economic Community, the EU's relations with the Third World have been structured as a system of hubs and spokes determined by the pre-eminence of certain member states on issues related to specific countries or areas outside the Union. In general, the former colonial powers craft the policies—at least in general terms but often in specific terms—toward their former colonies. Spain has been the hub of EU policy toward Latin America and specifically toward Cuba. The other members either support the consensus so constructed, or they oppose it through various negotiations. The result is a minimal and quite variable common denominator, especially in cases where there is no clear, settled, and continuing EU policy that member states fully support.

These elements explain the ambiguities of EU "policy" toward Cuba, and the EU policy's difficulty in competing with policies undertaken by successive U.S. administrations or addressing the sustained consistency of Cuban policy toward the EU. Cuban policy has been based on the following key elements: refusal to accept preconditions for relations; development of bilateral relations with member states (not rejecting the goal of normalizing the tie with the EU but not sacrificing bilateral relations to this goal); non-discriminatory dialogue based on equal sovereignty; and identification of areas of common interest for cooperation as determined by national priorities.

The level of maturity achieved in the EU between member states regarding economic integration is reflected only dimly in the shaping of a common EU foreign policy. The Union continues to be an economic giant and yet a political dwarf with little influence, especially on issues that, in any special way, involve the interests of the United States.

An example is the EU's inability to effect any change in the U.S. policy of blockade against Cuba, despite the Union's opposition to extraterritorial coercive measures.[5] In practice, the EU agrees with the United States that the blockade should be considered a bilateral issue.[6] Nor did the EU succeed in blocking specific points about Cuba imposed by the administration of George W. Bush in the declarations of the Transatlantic Summits of 2007 and 2008. In 2008, it did succeed in getting the United States to withdraw a parallel reference to Venezuela from the draft declaration, but not the reference to Cuba. In EU–U.S. relations, Cuba remains a dependent variable. EU policy toward Cuba, which is quite vulnerable to the influence of Washington, takes account not only of the state of U.S.–Cuban relations, but also of U.S. positions and sensibilities on this issue, to the point where one may say the EU policy is constructed "in its shadow."[7]

A paradigmatic case is the 1998 EU–U.S. Understanding about the U.S. Helms–Burton Act. Some authors hold that, in practice, this agreement nullified the Act's provisions affecting properties and visas.[8] Logically, that is not the Cuban reading of a transaction that "in practice signified Europe's renunciation of its opposition to the Helms–Burton Act and its support for the policy of subversion being carried out by the United States, while getting nothing in return."[9] The agreement avoided a trade war between the European Union and the United States because of Cuba (a matter of high political salience), without eliminating the law's chilling effects on European investment, as seen by the fact that the EU's tunnel vision challenged the extraterritoriality only of Titles III and IV of the Act. For the United States, this Understanding has been a win–win proposition: the Title III waiver was a domestic imperative in any case, it did not fulfill its improbable commitments with respect to Title IV, and it managed to block the EU's complaint to the World Trade Organization (WTO). The Understanding was possible, fundamentally, because Cuba was not worth a trade war between the world's two largest economies.

Cuba matters for U.S. policy because it is an issue in U.S. domestic politics. Cuba matters less for EU foreign policy because it is not generally an issue in domestic politics in European countries outside Spain. The Island's low priority among the EU's external concerns means that any cost-benefit analysis will, as a rule, privilege the quality of EU ties with the United States over those with Cuba.

Last but not least, one must bear in mind the ideological congruency between the United States and the European Union and their respective incongruencies with Cuba. EU relations with the Island are a by-product of the restructuring of the international system after the breakdown of the Cold War equilibrium. The new context strengthened tendencies toward globalization structured around a fundamentalist model of liberal democracy and market economy. After the fall of the Berlin Wall, the EU became, by default, the only factor in Europe offering any equilibrium in relation to U.S. political-military hegemony; its Cuban ties were born under political pressures for a "transition" similar to the Eastern European one. This coincided with a period in which the Island most strongly felt the negative impact of U.S. policy, which since the mid-1980s had involved a strategy of securing condemnation by international bodies, most notably the United Nations Human Rights Commission. Thus, an ideological and political component has played a fundamental role, with antecedents in Cuba's early ties to the former Council for Mutual Economic Assistance (CMEA) and continuity in the survival of its socialist system. That component is reflected in the mutual perceptions of the EU and Cuba, and it has flared up, to varying degrees of intensity, in EU–Cuba relations, sometimes in a determining fashion.

Although EU policy toward Cuba cannot be completely explained in terms of an unconditional strategic alliance with the United States—given that such an analysis fits primarily into a Cold War context and conveys an incomplete understanding of the European integration process—still that alliance does exist and continues to be strategic, even if its object has changed. Neither can the policy be justified in terms of the EU's customary discourse of democracy and human rights, which has been delegitimized by double standards in the Union's foreign policies. That lack of coherence reveals itself in dissimilar attitudes toward different counterparts, in accordance with the interests of the EU. Examples abound, with Cuba as a paradigmatic case, involving—additionally—the imposition of preconditions on the negotiation of any contractual arrangement.[10]

All this is hard to explain on anything other than ideological grounds. Cuba is the only country in Latin America or the Caribbean, and one of only a few in the world, without an agreement linking it to the EU. It is the only country in its region subject to a Common Position that establishes preconditions for future progress in cooperation, although that position does declare in its third point that the EU "will evaluate developments in Cuban internal and foreign policies according to the same standards that apply to European Union relations with other countries."[11] This contrasts with the EU's cooperation with countries whose behavior in terms of democracy and human rights is frankly deplorable. An additional element is the exaggerated and strident presentation of certain events in Cuba within the EU, and especially within the European Parliament, while no mention is made of all sorts of other events on the world scene.[12] All evidence indicates that this is due to political factors.[13] Though the means employed may be more or less nuanced, still in the end the policies of the United States and the European Union do have a common goal. Clearly, the goal is more extreme for the United States since it seeks the re-imposition of its hegemony over Cuba and a recovery of power by the oligarchic, anti-national bloc displaced by the Revolution; one should not assume this to match the objectives of the EU. But the point of convergence is in promoting a modification of the basis of the Cuban political and economic system, a "regime change." This hypothetical "peaceful transition to democracy" is open to various interpretations.[14] The European strand of this political discourse, especially the Spanish one, tends toward shopworn and untenable comparisons of systems that are, in fact, antagonistic, like the Cuban Revolution and Francoism, a murky mass-media cliché converted into an incontestable truth,[15] whose corollary is to take the Spanish transition as a paradigm for the proposed "peaceful transition" in Cuba. As might be expected, there is an irresolvable contradiction between this goal, the means employed to reach it, and Cuba's own interests and desires.

Lost Opportunities?

The period from 1988 to 1995 was characterized by many ups and downs in the relationship,[16] yet the end of that time offered a glimpse of possible negotiations toward the eventual signing of an economic and trade cooperation agreement. This process moved forward rapidly between June 1995 (a communiqué issued by the European Commission about developing relations with Cuba)[17] and December of that same year (a mandate issued by the European Council to prepare guidelines for the required negotiations).[18] However, it was ultimately frustrated by a combination of factors.

Spain was enjoying the six-month presidency of the Council during the final days of the Socialist Party administration of Felipe González, who had carried out a very active foreign policy with respect to Cuba. His intense negotiations within the heart of the EU were allowing the *dossier* to advance quickly. González was counting on a favorable attitude from the United States; although there was no evidence of an actual agreement, "the harmony between Brussels and Washington at the time was evident, and there had been repeated close consultations between the officials in charge of Cuba policy in the United States, Spain, Italy, and France."[19]

In February 1996, Manuel Marín, the European Commission Vice-President, made a sudden visit to Havana; his goal was to obtain certain political commitments from the Cuban side before the opening of formal negotiations, in spite of previous assurances that there would be no preconditions.[20] The basic points put forward by the EU included a reform of the penal code and recognition of the opposition—a serious obstacle to Cuban approval.[21] From the start, this attempt to apply conditions to the negotiations was doomed to fail. Nonetheless, Marín later blamed the fruitlessness of his personal effort on supposed disinterest from the Cuban side, despite the fact that the EU then represented more than a third of Cuba's foreign trade and more than half of tourism and foreign investment flows.[22]

Richard Nuccio, who arrived in Brussels twice, first less than 24 hours after the approval of the Commission communiqué and then slightly before Marín's trip to Havana, gave a press conference at the end of his second visit in which he clearly acknowledged the fragility of the consensus among the EU member states about the Cuba issue and his doubts that the process would yield concrete results. Later he said that, in strategic terms, the project failed because it was interpreted as an offer made in coalition with the United States, something which Castro was in no way ready to accept.[23]

The EU's suspension of this process was also affected by important changes in context during the first half of 1996: the Cuban Air Force shot down two small planes flown by the Brothers to the Rescue organization; the United States enacted the Helms–Burton Act which in turn highlighted the "structural weaknesses" of the EU and the ambiguity and fragility of its Cuba policy; and changes of administration occurred in Spain and in France.

At the end of the year, the European Council adopted the Common Position on Cuba based on the "catalogue of measures" presented by special U.S. envoy Stuart Eizenstat to Washington's European counterparts during a tour of various EU member countries in September 1996.[24] With reason, Cuba has repeatedly stated that the position was approved by the EU under pressure from José María Aznar on the basis of a draft originating in the U.S. State Department.[25] For some EU member states, this proposal constituted a mechanism of proportional pressure, while for others it was an act of obedience to the United States. For the U.S. Department of State, the Common Position was a cause for celebration.[26]

The adoption of the Common Position confirmed the conservative Spanish administration's alignment not only with Washington's policies but also with those promoted by the most reactionary sectors of the Cuban émigré community in Florida. When the EU adopted the Spanish position, in effect it became a hostage of Spanish policy, as it continues to be. In so doing, the EU drastically reduced its chances of influencing Cuba. Several later events corroborated that the Spanish government had become "the spearhead of North American interests within the framework of the EU."[27] The policy of George W. Bush's first administration and the effects of Europe's subordination to U.S. hegemony and unilateralism dovetailed with the policy of the Partido Popular (PP) administration in Spain to shape one of the most difficult and chilliest periods of the EU–U.S.–Cuba triangle. The high level of tension and charged ideological content spread into bilateral Spanish–Cuban relations, while the visible deterioration of EU–Cuba ties plunged these into the worst moment of their history.

The Spanish government offensive was felt in all the institutions of the Community, with Spain taking advantage not only of its leadership role on the Cuba issue but also of its position in majority groups within the European Parliament. It thus challenged Miami for the role of the center of the Cuban counter-revolution in exile.[28] Among the most important legacies of the Aznar administration were the stagnation of Cuba's political dialogue with the EU, which had been renewed the previous half-year under the presidency of Belgium; the indefinite suspension (instigated by European Commissioner Loyola de Palacio) of the procedure for considering Cuba's request for admission into the Cotonou Agreement; and the sanctions adopted by the EU Council in June 2003.[29]

In this adverse context, trade relations between member countries of the EU and Cuba not only were not interrupted, but were even advanced, which shows that these relations are not determined by bilateral political differences. In fact, commercial exchanges have not been subjected to political conditions. Its determinants lie, rather, in the evolution of international trade, Cuba's purchasing capacity,[30] protectionist elements implicit in the harmonization of markets within the Community,[31] and restrictions imposed by the U.S. blockade.

Thus, trade with the EU as a whole, which rose to account for more than a third of total Cuban foreign trade at the end of the 1990s due to the loss of preferential

TABLE 7.1 Annual average growth rates of Cuban foreign trade with selected partners, 1996–2002 and 2003–2008

	1996–2002	*2003–2008*
World	20.5	23.04
Europe*	13.2	9.72
EU-22**	NA	9.72
EU-15***	25.5	9.72
EU-5****	29.9	9.02
Spain	3.7	13.09
Venezuela	14.6	41.08
China	13.8	29.91

(*) This category refers to EU and non-EU states in the continent.
(**) The 22 trading partners among the 27 current member states of the EU reported individually in the Statistical Yearbook of Cuba: Austria, Belgium, Bulgaria, Czech Republic, Denmark, Finland, France, Germany, Greece, Hungary, Ireland, Italy, Latvia, Luxembourg, Netherlands, Poland, Portugal, Romania, Slovakia, Spain, Sweden, United Kingdom.
(***) The 15 member states of the EU until 2003.
(****) Cuba's five major trading partners in the EU are France, Germany, Italy, Netherlands, and Spain.
Source: Author's calculations from data published by Cuba, Oficina Nacional de Estadísticas, *Anuario Estadístico de Cuba*, 2001, 2006, and 2009.

trade ties with the former CMEA, did not suffer substantial change as a result of the application of the Common Position or the diplomatic sanctions of 2003. This is demonstrated in Table 7.1, which shows the annual average growth rates for the period between 1996 (year of the adoption of the Common Position) and 2002, and for the period between 2003 (year of the adoption of diplomatic sanctions by the EU) to 2008 (the latest year reflected in the most recent edition of Cuba's *Statistical Yearbook*). The slower average annual growth rate in the second period results, all evidence indicates, much more from significant increases in the Island's trade with other partners such as China and Venezuela.

The same may be said about the evolution of the shares of specific partners in Cuba's total international trade. The data in Table 7.2 use as samples the first years of four successive four-year periods, beginning with 1996. Despite the decrease in the relative shares of Cuba's main EU partners, the Union is still responsible for a fifth of the Island's international trade.

Spain has remained in a privileged position among Cuba's trading partners, even during the José María Aznar administration. It was displaced from the top rank by Venezuela only in 2000—after four years of Partido Popular government—and from the second rank by China only in 2005; this resulted from substantial increases in trade with those two countries, not from any appreciable drop in trade with Spain. Spain remains third in rank, which helps to explain why Cuba's trade with only

TABLE 7.2 Percentage of Cuba's foreign trade represented by selected trading partners in selected years (value expressed in thousands of pesos)

Partners	1996 Value	1996 %	2000 Value	2000 %	2004 Value	2004 %	2008 Value	2008 %
World	5,434,523	100.0	6,470,672	100.0	7,947,316	100.0	17,928,820	100.0
Europe*	2,467,303	45.4	2,809,742	43.4	2,709,425	34.0	3,981,762	22.2
EU–22**	NA	NA	NA	NA	NA	NA	3,499,828	19.5
EU–15***	1,538,802	28.3	2,268,294	35.0	2,350,219	29.6	3,365,476	18.8
EU–5****	1,323,532	24.4	1,957,650	28.6	2,142,022	26.9	3,045,217	17.0
Spain	570,393	10.5	893,338	13.8	819,138	10.3	1,430,502	8.0
China	275,857	5.0	524,301	8.1	670,439	8.4	2,159,833	12.0
Venezuela	334,221	6.1	912,409	14.0	1,509,776	19.0	4,892,548	27.3

(*) This category refers to EU and non-EU states in the continent.

(**) The 22 trading partners among the 27 current member states of the EU reported individually in the Statistical Yearbook of Cuba: Austria, Belgium, Bulgaria, Czech Republic, Denmark, Finland, France, Germany, Greece, Hungary, Ireland, Italy, Latvia, Luxembourg, Netherlands, Poland, Portugal, Romania, Slovakia, Spain, Sweden, United Kingdom.

(***) The 15 member states of the EU until 2003.

(****) Cuba's five major trading partners in the EU are France, Germany, Italy, Netherlands, and Spain.

Source: Author's calculations from data published by Cuba, Oficina Nacional de Estadísticas, *Anuario Estadístico de Cuba*, 2001, 2006, and 2009.

five EU member states represented more than three-quarters of all trade with the European continent and 17 percent of the Island's total trade in 2008. Four of those countries—Spain, Germany, the Netherlands, and Italy—rank among Cuba's ten most important trading partners in the world.

Similar points can be made about tourism. From 1996 to 2008, five of the ten top-ranking sources of tourism to Cuba have been members of the EU: the UK, Italy, Spain, Germany, and France. Although the share of visitors from these countries relative to the total inflow dropped (from 47 percent in 1996 to 26.9 percent in 2008), factors other than the ups and downs of political relations with the EU seem to be the cause: a diversification of the sources of tourists, and other market elements including Cuba's competitiveness in relation to other tourism locales.

European investment, especially investment from Spain and Italy, is also worth considering. Despite fluctuations, such investment has maintained a continuous presence since Cuban law opened sectors of the national economy to foreign capital. Although foreign direct investment (FDI) figures are not made public because of security concerns stemming from application of the Helms–Burton Act, Spain and Italy are, along with Venezuela and Canada, the sources of the greatest volume of FDI in Cuba. Spain, in particular, plays a very important role in the realm of hotel administration contracts. Clear examples are the contracts with the Sol-Meliá chain, which has chosen to remain present on the Island despite extraterritorial claims made by the United States under the Helms–Burton Act.

An Opportunity Seized

The conclusions adopted by the EU Council on June 23, 2008, though accompanied by the customary rhetoric about Cuba, were the most important turning point in EU–Cuban relations since 2003 because they definitively ended the sanctions that had been imposed on the Island.[32] Thus, they removed the main obstacle to resuming bilateral political dialogue and cooperation with the European Commission.

The process that led to the elimination of the sanctions began with a change in attitude provoked by the return of the Partido Socialista Obrero Español (PSOE) to power in Spain in the March 2004 elections. Although it could not overcome the domestic political rift over Cuba, from its first days the administration of José Luis Rodríguez Zapatero demonstrated clear interest in departing at all costs from the previous government's policy.

Zapatero "realigned" Spain with the leading advocates of regional integration (Germany and France) and brought the country back into a Europe that the PP had sacrificed to its alliance with the United States. This move provoked vociferous objections from the right, even though the new administration was carrying out a parallel policy—based on Europe's desire and need to "repair the broken crockery"— by "extending a hand" to Washington and trying to improve bilateral relations that had been damaged by the announcement that Spain would withdraw from Iraq.[33]

Spain's Foreign Minister, Miguel Ángel Moratinos, expecting Bush to adopt a more "multilateral" approach in his second term, proposed a "new transatlantic agenda."[34] He also expressed his interest in dialogue with Washington about all areas in which Spain could exercise any influence, such as Latin America. He said that there were "sufficient channels" through which to explain to the United States, for instance, a different vision of relations with Cuba. According to Moratinos, Washington "would fully understand" the Spanish position, as had previously occurred in difficult moments with Cuba, Venezuela, or other countries in the region. "Spain has enormous prestige throughout the American continent. It is an actor that must be respected and heard, as we ourselves want to hear and respect the United States."[35]

On the domestic front, efforts to reach a consensus with the PP, which in practice had been broken during that party's second term, failed.[36] Spain's conservative opposition began to apply intense pressure, which it also deployed in the following six years, taking advantage of any issue to attack and invalidate the PSOE's policy toward Cuba.

Some of the Zapatero administration's foreign policy problems with the United States stemmed from the contrast with the previous model of subordination to Washington put in place by Aznar. This distancing went beyond certain "signals."[37] Madrid ended the unconditional alliance with the United States, which had been a hallmark of the PP's foreign policy. It also began to rectify bilateral relations with Cuba and to express to the EU its opinions about the inefficacy of the 2003 sanctions and the need for political dialogue. Minister Moratinos visited Havana without holding any meetings with the so-called dissidents. In 2007, Spain and Cuba restored cooperation and agreed to carry out bilateral political dialogue.

Madrid also responded, on more than one occasion, to disagreements expressed by Washington. During a visit by Secretary of State Condoleezza Rice, who stated her government's opposition to Spain's engagement with Cuba, Spanish authorities defended their right to conduct their own foreign policy and expressed their opinion that the confrontation between the United States and Cuba was a thing of the past.

Close relations between Bush and Aznar, meanwhile, continued even after the change of administration in Madrid, especially around issues of "global security." Bush depended on Aznar in Iberoamerica, where as president of the Foundation for Social Studies and Analysis (FAES, according to its Spanish acronym) Aznar has sought to make this institution an influential force. Aznar sought to be a symbol for the Hispanic community in the United States; he has never hidden the fact that one objective of his firm alliance with Bush has been to strengthen the position of Spanish culture in the world's leading power.[38]

At the same time, Aznar and the former Czech president, Vaclav Havel, became European advocates for the Committee on the Present Danger (a U.S. foreign policy think tank that wielded significant influence under the most recent Republican administration), which the two former presidents joined to support the "global struggle against terrorism." The pair's political prestige in the Eastern European countries recently incorporated into the EU outlasted the period when Bush needed them to represent his "anti-terrorist" policy in Brussels and extended into other realms. Both of them, along with Lech Walesa, are members of the International Committee for Democracy in Cuba.

Similarly, the internal dynamics within the EU grew considerably more problematic as a result of the Aznarist legacy and the entrance of new member states. Despite Spain's traditional pre-eminence in the shaping of the Community's policies toward Latin America and Cuba, the expansion of the EU to the east diminished Madrid's influence and room to maneuver. Some of the new EU members, previously members of the former European socialist bloc, sought to maintain the legacy of the Aznar administration. The particular features of political transition in those countries, their attitudes with regard to Cuba, and their commitments to the United States (both larger and less responsible, in many cases, than those of some western EU partners) negatively influenced bilateral relations between the EU and Cuba, which turned more difficult, slower, and more complex. With the disappearance of socialism in the new member states from Eastern Europe, Cuba lost importance in their foreign policy agendas, which further diluted the already rather low priority the EU accorded to the Island. The visceral anticommunism that accompanied their transitions, and was the leitmotif of their slogans about "returning to Europe," threw more fuel on the fire. Together with conservative predominance inside the EU, this trend led to particularly intransigent attitudes toward Cuba.

That process unfolded in an era that combined strong Eurocentric introspection (determined by the breadth and complexity of the EU's domestic agenda) with a need to repair the transatlantic alliance. In a context dominated by the 2004 Report of the Commission for Assistance to a Free Cuba (the so-called "Bush Plan"), the EU had additional evidence of its inability to project a Cuba policy beyond the short term: the failure of projected Policy Paper on EU Medium-Term Strategy Toward Democracy in Cuba, a German initiative, with some accompanying events that were no less curious for being circumstantial.[39]

From the Cuban side, the suspension of cooperation with the EU and its member states as a response to the sanctions of June 2003 called some fundamentals of power in international relations into question. Additionally, the "freezing" of diplomats from EU governments that had joined in the policy of issuing invitations to the so-called dissidents sent a clear signal that an error of calculation had been committed in estimating the effectiveness of sanctions and a policy based on external pressure. Some specialists saw this situation as tantamount to a break in relations, though it did not really go that far. Little by little, EU member states began to realize how contradictory the policy their governments had agreed to in Brussels could be for their national interests.

Meanwhile, the transfer of the presidencies of the Council of State and Council of Ministers from Fidel to Raúl Castro did not represent a change in the nature of the Cuban political system or in Cuba's policy toward the EU. On the contrary, Cuba forged ever-closer relations with Latin America and the Caribbean, thanks to the political context that had grown up on a regional scale over the previous years. With Cuba's admission to the Rio Group, the Island now participated in all levels of intra-regional coordination. It remained excluded only from the inter-American system dominated by the United States.

The EU Council's decision in mid-2008 to end sanctions had the additional symbolic value of occurring before the end of the Bush era, in spite of great U.S. pressure.[40] The deterioration of the U.S. administration's position, its discredit among the majority of its European allies, and the prospective change in administration in Washington were decisive.

The influence of an "Obama effect" should be understood as a double perspective of change: in relation to U.S. allies and in relation to Cuba. It offered Europe a more comfortable atmosphere and more room to maneuver in its policy toward the Island, as reflected over the course of 2009 in at least three factors: improved Washington–Brussels relations, a less charged and aggressive discourse toward Cuba than under Bush, and the fulfillment of Obama's minimum electoral promises of policy changes toward the Island. The new administration did not question the European decision to end sanctions against Cuba. In 2009, for the first time in three years, no specific mention of Cuba appeared in the transatlantic summit declaration.

This entire process led to the following results:

- A relationship still unregulated by any agreement, whether bilateral or multilateral, of the sort that links the EU to its international counterparts and partners. The relationship thus retains a tendency to fall victim to contextual and circumstantial ups and downs, especially to domestic Cuban events that are taken up by the governments of member states or by a political sector within the EU as reasons to adopt or abandon certain lines of action.
- This bilateral relationship took more defined shape with the elimination of the sanctions the European Council had imposed on Cuba in June 2003. Though these were "suspended" in January 2005 at Spain's insistence, and though in some eyes they were never more than a mirage, in practice they continued in effect and were discretionarily applied by some member states. Cuba's own policy was clear: it could not sit down to negotiate with the EU except in conditions of equality, which the sanctions impeded and neither the EU nor its individual members would have accepted if the shoe were on the other foot.
- The relationship has three axes after the EU lifted its sanctions: 1) Bilateral political dialogue established through an exchange of notes during the French presidency of the Council (July–December 2008; 2) Cooperation with the European Commission, resumed during an October 2008 visit to Havana by Louis Michel, then the Commissioner for Development and Humanitarian Aid, with the signing of a Joint Declaration; 3) Maintenance of never-interrupted

access to the EU's Generalized System of Preferences (GSP) as a formula for trade cooperation.

- The above-mentioned political dialogue was instituted "on a reciprocal basis, with an unconditional and non-discriminatory character." As of June 2010, there had been four ministerial-level meetings between Cuba and the EU troika, headed in each session by that six-month period's rotating Council president (France, the Czech Republic, Sweden, and Spain, respectively) as well as two other actions in the realm of political dialogue in the first half of 2009.

- The resumption of cooperation with the European Commission relatively quickly mobilized some 40 million euros in Community budget lines for projects in specific areas of priority interest that the two sides had agreed upon. An additional 20 million euros were later added. This process was accompanied by the Commission's sending several technical delegations to Cuba and by the visits of four Commissioners, the most in the history of EU–Cuban relations.[41] These were: Louis Michel, Commissioner for Development and Humanitarian Aid, in October 2008 and March 2009; Benita Ferrero-Waldner, Commissioner for External Relations, in July 2009; and Karel De Gucht, likewise Commissioner for Development and Humanitarian Aid, in October 2009. In March of that year, the European Commission organized an event in Havana regarding cooperation with Cuba attended by more that 20 officials of the Community's executive branch, the largest simultaneous presence of this institution's officials in Cuba since the establishment of relations.

- In this context, bilateral cooperation with various member states has been renewed. Cooperation with Belgium had never been interrupted, and that with Spain was renewed in 2007. Austria, Cyprus, Italy, and Portugal later restored collaboration, and a broadening to include further countries is expected.

- The continued existence of the Common Position still remains to be dealt with.

Future Opportunities

When the Treaty of Lisbon came into effect on December 1, 2009, it introduced an institutional reform long sought within the EU but it also raised more questions than answers. Is a truly common EU foreign policy now more likely? Will the EU succeed in strengthening its supranational sovereignty in foreign policy? As long as there is no affirmative answer to this question, the Union will continue to be a stage on which the national interests of members confront each other while hiding their mutual rivalries from the rest of the world. In this arena, many of the states propose and apply policies and strategies that are inconsistent with those they employ when carrying out bilateral relations with third countries and that sometimes prejudice their own interests.

Another question is how the Europe that is emerging from the Treaty of Lisbon will relate to the power of the United States, which despite a global advance toward multipolarity remains the only "multidimensional" power.[42] How will Europe's weakness affect its competition with the United States in Cuba in a post-blockade scenario? The way the Treaty redesigns the EU's inter-institutional dynamic could be important to the Union's ability to redefine its policy toward Cuba to favor normalization of bilateral relations.[43]

What, in this context, does the term "normal relations" mean? It means non-discriminatory relations such as those the EU maintains with any other country. That is, though the relations are not free of conflict, they are subject to the rules, or what tend to be the rules, rather than objects of exceptional treatment. For Cuba, this includes elimination of the Common Position—the unresolved issue of the bilateral EU–Cuba agenda whose inefficacy is well known. The Common Position's replacement by a framework of bilateral relations—an agreement on economic and commercial cooperation—would be the most appropriate means to end this instrument's role as the EU's main reference point on relations with Cuba.

The big question is whether it is probable, or even possible, to eliminate the Common Position. Since the diplomatic sanctions of June 2003 were eliminated, political dialogue restored, and cooperation with the European Commission renewed, this instrument became the only obstacle to positive evolution of the bilateral relationship and its institutionalization in a contractual framework to offer stability and the opportunity to advance into new areas.

The moment would seem especially propitious:

- Since the last quarter of 2008, there has been a fluid institutional relationship between the EU and Cuba through diplomatic channels. At the level of public discourse, the confrontational tone has lessened somewhat.
- The institutional changes foreseen in the Treaty of Lisbon will gradually come into effect during a transition period. The beginning of this period coincided with the six-month presidency of Spain, which has been quite important in this process.
- In the second half of 2010, Spain was followed by Belgium, the only EU member country with which Cuba maintained cooperation during the 2003–08 period in response to Belgium's constructive position and its having distanced itself from the EU sanctions. Although less influential than Spain on the issue of Cuba and presiding during a more advanced stage of the Lisbon Treaty implementation, the Belgian presidency of the Council following Spain's marked 2010 as "good year," in contrast to 2009 when the presiding states were the Czech Republic and Sweden. A majority of the 27 EU members agree that the Common Position is ineffective but any decision to repeal it would require a unanimous vote, which will not be easy. Some European governments, like Sweden's, have made clear their disagreement with the Spanish intention of eliminating the Common Position.[44] Minister Moratinos' publicly expressed confidence that the Common Position would be replaced, as a result of Cuba's

release of most of the prisoners its government arrested in March 2003 who were still in jail in early 2010,[45] ran up against the resistance of a handful of fundamentalist member states.[46]

• Cuba does not accept the retention of the Common Position as the reference point for its relations with the EU. Thus, depending on how the EU Council proceeds, the possible scenarios range from the most positive and desirable (replacement of the Common Position by a framework of bilateral relations in the form of an agreement), through the status quo, to the most negative (a new impasse or confrontation).

The various U.S. administrations, for their part, have supported the Common Position, which was adopted when the Democratic administration of Bill Clinton occupied the White House and in the context of the adoption of the Helms–Burton Act. Although the Obama administration is headed by a different president in a different context and Obama has not openly defended the Common Position, he has not rejected it either, nor does he seem to support the Spanish government's public efforts to promote and win its elimination.

The clearest expressions of the Obama administration's views on the Common Position have been statements by Arturo Valenzuela, assistant secretary of state for western hemisphere affairs, who declared in early February, "At this time, in our judgment, we don't necessarily see a change in the Common Position as positive but it depends a lot on how changing it is handled." He stressed that an eventual change in the EU's stance must "make very clear that what is required" is an "expectation" of "a democratic opening in Cuba." "I think that is the objective we all have, going forward. To see a democratic Cuba," he said.[47]

Elimination of the Common Position would be an important step toward the normalization of EU–Cuban relations and would demonstrate what some call the EU's "constructive engagement" with the Island. Its political significance could be a source of conflict between the EU and the U.S., which could oblige Brussels to give Washington something in return. Although the move would place the Obama administration's limitations in sharper relief, it would probably not exercise any decisive influence on a shift in U.S. policy; on the other hand, a lifting of the U.S. blockade would indeed influence the policy of the EU. In that regard, there is an important precedent: the EU did not sign a cooperation agreement with Viet Nam (the negotiations dragged on for eight years) until after the United States lifted its embargo against that country.

On the other hand, there is quite a broad potential for collaboration within the framework of the U.S.–EU–Cuba triangle. Even in the absence of a bilateral accord, Cuba's cooperation with the European Commission includes sectors that lend themselves to eventual cooperation between Cuba and the United States (drug traffic, climate change, natural disasters, scientific and academic exchanges). The progressive renewal of collaboration with EU member states should contribute to reinforce this potential.

Given an agreement that would define areas of common interest and in accord with Cuba's development priorities, the fields for future collaboration are ample, with potentials in direct proportion to the end of the blockade and the normalization of relations with the EU and cooperation with its member states. Cuba not only has sufficient capacity in terms of economies of scale but also, given such new perspectives and a more open vision from each of the actors, its human resources, experience, and know-how in many areas of international cooperation could be joined with the material, technical, and financial capacities of the European Commission, EU member states, and the United States to explore and open important avenues of cooperation. Among the many dimensions that this collaboration could adopt, one interesting possibility could be to contribute to development programs in other countries through various multilateral mechanisms. Cuba has outlined to European countries more than a few proposals to explore fields of triangular cooperation.

The most recent and closest example of these possibilities is evident in Haiti, where some collaboration between Cuba and the United States has already occurred in the effort to confront the emergency created by the January 2010 earthquake. Washington requested Cuban permission for specific overflights of eastern Cuba to evacuate the wounded from Haiti and to bring in humanitarian aid. Meanwhile, there has been an exchange of information on this issue with Cheryl Mills, Hillary Clinton's chief of staff and coordinator of U.S. humanitarian aid efforts, which suggests the possibility of further collaboration.

Sadly, a negative factor was introduced into this process in 2010 by the crusade whereby European media and political parties made political use of the death of a common prisoner in Cuba, which created the context for the Resolution adopted by the European Parliament on March 11. The repeated utilization of Cuban domestic politics as a cover for undermining favorable trends in EU–*Cuba* relations cannot be coincidental. The avalanche of propaganda unleashed from Madrid and Miami has three main targets: the Cuban government, the efforts to eliminate or replace the Common Position, and the actions of the PSOE. Its greatest beneficiaries are all who, in any corner of the triangle, oppose dialogue between the United States and Cuba and between the EU and Cuba. The Spanish right wing, one of the most energetic actors, even holds up Obama as an example of opposition to transformation.[48]

The replacement of Moratinos, Spain's foreign minister under the Zapatero administration, by Trinidad Jiménez as part of a larger restructuring of the Spanish government a few days before the October 25, 2010 meeting of the EU Foreign Affairs Council, did not change the political stance of the Spanish delegation. The expected opposition of a handful of member States—Germany, Sweden, the Czech Republic and Poland—to the substitution of the Common Position avoided the required unanimity. The Council conclusions state:

Ministers held an exchange of views, over lunch, on recent political and economic developments in Cuba and on the options for the EU's policy towards Cuba.

They agreed to start a reflection and to ask the High Representative, *within the framework of the EU's common position on Cuba*, to explore the possibilities on the way forward for relations with Cuba, and to report back to the Council as soon as possible.[49]

Thus, the Common Position remains as the EU reference point for its Cuban policy. The prospects for normalization have diminished. The EU persists in conditioning its relations with Cuba and thus EU policy toward Cuba remains unsuccessful. In his remarks to the 65th session of United Nations' General Assembly, Cuba's Minister of Foreign Relations explicitly stated, "Now it is said that the so-called Common Position has been overcome. We will see. Facts will have the last say. But the European Union is delusional when it thinks it could normalize relations with Cuba while the Common Position is still in place."[50] The United States has not yet said a word.

Bearing in mind that "à la carte" changes in Cuba under foreign pressure are not under consideration and that the nature of the Cuban model is not up for negotiation in any bilateral dialogue, there are limited options for progress. Either the efforts for rapprochement, revived in 2008 will prevail, allowing forward progress in cooperation among the vertices of the triangle, or else the window will close "until further notice." To any halfway-lucid mind, the better alternative is clear.

Notes

1   Daniel S. Hamilton and Joseph P. Quinlan, *Partners in Prosperity: The Changing Geography of the Transatlantic Economy*, cited by Sandy Núñez Martínez, "EE.UU.-Europa: unidos hasta que la economía los separe," *Revista de Estudios Europeos* (Havana) no. 71 (September–December 2005): 5–30.
2   The EU was born in the Treaty of Maastricht (1987), which added to the European Communities (EC, Euratom, and ECSC, the pillars of economic and communitarian integration) two others of an inter-governmental nature: CFSP and Justice and Home Affairs (JHA). A series of expansions broadened European integration from the six founding members (Belgium, France, Germany, Italy, Luxembourg, and the Netherlands) to the twenty-seven as of this writing, with the incorporation of Denmark, Ireland, and the United Kingdom (1973); Greece (1981); Spain and Portugal (1986); Austria, Finland, and Sweden (1995); Cyprus, the Czech Republic, Estonia, Hungary, Latvia, Lithuania, Malta, Poland, Slovakia, and Slovenia (2004); and Rumania and Bulgaria (2007). See Eduardo Perera, "Impacto de la ampliación en las relaciones exteriores de la Unión Europea," *Revista de Estudios Europeos* (Havana) no. 69 (January–April 2005): 11–44.
3   Not by consensus, as is sometimes stated.
4   Consejo de Ministros de la UE, "Posición común de 2 de diciembre de 1996 definida por el Consejo en virtud del artículo J.2 del Tratado de la Unión Europea, sobre Cuba," 96/697/PESC, *Diario Oficial,* no. L 322 (December 12, 1996): 1–2.

5 The member states of the EU have never voted against the United Nations General Assembly resolution, "Necessity of ending the economic, commercial and financial blockade imposed by the United States of America against Cuba."

6 "The European Union believes that the United States trade policy towards Cuba is fundamentally a bilateral issue. Notwithstanding, the European Union and its member States have been clearly expressing their opposition to the extraterritorial extension of the United States blockade, such as that contained in the Cuban Democracy Act of 1992 and the Helms–Burton Act of 1996." See, "Informe del Secretario General de la ONU," A/59/150, July 16, 2004, available at www.cubavsbloqueo.cu. The results can be paradoxical: under the Torricelli Act, European branches of U.S. companies cannot trade with Cuba while their parent companies can do so if licensed; European ships that enter Cuban ports cannot enter U.S. ones within six months, while U.S. ships trading with Cuba are not subject to this restriction.

7 See Joaquín Roy, "European Views on Cuba (1959–2009): Milestones and Trends," paper presented at the conference of the Canadian Association for Latin American Studies (CALACS), Vancouver, June 4–7, 2008, p. 12, and also Susanne Gratius, "Cuba, los Estados Unidos y Europa: perspectivas de cambio," Política Exterior (Madrid), no. 130 (July–August 2009): 100, which states [translated]: "Relations between Cuba and the EU . . . have always been conditioned by the United States."

8 Joaquín Roy, 24; Jorge Domínguez, comment in the "Taller de autores de la revista Temas," February 11, 2010.

9 Pascual Serrano, "La democracia cubana no se agota en la representación formal, sino que incorpora mecanismos y formas de la democracia directa" (interview with Ricardo Alarcón), Rebelión, December 6, 2003, available at www.rebelion.org.

10 See Eduardo Perera, "Condicionalidad y condicionamientos previos en la política de cooperación al desarrollo de la Unión Europea," Revista de Estudios Europeos (Havana), no. 53–54 (January–June 2000): 3–32.

11 Cuba is one of the five countries to which this instrument is applied, along with Zimbabwe, Myanmar, Nigeria, and Iraq.

12 A recent example is the European Parliament passing a resolution on the death of Orlando Zapata ("Resolución del Parlamento Europeo, de 11 de marzo de 2010, sobre la situación de los presos políticos y de conciencia en Cuba," P7_TA-PROV(2010)0063, available at http://europarl.europa.eu), while it did not adopt a single resolution on the coup d'état in Honduras.

13 See Gerardo Arreola, "Ayuno de presos afecta el diálogo de Cuba con EU y la UE," (interview with Rafael Hernández), La Jornada (Mexico City), March 16, 2010, 20, available at www.jornada.unam.mx; and Salim Lamrani, "Cuba, los medios occidentales y el suicidio de Orlando Zapata Tamayo," Cubadebate, March 2, 2010, available at www. cubadebate.cu.

14 See Carlos Alzugaray, "Cuba cincuenta años después: continuidad y cambio político," Temas, no. 60 (October–December 2009): 37–47, pointing out that the concept of "transition" "is currently too 'charged' and presupposes a 'regime change.'"

15 José Manzaneda, "La guerra mediática contra Cuba y Venezuela necesita peones progresistas," Cubainformación, May 21, 2010, available at www.cubainformacion.tv.

16 See Eduardo Perera, "La Unión Europea y Cuba. Hacia un mayor realismo en las relaciones," Revista de Estudios Europeos (Havana), no. 31 (July–September 1994): 25–59.

17 European Commission, "Comunicación de la Comisión al Consejo y al Parlamento Europeo sobre las relaciones entre la Unión Europea y Cuba," COM (95)306, Boletín de la Unión Europea (Luxemburg), June 1995, 306.

18 Consejo Europeo de Madrid, "Conclusiones de la Presidencia," Boletín de la Unión Europea (Luxemburg), December 1995.

19 Joaquín Roy, "La Unión Europea ante Cuba y Colombia: de buenas intenciones y altas esperanzas a notables contradicciones y grandes frustraciones," *América Latina Hoy* (Salamanca), no. 31 (2002).

20 Response by José M. Anacoreta Correia, then director for Latin America in the Directorate-General I of the European Commission, to a question put to him during his presentation at the "III Encuentro Internacional de Estudios Europeos," Havana, October 1995; *Revista de Estudios Europeos* (Havana), no. 36 (October–December 1995): 10–61.

21 Ángel Viñas, "La Unión Europea y Cuba: historia de una acción de estrategia exterior en la posguerra fría," cited by Joaquín Roy, "La Unión Europea…"

22 In his speech to the VI institutionalized ministerial meeting of the Rio Group and the European Union held in Cochabamba, Bolivia in April 1996, Manuel Marín said, "We were making an offer to the Cuban government to reach a cooperation agreement with the EU, accompanied by an offer from the Rio Group, here in Cochabamba, to include Cuba as an observer country …The Cuban authorities are strictly responsible for Cuba's not being here today in Cochabamba and for a cooperation agreement with the EU not being possible." *Europe Bulletin* (Brussels), April 16, 1996.

23 See Richard Nuccio, "Cuba: A U.S. Perspective," cited by Joaquín Roy, "La Unión Europea…" op. cit.

24 For a comparison of the Spanish proposal, the one formulated by the United States for its major European partners, and the one adopted by the EU Council, see "Fidel-Aznar. Sigue la partida. ¿Y los cubanos qué?," *Cambio* (Madrid) 16, no. 1310 (December 9, 1996).

25 "Declaración del Ministerio de Relaciones Exteriores sobre las Conclusiones del Consejo de Relaciones Exteriores de la Unión Europea sobre Cuba," June 22, 2007, available at http://www.cubaminrex.cu.

26 State Department communiqué, December 3, 1996, cited by Joaquín Roy, "La Unión Europea…"

27 "Declaración del Ministerio de Relaciones Exteriores," *Granma Internacional* (Havana), December 4, 1996.

28 One indicator is the establishment in Madrid of the Fundación Hispano-Cubano, something of a branch of the Cuban-American National Foundation, with full participation of the PP leadership and employing the Casa de América as a meeting place.

29 These sanctions were a response to the prison sentences imposed by Cuban courts in March 2003 on 75 people charged with collaboration with a foreign power under Law 88 (Law on Protection of Cuba's National Independence and Economy).

30 According to Cuba's annual statistical yearbook, the Island's 2003 trade deficit was more than 3 billion pesos (1 Cuban peso, in the calculations of the yearbook, is equal to 1 U.S. dollar), and the 2008 deficit was 10 billion pesos. Additional problems include the foreign debt, calculated in 2007 at 8.9 billion pesos in active debt and another 7.6 billion pesos in immobilized debt, as well as the difficulty of obtaining foreign credit.

31 EU standards affect access to its markets for important Cuban products such as nickel, sugar, honey, alcoholic beverages, and tobacco, among others. These are some of the greatest barriers to the entry of Cuban products into the markets of the Community. They impose high taxes on exporters, which are derived from complex processes to certify the techniques demanded by the EU. The tendency to apply such requirements has grown over time. On the other hand, Cuba benefits from the EU's Generalized System of Preferences, although the list of products currently included in that system does not include the majority of Cuba's main exports to the EU.

32 Consejo de la Unión Europea, "Comunicado de Prensa, Sesión No. 2881 del Consejo Agricultura y Pesca," Luxemburg, June 23–24, available at www.consilium.europa.eu.

33 Andrés Ortega, "Dios, armas y ley," *Foreign Policy en Español,* no. 6 (December 2004).

34 Miguel Ángel Moratinos, "Nueva oportunidad," *Foreign Policy en Español,* no. 6 (December 2004).

35 Embajada de Cuba en Madrid, "Resumen de la prensa española," November 10, 2004.

36 Joaquín Roy, "Confrontación, irritación y desilusión: balance de las relaciones entre la Unión Europea y Cuba," *ARI* (Real Instituto Elcano de Estudios Internacionales y Estratégicos, Madrid), No. 165 (2004).

37 While George W. Bush was meeting Tony Blair in Washington and also receiving José María Aznar in private, without congratulating Zapatero on his victory, the executive branch in Madrid delayed naming an ambassador to the United States.

38 IBLNEWS (New York), November 10, 2004.

39 See Salim Lamrani, "La Unión Europea en el fondo del abismo," *Rebelión,* available at www.rebelion.org.

40 Some of these pressures were exemplified by the visits of Kirsten Madison, deputy assistant secretary of state for Central America and Cuba in the Bush administration, and Caleb McCarry, to the foreign ministries of several member states and by the 180-degree shift in the positions of the German delegation during the negotiation of the Conclusions of the Council after Bush's farewell visit to Germany.

41 Previously, Cuba had been visited only by Manuel Marín, Commissioner for Development Cooperation and Relations with Latin America (April 1994 and February 1996) and Emma Bonino, Commissioner for Fisheries and Humanitarian Aid (1995).

42 The United States is the only tri-dimensional power: economic, political, and military. Pedro Canales, "La cara de la nueva Administración será más cercana a Powell que a Rumsfeld," *La Razón* (Madrid), November 4, 2004.

43 The High Representative for Foreign Affairs and Security Policy will preside over the EU's Foreign Affairs Council; this implies a loss of importance for the six-month presidencies in the foreign policy realm. The reform will also affect the makeup of the EU troika, given that the High Representative is also the European Commission vice president in charge of foreign affairs. There is also a possibility that Cuba, currently attended by the European Commission's Directorate-General for Development (DG DEV), will instead be passed on to the Directorate-General for Foreign Relations (DG RELEX) presided over by Baroness Catherine Ashton, the High Representative. Ashton's role and abilities remain unclear, yet her office is vested with enormous power under the Treaty of Lisbon.

44 In October 2010, the director for Latin America in the Swedish foreign ministry, Elizabeth Eklund, said in the name of the Council presidency that she was "surprised" by the plans and declared her opposition: "Such a change would require the support of the Twenty-seven, and we do not support the change." See Aitor Hernández Morales, "La Presidencia española plantea cambiar la relación entre la Unión y Cuba," *El Mundo* (Madrid), available at www.elmundo.es. "The Spanish minister [Moratinos] defended his proposal when he traveled to Havana in the past month of October, but also admitted that any change would be difficult because of the hesitancy of countries such as Sweden, Holland, the United Kingdom, the Czech Republic, or Germany." "España desiste de cambiar Posición Común de la UE con Cuba," EFE, April 15, 2010, reprinted in various media including *El Nuevo Herald* and *Casa América.* See also, on the occasion of Moratinos' visit: "some European countries like Sweden, the Czech Republic, Holland, and Germany refuse to eliminate the common position unless Cuba makes some significant decision in the area of human rights, such as release of opposition prisoners." See Gerardo Arreola, "Llama canciller cubano a eliminar la Posición Común de Brusela," *La Jornada,* October 20, 2009, available at www.jornada.unam.mx.

45 "I think there is no longer any reason to maintain the common position. This is what my colleagues are requesting from me—that if we manage to clear away the question of

the prisoners, then logically the common position will be dropped," said Moratinos to a group of journalists during a tour of the Santovenia Nursing Home in the Cuban capital. EFE, July 8, 2010. As of October 2010, 39 of the 52 prisoners remaining from the 2003 arrests had been freed.

46 Governments of several EU member states—the United Kingdom, the Czech Republic, and Italy—lauded the news of the releases yet maintained tones of caution, or even of "this is not enough." The Italian government insisted that it expected new "concrete" gestures from Cuban authorities, while the Czech ministry of external relations welcomed the news but would remain cautious until the full promise is fulfilled, according to a spokesperson for the minister, Filip Kanda, who said that it "is still premature to speak of leaving the Common Position behind." AFP, July 8, 2010. The British foreign office official in charge of Latin America, Jeremy Browne, declared, "I welcome the Cuban government's commitment to release fifty-two political prisoners who have been detained since 2003. The release of political prisoners in Cuba has been a longstanding priority for the UK, and this is a welcome and positive step. I hope this will help lead to further human rights improvements, including the release of all political prisoners, in Cuba." "Jeremy Browne on release of political prisoners in Cuba," London, July 13, 2010.

47 "EE.UU. rechaza un cambio de la UE hacia Cuba, como pedía Moratinos," EFE-ABC, February 2, 2010. In relation to the announced release of 52 prisoners, the United States expressed through Secretary of State Hillary Clinton that it welcomed the news, although the action was somewhat "late." DPA, July 8, 2010.

48 The newspaper *ABC*, in its digital edition of April 3, 2010, argued: "Spain should be grateful for Washington's unmistakable position about what affects us most directly, and should draw the necessary conclusions from the fact that Cuba remains on the list of countries supporting terrorism . ... the Obama administration has not had any plan to smooth relations with Cuba other than its well-known effort to resolve migration problems." "Cuba y el terrorismo," *ABC*, April 3, 2010, available at www.abc.es.

49 Council of the European Union: "Press Release. 3041st Council Meeting, Foreign Affairs, Luxembourg, 25 October, 2010". Available at: http://consilium.europa.eu/App/Newsroom/.

50 Reply by Cuba's Minister of Foreign Affairs, Bruno Rodríguez Parrilla, to the Representatives of the United States and the European Union respectively during the General Assembly session under the item "Necessity of ending the economic, commercial and financial blockade imposed by the United States of America against Cuba" on October 26, 2010. Available at: http://www.cubaminrex.cu/english/Multilaterales/Articulos/Politicos/Other/Reply.html.

8

EUROPEAN UNION POLICY IN THE CUBA–U.S.–SPAIN TRIANGLE

SUSANNE GRATIUS

By Way of Preamble

European Union (EU) relations with Cuba have always been conditioned by the discord existing between the United States and the Island, but it would be wrong to say that Brussels' policies merely reflect those of Washington. The facts speak for themselves. The EU re-established relations with Cuba in the midst of the Cold War, carries out political dialogue with the government, continues at least a minimum level of cooperation, and is the Island's major trading partner, its second-largest investor, and its second-largest source of tourists.

Even so, by virtue of the EU's being a plural or multi-dimensional actor, its policy toward the Island is full of paradoxes and contradictions. The first of these is the outsized attention paid to Cuba in EU foreign relations compared to the Island's size and minor importance to Europe. Cuba has been the only Latin American country considered worthy of the creation of an EU common policy. Another paradox, certainly, is that ever since José María Aznar won adoption of the Common Position in 1996 (hereafter referred to as the Common Position), the EU Council has debated the Cuban case every single year. The Common Position, slightly more than one page long, foresees a peaceful and gradual transition toward democracy, preferably from within, and makes full re-establishment of relations contingent on visible progress toward democracy.

Given this Position, the EU has not signed a cooperation agreement with Cuba. That would be a reasonable decision, were it not for the fact that EU member states have signed more than 20 bilateral accords with Cuba. Similarly, the EU legation in Havana, unlike the 19 representations of its member states, lacks the status of an embassy (a situation, in this respect, shared with the U.S. Interests Section). It is also difficult to understand why Cuba has a dual identity in European Commission policy. For some purposes, it is seen as a Latin American country. For others, it is a Caribbean Island belonging to the ACP (African, Caribbean, and Pacific Group of States), yet not having signed a cooperation agreement.

This exceptionality of the Cuban case can be explained by three variables that have determined EU policy toward Cuba: the international context, the Cuba–U.S. conflict, and relations between Spain and Cuba. The EU's shifting posture emerges from this triangle and from the pressure applied by certain member states. International changes and the vagaries of Spanish policy toward the EU contrast with the relative continuity in Cuba–U.S. relations. For the EU itself in its relations with Cuba, there have been two variables and two constants. The variables are the Union's political position and cooperation around economic development, both of which oscillate in pendulum fashion between periods of honeymoon and divorce, while the constants have been diplomatic and economic presence.

Important Changes in the International System

The EU did not establish diplomatic contacts with Cuba until 1988, in the framework of its establishment of relations with the Council for Mutual Economic Assistance (CMEA).[1] During the Cold War, the EU and the CMEA were on opposite sides of the bipolar confrontation and saw each other through an ideological lens. The post-Cold War period opened up much more room for the development of relations, which reached their height in the mid-1990s when the EU became Cuba's most important economic partner and source of cooperation, replacing the former alliance with the socialist bloc while compensating for (and ignoring) the U.S. embargo. It was during these "golden years" that the EU established cooperation agreements, multiplied the number of high-level visits, and in 1995 approved a directive for negotiations toward a cooperation agreement with the Island, which because of political differences never came to fruition.

Over those 22 years, EU–Cuba relations have reached a certain maturity but progress on a shared agenda has been scarce. The Common Position's prerequisite for democracy continues to block full relations, including a juridical framework, an EU–Cuba cooperation agreement and more resources for development. Since the late 1990s, relations have been characterized by a constant alternation between rapprochement and distance, in an international context marked by two different periods. The first was the unipolar era of George W. Bush's post-9/11 "hard years," when the United States set the tone for relations. In the second period, Bush's second term, the global financial crisis, and the arrival of the Barack Obama presidency paralleled a slow decline in the superpower, while the changing international order marked by the rise of China and other emerging powers offered space for more flexible relations in a context of relative *détente* between Cuba and the United States (see Table 8.1).

TABLE 8.1   Cuba–EU relations

Cuba–EU in the unipolar world:

1988–1990:	Establishment of diplomatic relations and first discussions of an EU–Cuba cooperation agreement
1990–1993:	Freezing of relations, fall of the socialist bloc, and "embassy crisis"
1993–1995:	Inclusion of Cuba in EU cooperation, visit to Cuba by a European Parliament delegation, directive to the Commission to negotiate a cooperation agreement
1996–1998:	Freezing of relations after visit by then European Commission Vice-President Manuel Marín and the downing of two small "Brothers to the Rescue" planes, "Centro de Estudios sobre América" case, approval of the Helms–Burton Act and the Common Position
1998–2000:	Inclusion of Cuba in the ACP and opening of negotiations on Cuban membership in the ACP Cotonou Agreement
2001–2003:	Freezing of relations after resuming political dialogue, Cuba does not join "Cotonou," arrests of 75 dissidents, and EU approval of "four measures" that form a new obstacle to relations

Cuba–EU in the multi- or bipolar world:

2004–2010:	Phase of opening, elimination of the four measures, resumption of political dialogue and reopening of cooperation with Cuba by Spain and the European Commission, Spain proposes eliminating the Common Position
2010:	Death of a prisoner of conscience and hunger strike by other dissidents; release of most political prisoners and flexibilization of relations

In principle, the current international context seems more propitious for progress in EU–Cuba and U.S.–Cuba relations. In the first place, we are no longer living in the American Century but rather—thanks to the simultaneous rise of China and India—entering the Asian Century. In this new world where the global South has more influence and the North has less, it is no accident that Cuba is almost completely accepted in the international community. We are in a transition period toward a different geopolitical context, where traditional powers like the U.S. and the EU have lost power (a gradual process accelerated by the international financial crisis) and others, especially China, but also Brazil, India, and Russia, are growing in global influence.

In the Americas, the United States and the EU have somewhat less importance than previously, and Brazil and China have somewhat more. It was Brazil that pushed to admit Cuba to the Rio Group during the Costa de Sauípe presidential summit of December 2009. It was also Brazil, together with Venezuela, that during the April 2009 Summit of the Americas pressured the United States to drop the discriminatory clause, which had prohibited Cuba's return to the organization. Today, Cuba has diplomatic relations with every Latin American country, not conditioned by any prerequisites, and the critical voices seem to have subsided. The regional isolation of the 1980s and 1990s has little by little been replaced by a policy of unconditional engagement. Among other factors, this has resulted from the simultaneous coming to power of leftwing administrations in the region, the regional leadership of Lula, greater Chinese presence, Venezuela's influence, and the Chávez–Castro alliance within the ALBA framework.

In this new multipolar arena, Cuba has been able to re-engage with the region without having to make changes in its political system. At the same time, the diversification and normalization of its foreign relations (with the exception of those with its historical enemy) also reflect a certain resignation on the part of the international community after more than 50 years of continuity in policies that failed to modify the Cuban political system. Finally, as an effect of September 11, 2001, and the Cuban government's immediate condemnation of that terrorist attack, there is a greater sense of the Island's being part of "the West."

The diversification of political and economic models due to the rise of China and more generally the BRIC (Brazil, Russia, India, and China) countries has also influenced U.S., Latin American, and EU policies toward Cuba. As a result, "engagement" becomes the lowest common denominator among external actors with regard to Cuba:

- With the lifting of some restrictions on exporting food and medicine, the United States applies a policy of "sanctions and engagement";
- Canada, notwithstanding changes in administrations, barely varies its policy of "constructive or critical engagement," maintaining a consistent state policy;
- The EU applies an ambiguous policy of "conditional engagement," which varies between opening and shutting off dialogue and cooperation with the Cuban government;
- Latin America and Spain moved from conditional engagement to "unconditional engagement";
- China and Venezuela support the Cuban regime and are Cuba's major economic and ideological allies.

In this many-hued global scenario, Cuba–U.S. relations are no longer a bilateral conflict but rather one that represents a past hegemony confronting new powers for whom normalizing relations with Cuba is a way to differentiate themselves from the "superpower" in decline. It is worth remembering that China and Russia are not democratic powers but rather, leaving aside their differences, autocracies with a strong state role. Their international importance also changes the Western or Euro–U.S. view of promoting democracy as a universal model. In this different world, the paradigms of democracy promotion and a market economy have clearly been weakened in relation to other political and economic options.

The Constant: Discord Between Cuba and the U.S.

The major changes in the international system over the past 50 years contrast with the barely altered bilateral relationship between the U.S. and Cuba. Although over the past five decades there have been continual modifications in the number of and degree of channels of contact between the two countries, the levels of bilateral conflict have not changed. Cuba maintains its verbal war with Washington and blames the United States for the Island's economic crisis; the United States maintains its sanctions and conditions, and it still has not authorized its citizens to travel to Cuba nor repealed the Helms–Burton Act. In this context, there has been little room for change. Despite some predictions, President Obama's taking possession of the White House did not lead to a return to Carter's policy of opening toward Cuba, but rather to the "Clinton era" of people-to-people contact.

This continuity reflects the fact that bilateral relations can develop on the periphery of the international context. Neither the end of the Cold War, nor that of the subsequent U.S. hegemonic era, nor the current process of transition toward a G-20 multipolar world or a G-2 bipolar one have had visible repercussions in the Cuba–U.S. conflict. This phenomenon confirms the bilateral nature and longevity of a conflict whose resolution does not depend on changes of political administrations within the United States but (as Washington sees it) on a political regime change in Cuba and (as Havana sees it) on the renunciation of a hostile and imperialist policy.

The initial and mutual offers of dialogue put forward by both Presidents Raúl Castro and Barack Obama have not had any effect. After a brief phase of mutual openings and expectations, relations returned to business as usual. Caution has characterized both presidents' policies: in a moment of crisis and decline, Raúl Castro needs the excuse of an external threat to justify the continuity of his political project, and for Barack Obama the costs of lifting the embargo on Castroist Cuba (costs in image, credibility, internal disputes, and immigration security) are greater than the benefits. The continuity of his policy demonstrates once more that the United States has a state policy toward Cuba based on an implicit agreement between Democrats and Republicans to continue the embargo.

Within that framework, since the partial lifting of embargo restrictions on exporting medicine and food in 2001, Democratic administrations have favored gradual movement toward the European position of conditional engagement. The lack of bilateral diplomatic relations has not kept the two countries from carrying out technical talks on sectoral issues of mutual interests such as border control, drug trafficking, migration, and shared history. Neither the embargo nor the Helms–Burton Act kept the United States from becoming Cuba's largest supplier of food. Even in the dark years of the G.W. Bush administration, which tightened sanctions, family contact was not interrupted nor was cooperation between the two countries' coast guards. Barack Obama not only re-established the frequency of remittances and visits from Cuban-Americans to pre-2004 levels but he also sent Deputy Assistant Secretary of State Bisa Williams on an official visit to Cuba in September 2009.

These measures of engagement did not eliminate sanctions, only softened them. The greater flexibility reflects the interests of the private sector and of part of the Cuban-American community, and it contrasts with the political position of the administration and Congress, which defend sanctions. To the degree that pressure from below for a change of policy increases, the embargo becomes "more of a tradition than a policy." The same is true of the larger bilateral conflict, which represents both a reflection of the past and the inertia of the present. Neither side dares to change it because the costs would be too high and the results of a policy of opening are too uncertain. Both the United States and Cuba are accustomed to living with the embargo and making use of it for domestic ends:

- The Cuban government makes use of the embargo to justify its political immobility by reference to the foreign enemy, and to keep alive the notion of a foreign threat. Thus, "the siege mentality works against any democratic opening toward a less centralized system."[2] The embargo converts democracy, human rights, and civil society into taboo concepts to be used only by the "enemy."
- The United States makes use of the embargo as a guarantee of stability and a concession to the exile community. It has adjusted to the situation: the embargo prevents the much-feared waves of immigrants and any abrupt political change with unforeseen consequences. Also, its existence demonstrates that the United States has a policy of promoting democracy (even if that policy has been mistaken and counter-productive). Within the general framework of the embargo, there are shades or accents in favor of more sanctions or more dialogue, depending on whether the administration is Republican or Democratic.

Something similar occurs with the Helms–Burton Act whose impact is much greater on the future of relations than on the present. Ending sanctions while a Castro is in power seems highly unlikely. Their shelf life depends on the reigning political project in Cuba, which determines Washington's position. Thus, President Bill Clinton's signing of Helms–Burton was a result of the downing of the U.S.-based airplanes and the detention of a group of dissidents. By the same token, the recent phase of rapprochement briefly visible during the Obama administration was interrupted by the death of a prisoner of conscience in Cuba, but restored by the subsequent release of most political prisoners.

Beyond the constant of the embargo, and similarly to the behavior of the EU, U.S. policy swings like a pendulum: phases of stiffening sanctions during Republican administrations alternate with phases of *détente* and dialogue during Democratic ones. After the hardliner Bush, Obama inaugurated a new phase of dialogue and detente. The result of such pendulum politics is immobility, and Obama is no exception to that rule. In his administration, no change of policy is taking shape beyond a return to the Clinton era.

The only U.S. president who was at the point of interrupting the logic of this continuity was Jimmy Carter, who had initiated a political dialogue without preconditions (and failed). Since then, his successors have learned that, unless there are changes on the Island, it is better not to alter the framework of relations with Cuba. The embargo is the major bargaining chip, and as long as neither country has a clear idea of what would happen if it were to disappear, it will not be lifted. That is the gentlemen's agreement between the two.

The Variable Relation Between Spain and Cuba

Since 1898, the two external axes radiating from Cuba have pointed toward the United States and Spain. For both countries, Cuba is an "intermestic" issue, which arouses interest in both domestic and foreign politics: in the United States because of the exile community, and in Spain for historical reasons and because of ideological debate between the two major political parties. For both Madrid and Washington, Cuba has an emotional connotation and it is a polarizing issue. However, their fields of action have been different. If the embargo has been the constant element in U.S. state policy, engagement is the element that no Spanish administration has ever questioned. Therefore, the "U.S. factor" tends to unite Cuba and Spain—historically by virtue of the Island's *de facto* annexation by the United States in 1898, viewed negatively in both countries, and since the 1960s by virtue of the embargo's being clearly rejected and condemned in both countries.

Since revolutionary victory in 1959, Spain maintained diplomatic relations with Cuba, which were not interrupted even during the Franco period.[3] Today, Spain is Cuba's most important European partner: the leader in aid, second in investments, and fourth in trade. Spain has the most important European embassy on the Island, and a cultural center. Besides relations with the central government in Madrid, there is a fluid network of cooperation between Cuba and the autonomous communities of Spain, especially the Basque Country, Catalunya, and Andalucía, and with civil society too.[4] There is also an important community of Cubans living in Spain; unlike that in the United States, it has very little political influence.

As is the case in the United States, Cuba's importance in Spanish politics ranks well out of proportion to the level of relations and the size of the country.[5] This demonstrates how cultural factors can create much more lasting ties—if also more conflictual ones—than the ideological component. In Spain, Cuba transcends the political sphere. It is not merely a foreign policy issue; it is also a domestic issue, with components that are emotional (family and post-colonial), nostalgic (the leftwing myth), and resistance (shared external enemy).

Parallel to what happens in Washington, Spain's policy of economic engagement goes through swings of the pendulum. It has been more conditional under the

Partido Popular (PP) administrations, which have imposed prerequisites, and it has been more engaged under the PSOE administrations. The trajectory of these relations demonstrates that this is a zero-sum game yielding scant results.

Constructive engagement (or critical engagement) under President of the Government Felipe González (1982–96) signaled a new relationship with Cuba. González began a dialogue with the Cuban government including the human rights issue, increased cooperation on economic development, and strengthened economic and cultural exchange. During González's administration, Spain also took on an important role in advising Cuba about the economic reforms that began in the 1990s. It was on González's initiative, supported by some Latin American countries, that Cuba in 1991 joined the Iberoamerican Community of Nations. Three years later, Spain pushed for the European Commission to negotiate a cooperation agreement with Cuba. This policy of constructive engagement ended in March 1996, when Raúl Castro's speech reversed a period of opening in Cuba, the United States enacted the Helms–Burton Act, and José María Aznar was elected President of the Government in Spain.

Conditional engagement under José María Aznar (1996–2004) changed Spain's policy closer to the position of the Cuban-American National Federation (CANF) in Miami and that of the U.S. government. When Aznar suggested at the Iberoamerican Summit in Viña del Mar that it was up to Fidel Castro to "make a move" (*mover ficha*), he introduced a conflict that led to the temporary recall of Spain's ambassador in Cuba. After U.S. adoption of the Helms–Burton Act, Aznar proposed an EU Common Position on Cuba. His initial version was much harsher than the final one, which was approved on December 2, 1996, after having been softened by other member countries including Germany. At that time, the main goal and *raison d'être* of the Common Position was not to promote change in Cuba but rather to preserve European economic interests and achieve a truce with the United States in the immediate aftermath of its enactment of the Helms–Burton Act (this U.S.–EU truce would later become the "EU–U.S. Understanding"). In 1996, the Common Position was also a concession to the reigning "Atlanticist inclination" of Spanish foreign policy.[6] The conflictual phase in relations between Cuba and Spain was followed by a calming phase: the Spanish ambassador returned to Havana in April 1997, and Fidel Castro visited the Spanish government headquarters at Moncloa in 1998 to prepare for the Iberoamerican Summit, which would take place in Havana in 1999. That phase ended in 2003 when Aznar proposed the four EU sanctions (among them, inviting dissidents to celebrations of national holidays) as a response to the arrest that year of 75 dissidents in Cuba. Cuba responded by freezing official relations.

Unconditional engagement under President of the Government José Luis Rodríguez Zapatero changed Spain's policy to one of renewed engagement. Spain reopened bilateral channels of dialogue with Cuba (including over the controversial issue of human rights), re-established economic development cooperation, and convinced

EU member states to lift the four sanctions against Cuba. In addition to Minister of Foreign Affairs Moratinos (who visited the Island for the first time in April 2007), the symbol of the new policy was Ambassador Carlos Alonso Zaldívar, ex-member of the Spanish Communist Party who had joined the left wing of the PSOE. A changed political context (the Cuba–Venezuela alliance), made it difficult to return to González's approach of constructive engagement, as embodied in González's influence regarding domestic reforms. Nonetheless, Spain joined its Iberoamerican partners in their policy of engagement. It also took advantage of its term in the presidency of the EU (and of the transition toward a more cohesive EU foreign policy) to push for the elimination of the Common Position. In his speech at the Congress of Deputies on March 23, 2010, Minister Moratinos stressed the lack of results from the Common Position and argued that "The Common Position is a unilateral position, not a bilateral one; it involves no commitment by Cuban authorities to improve the human rights situation." Even if the Common Position were eliminated, however, the EU would revert to the *status quo ante* (before Aznar's policy, that is) without real progress in its Cuban relations.

These political vagaries demonstrate that the Cuba issue is a platform used in Spain to stake out differing ideological positions over the only foreign policy battlefield available to partisans in Spain concerning matters inside and outside the EU. Cuba is also a good instrument to measure distance from, or proximity to, Washington and thus to gauge the temperature of relations between Spain and the United States. The old Spanish saying *más se perdió en Cuba* (more we lost in Cuba) reflects the salience of the Cuba issue in Spain, the perception that U.S. policy toward Cuba is adverse to Spanish interests on the Island, and significance for Spain of exerting its influence on Cuba issues within the EU.

Past attempts to reach consensus on Spanish policy toward Cuba have not been successful.[7] However, in April 2010, Spain's major political parties achieved, for the first time, approval of a common statement by the Congress of Deputies that "condemns the death of prisoner of conscience Orlando Zapata" and "encourages a dialogue . . . to lay the basis for a future of national reconciliation" in Cuba. This could be the beginning of Spain's developing a common policy toward Cuba. A Spanish state policy toward Cuba would also put an end to the swings in the EU position, which have reflected the triangular relations of Cuba–U.S.–Spain.

EU Policy in Relation to the Cuba–U.S.–Spain Triangle and the Treaty of Lisbon

The EU is an infinitely more complex actor than the U.S. or Spain. Simple interpretations, such as the frequent Cuban assertions that the EU "plays Washington's game," fail to do justice either to the essence of European policy (clearly differentiated from that of the United States) or to the difficult process of seeking internal consensus. Approval of the Common Position was not a result of Stuart Eizenstat's visits. The four "sanctions" were not the product of the Bush administration's Cuba Transition Coordinator (a figure without much influence) but of the back-and-forth of Spanish policy toward Cuba, pressures from human rights groups, and the internal political moment within the EU.

Nonetheless, it is true that the EU's relationship to the Island is always under the shadow of Cuba–U.S. relations. It was no accident that the Common Position was approved the same year as the Helms–Burton Act—the two legal dispositions are closely related, though representing very different philosophies. Like Helms–Burton for the United States, the Common Position is the EU's chief bargaining chip, and its elimination would leave Europe without any levers to employ in negotiations. Only within the limits of this logic, which might also be said to reflect a tradition more than a policy, has the EU's pendulum swung this way or that. The policy constant has been the Common Position and its stipulation of conditions, which have prevented the signing of a cooperation agreement. The variable is whether to lean more toward preconditions or more toward dialogue.

Constant but Limited Economic Engagement

Cuba is the only market in which U.S. firms are not present, which is a historical exception and the result of the embargo, making Brussels and Washington more rivals than allies on the Cuba question. It is a commonplace to state that the EU and its member states have always rejected Washington's policy of sanctions because they consider it counter-productive to the goal of promoting democratic change in Cuba. While political dialogue between the EU and Cuba is conditioned by the Cuba–U.S.–Spain triangle, the EU has always maintained its economic engagement. The EU is Cuba's second most important trading partner, second-biggest investor, an important donor, and the second-largest supplier of tourists, after Canada (see Tables 8.2, 8.3 and 8.4).

The EU's role in Cuba is much more than symbolic. To be precise, the EU— together with China—guaranteed the Island's economic survival in the early 1990s when its main previous economic partners disappeared from one day to the next. Without the European Union, there is no doubt that the U.S. embargo would have had a much greater effect after the disappearance of the CMEA.[8] By the end of the new century's first decade, the EU had become somewhat less important. Economic reforms had slowed, there were fewer joint ventures, and Venezuela had entered the Cuban market as a replacement for Cuba's earlier alliance with the USSR. Compared with what Europe has to offer, however, the Cuban–Venezuelan alliance is a short-range phenomenon with little staying power. First, because Cuba cannot go on exporting its professionals, who are trained and demanded on the Island. Second, because the alliance with Hugo Chávez is a risk given the serious economic and internal security problems he faces.

TABLE 8.2   European tourists in Cuba, 2003 and 2008

	2003	2008
UK	120,866	193,932
Italy	177,627	126,042
Spain	127,666	121,166
Germany	157,721	100,964
France	144,548	90,731
Netherlands	29,451	33,548
Portugal	28,469	25,542
Poland	5,562	21,730
Belgium	24,318	15,681
Austria	18,739	13,450
Czech Rep.	7,777	11,214
Denmark	6,327	10,179
EU total	849,071	764,179
Percentage of total	44%	33%

Source: Cuba, Oficina Nacional de Estadísticas de Cuba

TABLE 8.3   EU participation in Cuban trade in 2005 and 2009

Imports		Exports	
2005	2009	2005	2009
25.8%	19%	38.7%	20.7%

Source: Eurostat

TABLE 8.4   Cuba's trade partners in 2007 and 2009

2007		2009	
Venezuela	22.3%	Venezuela	24.9%
China	15.1%	EU	19.4%
Spain	9.8%	China	17.4%
U.S.	5.8%	Canada	6.9%
Canada	4.3%	U.S.	5.5%
Germany	3.9%	Mexico and Brazil	3.2%
Italy	3.9%	South Korea	3.1%
Brazil	3.9%	Russia	2.0%
Russia	2.9%	Algeria	1.6%
Vietnam	2.7%	Dominican Republic	1.0%

Source: Eurostat

Because of the absence of the United States, the EU's role in the Cuban economy is probably exaggerated, however. The economic outlook for this role is limited by several factors: in the first place, by the absence of a cooperation agreement, which would create a shared legal framework, and also by the systemic differences that prevent the entrance of a socialist Cuba into the EU–Caribbean free-trade agreement; in the second place, by the internal limitations of a still modest economic opening and the absence of large-scale business opportunities, given that Cuba is a small country without strategic resources; in the third place, by relations of a classic North–South type—raw materials in exchange for technology and manufactured goods: while in 2009 the EU was Cuba's second trading partner and represented almost 20 percent of Cuba's trade, Cuba accounted for barely 0.1 percent of the EU's imports and exports and ranked as only its 79th largest partner; and in the fourth place, because the Helms–Burton Act remains a sword of Damocles that places conditions not only on future negotiations between Cuba and the United States but also on EU–Cuba relations.

The potential threat of U.S. sanctions that could be imposed on European companies under the U.S. Helms–Burton legislation has led to a kind of "economic self-censorship" which, together with the limits that stem from the fact of different political regimes in Cuba and the European Union, gets in the way of greater progress in economic relations. Few European companies are willing to run the risk of paying millions in damages to former owners of Cuban businesses living in the United States; consequently, investments have dropped. Property rights will be a key issue at any future negotiating table, where Europe will play a role (albeit secondary) by virtue of its investments in Cuban firms whose nationalization the United States does not recognize. So far, Brussels and Washington are guided by the Understanding reached in 1997.[9] Although European companies will remain on the scene, it is clear that, given proximity and low shipping costs, the United States would be too strong a competitor for them if the embargo was lifted.

Cuba's Abnormality in EU Politics

Approving a Common Position as a tool for carrying out a common foreign policy is the exception rather than the rule in the EU. The EU has common positions on Burma, Iraq, Nigeria, Zimbabwe, all considered "problematic states"—and Cuba. The Common Position points to Cuba's exaggerated role in EU politics, which stems from the historical quarrel over the Island between Spain and the United States. The EU applies a contradictory policy, one hijacked by Spain and embedded in the transatlantic relationship. Those are two axes that make EU policy toward Cuba highly incoherent and subject to continual variations within the constants of rejecting the embargo and remaining economically present.

Since establishing diplomatic relations, the EU still has not defined where Cuba belongs in institutional terms. It is a member of the ACP Group but not part of the regional agreements or of the Cotonou Agreement. Up to the approval of the Treaty of Lisbon, which has modified the institutional structure of the European community, the EU saw the Island as part of its Directorate-General for Development, although it was the Directorate-General for External Relations (DG Relex) that negotiated political dialogue. Thus, Cuba is treated as a Caribbean country although it actually has a Latin American identity. The Common Position introduces another peculiarity: double conditionality, given that all EU cooperation agreements with third countries include a democracy clause but, in Cuba's case, normalization of relations and the signing of a cooperation agreement require, as an additional and prior condition, visible democratic advances on the Island. This is the European response to Helms–Burton and, like the U.S. embargo, a negotiating chip for the EU vis-à-vis Cuba.

Since EU policy is designed by 27 member states, the European Commission and its various Directorates, and the European Parliament, the Common Position imposed by Spain is nothing more than a general guideline that permits various interpretations within the limits of rejecting sanctions. There are various contradictions within the EU:

- Cuba is part of the Iberoamerican Community and participates in its summit meetings but is the only country without an EU cooperation agreement.
- There is an EU delegation in Cuba but it does not have embassy status even though 12 member states have opened embassies on the Island.
- More than 20 bilateral accords have been signed but none between the EU and Cuba.
- There is a Common Position but the member states carry out a variety of policies within the framework of conditional engagement; this is true even within the European Commission itself (before the Treaty of Lisbon) with DG Development and DG Relex.

Consensus and Dissension Among the Actors

On this last point, depending on various possible politico-electoral circumstances, four positions on the Cuba question are discernible within the EU.

- The human rights fundamentalists who demand release of all political prisoners before any progress in relations;
- The U.S. allies who prioritize their relations with Washington and therefore act cautiously;
- The anti-Castro converts who demand special dialogue with the dissidents and more political pressure; and
- The engagement proponents who want a policy of critical or unconditional engagement, either out of principle or out of anti-Americanism.

TABLE 8.5 Cuba in the EU agenda

Common positions	Divergent positions

Reject sanctions and embargo
Maintain a presence in Cuba
Maintain economic relations
Promote internal change on the Island
Respect national sovereignty
Recognize realities of property ownership
Improve the economic situation and
  support a reform process
Gradual and peaceful transformation from
  within
	Preferential vs. secondary treatment for
	  dissidents
	High vs. low levels of cooperation
	Coordination with the United States vs. an
	  independent policy
	Preconditions and required gestures, vs.
	  none
	Maintaining vs. repealing the Common
	  Position
	How to treat the foreign debt
	Coordinate EU policy with Latin
	  American partners, or not (Spain does
	  this in the Iberoamerican framework)
	Degree of political dialogue with the
	  Cuban government

The engagement proponents are clearly a minority. On October 25, 2010, the Common Position was reviewed yet again. Although its elimination seemed more likely than it did a year earlier, some member states, such as Germany and the Czech Republic were reluctant to lift it. Spain has been actively promoting the approval of a framework for negotiating a cooperation agreement and the replacement of the Common Position. Its arguments were clear: the release of political prisoners and some signs of economic opening (like the authorization of a new list of private activities). Nonetheless, bearing in mind the four groups within the EU, this time, the Spanish demand was not successful. This indicates a constant loss of Spanish influence in EU foreign policy, proportionally to its diminishing economic weight.

Spain has declared that it will continue to try to change the Common Position, but eliminating or replacing it with a different document requires unanimity among 27 states. With favorable signals from Havana, the engagement proponents have more arguments to offer the anti-Castro forces, the fundamentalists, and the U.S. allies. As the different positions about different aspects of the Cuba issue demonstrate (see Table 8.5), the EU lacks a common policy toward Cuba and, although the disagreements are not fundamental, it will be hard to define a coherent strategy approved by all the actors.

Faced with a post-Lisbon EU which strengthens its common foreign policies, Cuba would have to keep relying on Spain, but without neglecting its relations with Brussels and other member states. Looking toward the future, Cuba has the advantage of having had intense historical relations with many Eastern European countries that are now EU members and could serve as portals to a more favorable relationship with Europe. Although these relationships tend to be negative in the current context—because the Czech Republic, Poland, and others compare Cuba with their own transitions and are close U.S. allies—the ties created in the past could be revived in some future moment to raise again the Cuba issue on the EU agenda.

Cuba in the Post-Lisbon Agenda

There is a certain frustration in the EU over the snail's pace of progress in relations with Cuba, and also a certain "Cuba fatigue" visible even during the Spanish presidency. In the first half of 2010, Spain held the last EU presidency that afforded a member state a six-month leading role in European foreign policy before a "new EU" less dependent on national agendas came into being. From then on, the EU's High Representative for Foreign Affairs, Catherine Ashton, will be responsible for relations with Cuba. The Island has never been a high priority but in the post-Lisbon EU it will be even less so.

The approval of the Treaty of Lisbon changed the makeup of the EU cast. None of the new actors (Karel Gucht, Commerce; Kristalina Georgieva, Humanitarian Aid; and Ashton) has any special interest in Cuba. Spain is much less prominent in the new structure. Javier Solana is gone, and no Spaniard holds an important post. This could lead to either of two scenarios: greater bilateralization, with Spain as Cuba's main partner, or greater "Europeanization," with a reduced Spanish role and less Spanish interest. The bipartisan compromise in the Congress of Deputies about issuing a denunciation of the death of a political prisoner points in the latter direction.

Finally, one must understand that "the common policies of the EU" always result from compromises among the positions of the member states, the European Commission, and, from now on, the three major representatives: Ashton as High Representative for Foreign Affairs and Vice-President of the Commission; Herman van Rompuy, EU President; and João Barroso, President of the Commission. The complex process of seeking consensus involves more than 30 official actors as well as representatives of civil society. It will be difficult for that process to lead to clear policies. More likely, there will be lowest common denominator positions. In the best of cases, the result will be a "Europe of quotas," one that seeks a representative balance among member states, demographics, and political positions. Thus, Washington neither has been, nor will be the determining element in EU policy toward Cuba, but only one of several.

As the Treaty of Lisbon takes full effect, it eliminates the rotating EU presidencies that conduct foreign affairs and it creates a common "external action service" and EU embassies. These changes will have consequences for Europe–Cuba relations. Up until now, Spain has been a much more important actor than Washington when it came to defining EU policy; in effect, Spain had a monopoly on defining European policy toward Cuba, promoting in turn the Common Position, the four measures implemented in 2003, the later elimination of those measures, and the subsequent debate on a new policy of engagement.

To the extent the EU manages to define common positions beyond those determined by member states, and to the degree the Union keeps growing and admitting countries with no interest in Cuba, Spain will lose its previous room for maneuver. "Europeanization" will most likely also reduce Cuba's outsized prominence in the Union's foreign agenda. This will lessen outside pressures but it will also reduce the EU's engagement with the Island.

The Future of the Transatlantic Agenda

The EU and the United States have carried out policies that have seemed irreconcilable. Engagement including political dialogue and a presence on the Island predominated in the EU, while sanctions and diplomatic isolation continued to be the linchpins of U.S. policy. Within these differing logics, however, both have reduced their pressure on Cuba. Without eliminating the requirement for democratization expressed in the fruitless Common Position, the EU seems less and less inclined to enforce it. The United States, meanwhile, has undermined its own embargo through engagement measures including travel and remittance permission for Cuban-Americans, dialogue on migration, food exports, bilateral coordination on drug trafficking and border control, contacts between Cubans in exile and those on the Island, and academic exchanges.

The Common Position in the EU's case and the sanctions in the U.S. case increasingly reflect *realpolitik* less and more just the weight of the past. When the exiles determined Washington's policy, Cuba and the United States could not have state-to-state relations; rather, the conflict between the Cuban government and its opposition was transferred or "extraterritorialized." Something similar occurred in the EU, demonstrating thereby the lack of supranationality in its foreign relations. The EU's policy was hijacked by Spain, and only internal Spanish politics can explain the policy's existence. To the extent that the hardliners' influence in the United States weakens, that Spain begins to develop a truly state position, and that the EU strengthens its common foreign policy, Europe and the United States could narrow the gap between their policies regarding Cuba. Such a change toward applying less pressure would also bring them closer to Latin American policy, as expressed in the recent inclusion of Cuba in the Rio Group despite the clause calling for democracy. In the medium and long terms, the days of both the embargo and the Common Position are numbered, especially if changes take place in Cuba.

In the short run, the two stances will continue to differ. In terms of goals, the EU wants to promote change from within toward a peaceful transition, while the United States wants to bring an end to the Cuban regime; these two opposite visions find common ground in criticism of the human rights situation and especially freedom of expression and association. In terms of their choice of dialogue partners, the EU talks primarily with the Cuban government, consigning the dissidents to a second rank, while U.S. policy is oriented to the interests of the exiles and the dissidents and has barely opened up channels of dialogue with the government.

Another fundamental and important difference for the future is the fact that the EU recognizes Cuba's sovereignty and its property nationalizations, while the United States does not. This difference presages a prolonged conflict over their shared economic interests in Cuba. In response to pressure from its farm interests, the United States dropped some sanctions and became Cuba's fifth trade partner. Because of the absence of the United States from the Cuban market, the EU acquired a privileged position as Cuba's main trading partner. Thus, the policy tools are not as different as they seem: the EU's main policy toward Cuba is one of economic presence, and the United States is following that same path by sending remittances and selling food. The two approaches also share a sanctions component: because of its double conditionality, the EU has not signed an agreement with Cuba, and the United States retains the embargo. Though the degrees differ, and though the Europeans are not in favor of sanctions, the ingredients are similar.

Although continuity is the main trend, something has changed in recent years: Cuba has stopped being a locus of open transatlantic conflict between the EU and the United States, and there is a consensus about engagement. Europe's experience with dialogue and negotiation in Cuba and its knowledge about the reality of the Island constitute its main capital vis-à-vis the United States. During more than 50 years of relative isolation, the distance between the United States and Cuba has grown, and each side continues to see the other through the prism of the Cold War and historical memory of the late 1950s. This policy has carried a high price for the United States: ignorance of Cuban reality and the application of a policy of science fiction created in the anti-Castro imaginations of the first-wave of exiles.[10] Reconstructing the present and constructing the future are among the enormous challenges facing Cuba and the United States. In this process, Europe can help, but it will always play a minor role, with the sole exception of Spain which will continue to have a presence on the Island.

The U.S. embargo is the key to the future. Less external pressure can increase the internal pressure. Lifting the embargo would speed up an opening inside Cuba, reduce the EU's role to its real dimensions (with no Common Position), and return the United States to the center of Cuba's foreign relations, where it has always been albeit in the form of an empty chair.

The EU's policy toward Latin America has been reactive. If the United States lifts the embargo, the EU will definitely eliminate the Common Position. And within a short time, the EU will become Cuba's second economic partner after the United States. The EU does not have a leading role to play in Cuba, but it does offer a constant presence and long experience in political negotiation which can be useful in U.S.–Cuban relations, not as a mediator but as an example.

Notes

1 Soviet-era Council for Mutual Economic Assistance, also known in English as COMECON; Spanish initials CAME.
2 Rafael Hernández, "¿Tendrá Estados Unidos una política latinoamericana (y caribeña) que incluya a Cuba?," *Foreign Affairs Latinoamérica* 8, no. 4 (2008): 50.
3 Francesc Bayo, *Las relaciones políticas entre España y Cuba: continuidad histórica y ajustes frecuentes* (Barcelona: Documentos CIDOB América Latina, no. 16, 2006).
4 Francesc Bayo and Christian Freres, *An Overview of the Linkages Between Spain's Regions and Cuba* (Ottawa: FOCAL Background Briefing, 2005).
5 Joaquín Roy, *The Cuban Revolution (1959–2009): Relations with Spain, the European Union, and the United States* (New York: Palgrave Macmillan, 2010).
6 Celestino del Arenal, "La dimensión regional en la política iberoamericana de España," *Revista de Pensamiento Iberoamericano* 19 (2008): 27–36.
7 One of these was an initiative by the Fundación FRIDE in Madrid, which organized three meetings that included members from the major political parties. See Jorge I. Domínguez and Susanne Gratius, *La política española ante la Cuba del futuro* (Cambridge, MA: DRCLAS Working Papers América Latina, no. 6, 2006).
8 Susanne Gratius, *¿Ayudando a Castro? Las políticas de EE.UU. y la UE hacia Cuba* (Madrid: FRIDE, Documento de Trabajo 15, 2006).
9 Joaquín Roy, *Cuba, the United States and the Helms–Burton Doctrine: International Reactions* (Miami: University Press of Florida, 2000).
10 Susanne Gratius, "Cuba, EE UU y Europa: perspectivas de cambio," *Política Exterior* (Madrid) 23, no. 130 (July–August 2009): 93–103.

9

U.S.–CUBA RELATIONS

THE POTENTIAL ECONOMIC IMPLICATIONS OF NORMALIZATION

ARCHIBALD R. M. RITTER

By mid-2010, the obstacles to the normalization of relations between the United States and Cuba appeared to be almost insurmountable. While there had been optimism in the early months of the Obama Presidency that a process of normalization was being set in motion, the process seemed to reach an impasse after the early moves of the Obama administration liberalizing remittances and travel for Cuban-Americans. The failure to move towards rapprochement is unfortunate for many reasons. The economic cost of continuing stalemate is immense.

The objective of this essay is to explore the potential economic benefits and costs of normalizing relations between the United States and Cuba. The direct economic benefits of normalization would operate through a number of channels, including the movement of people, trade in goods and services, foreign direct investment, financial flows, and technological transfer. These would have a variety of impacts on economic efficiency, income levels, standards of living and income distribution. The impacts of normalization will be sketched using two scenarios. In the first, it is assumed that normalization occurs with no other domestic economic policy changes within Cuba. In the second, it is imagined that Cuba adopts a number of economic reforms resulting in a reasonable degree of economic liberalization.

This essay does not analyze how to achieve normalization or suggest a road map in this direction, tasks undertaken by other individuals and institutions in the United States, for example by the Brookings Institution.[1] Nor does it examine the current economic relationship between the United States and Cuba or the important political consequences of normalization for both countries. Instead, the purpose is to explore the possible economic consequences of normalization in the two scenarios.

Normalization refers to re-establishing diplomatic relations, ending the embargo and establishing an open trading relationship, a mutual *apertura* to foreign direct investment (FDI), and a liberalizing of the movement of people and of financial flows. It would include the elimination of the numerous restrictions on trade, communications, internet linkages, and travel that now characterize U.S. policy towards Cuba plus the closure of Radio Marti.

Normalization Within the Economic Policy Status Quo in Cuba

In the first scenario, normalization occurs, but within the current public policy framework in Cuba. The current economic policy environment includes the following:

- The dual monetary and exchange rate systems;
- The restrictive regulatory environment and onerous taxation on self-employment;
- The prohibition of private sector small, medium, and cooperative enterprise (SMCEs);
- Bureaucratic protectionism and "state trading," that is, controls on imports of goods and services rather than decentralized market determination;
- Foreign investment restricted to joint ventures plus a case-by-case admission process;
- Restrictions on foreign investment regarding hiring and remuneration, profit repatriation, and limitation to foreign exchange earning activities (discussed below);
- Labor law prohibiting independent unions, unfettered collective bargaining and the right to strike;
- Limitations on movements of Cuban citizens wishing to leave and re-enter Cuba.

Given this context, what would be the impacts of normalization? In this first case, it is assumed that the main features of economic management are unchanged and that Cuba makes no policy changes regarding trade and foreign investment policy, freedom of movement, and financial flows.

Trade

With normalization, trade between the two countries would expand considerably, with beneficial consequences for economic performance and well-being for the citizens of both countries but most importantly for Cuban citizens. Given the rapidity with which agricultural imports to Cuba from the United States expanded after food and medicines were exempted from the embargo, geo-economic gravitational forces—i.e. proximity, complementarity, and lower transportation costs—between the two countries, together with the diversified range of goods and services that the U.S. economy can provide will lead to a rapid expansion of a broad range of U.S. exports to Cuba. Moreover, many Cuban-Americans in particular, and notably those based in Florida, are poised to play a major role in facilitating economic interaction between the two countries. This community includes people with a strong interest in promoting such interactions together with the financial resources and a broad range of business-oriented experience and talent to do so.

Despite these positive factors, Cuban merchandise exports to the United States likely will increase, but only modestly due to supply side constraints. In contrast, Cuba's service exports to the United States—notably tourism—should increase significantly.

A normalization of relations would be of major benefit to the United States, which would acquire a nearby market for its merchandise exports. With some intermediation by the Cuban-American as well as a broader business community, U.S. exports of many types of products would increase quickly. Such exports would partly displace some products currently imported by Cuba from Europe, Latin America, and Asia as well as Canada. One indication of how quickly U.S. exports to Cuba would increase is provided by the U.S. liberalization of agricultural and medical exports in 2002. From 2001 to 2008, agricultural exports increased from $4.6 million to almost $700 million (see Table 9.1). Cuba's increased foreign exchange availability was partly responsible for this increase in food imports. In effect, U.S. farmers, exporting enterprises, the producing states and the U.S. economy generally were benefitting from greater Cuban prosperity.

A wide variety of U.S. exports to Cuba would increase following normalization. Capital goods including electrical generation and transmission equipment; construction equipment; specialized vehicles of many sorts; light trucks and transport trucks; telephone, internet and communications equipment and systems; road and rail maintenance equipment; petroleum exploration, extraction and processing equipment; cement making equipment; aircraft; and many integrated production systems would all find potential markets in Cuba. Intermediate products such as specialized chemicals, plastics, mineral products, specialized oils and fuels, semi-fabricated metal products, lumber and wood products, other building materials, semi-finished paper products and many others would also have good market prospects. Some types of consumer good exports would increase, including such things as household furnishings, home repair and "do-it-yourself" equipment, processed foods, and automobiles.

When one examines U.S. trade with somewhat comparable countries in the region such as the Dominican Republic and Costa Rica, one can acquire an idea of the trade potential with Cuba. For example, U.S. exports to Costa Rica, a country with a population a little less than one-third that of Cuba and an income per capita somewhat higher, were $5.7 billion in 2008. For the Dominican Republic—with a population of about 9.5 million, smaller than Cuba's, and a lower per capita

TABLE 9.1 U.S. agricultural exports to Cuba, 2001–09

Commodities exported	Values in thousands of current U.S. dollars								
	2001	2002	2003	2004	2005	2006	2007	2008	2009
Bulk total	2,327	72,774	119,256	217,993	186,559	173,316	246,405	400,675	259,110
Consumer oriented total	2,247	25,723	39,902	96,876	101,056	75,387	88,921	173,128	164,918
Intermediate total	0	41,316	88,413	69,001	58,429	72,145	95,868	111,650	101,837
Forest products	0	15	801	4,611	5,309	7,345	8,960	9,666	1,744
Fish products	0	0	61	196	74	0	0	27	0
Total	4,574	139,828	248,433	388,676	351,427	328,192	440,154	695,146	527,609

Source: U.S. Department of Commerce, Census Bureau, *Foreign Trade Statistics*. Product Group: BICO-HS10 and U.S. Department of Agriculture, Foreign Agricultural Service, http://www.fas.usda.gov/gats/ExpressQuery1.aspx, accessed February 25 and March 5, 2010.

income—U.S. exports in 2008 were $6.6 billion.[2] These numbers would suggest a possible 10-fold increase in U.S. exports to Cuba from the approximate 2008 level of $700 million.

U.S. exports would undoubtedly increase significantly with normalization. However, bureaucratic control of trade and a proclivity to trade with like-minded countries such as ALBA partner Venezuela may limit U.S. export penetration of the Cuban market for a period of time. On the other hand, Cuban decisions to import also appear to be based significantly on price and quality considerations—witness the rapid switch from Canada to the United States as the principal agricultural product source. Ending the embargo will thus have a major positive impact for the United States through its exports, small perhaps relative to the overall size of the U.S. economy but reasonably large in absolute terms.

The United States will also gain to the extent that Cuba is able to develop its export markets there—through some lower cost products, or better quality or more diverse product varieties. Nickel exports to the United States in particular may prove valuable, although the particular refining capacity needed for Cuban nickel concentrate seems lacking at this time. But U.S. access to Cuban nickel concentrate that is refined in Canada or the Netherlands would be useful.

Initially, the embargo did major damage to the Cuban economy, because many of the supply chains were with the United States. U.S. products were particularly attractive in terms of price, quality and convenience, the transportation grid and storage/warehousing system was designed for short-haul trade with the United States and, when replacement parts became unavailable, the capital stock deteriorated faster. While in the 2010s and despite the embargo, Cuba can import virtually everything it needs from non-U.S. sources (see Table 9.2), ending the embargo will have a number of major beneficial economic consequences for Cuba. First, the prices of some products and services imported from the United States are likely lower than the prices from other sources—taking quality into consideration. Second, transportation costs with the United States are lower than with Europe, Asia, much of Latin America and Canada. The Gulf ports—New Orleans, Houston, Mobile, and Miami—are relatively close to Cuba. With normal shipping connections, many products ordered on one day could arrive in Cuba a day or two later from the nearby U.S. ports, while shipping times with other regions of the world are much longer. Repair, maintenance, and replacement part availability are also more convenient and likely cheaper in many cases. The result—seen already for agricultural products—will be a better price–quality combination and lower shipping costs as well as reduced storage costs.

However, bureaucratic controls within Cuba could continue to limit imports from the United States. The importation of goods is not "free" in the sense that anyone can import anything from anywhere as long as it is within the law and the regulatory and fiscal framework. Instead, by and large, the government, through its Trade Ministry, determines what is imported and from where. Politically motivated

TABLE 9.2 Cuba's major trading partners, 2000–08 (millions of Cuban pesos)

	2000	2001	2002	2003	2004	2005	2006	2007	2008
Cuba's major sources of merchandise imports									
TOTAL	4798.6	4793.2	4140.8	4672.7	5615.2	7604.3	9497.9	10079.2	14249.2
Africa	24.6	20.0	10.2	86.1	69.9	147.7	235.8	239.8	289.5
Asia	783.9	887.4	822.4	931.2	1101.0	1600.1	2310.3	2568.6	2883.7
China	443.7	548.5	516.9	506.1	590.3	891.4	1571.1	1518.1	1482.7
Europe	1819.1	1679.6	1437.5	1575.9	1554.5	1914.3	2637.0	2659.4	3269.4
Spain	743.2	693.7	564.9	594.7	645.0	667.9	859.6	952.3	1233.1
Russia	111.3	81.7	74.5	59.1	74.7	137.3	142.1	291.8	268.9
Western Hemisphere	2163.4	2145.0	1812.0	2029.8	2835.3	3872.4	4251.1	4525.1	7778.6
Canada	311.1	364.1	240.1	240.2	268.2	339.9	351.6	436.7	655.8
United States	0	4.4	173.6	327.3	443.9	476.3	483.6	581.7	801.1
Venezuela	898.4	951.5	725.3	684.1	1142.7	1863.7	2232.4	2343.2	4477.8
Cuba's major merchandise export markets									
TOTAL	1675.3	1621.9	1421.7	1688.0	2334.2	2159.4	2924.6	3685.7	3679.6
Africa	12.9	16.0	25.7	16.8	7.6	20.0	10.5	60.8	288.1
Asia	204.5	147.6	170.7	142.4	150.2	171.4	405.4	997.4	886.1
China	80.5	73.7	74.6	77.3	80.1	104.8	244.0	928.3	677.1
Europe	990.6	1077.0	864.2	924.6	1155.0	953.9	1241.5	898.5	812.4
Russia	324.6	404.7	278.4	132.1	120.8	52.5	136.7	70.6	53.1
Spain	150.2	143.6	144.5	178.7	174.2	160.6	157.0	172.5	197.4
Western Hemisphere	466.7	380.8	368.8	603.1	1017.2	1012.8	1265.0	1725.2	1690.2
Canada	277.9	228.3	203.2	266.8	487.0	437.9	546.4	963.0	767.5
United States	0	0	0	0	0	0	0	0	0
Venezuela	14.0	21.9	19.4	191.6	367.0	401.5	408.8	450.4	414.8

Source: Cuba, Oficina Nacional de Estadísticas, *Anuario estadístico de Cuba, 2001, 2005, 2008 and 2009*, Table 15.11, http://www.one.cu/ accessed March 10, 2010.

"state trading" with Venezuela for example, can override economically motivated trade. However, at the same time, some of the larger conglomerate enterprises that are publicly owned but operate with considerable independence within both the old peso economy and the convertible currency economy, have considerable latitude to import what they need for retailing in the formerly labeled "dollar stores" or "Cuban convertible peso" (CUC) stores in the domestic hard-currency economy. The volume of imports from the United States as elsewhere would also be limited by the foreign exchange earned by the Cuban economy from export of goods and services or by capital inflows or loans of various sorts. There are serious constraints that impede production increases for exportation, as argued below.

Import volumes are also affected by the availability of credit. Cuba has been successful historically in obtaining credits from various countries, most notably the Soviet Union from 1970 to 1988 (never to be repaid) and more recently from Venezuela. However, subsidized credits from Venezuela depend on the largess of President Chávez as well as its oil revenues, which in turn depend on prices and export volumes. Venezuela's oil export volumes are unlikely to increase soon despite Venezuela's vast reserves, and prices may not return to the peak levels of 2007–08 for some time. The sustainability of the credits from Venezuela is thus ambiguous. Moreover, due largely to U.S. policy, Cuba is not at this time a member of the major international financial institutions such as the Inter-American Development Bank or the World Bank so that credits for the purchase of imports from the United States or elsewhere are not yet forthcoming from these sources. But after normalization, membership and credit facilities would become available.

A long-term risk for Cuba, echoing historical patterns, would be an excessive concentration of trade ties with the United States, so one might expect continuing efforts by Cuba to ensure diversified trade relations.

Cuba's exports of goods and services to the United States would also increase with normalization under the current public policy status quo, but again, by less than could occur with key economic reforms. Cuba's merchandise exports are currently limited by a weak production capability. The sugar sector has shrunk by over 80 percent from the late 1980s to the late 2000s and shows little sign of recuperation in the short term.[3] This could change in the longer term, but only with massive investment and technological transfer from countries like Brazil in sugar and ethanol production. In the short term and again with no policy reforms, coffee production for export would be unlikely to increase, as a substantially higher real producer price is needed together with well-functioning markets for inputs and the final product. Tobacco exports—especially fine cigars—could find a significant market in the United States despite health concerns, but good high-quality cigars from other sources are also available in the United States. However, the curiosity value of Cuban cigars in the U.S. market should lead to increases in export sales. While the small farmers who produce high-quality tobacco could certainly produce more under the right conditions, the question is whether appropriate pricing policies and input-provision will provide the necessary incentive framework for increased production. Rum exports to the United States would also likely increase significantly, although one can expect continuing legal complications over the use of the trade name "Havana Club." There is some potential for exports of Cuban pharmaceuticals to the United States, but testing is arduous and time consuming so market development will take some time. Nickel exports to the U.S. market—or to other markets—could increase but the gestation period for new nickel mining and concentrating projects is long. Cuba does have the potential for increasing mine production and concentrate exports so this could in time be a significant export to the United States.

New manufactured product exports are improbable within the current policy environment, notably the blockage of small and medium scale enterprise and the innovative activities that such a sector could engender. Moreover, the dysfunctional dual exchange rate and monetary systems impede production for export as long as enterprises are compensated for their export earnings at 1.00 Cuban peso (*Moneda Nacional or "MN"*) to $1.10 worth of products exported—while the real exchange rate of relevance to Cuban citizens is around 22 *MN* pesos to $1.00.

In summary, ending the embargo will be of major benefit to the United States with respect to the expansion of its merchandise exports to Cuba despite some potential obstacles. Cuba will benefit with respect to the real purchasing power of its foreign exchange earnings. Cuba also will benefit from the availability of imports from the United States, as these will be of better quality and relatively lower price when they displace imports from other sources. But Cuba is unlikely to be able to expand its merchandise exports to the United States quickly when the embargo ends due to supply side problems. However, in time, the U.S. market for such things as pharmaceuticals, beverages and tobacco should improve.

Cuba will likely experience some significant increases in service exports to the United States over and above tourism. Cuba could provide medical services to some U.S. citizens or their medical insurance companies wanting lower cost and good quality medical attention. One could expect also increases in service exports in the realms of music and the arts, as well as sports, especially baseball. Cuban citizens would also benefit through better communications and internet access with a better linkage with the United States.

The United States would also benefit from the provision of services of various sorts to Cuba. One could expect that a wide variety of specialized professional and business service exports would begin to flow from the United States to Cuba and would reach significant levels quickly. Such service exports could include engineering consulting, architectural services, information, computer and communications services, legal services, financial services, and environmental consulting, to name only a few. Again, Cuban-American citizens probably would be prominent in such activities. The export of such services would be of benefit to the United States whose citizens and enterprises would earn income in Cuba. Cuba also would benefit from the importation of high-tech knowledge and skills.

The Movement of People

Normalization of relations with the United States, even with no changes in the policy environment, will generate a tourism bonanza for Cuba. Already in the decade of the 2000s there has been significant tourism from the United States reaching almost 85,000 in 2003 before the tightening of travel restrictions by the Bush administration (Table 9.3). Much of the U.S. tourism to Cuba in the 2000s was legal, of a family reunification or educational variety. But some proportion of the tourist numbers in Table 9.3 was illegal, travelling through Canada, Mexico or other countries, unrecorded in the United States but recorded in Cuba.

The increases in tourism following normalization could be spectacular. Indeed, freedom of U.S. citizens to travel to Cuba may be implemented before full normalization occurs.[4] One could anticipate increases in the following types of tourism, all of these being important foreign exchange earners:

* *Curiosity tourism.* There could be a huge tourist influx of U.S. citizens wanting to see Cuba for the first time in decades. Relatively few U.S. citizens appear to have broken U.S. travel restrictions, so the pent-up demand would be enormous.
* *Family reunification tourism.* When all controls are lifted on the U.S. side for travel to Cuba, a large increase in short-term visits by Cuban-Americans for family purposes is likely to occur. Such an increase already occurred in 2009–10.
* *Sun, sea and sand tourism.* Many U.S. citizens, especially from the northeastern and central parts of the country, will likely follow the winter-escaping Canadians to Cuban beaches for one- to two-week periods.
* *"Snow-bird" tourism.* Some U.S. citizens, mainly retirees, will spend several of the winter months in Cuba. This will be limited until accommodation arrangements such as time-share condominium arrangements are possible.
* *Medical tourism.* There may be some travel to Cuba for access to medical services which will likely continue to be inexpensive relative to the United States.
* *Convention tourism.* Short-term visits for conventions could increase significantly.
* *Cultural and sport tourism.* One might expect more visits for purposes of interacting with and experiencing Cuban art, music, cinema, and sports.
* *Educational tourism.* It is likely that U.S. students and teachers at various levels would enroll or visit Cuban institutions of higher learning or cultural and sports centers for courses, years abroad, sabbaticals, language training, etc., in much greater numbers than have been possible under the embargo.
* *"March-Break" tourism.* Students from the United States are likely to try a visit to Cuba for the March Break, instead of the Maya Riviera, Florida or elsewhere.

When normalization occurs, it is likely that significant numbers of retirees will move to Cuba on a semi-permanent basis when this is possible. While this perhaps may not be "tourism" narrowly defined, its economic consequences are the same,

TABLE 9.3 U.S. and Canadian tourism in Cuba, 2003–09

	2003	2004	2005	2006	2007	2008	2009
Total	1,905,682	2,048,572	2,319,334	2,220,567	2,152,221	2,348,340	2,425,000
Canada	452,438	563,371	602,377	604,263	660,384	818,246	932,800
United States	84,529	49,856	37,233	36,808	40,521	41,904	300,000ᵉ

Note: e. indicates a preliminary estimate.

Source: Cuba, Oficina Nacional de Estadísticas, *Anuario estadístico de Cuba, 2008*, Chart 15.5 and *Panorama Económico y Social de Cuba, 2009*, "Turismo. Indicadores Seleccionados 2009."

namely the earning of foreign exchange by providing services to foreign nationals. Some Cuban-Americans, especially from the northern United States and some other citizens may choose to spend half or more of the year in Cuba—as they often do now in Mexico, Costa Rica or southern areas of the United States.

In sum, Cuba will likely experience a tourist boom that may be immense at first, then tapering off somewhat as the "curiosity tourism" begins to wane, but remaining at relatively high levels. One could imagine U.S. tourism quickly doubling the already high Canadian level and then redoubling in a decade or so following normalization, as Cuba's capacity to accommodate larger numbers of tourists expands. This also would lead quickly to large increases, perhaps a doubling of Cuba's total foreign exchange earnings from tourism within a decade, which were already at 2.36 billion convertible pesos (CUCs) or about $2.6 billion by 2008.[5]

On the down-side for the United States, some increases in travel by U.S. citizens to Cuba may be at the expense of U.S. destinations, especially South Florida. This could be the case especially for "snow-bird" tourism, "sun and sand" tourism, "retiree" tourism and even convention and "March-Break" tourism. But on the other hand, Miami could become a major transit center for travel to Cuba by high-speed hydrofoil and conventional ferry boat. One can imagine also joint Miami–Havana tourist packages as well so that Miami and South Florida could gain from symbiotic or cooperative tourist ventures with Cuba.

With normalization, Cuban tourism to the United States will also be facilitated. However, without some changes in policy in Cuba, the current limitations on the movement of Cuban citizens to the United States—as elsewhere at this time—would continue. At present, a Cuban citizen wishing to travel abroad in a personal capacity must first be invited by a foreign citizen who must pay a high-priced consular fee (plus an additional sum for the Cuban Consulate to e-mail the relevant *Consultoría Jurídica Internacional* in Cuba).[6] The foreign host must also agree "to guarantee all the expenses related to the trip as for lodging, maintenance, health insurance, etc., so the person invited is legally covered during his/her stay."[7] Visa fees are also likely to be charged to Cuban citizens visiting the United States. These restrictions and fees, if they were maintained after normalization, would limit the number of Cuban citizens that would be able to visit the United States, thereby limiting the benefits for the host country and for Cuban citizens themselves.

Moreover, the dual monetary system makes it almost impossible for most Cuban citizens to travel abroad as the *Moneda Nacional* (*MN*) that they earn in their normal work is inconvertible at the official rate of exchange (1 peso *MN* = $1.10) or a reasonable rate of exchange. Moreover, the average salary in 2008 was 415 pesos (*MN*) per month[8] or about $20–21 at the exchange rate relevant for Cuban citizens. At this level of income, access to travel outside Cuba is not possible unless citizens have foreign sponsors, state support, or large convertible peso earnings.

In summary, with normalization, U.S. citizens will benefit from being able to visit Cuba freely. Cuban tourism to the United States will likely be minor for some years to come barring changes in economic policy affecting the dual monetary system within Cuba and liberalization of the right to travel on the part of Cuban citizens.

Prospective U.S. Foreign Direct Investment in Cuba

Major potential exists for U.S. foreign direct investment in Cuba following normalization. The range of areas where such investment could occur is broad, encompassing many types of economic activity, including the production of some consumer goods, custom capital goods, food processing, agriculture, professional services, financial and business services, construction, and transportation, for example. One would expect that the Cuban-American community in particular would have a major interest and the vision necessary to see and cultivate the emerging opportunities.

Offshore petroleum is one particular area where some U.S. enterprises have expertise and experience that could benefit Cuba. Proximity, necessity, and opportunity together would promote such investment. The deep-sea petroleum regions also are in contiguous waters of the Florida Straits and the Gulf of Mexico so that cooperation in exploration, extraction, and environmental protection are mutually desirable for Cuba and the United States.

Such foreign investment has major benefits, but also some costs. The benefits would include the transfer of entrepreneurship, managerial know-how, technical expertise, financial resources, market access, and capital equipment in integrated "packages" that can be implemented rapidly and organically. The costs would include the repatriation of profits, and the shift of some decision-making authority offshore. Do the benefits exceed the costs? Most governments—including the Government of Cuba since 1992—judge this to be the case and for this reason welcome foreign investment, though within regulatory and tax frameworks of varying intensity. The example of Sherritt International is instructive in this case. Sherritt has earned profits that have been repatriated—though with some difficulty in 2009—but it has generated immense benefits for Cuba in terms of technological transfer, improved productivity, improved environmental and health and safety standards, tax revenues, and foreign exchange earnings for.

Would U.S. investment actually be forthcoming if relations were normalized but with no policy changes in Cuba? Probably some projects would occur within the current joint venture arrangement and regulatory system. However, there are a variety of restrictions, problems and uncertainties that reduce the attractiveness of investing in Cuba. These limit foreign investment from all countries now and will continue after normalization.

First, there is uncertainty about the commitment of the Cuban government to the course adopted regarding foreign investment. Although official documents destined for international consumption have welcomed foreign investment, other statements from the media raised questions regarding its future role. Moreover,

President Fidel Castro waged an "anti-globalization" campaign with annual international conferences in Havana from 1999 to 2007, often with himself as the principal personage at the podium. Even Sherritt International has not felt itself immune from the uncertainties in Cuba:

> However, there can be no assurance that this attitude to foreign investment and profit repatriation will continue or that a change in economic conditions will not result in a change in the policies of the Cuban government or the imposition of more stringent foreign investment restrictions. Such changes are beyond the control of Sherritt and the effect of any such changes cannot be accurately predicted.[9]

Second, while the Foreign Investment Law outlines "rules of the game" for foreign investors, in fact, during the 2000s, each foreign investment has been determined on a case-by-case basis. Each potential project must be negotiated with the counterpart enterprise and the Ministry of Foreign Trade and Foreign Investment. After delays and significant investments of time and money, foreign investors can be turned down for a variety of reasons.

A third general limitation on foreign investment is that those activities oriented to domestic consumption in the "Cuban-peso" economy earning *Moneda Nacional* are essentially closed to foreign investors. In effect, only those activities that earn foreign exchange directly through exportation of goods or services and some activities that service the tourist sector for hard currency are worth entering because profit repatriation cannot otherwise occur.

Fourth, recruitment and selection of employees must be done through the *Agencia de Contratación a Representaciones Comerciales* (*ACOREC*). The wage structure is also determined by the government. Moreover, foreign enterprises must pay wages and salaries in "convertible pesos" or CUCs, at the exchange rate of CUC 1.00 per U.S.$1.10, while the workers are paid in "Cuban pesos" (with the relevant exchange rate for Cuban citizens in recent years at 1.00 *MN* = \$0.04). This means that the state makes tax-like levies on the wage payments by foreign firms to their workers at an average rate of around 96 percent so that the real cost of labor is relatively high.

Fifth, the repatriation of profits can be problematic. When foreign exchange earnings decline due to reduced export prices or volumes, the Government of Cuba postpones the payment of profits in foreign exchange rather than cutting import purchases.

A further potential problem that may produce unease for foreign enterprises operating in Cuba is that Cuban workers do not have the right to undertake independent collective bargaining, negotiation with their employers, or to strike. These rights are enshrined in the International Labor Organization (ILO) and UN Declarations; the government has not allowed attempts to create independent unions to exercise them.[10] Only official government unions are legal. If U.S.

enterprises were to enter Cuba under current conditions of labor law, there could be a reaction against them in the United States, spear-headed mainly by components of the Cuban-American community. On the other hand, U.S. and other countries' enterprises have no compunction regarding investing in China, which has similar labor laws to Cuba. The difference may be the existence of the Cuban-American community, which may make an issue regarding investing in Cuba. One could imagine boycotts and publicity campaigns against U.S. enterprises operating in Cuba under current conditions. The potential loss of market share in the United States and the bad publicity could reduce prospective investment by U.S. firms.

It is worth noting that Cuba is also a foreign investor. The joint venture with the Canadian enterprise Sherritt International involves Cuban 50 percent ownership of the nickel refinery in Fort Saskatchewan, Alberta, in exchange for 50 percent ownership by Sherritt of the Moa mine and concentrating plant in Cuba. Would the current leadership of Cuba accept this formula for opportunities in the United States following normalization? The answer is probably "yes" allowing for a period of adjustment following normalization.

Financial Flows

Normalization with the United States will also generate a variety of new types of financial flows. These will be largely from the United States to Cuba. Flows from Cuba to the United States will be so small for some time after normalization that they can be ignored here. Already, of course, family remittances constitute a large flow of foreign exchange into Cuba and may be somewhere in the area of $1 billion at this time.

New financial flows to Cuba potentially could include:

* Informal loans or donations to friends or relatives;
* Credits provided by NGOs for specific purposes such as to finance a micro-credit program for small farmers or small non-farm enterprises;
* Suppliers' credits, provided by U.S. exporting firms to Cuban buyers for the purchase of U.S. products;
* Commercial bank loans to Cuban importing firms or productive enterprises for investment purposes;
* "Portfolio investment" or the purchase of shares or equity in Cuban enterprises;
* The Export–Import Bank of the United States, which may extend credits to Cuban purchasers and support small U.S. enterprises exporting to Cuba (against non-payment, for example);
* U.S. Agency for International Development grants or loans on soft terms;
* Financing from the Inter-American Development Bank or the World Bank, assuming that membership in these organizations will follow normalization with the United States.

These types of financial flows are all potentialities only. Will Cuba permit such flows to occur? Or, is the existing policy environment appropriate for the financial flows to become operational?

Informal loans and donations among relatives already occur through the remittance process. They will continue and expand if the opportunities to use such funds productively also expand. Lending through NGOs might occur under the current policy framework, but only if the NGOs and their programs were politically acceptable.[11]

Suppliers' credits and commercial bank lending to Cuban enterprises could certainly occur after normalization. If Cuba were to treat the United States as it treats other countries after normalization, then the purchase of equity in Cuban firms by U.S. firms under joint venture arrangements also would be possible. Cuba could utilize loans from the Export Import Bank of the United States. Would Cuba under its current leadership or its immediate successor accept assistance from USAID? This may be conceivable but seems unlikely. Would Cuba under the administration of Raúl Castro or his successor join the World Bank, IMF and IADB after normalization with the United States? This would become a possibility. The advantages to Cuba of obtaining such credits would suggest that these facilities, or at least the World Bank and the IADB, would be utilized quickly if they became available. In sum, within the existing policy and political environment, some types of financial flows would come to life, some might be blocked, and some other types of flows are unclear.

The liberalization of the financial flows to Cuba from the United States would have some useful results. The Cuban national economy in 2010 is desperately short of foreign exchange and many kinds of capital equipment necessary for increasing productivity and levels of output necessary for improving the material well-being of its citizens. It is imperative that investment in the Cuban economy increases, as it has been very low with gross investment as a percentage of GDP averaging 8.6 percent from 2000 to 2008 in comparison with 18.7 percent for Latin America as a whole.[12] The provision of a variety of types of credit can help to improve this situation and to provide much-needed foreign exchange for the purchase of imported capital equipment.

A final benefit for the United States in establishing completely normal relations with Cuba would be the elimination of the bureaucratic apparatus necessary to enforce the regulations on trade, travel, and financial flows that apply to Cuba almost uniquely together with eliminating Radio Marti. The budgetary savings—reflecting the real resource savings—from these cuts would not be insignificant.

Normalization in the Context of Economic Liberalization

The gains from normalization for Cuba would be augmented considerably if this occurred prior to, simultaneous with, or shortly after a process of economic policy reform within Cuba. Greater prosperity for Cuba would then result also in increased interaction and benefits for the United States as well.

Imagine that the following types of reform were implemented in Cuba:

- Unification of the dual monetary and exchange rate systems;
- Relaxation of the tax burden and restrictions on self-employment;
- Establishment of a supportive regulatory framework for small enterprise;
- Legalization of private sector small, medium and cooperative enterprises (SMCEs);
- Relaxation of bureaucratic controls on imports, within the context of a realistic exchange rate;
- Modification of policy towards foreign investment permitting majority ownership in some sectors with a rules-based legal environment regarding admission;
- Relaxation of controls on foreign investment regarding hiring and remuneration, etc.;
- Relaxation on controls of funds flowing through NGOs;
- Relaxed commercial bank lending.

Implementation of these policy modifications would result in the Cuban economy approximating that of China, characterized by economic liberalization within a one-party system. Some of these policy changes have been under discussion within Cuba for some time. Monetary and exchange rate policy have been under discussion in academia and the *Banco Central de Cuba* since the 1990s, with an excellent analysis of the issue published in 2009.[13] The conversion of hundreds of state-run beauty shops and barbershops to employee-run cooperatives in April 2010 also suggests that a process of reform in the regulatory environment for small enterprise may be beginning. Though admittedly a modest change, this may have major implications for small and medium enterprise in the longer term.[14]

Economic changes such as the ones listed above would augment and improve Cuba's interaction with the world including the United States and have salutary effects on the domestic economy. The unification of the monetary and exchange rate systems and establishment of a realistic exchange rate would end the dysfunctional and counter-productive incentive structure that has deformed the economic behavior and lives of citizens for almost two decades. A realistic exchange rate is also necessary to link the domestic economy with the rest of the world in a rational manner. Monetary and exchange rate unification would provide the incentive structure and the resources for domestic enterprises, public and private, to export effectively, as they would receive the foreign exchange earnings from their foreign sales at a reasonable rate of exchange. The result, in time, would then be increased exports to the United States and the world, and increased substitution of imported products with domestically produced goods and services. Such unification would also permit foreign investors to have the possibility of investing in sectors servicing the domestic economy as well as foreign exchange-earning markets outside Cuba.

The relaxation of restrictions on self-employment and the legalization of private sector SMCEs would permit a flowering of ingenuity and entrepreneurship. One would expect that small-scale enterprise would enter many goods and service producing areas and would lead to the cultivation of niche markets and the formation of "clusters" of similar, inter-related and complementary enterprises. The volumes and diversity of products would expand rapidly—witness the explosion of entrepreneurial activity and resulting improvements in employment, income generation, and production of needed goods and services that occurred after the legalization of self-employment in 1993. This would be of benefit to Cuban citizens from numerous perspectives. Among the benefits would be productive job creation and income generation; improvement of quality, quantity, and diversity of goods and services; improved productivity permitting higher real incomes; shrinkage of the underground economy; increases in tax revenues; promotion of innovation; increased competition and lower prices generally; the development of a culture of respect for public policy rather than illegality, and generally an improved quality of life.

Of particular relevance here, however, is that a proliferation and expansion of SMCEs would lead to the cultivation of export markets to the United States and elsewhere. Moreover, such enterprises would produce a range of better quality goods and services that would replace imports. Such enterprises would make Cuba an even more attractive tourist destination. It is useful to note that, when legalized, the production of arts and crafts mainly for the tourist sector improved exceedingly rapidly in terms of quantity, quality and diversity. This is likely to occur in all areas when SMCEs are legalized—assuming a reasonable regulatory framework. Furthermore, legalization and the expansion of SMCEs will also provide an avenue for financial flows and direct investment to enter Cuba, which in turn would accelerate the expansion of the sector.

Changes in the legal environment within which foreign firms could invest in Cuba (a rules-based system, full ownership, and control over hiring and remuneration systems) would encourage U.S. and other nations' enterprises to invest in Cuba in ways in which they will not invest at the present time. This would promote the transfer of technology, financial resources, and managerial and entrepreneurial know-how which in turn would promote increased productivity, economic diversification, and volumes of output for export and/or domestic use.

If a monetary-exchange rate reform occurred successfully and if SMCEs were encouraged, some types of financial inflows to Cuba from the United States and the world would increase following normalization. One might expect increases in portfolio investment, suppliers' credits, commercial bank lending, and informal lending in this case. With a unified currency, a reasonable regulatory framework for foreign direct investment, and the legalization of SMCEs, opportunities for inflows of funds would expand quickly as well. Such inflows would help promote investment in old and new areas of economic activity, promoting increased quantity, quality and diversity of the output of goods and services. All of these effects would help generate greater productive employment and higher real incomes and living standards for Cuban citizens. Such enhanced Cuban prosperity also would have a positive feedback effect for the United States through increased Cuban demand for U.S. imports.

The consequences of the more intense economic interaction that would result from U.S.–Cuba normalization within the context of the economic policy environment of this second scenario can be summarized quickly. First, from Cuba's perspective, merchandise exports would increase significantly with exchange rate reform, liberalization of small and medium enterprise, and facilitated FDI and financial inflows. These changes would also promote increased import-substitution for some products and increased exports of services. Imports would increase, made possible by the expansion of exports. Increased imports of machinery and equipment would promote investment and increased resource productivity. Expanded intermediate goods imports would permit increased and diversified domestic production and increased consumer goods imports would help raise people's material levels of living directly.

The above-mentioned policy changes would also help promote service exports— tourism in particular, but also other types of service in the artistic and sports areas and before long in business and personal services. With liberalized travel for Cubans in the United States, assuming changes in Cuban regulations on travel by Cuban citizens, the earnings of Cuban citizens in baseball and the arts in particular will increase and be repatriated to Cuba.

Increased FDI and the various types of financial inflows would promote investment in all sectors of the Cuban economy, including the state sector, mixed enterprises, SMCEs and self-employment. These would promote enterprise development, increases in the capital stock, technological transfer (through importation of machinery and equipment, importation of complete integrated production systems, and movement of people) and managerial and entrepreneurial transfer and learning. Again, the result would be increased productivity of resource use in Cuba and higher levels of productive employment and higher real incomes.

Greater economic prosperity for Cuba will increase the potential level of tax revenues, which will empower the Government of Cuba to invest more in public goods such as infrastructure of all sorts. Education and health could be strengthened with greater investment of public revenues. The incomes of educational, health and all other public sector employees, currently woefully inadequate, could be increased steadily. Greater economic prosperity generally and higher public revenues specifically would permit incomes and levels of human development to rise. The government and Cuban citizens themselves would be able to invest more in human development activities.

Careful social policy measures would be required to maintain an acceptable level of equity in income distribution.[15] This would be difficult, because in any process of economic change, some individuals are better able to capture the new income-earning possibilities than others, so that the rising tide does not lift all boats at the same rate.

There would also be gains for the United States from normalization of relations plus Cuban economic reforms. As the Cuban economy prospered, U.S. exports would increase further. The United States would gain from the expansion of imports from Cuba as the Cuban economy and its exports diversified. In time, the United States would gain from a bonanza of tourists from Cuba. It has been most difficult for Cuban citizens to visit the United States or anywhere else for the past half century. With currency reform and growing prosperity in Cuba, plus reforms of Cuba's regulations on travel of its citizens outside Cuba, one could expect a wave of Cuban visitors to the United States—pent-up curiosity tourism, conference tourism, family reunification tourism, geographically-oriented tourism, etc. This will benefit Cuban citizens and the United States.

Conclusion and Policy Implications

The normalization of relations between the United States and Cuba—defined as ending the embargo, re-establishing diplomatic relations, and permitting financial flows, foreign investment and free movement of people—will generate important net benefits for both countries. The benefits would be even greater if normalization were accompanied by some economic reforms within Cuba.

Normalization will quickly lead to an immediate influx of tourists from the United States to Cuba of bonanza dimension. U.S. exports to Cuba will expand quickly, displacing those of other countries that are less competitive in terms of quality, price and convenience. Foreign investment and various types of financial inflows to Cuba will promote Cuban economic expansion and diversification and will be of benefit to the U.S. interests involved. Normalization plus a set of economic reforms in Cuba would promote more intense interaction between Cuba and the United States and the rest of the world, and generate greater prosperity for Cuba, and also for the United States.

The gains for both countries from U.S.–Cuba normalization are so significant that both countries would be wise to facilitate and promote the process. The Obama administration began a process leading towards normalization with the relaxation of the Bush administration's tightening of travel and remittance restrictions. The Government of Cuba could have responded by removing the 10 percent tax on remittance payments from Cuban-Americans which had been imposed in response to the Bush measures. This would have signaled to the U.S. administration that it wishes to facilitate the process of normalization. But the release of some political prisoners in July 2010, brokered by the Roman Catholic Church, also presents a positive response to the Obama administration's earlier initiatives so that it perhaps is now for the United States to undertake significant conciliatory moves such as permitting freedom of travel for all U.S. citizens to Cuba.

In view of the prospective economic benefits for both countries, movement towards normalization by the United States and Cuba is imperative. Both countries could promote the process by a mutually responsive and supportive sequence of actions that could include major measures on the U.S. side such as permitting free travel by U.S. citizens and dropping the embargo and on the Cuban side by dropping the 10 percent tax on U.S. dollar remittance payments and instituting other measures to foster broad change.

Notes

1   Vicki Huddleston and Carlos Pascual, *Learning to Salsa: New Steps in U.S.–Cuba Relations* (Washington DC: The Brookings Institution, 2010).
2   Office of the U.S. Trade Representatives, http://www.ustr.gov/ accessed March 5, 2010.
3   Early indications place the sugar harvest for 2010 around 1 million tons, an all-time low.
4   A bill entitled the "Travel Restriction Reform and Export Enhancement Act, H.R. 4645" had been making its way through the U.S. House of Representatives with a Hearing on March 11, 2010. The bill would end all restrictions on travel by American citizens to the island and remove barriers to increasing agricultural exports. By end 2010, the passage of this bill appeared unlikely.
5   Oficina Nacional de Estadísticas, *Panorama Económico y Social de Cuba, 2009*, Table 15.11, http://www.one.cu/panorama2009.htm, accessed March 1, 2010.
6   Embassy of Cuba in Canada, Consular Section, "New Procedure to Invite a Cuban National to Come Visit Canada," http://embacu.cubaminrex.cu/Default. aspx?tabid=1188, accessed March 3, 2010.
7   Ibid.
8   Oficina Nacional de Estadísticas, "Cuba: Turismo. Indicadores Seleccionados 2009," *Panorama Económico y Social de Cuba, 2009*, Table 7.4, http://www.one.cu/panorama2009. htm, accessed March 1, 2010.
9   Sherritt International, Annual Report, 2000, 23, http://www.sherritt.com/Investor_ Relations/Financial_Reports/Annual_Reports.html, accessed September 2007.
10 The International Labor Organization's Declaration on Fundamental Principles and Rights at Work includes, as the first fundamental right of labor, "freedom of association and the effective recognition of the right to collective bargaining" (International Labor Organization, Declaration on Fundamental Principles and Rights at Work, http://www. ilo.org/declaration/lang--en/index.htm, accessed March 29, 2010). The UN Universal Declaration on Human Rights (Articles 13, 19 and 20) also emphasizes freedom of mobility, expression and assembly.
11 However, the provision of credits to the self-employed in Cuba is not acceptable in Cuba at this time. Moreover, small and medium scale enterprise is not yet possible within the current regulatory framework.
12 CEPAL, Naciones Unidas, *Balance preliminar de las economías de América Latina y el Caribe 2009*, p. 160, http://www.eclac.cl/cgi-bin/getProd.asp?xml=/publicaciones/ xml/2/38062/P38062.xml&xsl=/de/tpl/p9f.xsl&base=/tpl/top-bottom.xsl, accessed February 2, 2010.
13 Pavel Vidal Alejandro, "Política Monetaria y Doble Moneda," in *Miradas a la economía cubana*, ed. Omar E. Pérez Villanueva, Pavel Vidal Alejandro, Armando Nova González and Luisa Iñiguez Rojas (Havana: Editorial Caminos, 2009).

14 Marc Frank, April 12, 2010. "Cuba handing beauty, barber shops over to workers." Havana: *Reuters*.
15 President Raúl Castro seems to have modified Cuba's social justice objective from equality of income to equality of opportunities, stating: "Socialism means social justice and equality, but equality of rights, of opportunities, not of income." Will Weissert, "Raúl Castro: Communism is Not Egalitarianism" Associated Press, July 15, 2008.

10

U.S.–CUBA ECONOMIC RELATIONS

THE PENDING NORMALIZATION

JORGE MARIO SÁNCHEZ EGOZCUE

The subject of normalizing economic relations between Cuba and the United States tends to provoke extreme reactions whenever it is discussed in either country. For many in Cuba, any link between the two countries represents a threat because it is associated with a chain of concessions that affect sovereignty or a reversion to the past. Others presume that they would have to confront an avalanche of U.S. tourists and merchandise for which Cuba lacks the necessary infrastructure and technical-cultural capacity, and that they would face potential dislocation of the Island's economic and social policies.

Something similar can be said about the reaction in the United States. Some are convinced nothing can happen without changing the Cuban government to meet the demands of a faction holding extreme views, which is unwilling to connect with the country as it really exists. At the other end of the spectrum there are those who have engaged with Cuba as it exists and who make projections based on their anecdotal experiences. They tend to assume that the only feasible economic relations are those based on special deals that avoid the usual legal hurdles—licensed exceptions that, in the end, consolidate existing distortions in the Cuban economy.

The result of this polarity is the absence of a middle ground on which both governments could create a consensus. Therefore, the only realistic path seems to be one based on a series of steps regarding specific issues to foster pragmatism and thereby increase each party's adaptability. So far, the areas in which some improvement has been achieved (migration agreements, commercial exchange, family visits, and delivery of remittances) have all involved bilateral arrangements, none of which could be categorized as "normal" relations.

Assessments of normalization of economic relations between the two countries should not be reduced to estimates of the number of tourists, the volume of remittances, trade in goods, or possible investments. Rather, these relations should be seen as part of a spectrum in which favorable and adverse effects are intertwined, encompassing issues such as political relations, preservation of cultural identity and of the environment, adaptations in the socio-economic development model, and sports, science, and religion.

This essay summarizes the most immediate possibilities in the realm of economic relations between the two countries that could produce greater linkages while leaving aside the no-less-important question of when and how the current restrictions could be relaxed, whether as the result of political dialogue or unilateral U.S. government actions. Instead of a "political weather forecast" regarding changes in the key variables of bilateral relations and their implications for the economic sphere, I assess on the basis of empirical evidence the relative importance of the components that define each party's immediate capacity to respond to the other. This approach also considers the inertial effect of recent precedents, the regional context, institutional factors, and Cuba's current "business culture."

Many other studies repeat some assumptions that reveal how the lack of contact between the two societies has led to oversimplified stereotypes. The most common of these is the "light switch" approach, which implies a quasi-automatic process of connection and fluidity in mutual economic relations that would unfold almost spontaneously as soon as current restrictions were lifted and in which conflicts of interest would never appear. Other writings take for granted a more-or-less speedy transfer of standards and practices whose compatibility with actual conditions remains unexamined, despite the two countries' differences in technology, business culture, and institutional environment. They envision Cuba in the role as passive receiver. They fail to consider internal visions of development strategy and insertion in the international economy, previous Cuban experience with trade and investment involving Canada and the European Union, or lessons derived from regional experiences.

If the attractions of the Cuban market are judged by conventional indicators—Cuba's high-risk rating by international agencies, the size of its foreign debt, the high initial costs and long bureaucratic delays that a foreign firm encounters when it attempts to set up operations on the Island—then it becomes impossible to understand how, in a relatively short period and in spite of strict limitations on authorized commercial operations, the United States has managed to occupy fourth place among countries trading with Cuba in recent years. Conventional logic, based on notions of competitiveness, benefits, complementarities, etc., is not sufficient to explain fully these recent concrete developments. The future will probably bring similar surprises given that we are talking about a context where inertia and rupture coexist.

Further complicating the analysis is the lack of consensus between the two sides about the meaning of "normalization." Each country acts according to its own calculations of risk or influence, making it hard to find a mutual basis on which to consolidate and extend ties. This happens because the respective visions of each perspective are historically rooted in a "legacy of mistrust" that is impossible to ignore. Therefore, the relations established so far exist within a dysfunctional framework that has to be changed. It is no accident that almost all proposals for loosening the embargo presented to the U.S. Congress rely on arguments related to the promotion of internal change in Cuba or the securing of unilateral profits in specific sectors. Proposals have yet to appear that advance the notion of mutual benefits, common between other nations.

Nonetheless, the decisive factor in this process is domestic Cuban reality. Within the country, a generational change in leadership is under way, and so too is the beginning of a process of reforms to repair the economy, which has been stifled by rigidity and inefficiency resulting from an excessive degree of state control, as well as by accumulated distortions, the effects of climatic events, and the difficult conditions of the international market. This reform process is an unavoidable necessity; as it expands, it may lead to deep transformations. Its dynamic may run faster or slower, as determined by its results and by a perception of stability or risk that will depend on the external context including relations with the United States. The last factor, however, is not an indispensable ingredient. In fact, it is far easier to live with the continuity of the U.S.–Cuba conflict than to adapt to its solution. Therefore, what happens in the future of bilateral economic relations depends largely on Cuba's capacity to change itself and on how the United States reacts to those changes.

Normalization of economic relations between the United States and Cuba represents a challenge because, besides the two countries' asymmetry of power and their political differences, this exchange has developed on the basis of mechanisms that must be replaced. Experiences in the region have shown that "normal economic relations" with the United States do not preclude disagreements, and that differences are not always easily resolved. In any case, without renouncing sovereignty, bilateral relations will not amount to the panacea that some foresee, nor the abyss that others predict.

Recent Precedents and Results

Since the 1990s, commercial exchange between the two countries has been characterized by a low degree of diversification. Trade has been concentrated almost exclusively in Cuban purchases of food and other agricultural products subject to special rules about payment and restricted by a U.S. regulatory and oversight regime in which permitted transactions are licensed exceptions to the limits imposed on U.S. entities to engage in trade with an enemy nation. The other two components of the economic relationship have been tourism and remittances.

The current U.S. presence in the Cuban economy began almost invisibly in the late 1980s with certain exchanges of medicine, equipment, and food that were imported from U.S. subsidiaries based in third countries. These imports did not grow significantly until the early 1990s, with the disappearance of the socialist bloc, when they reached just above $700 million. This flow stopped upon the 1992 enactment of the Torricelli Act—the Cuban Democracy Act (CDA)—based on the expectation that, deprived of relations with the socialist bloc, the Cuban government would face a "domino effect" from its inability to reinsert itself effectively in the international economy. The CDA also included provisions that could permit the export of farm products and pharmaceutical drugs to NGOs, academic and sports exchanges, telephone communications and the sending of remittances.

In comparison to the previous decades of reciprocal isolation, the changes in the 1990s stimulated U.S. business circles to seek openings within existing restrictions. This activism facilitated later steps, especially by academic sectors and by some companies, to commission assessments and proposals. No less than 30 such studies of potential markets in Cuba were carried out, examining specific areas such as mining, fishing, farming, tourism and related services, and others.[1]

Before 2001, Cuba–U.S. trade was perceived more as an object of academic speculation than a short-term reality for companies.[2] Even the most optimistic U.S. business executives opted for other opportunities in the region rather than investing time, money, and energy in something that seemed so uncertain. This perception changed drastically toward the end of 2001, when conditions shifted favorably due to severe damage caused by Hurricane Michelle. When Cuba rejected Washington's offer for humanitarian aid because of the conditions attached to such aid, the Office of Foreign Assets Control (OFAC) of the U.S. Treasury Department was commissioned to establish a mechanism to grant licenses for food purchases based on the 2000 Trade Sanctions Reform and Export Enhancement Act.[3] The first $35 million of sales occurred in December 2001. The following September, the first U.S.–Cuba Agricultural Fair was held in Havana, attended by 750 representatives of 288 companies from 33 states. Signed contracts totaled $112 million.[4]

Between 2001 and 2006, using the loophole opened by such special licenses, more than 4,350 companies and 132 agricultural associations and federations visited the Island to explore market opportunities. Contracts were signed with 159 companies from 35 states, involving 23 ports in these transactions. Cuba became the 25th most important market, in absolute terms, for U.S. exports in these sectors.

In a relatively short time, the United States became Cuba's major supplier of imported food and agricultural goods, reaching a peak of $710 million (nearly 3.5 million tons) in 2008. Despite the reduction resulting from the tightening of payment terms after George W. Bush's re-election in 2004, this represented 27 percent of Cuban imports. The most important increases were due, however, to price increases (61 percent from 2007 to 2008 alone) rather than to the physical quantities acquired.

Despite legal restrictions, the acceleration of this trade can be explained by several factors. Besides lower shipping and insurance costs resulting from geographic proximity and relatively better prices, there was also (for various reasons) a sharp deterioration in the efficiency of Cuba's domestic food production that contributed to increased imports. Therefore this evolution is not attributable solely to trade shifts or market substitution. Rather, an effect of the contraction of domestic supply was superimposed on top of lower relative costs.

From the record $963 million spent in 2008,[5] Cuban purchases of U.S. agricultural goods dropped to $675 million in 2009. The drop is attributable to Cuba's complex economic situation and the effects of the international economic crisis. By January 2010, U.S. exports of food and agricultural goods were reported to be 24 percent lower than the year before, reaching only $513 million.[6]

In March 2010, OFAC announced an exception that loosened the rules governing food sales to Cuba—specifically, a reinterpretation of the criteria stipulating Cuban advance cash payments for U.S. imports.[7] By allowing Cuban buyers to pay for goods just before they are unloaded in Cuba, the change lowers transaction costs in third-country banks, though this change will probably not have an immediate effect in Cuba given its difficult financial circumstances. Current restrictions still block Cuba from importing other products such as raw materials, intermediate goods, equipment, diversified manufactured goods, and special services (marketing, legal, consulting, environment, biological controls, etc.).

The second component of economic exchange in recent years has been tourism. From 1990 to 2007, Cuba received some 24 million tourists, with revenues exceeding $25 billion. Hotel capacity grew from 13,000 to 47,000 rooms, half of them managed by international firms, with occupancy rates between 60 and 80 percent. In 2009, the total of visitors to the Island reached 2.5 million[8]—half of them Canadians or Cuban-born emigrants. Some 50,000 came from the United States.[9] Of the visiting Cubans living abroad (12.3 percent of the total), in 2008 those coming from the United States represented 55 percent. A recent novelty was the announcement by the Cuban minister of tourism that U.S. hotel chains would now be allowed to administer hotels in Cuba.[10]

The third component has been remittances. These began to have an important effect in the 1990s and have become the country's third largest revenue source. Estimates of the total vary according to the source and methodology, but the range is somewhere between $700 million and $1 billion annually. Their impact is mixed. On the one hand, they helped to compensate for the drop in economic activity that followed the collapse of the socialist bloc, allowing growth in family consumption and serving as input for the growth of small private businesses. On the other hand, once the funds flowed into state channels when remittance-receivers shopped in hard-currency stores or changed money in the currency exchange booths, they financed part of the country's productive activity. The most recent calculation of such funds sent from the United States has estimated the total in the order of $360 to $600 million (53 percent of total remittances from abroad).[11] The majority of studies have confirmed that the main destination of remittance funds is consumption (food, clothing, household appliances, etc.), while they are used to a lesser extent for other ends such as home repair, savings, and micro-investment in small businesses.

Estimated Projections and Legislative Proposals

Using a variety of methods, researchers have arrived at a number of estimates of the potential for bilateral trade. The U.S. International Trade Commission (USITC) has, at the request of Congress, presented two estimates. The most recent,[12] employing a version of the "gravity model" used by the World Trade Organization (WTO), estimates potential trade under two different scenarios. The first envisions lifting of financial restrictions, which impose extra costs ranging from 2.5 to 10 percent. In that case, the U.S. share of Cuban farm, fishing, and forest product imports could rise by two-thirds of its current level or even double in size. Of the 17 product groups studied, food exports would show significant annual increases—fruits and vegetables from $34 to $65 million, powdered milk from $14 to $41 million, processed foods from $18 to $34 million, wheat from $17 to $33 million, beans from $9 to $22 million—with market shares ranging from 10 to 90 percent depending on the product.[13] The second scenario posits the simultaneous end of restrictions on both financing and travel. In that case, the additional demand created by tourism would imply additional increases of from $1 to $8 million for at least four kinds of goods.

Other estimates have predicted that total bilateral trade in the first year of legalized trade between Cuba and the United States would reach some $2.6 billion,[14] which matches the range obtained in earlier studies using different premises.[15] These and other assessments all agree that Cuba would most likely import more than it could sell to the United States. The anticipated trade deficit of 15 to 30 percent could be partially or totally made up by income from tourism and investments.

In the case of tourism, USITC's 2007 study estimated that U.S. visitors would rise from an initial 171,000 to between 554,000 and 1,000,000, with an annual increase ranging from 226,000 to 538,000 and a direct effect on revenue between 13 and 33 percent. A forecast by the American Society of Travel Agents (ASTA) calculated that, two years after an end to the travel ban, some 850,000 U.S. residents would travel to Cuba to stay in hotels and another 500,000 would stay on cruise ships.[16] If such quantities were to displace tourists from other countries or if they could be distributed throughout the year, Cuba could handle them immediately. If they were to represent additional demand during peak seasons, however, more lodging capacity would be required.

Without new hotel investment, available reserves could allow for an increase in private sector renters (bed-and-breakfasts), which today take in about 20 percent of the market—or nearly 500,000 visitors—and other existing facilities could be reoriented to house tourists if the bulk of the growth is in midrange-price tourism. Demand for top-level facilities, limited at present, would require new investment. Of course, a policy of tourist-industry growth on such a scale would also require improvement of social and private infrastructure (airports and related service, transportation fleets and road maintenance, telecommunications, automated process-control systems, etc.) as well as adequate supplies of inputs (construction materials, furniture, machinery, replacement and repair parts, natural and semi-processed foods, beverages and collateral services). In the 1990s, these necessities were met in part through foreign investment. If conditions change, participation by U.S. investors can also be expected.

The Cuban tourist draw is primarily sun and sea and, to a lesser degree, culture and history in the cities. The hotel structure has been tending toward the regional pattern, with medium-sized four- and five-star hotels. Other alternatives for diversifying the market, such as visits for business, educational, ecotourism, sport, religious events, or for medical treatment are feasible but will require more infrastructure investments (ATMs, restaurants, car rental, etc.) and increased capacity for international bookings over the internet and for credit card payments to be able to compete with neighboring countries of a similar profile. On the other hand, these alternatives would offer greater variety in supply and higher standards of quality, with higher revenue yield per visitor.

In any case, specialists agree that in the short term U.S. tourists would replace those from other countries before creating any abrupt expansion. The notion of a tsunami of U.S. tourism is not due to travel by Cuban-born residents of the North (whose rate of repeated visits is already much higher than that of conventional tourists); rather, it would stem from the surge that would arise from the elimination of the legal prohibition against U.S. citizens traveling to Cuba. These expectations, however, do not match the observable trend of U.S.-origin tourism to other Caribbean countries where such restrictions are not in effect. In immediate terms, the international crisis has partly dampened growth in this sector, though the market could tighten if there is a speedy expansion following an opening. So far, growth in the tourist industry has depended on expansion in lodging capacity yet, from a strategic point of view, excess investment could create profitability problems over the medium term if unaccompanied by efficiency gains in income per visitor, which is an indicator that has trended down in recent years.

Overall, sectoral studies emphasize the potential gains for traditional Cuban exports (tobacco, rum, nickel, tropical fruits, seafood, etc.) from trade with the United States.[17] Because of their spillover and multiplier effects, the areas of greatest impact are those tied to Cuba's most recent generation of export products that take advantage of new capacities developed in recent years (biotechnology, medical-pharmaceutical, software, some manufactured goods, and hydrocarbons and their derivatives). These could rapidly absorb investments that would allow for quality improvements and expansion into new markets. Even less studied are latent reserves for re-export of manufactured goods. The attempts in the early 1990s to create free trade zones created infrastructure that is now under-utilized but that undoubtedly offers potential advantages. The use of this potential capacity ought to be studied, with an eye to how Cuba's well-qualified labor force can assimilate varied technologies, from electronics production to those for making components for tourist facilities, to cite two sectors that Cuba has not yet entered but whose worldwide sales have grown consistently over the past ten years.

So far, few of these alternatives have been seriously considered in the United States. In early 2009, a report by the Senate Foreign Relations Committee offered recommendations as part of an assessment of the viability of joint action by the executive and legislative branches to broaden commercial relations between the two countries. These included:

1. Reviewing the requirement that Cuba make cash payments in advance for food procurement.
2. Allowing private financing of agricultural sales.
3. Expanding the categories of permitted sales to include agricultural machinery and supplies.
4. Authorizing general travel licenses for purposes of marketing, business negotiations, and delivery of agricultural goods.
5. Granting visas to Cuban officials to carry out activities related to purchases, including sanitary inspections.[18]

Other recommendations made to the Obama administration by a variety of institutions include using its executive authority to allow licenses for the import of Cuban art works and artistic products; restoring the authorization that allows travelers to bring back limited quantities of Cuban goods; revoking section 1705(d) of the Helms–Burton Act that requires on-site verification of the uses to which medicine and medical equipment exported to Cuba are being put (or, at least, easing the regulatory interpretation of this provision); authorizing the sale and/or lease of U.S.-produced machinery for use by Cuban or third-country firms that extract oil from the Gulf of Mexico; and, commissioning a study to assess the losses suffered by the U.S. economy as a result of the Cuba embargo.

As has been pointed out, proposals that seek in one way or another to link a loosening of the embargo to internal political changes introduce complexity into this process.[19] There are, however, some cases that do not fall into this category. Quite a number of bills to partially reduce restrictions have recently been introduced in the Senate and House: some are broad, while others would loosen the travel ban, allow educational travel, cover agricultural and medical exports, deal specifically with hydrocarbons, or modify restrictions on trademark registration.[20]

The concrete steps taken by Barack Obama to loosen some aspects of the embargo in accord with his campaign promises include relaxation of some regulations tightened during George W. Bush's second term so as to restore OFAC regulations to 2004 levels (eliminating restrictions on travel by Cuban-Americans, raising the ceilings on travel expenditures, remittances, and parcel post shipments, issuing visas for academic and cultural exchange), and one innovation: licensing the provision of private services or the signing of telecommunication contracts (for use or provision of cellular phone, cameras, computers, and satellite, internet, and fiber-optic communication).[21] In a general sense, the new measures represent a partial decompression, characterized by Cuba as "positive, but minimal." The exceptions are those adopted for travel and communications, which have progressed beyond what was accomplished during the Jimmy Carter and Bill Clinton administrations.

With respect to worldwide or international financial institutions, there is no possibility of Cuban participation in the immediate future. Not only does the United States have veto power but the Cuban government has explicitly rejected any recourse to these bodies. Thus, unlike the situation with other Latin American countries, the main source of financing for trade and investment would be the private sector. If Cuban exports were allowed into the United States, the capacity to respond would be seriously limited by two factors: access to domestic or foreign financing and the fact that Cuban products are artificially overpriced. There is also the issue of the competitiveness required to displace the countries already established in that market. Still, there are numerous possibilities.

Viewed from a regional perspective, Cuba shares various traits with its Caribbean neighbors insofar as the composition of part of its exports, and it shares the same challenges insofar as the effects of any commercial liberalization. There are three different profiles in the region. The first is based on the experience of the Dominican Republic, which joined the Central American Free Trade Agreement (CAFTA) and accounts for one-fourth of regional trade with the United States. It relies on trade in machinery and tourist services. A second model is based on the experience of Trinidad and Tobago and their petroleum and natural gas exports. Finally, a third model of Jamaica and the Bahamas focuses on tourism. The remainder of examples—based on smaller countries or those in marginal positions—suggest a more skeptical position with respect to the impact of commercial openings by way of CARICOM (the Caribbean Community) or the Association of Caribbean States because of the undesirable impacts for intellectual property rights and financial, tourist, or technological and professional services. These examples instead reinforce the notion that the special and differentiated trade treatments should be preserved as much as possible.

In 2000, the Caribbean Basin Trade Initiative (CBTI) was approved, replacing the 1980s Caribbean Basin Initiative (CBI). This new measure established temporary tariff treatment relatively close to that of a free trade agreement, especially for exports of textiles and manufactured goods. Cuba has no connection with those arrangements, nor does it have a complex structure of tariff and other barriers, nor any specific policies to promote exports of textiles or home appliances (another alternative adopted by some countries in the region). As for insertion in the sphere of international financial services, as some other nations in the region have done, Cuba's relative backwardness in communications infrastructure and legal system make this possibility unlikely in the short run.

OFAC's Current Regulatory Framework

Even assuming a scenario of normalizing economic relations with the United States without severe complications, the implied adjustments in Cuba's commercial and economic arrangements with other countries would present a sizeable challenge. In practice, Cuba faces a tradeoff between its gains in stability and risk diversification, on the one hand, and the benefits of access to a geographically closer market with lower transport and insurance costs and higher quality standards, on the other. However, the latter benefits could be annulled by the executive branch, as occurred in 2004 when the advance cash payment requirement was imposed. Therefore, purchases in the U.S. market involve a food-security component that is not present in the case of other suppliers. An immediate and uncontrolled expansion of such imports would not be very prudent because, to the same degree that the imports grew, Cuba's vulnerability to changes in U.S. political winds would increase as well.

OFAC's current regulatory framework consists largely of two processes: travel licensing and regulations about finance and payment for U.S. exports to Cuba. The first probably gets more attention because of its connection to tourism but the second has, up to now, shaped existing commercial exchange. Cuban exports to the United States are prohibited; the permitted U.S. sales to Cuba are limited to a few kinds of goods (mostly food) subject to abnormal conditions. Because of the requirement for advance cash payment, goods awaiting transport automatically become Cuban property while they are still in U.S. ports. Thus, they become vulnerable to confiscation in the case of lawsuits by Cuban-American residents.[22] To reduce this risk, Cuba has turned to payment through letters of credit.

Routing payments through European banks, however, raises costs by 25 percent per transaction. Also, any delay causes charges for extra ship time in port (between $20,000 and $40,000), which Cuba has to pay. Similar problems occur in administrative procedures, which present additional complications in Cuba's case.[23] First, given that they are governed by special regulations, they can be changed without prior notice. Second, Cuba's commercial operations with the United States must abide by measures stipulated in the Administrative Procedure Act, which does not allow any delay in payments, while other countries may have recourse to an alternative (the Regulatory Flexibility Act) that gives them additional room for maneuver. The result for Cuban buyers is that they cannot count on prompt service by the U.S. exporter, and any unforeseen bureaucratic delay results in quickly multiplying operational costs, as has happened in the past.

Similarly, U.S. companies doing business with Cuba are barred from the use of Federal Farm Promotion Program "Check-Off" funds and the Market Access Program, which provide access to collective financing for promotion, technical assistance, research, and industry and consumer information to maintain or expand markets. Also, representatives of Cuban buying agencies are barred from visiting the United States to inspect sanitary conditions, a standard international practice for such operations. Thus, even without additional political complications, there is already a set of regulations that inhibits normal commerce and generates deformations leading to higher costs and risks.

Paradoxically, despite all the above, trade between the two countries reached its highest level just when sanctions and political tensions peaked during Bush's second term. Some analysts have viewed Cuba's practice of distributing its purchases of a single product among several states as a policy designed to stimulate the business lobby's interest in loosening regulations. In fact, once a license has been granted, the incentive to support such lobbying efforts decreases because access to the Cuban market has been achieved. Besides the benefit of receiving advance cash payments, the sellers also enjoy unusual negotiating conditions (a single contract with the government agency Alimport gives them access to the entire market, without having to deal with multiple companies and complex legal procedures); additionally, the embargo itself protects these companies from competition by other U.S. companies that lack export licenses.

These elements contribute to a conflicted and counterproductive environment because the greater benefits and lower risks associated with the special license mechanism generate short-term incentives to continue the status quo rather than engaging in the difficult process of policy change. This dysfunctional relationship creates an institutional inertia which can only be altered by initiatives that would succeed in progressively loosening some areas of the restrictions. Given current political circumstances, this process seems unlikely. Therefore, it is important to study the closest precedent as a point of comparison. Cuba's patterns of economic exchange with Canada and the European Union are not free of contradictions; nonetheless, for more than a decade commerce and investment with Cuba has expanded to unprecedented levels and in strategic areas. The result has been a business culture with its own idiosyncrasies. Might such know-how be "transferable?"

Foreign trade and, by extension, international economic relations are a useful "channel" for exploring spaces of possible cooperation as long as, in accord with international norms, they feature disagreement and negotiation to reach an understanding. Part of Cuba's education in business culture took place in the 1990s with the opening to foreign markets, investment, and banks. This process required coming up to date regarding international standards and regulations about legal, environmental, and agricultural-sanitary aspects, among others. A "local business culture" emerged, which is summarized in two guides about doing business in Cuba, one produced by the Canadian embassy and another by the firm of Ernst & Young. These recognize that, "The regulatory process can be considered both bureaucratic and time-consuming … the process is flexible to some extent, especially to businesses which have a business plan of particular interest to their Cuban partner."[24] This hybridization of modern legal standards with practices that leave a large margin for discretion is not always well understood by foreign executives. For some, it demonstrates a need for further knowledge transfers by way of consulting services and training, but it is undeniable that this culture has achieved results and that in many ways it is much closer to "normal" processes at the international level than the mechanism currently regulating exchanges between Cuba and the United States.

New Alternatives on the Horizon, Pending Claims from the Past

Beyond tourism, remittances, and trade in food products, there are three relatively new areas with important potential: energy, telecommunications, and advanced medical products and medical services such as biotechnology, vaccines, and software.

In the energy field, two areas of reciprocal interest stand out. The first has to do with the discovery of hydrocarbon reserves in the Gulf of Mexico within Cuban territorial waters, which were mutually agreed to in accords with the Carter administration. The second is the modernization of Cuba's energy grid and infrastructure, which has begun to introduce renewable energy projects with the support of the United Nations Development Program.

The oil underneath the deep waters of the Gulf will have a strategic impact on future economic relations between the two countries, if the necessary conditions appear. Extraction and processing of these considerable reserves of crude oil would in itself expand investment and trade; this could further extend to the production of derivatives, chemicals, and lubricants, as well as to re-export within the Caribbean. A study of these reserves carried out by the U.S. Geological Survey estimated their potential at 4.6 billion barrels of petroleum and 9.8 trillion cubic feet of natural gas.[25] These estimates are approximately equivalent to the reserves of Ecuador and, in principle, they would make Cuba a potential exporter that could rank between fourth and sixth in Latin America in the long run. As a result, executives in this sector have been searching for means of access to a market that would be attractive to producers, distributors, and consignees. So far, Cuba has signed exploration contracts for these waters with companies from Spain (Repsol), Norway (Norsk-Hydro), India (ONGC), Venezuela (PDVSA), Malaysia (Petronas), Viet Nam (Petrovietnam), Brazil (Petrobras), and Russia (Zarubezhneft).

A bill introduced in the U.S. Senate in July 2009 about states' shares of income from petroleum extraction in federal waters would, for the first time, allow executives and employees in this sector to travel to Cuba thanks to an amendment proposed by Senator Mary Landrieu (D-LA).[26] According to press reports, the amendment was encouraged by the Petroleum Equipment Suppliers Association, whose members include Halliburton Corporation. Analysts who have studied the issue assert that current investors' operations and logistical costs are 30 to 40 percent higher than they would otherwise be because the embargo requires them to buy repair and replacement parts in Mexico, Brazil, or Venezuela rather than Texas or Florida. At the same time, the projects' viability depends on high international oil prices; too big a drop in prices would make deep-water drilling economically unfeasible.

Further, the recent British Petroleum disaster could temporarily inhibit interest in such exploration.

As for projects to develop and replace energy generation and distribution infrastructure, the past few years have seen the introduction of small-scale generating systems using solar panels and hydropower in farming and mountain communities. These have received financial support from international bodies and NGOs. There has also been recourse to a redistributed generation model, which replaces old electrical generating plants with smaller groups to reduce the effects of hurricane damage. Still, in the longer run there will be need for a second generation of investment in more efficient plants with sufficient capacity to meet future increased demand from the private and productive sector while conforming to environmental standards.

In telecommunications, much remains to be done. A joint venture company (60 percent Venezuelan and 40 percent Cuban) is already undertaking a $70 million project to lay a 1,550 kilometer fiber-optic cable to connect Cuba, Jamaica, Haiti and Venezuela that is scheduled to become operational in 2011. A later phase could include Trinidad and Tobago as well. This investment will multiply Cuba's internet access 3,000-fold to a capacity of 640 gigabytes, which can support some 20,000 simultaneous telephone calls. Currently, 90 percent of world information traffic travels over such channels. That project coincides with the Obama administration's permission for OFAC to license contracts, payments, and travel related to establishing cell phone, telecommunications, satellite, and fiber-optic cable service as well as the re-export of goods and technologies in this sector.[27] Although nothing concrete has happened so far, many firms in Florida and the Caribbean are exploring possible proposals.

In the field of advanced medical products and services, the international scientific community has recognized Cuba's efficiency in the production of vaccines for meningitis and hepatitis B and in epidemiological prevention. Cuba's capacity for research into tropical diseases, biotechnology, and biodiversity offers highly attractive alternatives for U.S. research centers interested in creating joint cooperation programs like those currently underway with Britain, Brazil, Mexico, China, and India.[28] The situation is similar regarding production of specialized software for medical uses or of process control systems. Given its resources and the international recognition already achieved, Cuba's potential capacity to export such services to the United States is significant. In a rare exception to the existing rules, in 2004 the Treasury Department authorized the California firm CancerVax to carry out clinical trials of three anti-cancer vaccines along with Cuba's Center for Molecular Immunology. If they were to be approved, these and other products could count on a steady demand.

There is growing interest in opportunities linked to Cuban exports of medical goods and services, even though such goods and services would require protocols before they could be certified as well as guarantees of intellectual property rights to research results, all of which are still in early stages. If certification of medical services could be achieved and if U.S. medical insurance policies would cover payments to

Cuban agencies, then U.S. citizens could benefit from this alternative. Patients from other regions have come to Cuba for years, traveling to see the country and to be operated on or receive specialized treatment, often at prices much more competitive than those in their countries of origin.

The pharmaceutical industry also offers favorable conditions for expanding Cuban sales in the short run, without the need for large new investments, by making use of existing facilities. Possibilities include cooperative production via joint ventures or encouraging foreign investment in this sector, as neighboring countries have done. There are also barely explored options in software production of integrated systems for various uses—medical, hotel management, industrial processes, climate control, specialized agriculture, etc.—in which Cuba has specialized and has been able to place competitive products in the world market.

One important factor involving Cuba and the United States is the existence of reciprocal demands for compensation. Cuba demands indemnification for the cost of the embargo. Although it is difficult to quantify this effect with precision, its multiple forms include market reorientation (with implicit costs of secure transportation) and the losses involved in reorienting exports, tourism, and commercial flights; technological impacts; higher costs of financing the foreign debt; and emigration of skilled workers and professions, to list only the most recognized results. Its effect has also extended to third countries, with serious consequences. Cuba's accumulated losses, by official figures, total more than $96 billion.

Also pending on the agenda of both governments is compensation for the nationalizations carried out by Cuba in the 1960s. This is a most complicated issue because it has so many aspects, many of which require some type of political-juridical negotiating framework that would establish definitions, methods of assessing value, and compensation procedures, without which normalized economic relations in a broad sense would be very difficult to achieve. A related issue is any link between the income generated by current commercial operations and the pending compensation claims, which could become serious impediments to the growth of these operations.

Some suggestions made to the Obama administration about this issue include rescinding rules that prohibit sale or inheritance of properties involved in the claims against Cuba without special authorization by OFAC or the Congress; authorizing the owners of such properties to negotiate individually with the Cuban government, which would require Treasury licenses so they could receive compensation in cash or in stock in Cuban entities; specifying in a public declaration that the government will concern itself only with compensation to owners who were U.S. citizens at the time of the expropriation; approaching the Cuban government about bilateral negotiations via the Foreign Claims Settlement Commission; and repealing Section 211 of the 1999 Appropriations Act, which denies the right to register or renew trademarks associated with nationalized properties.[29]

In the dynamic of changes in Cuba's international economic position over the past two decades, relations with the United States have had a curious character.

In the 1990s, when exchange revolved mainly around the axes of the European Union and Canada in an environment marked by financial volatility and high costs, exchanges with the United States offered a conjunctural alternative that was decisive for survival after the collapse of the socialist bloc. Tourism became the leading source of income, and a significant part of that tourism came from the United States. Remittances became the third largest income source and, in the beginning, almost all of these came from the northern neighbor. After 2000, the axis shifted toward China and Venezuela within a new framework of relations characterized by inter-governmental agreements and more financial stability conferred by credits and agreements within the Bolivarian Alliance for the Americas (ALBA). This concentrated a high volume of purchases in those two countries. Meanwhile, food purchases from the United States expanded to the point of making the United States Cuba's fourth largest trading partner, just when restrictions were tightest. The framework of Cuban foreign economic relations was particularly unfavorable to broadening trade with the United States during either of the Bush terms, yet such was the result. Can any lessons be drawn from these developments? One is that, despite the stubborn U.S. policy of trying to isolate Cuba over the past 50 years, both countries have moved progressively toward alternative mechanisms that, without changing the legal framework, make it more porous over time.

Continuity and Change: Proposing Some Tentative Scenarios

The tendency in making predictions is to project the present into the future while underestimating radical innovations that—even after a prolonged status quo—may occur. That is the lesson of the 1990s, with the transformations that followed the collapse of Soviet socialism, and it is the lesson of the 2000s with growth in economic exchange between Cuba and the United States. The imagination of scenarios of agreement can of course lead to wishful thinking, but it is still a useful way of exploring some alternative options. Months before the end of the Obama electoral campaign, the well-known intellectual Ignacio Ramonet pointed out that, if he were elected and if he really tried to replace the philosophy of "Cuban regime change" with one of more-or-less flexible coexistence, then, "that would signify a Copernican Revolution for the Cuban political system," which would have to redefine its historic enemy in terms compatible with a more pragmatic policy of "normalization" of relations.[30] More than a year has gone by and events have deflated this hope.

From the U.S. side, there are at least two factors to consider. First, Obama has fulfilled the promises he made about Cuba policy during his campaign. Now he faces more pressing concerns: economic crisis, war, and domestic concerns. Second, the process of changing foreign policy, in and of itself, offers a chief executive very little margin to make profound changes in a short time. As Henry Kissinger has pointed out:

[Obama's foreign policy] must navigate between two kinds of public pressures toward diplomacy endemic in American attitudes. Both seek to transcend the patient give-and-take of traditional diplomacy. The first reflects an aversion to negotiating with societies that do not share our values and general outlook. It rejects the effort to alter the other side's behavior through negotiations. It treats compromise as appeasement and seeks the conversion or overthrow of the adversary. The critics of this approach—now dominant—emphasize psychology. They consider the opening of negotiations an inherent transformation. For them, symbolism and gestures represent substance.[31]

Tacit recognition of the need to remake the international image of the United States, and the president's efforts to undertake less aggressive diplomacy than that of his predecessor, does not mean that the balance of power in the U.S. Congress shifted enough to leave behind the first of these two perspectives, which prevailed over most of the decade.

Some restrictions could be eliminated quickly. Others require gradual dismantling but there is no guarantee that the U.S. Congress is inclined to go too far. Proof of these challenges is how slowly negotiations to garner enough support for the bills presented so far in Congress have proceeded. Therefore, even assuming an explicit desire to partially loosen prohibitions, there is no reason to expect that the Obama administration will embark on an endeavor to rework U.S. Cuba policy. It neither aspires to do so, nor does it have strong motives to make this a priority.

In the case of economic relations between Cuba and the United States, there is still some "room to maneuver." Given the elements described above, and considering the inertia of the processes underway and the lack of incentives for either side to make substantive immediate innovations, in the current context the most probable outcome is a "soft prolongation." There will be no strategic reformulation of bilateral relations to establish a new road map of steps to be taken; gradual changes seem more viable than drastic ones. *Grosso modo,* the scenarios might be:

1. Obama *"clintonized"* or *"decaffeinated"*: As occurred with the Clinton administration, a relatively liberal agenda at the start is modified substantially as the president hurries toward the political center to preserve his chances of winning a second term. Within such a framework, there is still room for a modest restoration of academic and cultural exchange as well as remittances and travel by Cuban-Americans. Scientific exchange and food sales will remain limited, as will travel by non-Cuban-born citizens, generally under discretionary authorization through general licenses. There will be no rethinking of the basis of relations. Attempts within the U.S. Congress to permit all travel will continue but without great likelihood of success. The result is a loss of opportunities and incentives for both Obama and Cuba, occasional disagreements, but

without a sharpened confrontation. A second term, if there is one, might bring new initiatives. A drop in levels of bilateral trade is one outcome from the international crisis; remittances will not grow very much for the same reason; tourism by Cuban-Americans will remain at current levels. In this scenario, the relative position of the United States in the Cuban economy (trade, tourism, and remittances) will change very little.

2. Moderate incentives (*allegro ma non troppo*): There will be greater flexibility in areas for which there is some precedent, such as tourism, academia, religion, and culture, thanks to a change in the balance of power in the U.S. Congress. Such increased incentives could bring sharper conflict with the regulations, which would lead to revision of their interpretation following the recent pattern around cash payments. In this context, the non-institutional actors of both governments (NGOs, academics, press, cultural figures, etc.) have a key initial role to play in promoting dialogue. The re-establishment of academic and cultural exchange programs between both countries could generate a constructive climate for formal cooperation in other areas of mutual interest. The benefits from an expansion of tourism would be important to Cuba not only in increasing income, but also in generating spillovers to linked sectors. Commercialization of "intellectual goods" (music, consulting services, training, etc.) could lead to some agreement regarding reciprocal protection of intellectual property. In spite of continued differences, the current discourse of regime change would have to be modified toward one of support for "exchange" in broad terms. In economic terms, Cuban income could rise by at least a third without the need for large investments. Some level of synchronization with regional standards might be required.

3. Evolutionary/optimistic scenario (the least likely in the long run): Fundamental differences in political systems and in positioning in the world context will not disappear. Still, a scenario of coexistence without sustained confrontation could be achieved, as has occurred between the United States and China and Viet Nam, for instance. In that context, gradual progress to change the center of gravity could occur, which would make enforcement of the Helms–Burton Act porous enough to require a reformulation. In the economic sphere, there could be a partial deregulation in trade and energy as well as financing and limited investment in selected sectors. This scenario would require more time than the term or terms of a single administration, so it could be very vulnerable to political changes in the United States. Basically, it would require ending the application of the Trading With the Enemy Act, section 5(b), to Cuba, as well as most of the regulations in the Export Administration Regulations and, at least, the prohibitions of private financing of exports to Cuba and Cuban exports to the United States in the Trade Sanctions Reform and Export Enhancement Act of 2000. The resultant economic effects would be important to both countries.

Conclusions

Unless the frame of reference for political relations changes, the potential for economic relations remains hypothetical, as it has been in recent years. However, Cuba's prosperity does not depend on having economic relations—good or bad—with the United States. It depends on Cubans' capacity to reinvent their country. Thus, the positive side of such bilateral relations (if they become a reality) would be a welcome complement, and the negative side could be managed without recourse to extraordinary sacrifices that would mortgage the future. For both governments, a process of normalization will not be viable without passing through gradual stages. Therefore, it is essential to preserve flexibility to adapt to new circumstances without implying, from the Cuban side, ceding national sovereignty or paying unacceptable social costs.

The challenges such processes would pose do not exceed current Cuban technical capacities, nor do they pose new problems that would require rebuilding support at a public and governmental level. Cuba has already established such ties with other developed countries in past decades, and the results show that—given minimum acceptable conditions—important advances in strategic economic sectors are possible. In the case of the United States, the differences that stem from the asymmetry of power, the political systems, and the historical legacy will not vanish in the immediate future. Neither, however, is it necessary to assume that the conflict between the two countries is a dead-end street because there are accessible solutions to issues of common interest, even if as yet there is no political framework appropriate to achieve them. The normalization of economic relations between the two nations should not be reduced to a polar conflict between sovereignty and benefits. Complex as it may be, we can and must work to advance beyond what has been achieved so far, for the benefit of both nations.

Notes

1 Specialized centers within the University of Havana and those in Austin, Texas, and Gainesville, Florida, also undertook related research projects.
2 Jorge Mario Sánchez Egozcue, "Economic Relations Cuba–U.S., Bilateralism or Geopolitics?" paper presented at the XXVII Congress of the Latin American Studies Association (LASA), Montreal, 2007.
3 Public Law 106-387, October 18, 2000, in 22 USC 7201–7209.
4 Report by Alimport Cuba, Cuban Ministry of Food Industry (MINAL), and the United States International Trade Commission (USITC), "U.S. Agricultural Sales to Cuba: Certain Economic Effects of U.S. Restrictions," Investigation no. 332-489, July 2007, available at www.usitc.gov.
5 The totals reported by Cuba differ from others cited from U.S. sources because the Cuban numbers include the cost of shipping, insurance costs, banking transaction fees, and others.
6 Economic Eye on Cuba, "2010–2011 U.S. Export Statistics for Cuba," U.S.–Cuba Trade and Economic Council, March 2010, available at www.cubatrade.org.

7   FY2009 Omnibus Appropriations Measure (P.L. 111-8); Reuters, "EEUU flexibiliza reglas de pago para venta de alimentos a Cuba," March 9, 2009.

8   José Luis Perelló Cabrera, "Factores de éxito, impactos y amenazas en el modelo de desarrollo turístico cubano, 1990–2009," Centro de Estudios Turísticos, Universidad de La Habana, 2009, 9–14.

9   Leticia Pineda, "Cuba y empresarios de los Estados Unidos exploran llegada libre de turistas a la isla," AFP, March 25, 2010.

10 Gerardo Arreola, "Cuba abre la puerta a cadenas hoteleras de los Estados Unidos." *La Jornada,* Mexico City, March 26, 2010.

11 Author estimates from The Economist Intelligence Unit, *Country Report* (January 2010): 14. See also, Manuel Orozco, "The Cuban Condition: Migration, Remittances, and its Diaspora," paper presented at the conference, "El Caribe en su inserción internacional," Inter-American Dialogue, San José, Costa Rica, February 3–4, 2009. Difficulties in estimation derive from the overlap of remittances with other hard-currency flows, such as "spillover" from tourism, income that entertainers, artists, and other professionals earn from contracts abroad, hard-currency bonuses paid within Cuba, and other interactions involving internal recirculation of currency.

12 USITC, "The Economic Impact of US Sanctions with Respect to Cuba," Investigation no. 332-413, available at en www.usitc.gov.

13 USITC, "U.S. Agricultural Sales to Cuba," viii, Table ES.1.

14 Jorge Mario Sánchez Egozcue, "Challenges of Cuba's Insertion in Caribbean–U.S. Trade," in *The Cuban Economy at the Start of the Twenty First Century,* ed. Jorge I. Domínguez, Omar E. Pérez and Lorena G. Barberia (Cambridge: Harvard University Press, 2004).

15 USITC, "The Economic Impact;" Claudio Montenegro and Raimundo Soto, "How Distorted is Cuba's Trade? Evidence and Predictions from a Gravity Model," *Journal of International Trade and Economic Development* 5, no. 1 (1996): 45–68.

16 EFE, "Cancún flujo turístico a Cuba," March 24, 2010.

17 U.S. Department of Agriculture, "Cuba's Food & Agriculture Situation Report," March 26, 2008, available at www.fas.usda.gov.

18 Committee on Foreign Relations, United States Senate, "Changing Cuba Policy in the United States National Interest," 111 Congress, February 23, 2009, available at www.access.gpo.gov.

19 Carmelo Mesa-Lago, "Posible restablecimiento de relaciones económicas entre Cuba y Estados Unidos: ventajas y desventajas," *Espacio Laical,* Havana, no. 2 (2008).: 36–38

20 Mark P. Sullivan, "Cuba: Issues for the 111th Congress." Congressional Research Service Report R40193, January 13, 2010, available at www.crs.gov.

21 U.S. Department of the Treasury, Office of Foreign Assets Control, "Treasury Amends Cuban Assets Control Regulations to Implement the President's Initiative on Family Visits, Remittances, and Telecommunications," September 3, 2009, available at www.treasury.gov.

22 Ana Radelat, "In Wake of Tough New OFAC Regulations, Food Exporters Turn to Letters of Credit," *CubaNews,* March 1, 2005.

23 USITC, "U.S. Agricultural Sales to Cuba ...," note 47.

24 Embassy of Canada in Havana, Cuba – A Guide for Canadian Business (March 2001); Ernst & Young Caribbean Services, A Business Guide to Cuba (January 2006) (quotation is from the latter).

25 U.S. Energy Information Administration, "Country Analysis Briefs: Caribbean," October, 2008; U.S. Geological Survey, "Assessment of Undiscovered Oil and Gas Resources of the North Cuban Basin, Cuba, 2004," February 2005.

26 Leslie Moore Mira, "Senate Bill Eases Cuba Restrictions for US Oil, Gas Industry," Platts, New York, January 8, 2010.

27   OFAC, "Treasury Amends."
28   Michael T. Clegg and Sergio Jorge Pastrana, "U.S.–Cuban Scientific Relations," *Science* 322, available at www.sciencemag.org.
29   Omnibus Consolidated and Emergency Supplemental Appropriations Act, 1999.
30   Jorge Halperín, "Obama puede provocar un sismo en el futuro de Cuba (Diálogo con Ignacio Ramonet)," *El Mundo,* Madrid, March 2, 2008.
31   Henry A. Kissinger, "Obama's Foreign Policy Challenge," *The Washington Post,* Washington, April 22, 2009.

11

U.S. IMMIGRATION POLICIES TOWARD CUBA

LORENA G. BARBERIA

There has been a significant migration of Cubans to the United States since the nineteenth century but the numbers of Cuban nationals arriving in the United States increased significantly after the 1959 revolution. In contrast to migrants coming from other neighboring Latin American countries, the flow of Cuban migrants arriving in the United States has not been steady across the last five decades. Instead, concentrated flows of émigrés have arrived in specific periods on U.S. soil and mainly settled in the State of Florida. Following the end of the Cold War and the onset of a profound economic crisis in Cuba, the numbers of Cubans arriving in the United States began to increase significantly starting in 1994. This wave of Cuban migration, which is ongoing and has transpired for more than a decade and a half, represents the longest and largest in magnitude of the four waves of migration that has taken place since Cubans began leaving the Island in the early 1960s. Indeed, the United States remains the top destination for Cuban nationals leaving the country and the last U.S. Census revealed that nearly one-fifth of the Cuban-born population in the United States had arrived between 1994 and 2000.[1]

The different explanations that have been offered for the variation in migration policies toward Cuba adopted by the United States have concurred that international factors drove policy responses in the early decades of the Cuban revolution.[2] In adopting migrant-accepting policies, Presidents Eisenhower, Kennedy, Johnson and Nixon embraced Cuban émigrés as part of traditional U.S. anticommunist immigration ideology. Strategically, the U.S. government also recognized that exiled Cubans would be an opposition force that would contribute to its strategy to isolate Cuba. Starting in the 1980s, scholars also concur that there was a major turning point in U.S. migration policy towards Cuba. The United States began to adopt restrictive policies in the 1980s as its strategic interests shifted and it sought to weaken Cuba's unilateral power to set U.S. immigration policy.[3]

The scholarship that has aimed at explaining the variation in U.S. migration policy toward Cuba in the post-Cold War era, in contrast, has emphasized that domestic policy considerations have begun to drive U.S. foreign policy decisions.[4] While not discounting that the Cuban-American lobby and domestic politics in the United States have increased their influence on the migration policies the United States has adopted toward Cuba in the post-Cold War era, this chapter argues that U.S. foreign policy considerations continue to play an important role in driving U.S. migration policies toward Cuba in the post-Cold War era. The United States has placed a higher priority on defending its interests in protecting its borders from the unregulated arrival of mass influxes of Cubans during periods of crisis in migration relations. In addition to strong pressures from the Cuban-American lobby and domestic political pressures, this chapter argues that the Clinton administration chose cooperative policies in bilateral migration disputes with Cuba in the 1990s during both the rafter and the Elián González crises because these outcomes were in alignment with U.S. national interests. Moreover, the United States continued to cooperate with the Cuban government on migration during the George W. Bush administration. Indeed, even during this eight-year period, in which bilateral relations were considerably strained and even as the United States tightened the trade embargo, imposed stricter limits on family visits, cash remittance flows, travel, and professional exchanges to the Island, charged its government with having developed an offensive biological warfare program, and launched a democratic transition program aimed at assisting in the organization of the Cuban government after the removal of Fidel and Raúl Castro, the United States adhered to policies made by the Clinton administration on Cuban migration though it cut off semi-annual consultation talks and failed to meet the visa minimum ceilings in some years.

The reason that the United States has chosen to cooperate with Cuba on migration policy is best explained by understanding that the notion of national security expanded in the post-Cold War era to include nonmilitary threats. In other words, this chapter argues that the proximity of Cuba coupled with the volatile outflows of Cubans that continue to attempt entry into the United States has driven the United States to cooperate with the Cuban government and this factor continues to drive the U.S. policy response in the period from 1989 to the present. At the same time, the chapter recognizes and shows how domestic interests have shaped the U.S. policy response. Cuban-Americans have pressured the United States to reduce migrant-restricting policies and have secured some important victories in both the policy formulation and implementation stages but have not been able to prevent cooperation. Domestic political pressures from voters outside Miami have strengthened U.S. foreign policy goals geared to limiting Cuban migration and this alignment has worked to reinforce the migrant-restricting policy response adopted by the United States towards the arrival of Cuban émigrés onto U.S. borders.

This chapter adopts a historically-grounded approach to analyzing the policies that have been implemented by the U.S. government towards those seeking to leave Cuba. It begins by tracing how the United States gradually began to shift its migration policies for strategic reasons during the period between the Cuban revolution in 1959 and the onset of the "special period" in Cuba following the collapse of Cuba's trade with the Soviet bloc. Subsequently, it describes and analyzes the migration policies implemented by the United States in the last two decades. It argues that there has been a great deal of continuity in the post-Cold War era with respect to the U.S. migration policies towards Cuba that were adopted in the 1980s. The following sections illustrate how domestic and foreign policy considerations have influenced U.S. migration policy. In terms of U.S.–Cuba relations, the migration of Cubans to the United States continues to be a highly contested area in which there are significant disagreements on what policies should be pursued by both the receiving and sending countries. Therefore, in the final section of the chapter, policy areas that represent major points of conflict between both governments are reviewed with the aim of drawing attention to the policies that could be adopted by either government that could further improve U.S.–Cuba relations on migration.

U.S. Policy: A Shift from Open Borders to Restrictive Policies

The post-Cold War migration policy of the United States government toward Cuba is best understood as rooted in the fundamental policy reversal that took place starting in 1980 when U.S. policy shifted for the first time to restricting the inflow of Cubans into the United States. In contrast to the preceding two decades when the United States allowed, encouraged, assisted and sponsored mass migration of what were considered refugees fleeing from communism on the Island, the United States began to shift its policies toward Cubans choosing to leave the Island in the early 1980s.[5] Beginning with the Carter administration and consolidated during the Reagan administration, the United States shifted its policies from migrant-accepting to migrant-restricting as it sought to prevent the arrival of massive flows of Cubans on U.S. shores. During and in the aftermath of the 1994 rafter crisis, the United States further adjusted its migratory policies toward Cubans in order to guarantee orderly Cuban migration into its territories. Nonetheless, the United States has been limited in the migrant-restricting reforms it has been able to implement toward Cuban migrants, as increasingly U.S. administrations have had to balance their policies to regulate Cuban migratory flows with the interests of the concentrated and influential base of Cuban émigrés located mainly in South Florida and for domestic political considerations.[6] Recognizing that these forces have moderated the U.S. migration-preventing policy response, this chapter adopts the view that they have not prevented this outcome from prevailing as the fundamental outcome during the post-Cold War period.

TABLE 11.1   Year of arrival of foreign-born Cuban population in the United States

Year of arrival	Number	Percentage of Cuban-born U.S. population
Before 1960	65,602	7.43%
1960–64 (early exiles)	133,992	15.17%
1964–74 (Camarioca and freedom flights)	247,726	28.04%
1975–79	29,508	3.34%
1980–81 (Mariel crisis)	101,837	11.53%
1982–93	130,337	14.75%
1994–96 (rafter crisis)	96,168	10.89%
1997–2000	78,269	8.86%
Total	883,439	100.00%

Source: Table is reproduced from data based on U.S. Census microsample data. Pérez, Lisandro. "Cuba" in *The New Americans: A Guide to Immigration since 1965*, edited by Mary Waters, Reed Ueda, and Helen B. Marrow. Cambridge: Harvard University Press, 2007.

Following the Cuban revolution and in the heat of the Cold War, the United States embraced nearly half a million Cubans fleeing the Island in the early 1960s and 1970s (see Table 11.1). In the early years, émigrés were admitted as "refugees fleeing from communism" under the auspices of the Walter–McCarran Act and provided with benefits under the Cuban Refugee Program established in 1961 by President John F. Kennedy. Driven by the belief that opening its borders to Cuban émigrés weakened the Cuban government, the United States government subsequently passed the Cuban Adjustment Act (CAA) in 1966. In contrast to U.S. policy that has tightly regulated the entry of migrants into its territory since the early twentieth century, the legal provisions of the Cuban Adjustment Act of 1966 conceded unique privileges to those Cubans seeking to enter the United States.[7] The CAA gave the U.S. Attorney General the discretionary authority to grant exemptions to Cuban nationals from national immigration quotas in effect at the time in the United States for other migrants and to confer them with legal permanent residency after only one year's presence in the United States.[8] Throughout this period, the United States also continued to renew support for Cuban refugee programs and to subsidize the financial burden of resettling refugees for South Florida.

A major shift in U.S. policy, restricting for the first time the inflow of Cuban nationals, was sparked by Cuba's opening of the Mariel port in 1980, which represented the second incident in which Cuba opened a port and issued a call to Cuban-Americans to retrieve those seeking to leave for the United States. The United States admitted the approximately 125,000 Cuban émigrés brought to Florida on private vessels, just as it had admitted a smaller number in the 1965 Camarioca port boatlift. However, for the first time in two decades, the Carter administration determined that Cuban nationals seeking entry into the United States would be processed under the recently passed 1980 Refugee Act and thus would no longer be automatically admitted as refugees or asylees.[9] Instead, émigrés that arrived on U.S. shores during the Mariel boat exodus were labeled as "Cuban–Haitian Entrants (Status Pending)."[10] While *Marielitos* were eventually granted legal permanent residency under the Immigration Reform and Control Act (IRCA) of 1986, the definition of the legal status of these émigrés as distinct from earlier groups of exiles represented a fundamental shift in U.S. policy.

The Mariel crisis brought about a turnaround in how the United States viewed the coherence of its migration policy with its foreign policy objectives toward Cuba. From 1960 to 1980, U.S. administrations had chosen to advocate an open border policy as consistent with an overall strategy to weaken the government of Fidel Castro. Consensus began to emerge in the U.S. government that it was in the national interest to prevent Cuba from being able to determine unilaterally when massive flows of Cubans would arrive on Florida shores.[11] The political, social, and economic costs borne by the United States for absorbing Cuban émigrés also began to be viewed as too significant in relative terms. In response to these pressures, the United States decided to maintain its commitment to close the Cuban Refugee Program in 1981 despite being in the midst of the process of resettling the *Marielitos*.

The view that U.S. national interests were best served by policies that restricted Cuban migration was further consolidated by the 1994 rafter crisis, which coincided with the re-election campaigns of Florida Governor Lawton Chiles. In contrast to the Camarioca and Mariel crisis in which the United States had immediately agreed to admit Cuban nationals, the Clinton administration reversed its admission of Cuban rafters into the United States as the influx of rafters began to grow two weeks after the crisis began. Instead, the administration ordered U.S. Navy and Coast Guard officials to begin taking Cubans intercepted at sea to the U.S. Naval Base in Guantanamo and to safe haven camps in Panama.[12] By maintaining nearly 29,000 Cuban nationals as detainees outside its national territory, the United States enhanced its negotiation position and both countries quickly began conversations that culminated in the signing of a migration agreement in September 1994.[13]

Under the 1994 accord, the two countries agreed to cooperate to guarantee "safe, legal, and orderly immigration" from the Island to the United States.[14] Both governments also agreed that Cuban nationals departing on boats and rafts would be taken to the U.S. naval base in Guantanamo and the Cuban government committed itself to implement measures to discourage unsafe departures. In statements immediately after the agreement had been signed, President Clinton notably called attention to the fact that the agreement made advances in deterring what he termed as "illegal immigration" by Cuban nationals. Specifically, President Clinton stated that "[the accord] will help insure that the massive flow of dangerous and illegal migration will be replaced by a safer, legal and more orderly process."[15]

Six months later, the U.S. government concluded a new migration accord with the Cuban government. The May 1995 agreement established what would come to be denominated as the "wet-foot, dry-foot policy." It represented an even larger departure from the changes in U.S. migration policy toward Cuba that had been announced during the Mariel boat exodus. For the first time in 28 years, the U.S. government announced that those Cubans intercepted at sea would be treated as migrants attempting to enter the United States from other countries and therefore would be repatriated to the Island with the exception of those deemed to have a legitimate asylum claim that would be taken to a third country. At the same time, the Clinton administration also included a mechanism to ensure that the United States would continue to adhere to the Cuban Adjustment Act. Cubans reaching U.S. shores on "dry feet" retained the right to qualify for resident status and ultimately for U.S. citizenship under the Cuban Adjustment Act. In crafting the "wet-foot, dry-foot policy," the U.S. government developed a way of responding to the rafter crisis that ended the automatic parole of Cubans into its territory. The United States began repatriating the majority of "wet-foot" Cubans to the Island starting in September 1994. From May 1995 through July 2003, the United States placed about 170 Cuban refugees in 11 different countries.[16]

The May 1995 agreement was the sixth migration accord signed by Cuba and the United States since 1959 and the fourteenth round of talks that took place between both governments since conversations began in May 1984. The United States made no additional concessions in 1995. Instead, the United States agreed to abide by the spirit of the 1984 accords by agreeing to grant *at least* 20,000 visas per year. As during the Cold War, both governments made the greatest progress in advancing negotiations aimed at establishing safe, legal, and orderly migration immediately following a migration crisis. Indeed, the United States and Cuba had signed formal migration agreements in 1965, 1978, 1984 and 1987.[17] Of these, the migration agreement signed in 1984 in response to the Mariel crisis had been the most far reaching in terms of the changes it introduced in U.S. migration policy towards Cuba. As part of the accord, the Reagan administration removed the exemptions granted to Cuban nationals from national immigration quotas during the passage of the Cuban Adjustment Act in 1966. Although the 1984 agreement was subsequently suspended by Cuba in retaliation for Radio Marti broadcasts and only re-instituted in 1987, it included provisions that up to 20,000 visas would be issued to Cuban nationals per year. In the final years of the Cold War, however, the United States failed to increase the number of Cuban émigrés admitted. Indeed, as Table 11.2 confirms, the U.S. Interests Section in Havana issued only 11,222 immigrant visas from 1985 to 1994.[18]

In 1995, the United States agreed to admit no less than 20,000 immigrants from Cuba annually, not including the immediate relatives of U.S. citizens.[19] In contrast to the bilateral agreements that had been reached in 1984 and 1987, however, the United States has made a good faith effort to fulfill its 1995 commitment. In the

TABLE 11.2   Immigration visas issued by the U.S. State Department to Cubans, 1984–2001

Year	Immigration visas	Refugees*
1984	–	n.a.
1985	1,227	n.a.
1986	–	n.a.
1987	–	n.a.
1988	3,472	n.a.
1989	1,631	n.a.
1990	1,098	4,753
1991	1,376	3,933
1992	910	3,720
1993	964	3,065
1994	544	2,670
1995	26,453	6,133
1996	15,700	3,498
1997	15,899	2,911
1998	15,787	1,587
1999	24,149	2,018
2000	21,228	3,184
2001	20,133	2,944
2002	n.a.	1,919
2003	n.a.	305
2004	n.a.	2,980
2005	n.a.	6,360
2006	n.a.	3,143
2007	n.a.	2,922
2008	n.a.	4,177

*Those in the United States apply for asylum, while those abroad apply for refugee status.
Source: Data on immigration visas reported by Aja Díaz, Antonio. *Al cruzar las fronteras*. La Havana: UNPF and CEDEM, 2009. Data on the number of visas processed for refugees reported by the U.S. Department of Homeland Security, *2008 Yearbook of Immigration Statistics*. Washington D.C.: DHS, 2009.

three years following the signing of the agreement, the United States granted entry to more than 32,000 Cubans in addition to processing the cases of those Cuban nationals who had been detained at Guantanamo. The U.S. Coast Guard has also worked in closer cooperation with the Cuban Border Guard and repatriated rafters to Cuba.[20] A study by the University of Havana's Center for the Study of International Migration has estimated that 10,011 of the 21,900 Cubans, or nearly half of those who have attempted to leave Cuba covertly via maritime routes between 1995 and 2004, were repatriated to Cuba from the Bahamas, the Cayman Islands and the United States.[21]

Moreover, in response to concerns that an insufficient number of Cuban applicants would qualify under the provisions in the Immigration and Nationality Act that allowed U.S. authorities to grant entry to special categories of entrants (employment-based immigrants, e.g., persons of extraordinary ability, members of the professions, or skill-shortage workers and therefore the types of Cuban nationals that were frequently prevented from leaving Cuba by the Cuban government), the 1995 migration agreement established a lottery for Cuban nationals. The Special Cuban Lottery, which is only for citizens of Cuba, lowered the entry requirements for Cuban nationals by allowing them to qualify for admission to the United States under special criteria. The lottery gives Cuban citizens between 18 and 55 years of age who met two of the following three criteria: a) completion of either secondary school or a higher level of education, b) at least three years of work experience, c) have relatives residing in the United States, eligibility to enter the United States. Since the agreement was enacted, the United States has held three lotteries. In each lottery, the number of qualifying registrants has increased and it is well above the 20,000 visa ceiling. Indeed, U.S. State Department officials have confirmed that the number of qualified applications rose from 189,000 in 1994 to 433,000 in 1996 and 541,000 in 1998.[22]

U.S. migration policies implemented since 1994 and 1995, however, have only been partially effective in furthering the strategic interests of the United States in ending unsafe, illegal, and disorderly migration from Cuba. A case that vividly illustrated the dilemmas for the United States in responding to the continued flow of unauthorized migration from Cuba was sparked by the rescue of 6-year-old Elián González; he was rescued by two fishermen on an inner tube some 60 miles north of Miami on November 25, 1999.[23] As a Cuban minor rescued at sea with a father in Cuba, Elián should have been returned quickly to his father in compliance with the 1995 bilateral migration agreement and international law. The incident, however, soon turned into a diplomatic problem for the Clinton administration, given the asylum petition filed by the boy's relatives in Miami and their refusal to relinquish custody of the boy to the father. Elián was only able to return to his father in Cuba on June 28, 2000, more than two months after Attorney General Janet Reno had ordered that he be seized by U.S. Immigration and Naturalization Service (INS) officials in a raid on the home of his Miami relatives and only after the 11th U.S. Circuit Court of Appeals ruled in the father's favor and the U.S. Supreme Court declined to review the decision.

Moreover, by maintaining provisions that guarantee admissions to those entering on "dry feet," Cubans continue to have the incentive to attempt to enter the United States. Indeed, as Table 11.3 shows, though not as high as peak levels witnessed in 1994, the annual number of Cuban migrants interdicted at sea by the U.S. Coast Guard (USCG) has been increasing since 1999 and it is currently at levels that are as high as the years immediately preceding the 1994 rafter crisis.[24] If the number of apprehensions by U.S. Border Patrol is added to USCG interdictions, illegal migration to the United States is increasing at record high rates. Moreover, Cubans and Cuban-Americans in Florida have pioneered alternative routes via Mexico to circumvent U.S. patrols. For example, the Department of Homeland Security reported that 1,055 Cubans landed in South Florida and 2,868 were interdicted by the USCG in 2007. In the same year, 11,126 Cubans entered the United States at the Mexican border.[25]

TABLE 11.3   Apprehension of Cuban migrants on U.S. borders and at sea, 1989–2008

Year	U.S. Coast Guard interdictions at sea	U.S. border patrol apprehensions
1989	257	n.a.
1990	443	n.a.
1991	1,722	n.a.
1992	2,066	n.a.
1993	2,882	n.a.
1994	38,560	n.a.
1995	525	n.a.
1996	411	n.a.
1997	421	n.a.
1998	903	n.a.
1999	1,619	2,789
2000	1,000	2,405
2001	777	2,858
2002	666	1,541
2003	1,555	1,303
2004	1,225	819
2005	2,712	3,263
2006	2,810	4,021
2007	2,868	4,295
2008	2,199	3,351

Sources: U.S. Department of Homeland Security, "Alien Migrant Interdiction," http://www.uscg. mil/hq/cg5/cg531/AMIO/FlowStats/FY.asp/ accessed 10 March 2010; Wasem, Ruth Ellen, "Cuban Migration to the United States: Policy and Trends, Congressional Research Service Report R40566." Washington D.C.: Congressional Research Service, 2009.

The Cuban-American Community: Promotion of Migrant-Accepting Policies

Since the end of the Cold War, the presence in the United States of a concentrated, organized and vocal Cuban émigré community has complicated U.S. efforts to restrict migration from Cuba. Whereas Cuban-Americans were only a marginally influential political force during the 1980 Mariel event, they became a dominant force in Miami and South Florida politics and by the 1990s were well-connected in both Democratic and Republican circles in Washington DC.[26] In the post-Cold War era, the Cuban-American lobby has played an important role in shaping U.S. policy towards Cuba. Indeed, President Clinton went as far as responding that U.S. Cuba policy was the product of "the hardest-line people in Miami."[27] As will be argued below, Cuban-Americans have pressured the United States to reduce migrant-restricting policies and have secured some important victories in both the policy formulation and implementation stages.

During the rafter crisis, and even though some Cuban nationals spent as long as 18 months on the U.S. Guantanamo naval base, the approximately 38,500 Cuban rafters were eventually admitted into the United States as stipulated by the 1995 bilateral migration agreement.[28] Cuban-Americans were prominent in lobbying the U.S. government to admit Guantanamo refugees. As Carlos de la Cruz, a prominent Cuban-American businessperson and influential figure in politics noted, "I was dealing with the National Security Council and General John Sheehan [director of operations for the joint chiefs at the time]. I arranged to go to Guantánamo with the general and [Florida] Senator Bob Graham, talk to the rafters and to the White House. We got the deal and the media to understand that this was all under the radar, nothing written—but we got 2,500 rafters in."[29] Lobbying efforts continued and eventually all detainees in Guantanamo were granted parole.

Cuban-Americans effectively lobbied the United States government to not repeal the Cuban Adjustment Act. Instead, the U.S. Congress enacted language stipulating that the CAA could only be repealed when Cuba becomes a democracy; in addition, immigration caps on the number of Cuban admissions could not be used to limit the Attorney General´s authority to grant permanent residence to Cuban émigrés after only one year of residence in the United States.[30] Specifically, Section 606 of the Illegal Immigration Reform and Immigrant Responsibility Act of 1996, Division C of P.L. 104-208 states that "Public Law 89-732 is repealed effective only upon a determination by the president under section 203(c)(3) of the Cuban Liberty and Democratic Solidarity (LIBERTAD) Act of 1996 (Public Law 104-114) that a democratically elected government in Cuba is in power." In addition, the Cuban-American community has continued to pressure the U.S. government to admit Cubans into the United States as political refugees. In relative terms, they have been quite successful. The United States has continued to classify a significant share of Cubans seeking to migrate to the United States as refugees. In 1999, the top five refugee groups admitted to the United States by nationality were, in rank order, from Bosnia-Herzegovina, Yugoslavia, the former Soviet Union, Vietnam, and Cuba.[31] Nine years later, Cuba remains as the fifth highest country with the greatest number of refugees admitted to the United States after Burma, Iraq, Bhutan, and Iran.

In addition, the United States has not rescinded the special benefits introduced as part of the Refugee Education Assistance Act of 1980 for Cuban and Haitian boat rafters, providing these entrants with access to special federal programs, which are not granted to other migrants recently arrived in the United States.[32] Consequently, Cuban migrants are still treated as refugees and asylees for the purposes of the federal refugee resettlement program and also receive most other federal benefits and assistance, including supplemental cash and medical assistance. As a result, under current law, Cuban émigrés that meet all the requirements for eligibility including age, disability, or blindness requirements, or those falling below established income and resource thresholds are eligible to receive supplemental social security income for up to seven years after entry. In 2008, individual SSI beneficiaries could have received up to the maximum federal benefit rate of $7,644 per year, and married couples received up to $11,472 per year.

Furthermore, while restrictions on illegal migration from Cuba were tightened, the United States continued to introduce targeted programs that privilege specific categories of Cubans entering the United States. In 2006, the George W. Bush administration eased restrictions for the immigration of Cuban medical professionals, their spouses and minor children, who were working in third countries; it launched a new initiative denoted as the "Cuban Medical Professional Parole Program."[33] By 2007, Congressman Lincoln Diaz-Balart's office announced that 1,000 Cuban medical professionals, out of the 40,000 who are estimated to be deployed and working in 68 countries on medical missions sponsored by the Cuban government, were admitted under the program.[34] The U.S. recruitment of medical professionals is in marked contrast with the shift in the characteristics of Cuban émigrés that have entered the United States in successive waves. Whereas earlier waves of Cuban émigrés were mainly of upper and middle class origins, there has been a rise in the proportion of less-skilled workers admitted in each successive cohort of Cuban migrants.[35] Nearly half of Cubans entering the United States were semi-skilled and unskilled workers by 1997. Migrants from professional, semi-professional or managerial occupations, in contrast, represented only 9 percent of the 16,750 Cubans admitted into the United States.

In the post-Cold War era, the Cuban-American lobby has successfully advocated for U.S. migration policies that grant special privileges to Cuban migrants. The benefits accorded to Cuban migrants remain well above those that other immigrant groups, even political refugees, are able to obtain. Yet, as will be argued below, the power of the Cuban-American lobby has been limited. In particular, they have been less effective at influencing U.S. policy during moments of crisis related to migration issues. The Cuban-American lobby was not able to prevent the Clinton administration from pursuing migration talks or signing accords with Cuba during or in the aftermath of the rafter crisis. Similarly, the strong consensus in the Cuban-American community that favored keeping Elián González in the United States, despite his father's demands to the contrary, did not prevail over the administration's decision.

Domestic Politics: Support for Restrictions on U.S. Migration Policies Toward Cuba

One reason for the limitation on the influence of the Cuban-American lobby with respect to the policy response of U.S. administrations to migration disputes with Cuba in the post-Cold War period, in addition to the U.S. foreign policy concerns, has been the countervailing influence exerted by other domestic politics factors. Domestic political pressures from voters outside Miami have strengthened U.S. foreign policy goals geared to limiting Cuban migration, thereby reinforcing the migrant-restricting policy response adopted by the United States towards the entry of Cuban émigrés. These domestic pressures were critical in reinforcing U.S. government decisions in both the rafter crisis and the Elián González episodes.

During the rafter crisis, U.S. officials invoked the need to avoid repeating the same mistake made by President Jimmy Carter during the Mariel crisis, when the U.S. response was viewed as a sign of weakness, contributing to the defeat of Carter's re-election bid.[36] President Clinton, who in 1980 as Governor of Arkansas had been responsible for responding to the riots at Fort Chafee by Mariel refugees and who had also lost his re-election bid in the aftermath of the riots, sided with Florida Governor Lawton Chiles who had threatened to invoke a state of emergency and deploy the National Guard.[37] The Democratic Governor was locked in a tightly disputed re-election bid. In the middle of President Clinton's first term, the Democratic Party was also battling threatening midterm election opposition that eventually resulted in a 54-seat swing and the Republican Party's gaining of a majority of seats in the House for the first time since 1954. The Democratic Party and President Clinton were pressured to address the increasing concern over immigration issues expressed by the U.S. public opinion with an effective response that ended the unregulated arrival of Cubans on Florida Shores. An April 1994 CNN/USA Today/Gallup poll had revealed that 55 percent of the U.S. public disapproved of President Clinton's handling of immigration.[38]

On August 18, 1994 Clinton reversed the U.S. acceptance of the Cuban rafters that had been arriving in Florida in July and early August. He issued orders to the U.S. Coast Guard to detain Cuban rafters and transport them to U.S. naval bases in Guantanamo and Panama. The flow of Cuban rafters, however, did not end. As a result, President Clinton entered into migration talks with the Cuban government in September 1994. In the following months, the rafter crisis continued to pose problems for the administration. Paralleling incidents that had occurred in U.S. territory during the Mariel episode, U.S. troops were forced to quell 8,600 rioting Cuban refugees detained in Panama in December 1994. Fearing that a similar or worse incident could take place in Guantanamo, Clinton struggled with how to respond when the number of rafters surged in the spring and summer of 1995. The capacity and costs of detention at the U.S. naval base were mounting; U.S. admission of the new wave of rafters could re-ignite the crisis. A 1995 Gallup poll indicated that 62 percent of the U.S. public favored decreasing immigration into the United States.[39] In May 1995, the Clinton administration returned to the negotiating table and signed a second agreement with Cuba. As LeoGrande summarizes, "as the crisis wore on, the domestic cost of failing to find a solution escalated along with refugee flow, first prompting Clinton to impose the detention policy and later, when that was inadequate, to negotiate with Cuba."[40] Although the administration went against the interests of the majority of Cuban-Americans, Bill Clinton won the State of Florida by a 5.7 percent margin in his 1996 re-election bid and he won more than 40 percent of the Cuban-American vote centered in Dade County.[41]

Despite threats by the Cuban American National Foundation that Cuban-Americans could be pivotal in preventing a Democratic victory in Florida in November 2000, the Clinton administration returned Elián González to his father in April. In part, the administration adopted this bold approach because there were countervailing signals in the U.S. Congress and by the general public that indicated that this policy would be acceptable and perhaps even favored by strong majorities. During the crisis, despite being Republican-dominated, the Congress had been unable to pass or defeat any of the seven bills and resolutions that had been introduced in the House and Senate favoring the boy's return or retention. Moreover, the affair also coincided with a marked rise in the political influence of interest groups, including U.S. business and agricultural interests, which had started to lobby for changes in Cuba policy in the period immediately preceding and during the crisis.[42]

U.S. public opinion was generally supportive of the boy's return to Cuba. Indeed, the U.S. public had initially seemed evenly divided over the boy's return and the raid ordered by the administration, but subsequently shifted sharply toward favoring the course of action adopted by the Clinton administration. The misreading of the impact of the escalation of the conflict on the effectiveness of the lobbying power of the Cuban American National Foundation was noted by its president in an interview. As Francisco "Pepe" Hernández noted, "Everything changed after Elián. We made the terrible mistake of turning it into an issue between ourselves and Castro … We were unable to understand why the rest of the world didn't get it. But when it was all over, we conducted a poll: huge percentages against us over Elián; we were seen as inflexible, as people only interested in vengeance."[43]

Even in the Cold War era, domestic politics had started to influence U.S.–Cuba migration negotiations and the adoption of migrant-restricting policies.[44] In the post-Cold War period, these forces have become more vocal as the U.S. public has called for increased efforts by the government to protect its borders and control migration flows. While these pressures have focused on immigration and border protection in general terms, they are also more visible in discussions on Cuban migration to the United States. Increasingly, there is greater consensus in the U.S. government that there is a need for greater alignment between how non-Cuban and Cuban migrants are treated by U.S. law. These pressures reinforced U.S. foreign policy concerns that called for a shift in policy toward migrant-restricting policies for Cuban émigrés, most particularly during periods of crisis.

U.S. Migration Policy Toward Cuba and Foreign Policy in the Post-Cold War Era

As noted at the onset of this chapter, the current wave of Cuban migration to the United States represents the longest and largest of the four waves of migration that have taken place since Cubans began leaving the Island in 1960. In the post-Cold

War era, the United States mounted an effective response to dealing with the two most dramatic migration crises that took place. In both the rafter and Elián González crises, as well as in the aftermath of both events, the United States cooperated with the Cuban government to bring about orderly legal migration of Cubans to its territory. An analysis of U.S. government documents and testimony by government officials confirms that the potential security threat posed by uncontrolled migration from Cuba motivated the policies and actions adopted by the United States during these two events. Dan Fisk, for example, contends that this concern drove the Clinton administration's Cuba policy, explaining that the administration's policies can be interpreted as a coherent and consistent set of initiatives from 1993 to 2000 focused on sending signals to "reassure Castro that he need not unleash another Mariel and for mechanisms to encourage Cubans to remain in spite of the Island's dire economic situation."[45]

In the post-Cold War era, the United States significantly modified its security assessment of Cuba. In several instances over the course of the last 15 years, U.S. generals heading the U.S. Southern Command (Southcom) have relayed a similar assessment of Cuba's threat to U.S. national security. Since Cuba has downsized its armed forces and lost Soviet bloc economic and military assistance, its ability to project military power off the Island has been significantly reduced.[46] Despite its fading as a security threat, consensus also exists in U.S. security circles stressing that the United States must remain prepared for a mass exodus of Cubans. In 1997, during the Senate Armed Services Committee hearing on his appointment to be Commander in Chief of the U.S. Southern Command, General Charles Wilhelm responded that the only threat Cuba posed was that of migration in the immediate aftermath of the rafter crisis.[47]

Frequently, U.S. officials have linked fears of a potential migration crisis with the onset of a transition in Cuba. In statements delivered while heading the U.S. Interests Section in Havana, Michael G. Kozak explained the Clinton administration's Cuba policy in the following manner: "Today … our primary concern is the one that did not exist twenty years ago. That is the issue of stability [in Cuba]. [The United States] cannot permit the social dislocation in our country that would be associated with attempting to absorb a large portion of the Cuban population."[48] Retired Army General Barry McCaffrey, who was 1994–96 commander of Southcom, relayed this view in his response to the transfer of Cuba to the U.S. Northern Command (Northcom) in 2002. McCaffrey stated, "It probably makes pretty decent sense because you're going to have to coordinate local law enforcement, local health-care providers when Castro dies. Florida and the Gulf Coast states at every level will be engaged with the significant probability of a huge exodus from Cuba."[49]

U.S. fears of a potential migration crisis sparked by a crisis in Cuba have not subsided. Instead, partly in response to increased arrivals of Cubans at sea and on U.S. borders and partly due to the changes that have taken place in the leadership of the Cuban government, the United States increased border enforcement and developed plans to pre-empt another major boat crisis. As a pre-emptive response to the possibility of a new crisis of uncontrolled flows of Cubans leaving the Island on rafts and boats, the U.S. Coast Guard developed "Operation Vigilant Sentry" in 2003.[50] The plan proposes to "set up a perimeter around Cuba to intercept migrants and immediately return them to Cuba, in hopes of discouraging more departures;" it remains in effect.[51] After Fidel Castro officially handed power over to his younger brother, Raúl, in August 2006, in March 2007 the United States Department of Homeland Security carried out a massive two-day exercise in which federal, state and local agents from 85 law enforcement agencies simulated a response to a surge of 2,000 Cuban illegal migrants.[52]

During the George W. Bush administration, the United States continued to adhere to the migration accords with the Cuban government that were signed by the Clinton administration. And although the United States did not continue semi-annual consultation talks with Cuba or honor visa commitments, the United States deepened cooperation with respect to hijacking. Incidents that took place in 2003 are indicative of U.S. efforts to cooperate with Cuba.

In March 2003, U.S. officials permitted six Cuban men, who had hijacked a Cuban plane with more than 20 passengers aboard, to land in Key West as they had similarly done in the case of a crop duster plane that had landed in November 2002. Unlike the predecessor case, the six men were prosecuted in U.S. courts and received 20-year sentences.[53] Two weeks later, the head of the Cuban Interests Section, James Cason, interceded at Havana's José Martí International Airport in an attempted hijacking of a small, twin-engine propeller plane with 20 passengers, the hijacker, and his family. Although Cason was unable to reverse the hijacker's request to land in Key West with his family, U.S. and Cuban officials cooperated to escort the aircraft to a safe landing in the United States. In this incident, the hijacker was also arrested and sentenced by U.S. courts. When 12 Cubans hijacked a Cuban-government vessel in July 2003, U.S. Coast Guard officials boarded the ship in international waters prior to its arrival on Florida shores. After being assured by the Cuban government that the migrants would only be subjected to 10-year prison sentences, the hijackers were returned to Cuba despite the loud protests of Cuban-American legislators.[54] In a post-September 11 context and the onset of the U.S. invasion of Iraq, the Bush administration responded to the heightened risk of a wave of hijackings in Cuba by reinforcing the Cuban government's efforts to encourage Cubans to use legal channels of emigration, despite petitions filed by these Cubans with U.S. immigration authorities arguing that they had a reasonable fear of persecution if returned to their homeland.

Improving U.S.–Cuba Cooperation on Migration

Existing agreements stipulate that U.S.–Cuba migration talks should occur twice per year. While the United States continued to adhere to the major principles outlined in the 1994 and 1995 accords with Cuba, the George W. Bush administration suspended these semi-annual conversations in 2003. Following the election of Barack Obama, the United States and Cuba resumed migration talks; three meetings took place in July 2009, February 2010, and June 2010. This section summarizes the key issues on which U.S. immigration policy and Cuban government policies could improve bilateral cooperation over migration. Although this chapter has been centered on U.S. policy, changes in Cuba's migration policy are also highlighted because they are fundamental for bilateral negotiations to progress.

U.S. Policies

A) Cuban Adjustment Act (CAA)

Cuban refugees could be admitted to the United States under existing U.S. refugee law, rather than under the provisions in the CAA that give the U.S. Attorney General discretionary authority to admit Cuban migrants. As Robert Bach has noted, "The United States now has better ways to assist asylum seekers and humanitarian cases than the blanket procedures of 1966, including principles and procedures that apply to all nationalities. A modern U.S. asylum system provides protection from persecution through case-by-case review, and contains mechanisms for returning, if appropriate, those interdicted on land or sea to their country of origin."[55]

B) "Wet-foot, dry-foot policy"

The United States could use existing Justice Department authority to discontinue its "dry foot" policy whereby the discretionary authority of the U.S. Attorney General grants parole to Cubans who are smuggled or arrive on U.S. borders under the CAA. Instead Cubans who arrive to the United States by illegal means could be processed under the same principles as for illegal arrivals from all other nationalities.

C) U.S. immigrant visas for Cuban citizens

Given that the number of visas awarded to all types of Cuban nationals by the U.S. government has been targeted to at least 20,000 since 1984, the United States could increase the 20,000 annual cap and/or announce a new lottery for Cuban nationals.

D) Operation Vigilant Sentry

The U.S. Coast Guard could re-evaluate "Operation Vigilant Sentry" and revise current policies, which mandate that a perimeter be placed around Cuba to intercept migrants and immediately return them to Cuba during a massive boat exodus. Instead, the United States could transport émigrés departing the Island to a third country or provide them with temporary refuge in accordance with international law.

E) MULTILATERAL COOPERATION ON MIGRATION

The control of immigration can benefit from multilateral cooperation. In October 2008, Mexico and Cuba signed a migration agreement calling for increased cooperation between the Mexican Navy and the Cuban Border Guard on smuggling and illegal migration. Mexico has also agreed to return to Cuba those Cuban citizens in Mexico without proper documentation. The Cuban government could be invited to participate in discussions on multilateral cooperation with the United States and its neighboring countries.

Cuban Government Policies

A) EXIT AND TEMPORARY RESIDENCY PERMITS

The Cuban government could remove requirements that mandate that Cubans seeking to leave the Island must obtain an exit permit (*permiso de salida*). The permits have been required since 1962. In 1994, the Cuban government introduced reforms to give eligibility to any Cuban over the age of 18. The Cuban government could also grant temporary residency permits (*permiso de residencia en el exterior*) to those seeking to emigrate to the United States, which would allow those seeking to reside in the United States to remain abroad for up to 11 months while retaining full citizenship rights and privileges.

B) UNAUTHORIZED MIGRATION

Under current policy, those who choose to leave illegally, such as the estimated 45,000 Cubans who left between 1990 and 1994 during the rafter crisis, are not eligible for re-entry to the national territory for a period of 5 years. The Cuban government could adopt policies to allow for re-entry and re-integration for those who leave covertly and for those who are repatriated.

C) CUBANS DEEMED EXCLUDABLE FOR ADMISSION INTO THE UNITED STATES

Although Cuba has agreed to accept the return of excludable migrants on a case-by-case basis, its limited admission of migrants who have committed crimes in the United States has been a source of conflict.[56] The Cuban government could undertake increased efforts to repatriate these Cuban nationals.

Conclusion

During the Cold War, the U.S. and Cuban government policies on migration significantly influenced the timing and manner for the entry of Cubans to the United States. Since the Soviet bloc collapsed, U.S. foreign policy considerations have continued to play an important role in driving U.S. migration policies toward Cuba because the United States places a high priority on protecting its borders from the unregulated arrival of mass influxes of Cubans. The Clinton administration chose cooperative policies in bilateral migration disputes with Cuba in the 1990s during both the rafter and the Elián González crises. The United States responded in this manner because policy choices were in alignment with U.S. national interests and non-Cuban-American public opinion. Moreover, cooperation persisted during the George W. Bush administration.

The shift toward greater U.S. cooperation with Cuba is driven by the desire to control U.S. borders. Cuba's proximity and the volatile outflows of Cubans that continue to attempt entry into the United States have driven the United States to cooperate with the Cuban government. In the post-Cold War period, the United States has increased its efforts to combat nonmilitary threats to its national interests. These factors explain the decisions adopted by U.S. administrations in both the rafter crisis and the Elián González episodes. They will continue to be an important determinant of U.S. migration policy toward Cuba in the near and midterm.

U.S. domestic interests will continue to shape the U.S. policy response encouraging greater cooperation with Cuba on the control of migratory flows. The Cuban-American community's makeup is increasingly shifting, now including people that recently left socialist Cuba; the community's lobbying efforts have thus fragmented but its members will continue to advocate migrant-accepting policies. As Cubans arriving in the United States are increasingly viewed as economic migrants, however, domestic political interests will favor the government's adoption of migration policies that treat Cuban migrants under the same principles that guide the migrant-restricting policy response the United States has adopted more generally towards the immigration of Latin Americans—not automatically as a class of political refugees. In the near term, therefore, there is likely to be greater agreement between the two governments to resolve some of the outstanding issues that had made migration a source of contention in bilateral relations.

Notes

1 Lisandro Pérez, "Cuba," in *The New Americans: A Guide to Immigration since 1965*, ed. Mary C. Waters, Reed Ueda, and Helen B. Marrow (Cambridge, MA: Harvard University Press, 2007).
2 Jorge I. Domínguez, "Cooperating with the Enemy? U.S. Immigration Policies toward Cuba," in *Western Hemisphere Immigration and United States Foreign Policy*, ed. Christopher

Mitchell (University Park, PA: Pennsylvania State University Press, 1992); William M. LeoGrande, "From Havana to Miami: U.S. Cuba Policy as a Two-Level Game," *Journal of Interamerican Studies and World Affairs* 40, no. 1 (1998): 67–86.

3   Domínguez, "Cooperating with the Enemy? U.S. Immigration Policies toward Cuba."

4   LeoGrande, "From Havana to Miami: U.S. Cuba Policy as a Two-Level Game." LeoGrande analyzes U.S.–Cuba relations as a two-level game and hypothesizes that the outcome of the rafter crisis in 1994 was driven in large part by domestic imperatives. He cites U.S. public opinion and the Cuban-American lobby as key determinants on the outcomes of the crisis. Arguing that the interests of the U.S. public (e.g. favoring migration-restrictive policies) and the Cuban-American community (e.g. favoring migrant-accepting policies) are in conflict, LeoGrande concludes that U.S. public opinion prevailed over the interests of Cuban émigrés in 1994.

5   Domínguez, "Cooperating with the Enemy? U.S. Immigration Policies toward Cuba."

6   LeoGrande, "From Havana to Miami: U.S. Cuba Policy as a Two-Level Game."

7   The U.S. granted similar adjustment acts for refugees from other (mostly Communist) countries. In contrast to Cuban émigrés, however, these exemptions were repealed or superceded by subsequent legislation, primarily the 1980 Refugee Act.

8   The provision in Section 1 of the CAA states "That, notwithstanding the provisions of section 245(c) of the Immigration and Nationality Act, the status of any alien who is a native or citizen of Cuba and who has been inspected and admitted or paroled into the United States subsequent to January 1, 1959 and has been physically present in the United States for at least one year, may be adjusted by the Attorney General, in his discretion and under such regulations as he may prescribe, to that of an alien lawfully admitted for permanent residence if the alien makes an application for such adjustment, and the alien is eligible to receive an immigrant visa and is admissible to the United States for permanent residence."

9   Under the 1980 Refugee Act, asylum seekers from communist countries like Cuba were now required to establish a well-founded fear of persecution.

10   Ruth Ellen Wasem, "Cuban Migration to the United States: Policy and Trends, Congressional Research Service Report R40566" (Washington DC: Congressional Research Service, 2009).

11   Domínguez, "Cooperating with the Enemy? U.S. Immigration Policies toward Cuba."

12   Jon Nordheimer, "Flight from Cuba: U.S. will expand patrols to stop Cuban Refugees," *The New York Times*, August 23, 1994. A massive exodus of Haitian rafters preceded the Cuban rafter crisis in 1992. The largest exodus of Haitians to U.S. shores was triggered by the coup d'état of 1991, and the subsequent violent persecution of Aristide supporters. The U.S. Coast Guard reported interdicting 37,618 Haitians in 1992. The U.S. Coast Guard began taking Haitians to Guantanamo Naval Base during this period.

13   In contrast, the majority of the 21,000 Haitian rafters kept at Guantanamo during the crisis were repatriated to their country of origin as they were deemed economic migrants. "United States Coast Guard, United States Department of Homeland Security, Alien Migrant Interdiction," http://www.uscg.mil/hq/cg5/cg531/AMIO/FlowStats/FY.asp.

14   Wasem, "Cuban Migration to the United States: Policy and Trends, Congressional Research Service Report R40566."

15   John T. Woolley and Gerhard Peters, "William J. Clinton Statement on the Cuba–United States Agreement on Migration, September 9, 1994," in *The American Presidency Project*. Available from: http://www.presidency.ucsb.edu/ws/?pid=49056 (2010).

16   Wasem, "Cuban Migration to the United States: Policy and Trends, Congressional Research Service Report R40566."

17   Domínguez, "Cooperating with the Enemy? U.S. Immigration Policies toward Cuba."

18 Antonio Aja Díaz, *Al cruzar las fronteras* (La Havana: Centro de Estudios Demográficos, Universidad de La Habana and United Nations Population Fund, 2009); U.S. Department of Homeland Security, "2008 Yearbook of Immigration Statistics" (Washington DC: U.S. Department of Homeland Security, 2009).

19 Wasem, "Cuban Migration to the United States: Policy and Trends, Congressional Research Service Report R40566."

20 Randy Beardsworth, "U.S.–Cuba Functional Relationships: A Security Imperative," in *9 Ways For US to Talk to Cuba and For Cuba to Talk to US*, ed. Sarah Stephens and Alice Dunscomb (Washington DC: Center for Democracy in the Americas, 2009).

21 Aja Díaz, *Al cruzar las fronteras.*

22 Wasem, "Cuban Migration to the United States: Policy and Trends, Congressional Research Service Report R40566."

23 Two other refugees, Nivaldo Fernández Ferrán and Arianne Horta Alfonso, were also on the same raft and managed to swim ashore on Key Biscayne, just south of Miami Beach ("The War over Elián," 2000). Immigration officials granted both individuals admission to the United States.

24 U.S. Department of Homeland Security, "Alien Migrant Interdiction."

25 Mark Stevenson, "Cubans head for Mexico to dodge U.S. sea patrols," *Associated Press*, October 17, 2008.

26 Susan Eckstein and Lorena Barberia, "Grounding Immigrant Generations in History: Cuban Americans and Their Transnational Ties," *International Migration Review* 36, no. 3 (2002): 799–837.

27 Richard A. Nuccio, "Cuba: A U.S. Perspective," in *Transatlantic Tensions: The United States, Europe, and Problem Countries*, ed. Richard N. Haass (Washington DC: Brookings Institution Press, 1999).

28 Mireya Navarro, "Last of Refugees From Cuba In '94 Flight Now Enter U.S.," *New York Times*, February 1, 1996.

29 Ed Vulliamy, "Elián González and the Cuban Crisis: Fallout from a Big Row over a Little Boy," *The Observer*, February 21, 2010.

30 Wasem, "Cuban Migration to the United States: Policy and Trends, Congressional Research Service Report R40566."

31 United States, "2008 Yearbook of Immigration Statistics."

32 Wasem, "Cuban Migration to the United States: Policy and Trends, Congressional Research Service Report R40566."

33 U.S. Department of State, "Cuban Medical Professional Parole Program," http://www.state.gov/p/wha/rls/fs/2009/115414.htm.

34 Tal Abbady, "Hundreds of Cuban medical workers defecting to U.S. while overseas," *South Florida Sun-Sentinel*, October 10, 2007.

35 Eckstein and Barberia, "Grounding Immigrant Generations in History: Cuban Americans and Their Transnational Ties."

36 In retrospect, President Carter went further claiming the U.S. appeared impotent during Mariel. As he stated, "The refugee question has hurt us badly. It wasn't just in Florida, but it was throughout the country. It was a burning issue. It made us look impotent when we received these refugees from Cuba. See Domínguez, "Cooperating with the Enemy? U.S. Immigration Policies toward Cuba," 46.

37 LeoGrande, "From Havana to Miami: U.S. Cuba Policy as a Two-Level Game."

38 Those interviewed were asked the following question, "Thinking about some issues, do you approve or disapprove of the way President Bill Clinton is handling ... immigration?" Francine Segovia and Renatta Defever, "The Polls–Trends: American Public Opinion on Immigrants and Immigration Policy," *Public Opinion Quarterly* 74, no. 2 (2010): 375–394.

39 Ibid.

40   LeoGrande, "From Havana to Miami: U.S. Cuba Policy as a Two-Level Game," 79.

41   David Leip, "Atlas of U.S. Presidential Elections," http://uselectionatlas.org/; Katherine Q. Seelye, "Boy's Case Could Sway Bush–Gore Contest," *New York Times*, March 30, 2000.

42   Philip Brenner, Patrick J. Haney, and Walter Vanderbush, "The Confluence of Domestic and International Interests: U.S. Policy Toward Cuba, 1998–2001," *International Studies Perspectives* 3, no. 2 (2002): 192–208; Morris H. Morley and Chris McGillion, *Unfinished business: America and Cuba after the Cold War, 1989–2001* (Cambridge, UK, and New York: Cambridge University Press, 2002); Daniel P. Erikson, *The Cuba Wars: Fidel Castro, the United States, and the Next Revolution* (New York: Bloomsbury Press, 2008).

43   Vulliamy, "Elián González and the Cuban Crisis: Fallout from a Big Row over a Little Boy."

44   Domínguez, "Cooperating with the Enemy? U.S. Immigration Policies toward Cuba."

45   Daniel W. Fisk, "Cuba: The End of an Era," *Washington Quarterly* 24, no. 1 (2001): 95.

46   James T. Hill, "A Time to Normalize Relations Between the U.S. and Cuban Militaries," in *9 Ways For US to Talk to Cuba and For Cuba to Talk to US*, ed. Sarah Stephens and Alice Dunscomb (Washington DC: Center for Democracy in the Americas, 2009); Bantz J. Craddock and Barbara Fick, "Security Cooperation with a Democratic and Free Cuba: What would it look like?," *Cuban Affairs* 1, no. 4 (2006): 1–25.

47   In Wilhelm's testimony and responses to questions during the hearing, significant discussion centered on the threats imposed by illegal immigration from Latin America and the Caribbean, including Cuba, to the United States. United States Senate, "Committee concluded hearings on the nominations of Gen. Michael E. Ryan, USAF, to be Chief of Staff, United States Air Force, Adm. Harold W. Gehman Jr., USN, to be Commander-in-Chief, United States Atlantic Command, and Lt. Gen. Charles E. Wilhelm, USMC, to be Commander-in-Chief, United States Southern Command and for appointment to the grade of general, after the nominees testified and answered questions in their own behalf" (paper presented at the Committee on Armed Services Washington DC, September 16, 1997).

48   Fisk, "Cuba: The End of an Era."

49   Carol Rosenberg, "Southcom to Yield Cuba Role to New Command," *Miami Herald*, April 24, 2002.

50   U.S. Department of Homeland Security, "Fact Sheet-Operation Vigilant Sentry," United States Department of Homeland Security, http://www.piersystem.com/go/doc/1038/148670/.

51   Robert Bach, "Missteps and Next Steps in U.S.–Cuba Migration Policies," in *9 Ways For US to Talk to Cuba and For Cuba to Talk to US*, ed. Sarah Stephens and Alice Dunscomb (Washington DC: Center for Democracy in the Americas, 2009).

52   Jane Sutton, "U.S. Halts Imaginary Cubans in Security Drill," *Washington Post*, March 8, 2007.

53   Erikson, *The Cuba Wars: Fidel Castro, the United States, and the Next Revolution*. Fourteen of the 24 passengers requested and were granted permission by the Department of Homeland Security to remain in the U.S. The remaining 12 returned to Cuba.

54   Phil Peters, "Issue #5 The Imperfect Migration Accords at Work," *Cuba Policy Report*, July 14, 2003. The Cuban government ordered the execution of three hijackers in April 2003 for terrorism-related charges related to the seizure of a ferryboat in Havana.

55   Bach, "Missteps and Next Steps in U.S.–Cuba Migration Policies."

56   Wasem, "Cuban Migration to the United States: Policy and Trends, Congressional Research Service Report R40566."

12

U.S.–CUBA

EMIGRATION AND BILATERAL RELATIONS

ANTONIO AJA DÍAZ

In the last decade of the twentieth century and the first one of the twenty-first, very significant events in international relations have occurred. The disintegration of the socialist bloc, the end of the project of "really existing socialism," and the disappearance of the USSR represent deep changes in the correlation of forces on a world scale. Although the Cold War ended, confrontation between the United States and Cuba continued, as did an absence of dialogue, persistent hostility on the part of several U.S. administrations, and resistance by the Cuban revolution.

Within this context, the tendency of emigration from the Island to the North continued. In the contours of the bilateral relations between the two countries, migration talks have provided almost the only concrete channel of communication.

Main Tendencies in Cuban Emigration to the United States

From 1959 until today, the United States has been the main destination of emigrants from the Island, and the United States has used this pattern as part of its hostile policy toward the Cuban revolution in different eras and in accordance with the destabilization tactics of each.[1] A new such era began in 1989, with subdivisions covering the 1990s and the first decade of the twenty-first century. The unfolding of the "special period in time of peace"[2] under the impact of the deep economic crisis besetting the country imbues the 1990s with a special role in the following analysis, particularly because of the role that relatives abroad began to play in Cuban daily life. Their role gained new dimensions with a perception that linked having such relatives with the possibility of economic help in confronting the crisis.

In the 1990s, the flow of migrants was characterized by a mix of permanent and temporary emigration, as well as significant numbers of visitors to the Island (estimated at more than 100,000 between 1995 and 1996 alone). Legal emigration remained low until early 1995, while illegal departures mushroomed. In 1994 more than 50,000 people were involved in the latter process, successfully or not. The composition and motivation of the emigration during this decade was different from those of earlier waves. An economic component (including one of labor mobility) predominated alongside political factors and others such as family reunification or lack of confidence that the social project of the revolution would provide a way out of the crisis.

Since 1959, due to the politicized and ideological atmosphere surrounding the issue of Cuba–U.S. migration, the act of emigration was seen in Cuba as "abandoning the fatherland" and therefore it acquired levels of stigmatization in accord with the historical moment of revolutionary victory. Some of these levels still persist, as in the definition of "emigration without [possibility of] permanent return." The policies of both governments serve as influences that can stimulate or retard the migratory flow. They introduce elements of regulation and deregulation, and they even affect the practical means by which the emigrants carry out their journeys. In the United States, independently of the motivations of Cubans migrating to that country, these immigrants are seen as "fleeing political persecution," "escaping from communism," or "dissidents." Although these interpretations began to be questioned in the late 1990s, they remain essentially in force up to today.

In terms of potential normalization of migratory relations, 1995 represented a turning point. The signing of a new agreement suggested the possibility of regulating the legal migratory flow of Cubans to the United States and of trying to stop illegal emigration. This possibility was formalized and raised to a potentially definitive level when, on May 2 of that year, the "Joint Communiqué" on normalizing migratory relations was issued. That document, which resolved the issue of the Cuban emigrants being held at the Guantánamo naval base, reaffirmed a joint interest in avoiding "dangerous departures." These migratory accords, in attempting to solve the serious problem created by the interruption in legal migration, offered an opportunity for preferential treatment. Applying various provisions contained in the U.S. General Law of Immigration, during 1995 more than 26,224 visas were issued to Cuban citizens who applied for them.[3]

Emigration at the Start of the Twenty-First Century

The first six years of the twenty-first century may be classified as the second most important period of emigration since 1960–62 because of the size of net emigration from the country—226,078 individuals, of whom 54.5 percent were female. For 1994–2006, that figure is 407,145, of whom 51.1 percent were female.[4]

To better understand this dynamic requires analyzing international migration as a variable in the context of Cuban demographic tendencies. In brief, demographic figures show insufficient population growth, low birthrates, and a clear increase in the age of the population. Emigration's impact on this situation can be seen in the above-mentioned net outflow and the slight female majority among emigrants. In addition, the most common age groups among the emigrants are those between 10 and 29 years of age (46.6 percent).

In Cuban emigration at the turn of the twenty-first century, the presence of young professionals can also be observed. Professionals account for 12 percent of the total in the most recent five-year period, which locates Cuba within the current of "brain drain," the loss of important human capital.

Studies of a possible "return to Cuba" and the conditions that would propitiate such a return reveal that 40 percent of individuals who have considered a possible return, or had not previously thought about it, say they would go back if the country's economy improves or if they do not succeed in achieving their goals for life abroad. As far as political factors, 80 percent of subjects who do not reject the idea of returning say that possible changes in the country's political system do not play a significant role. Alongside this analysis we may note the growth over the last four years of attempts to return from the United States and from other parts of the world. Those making such attempts are mostly elderly people and emigrants who left the country since the mid-1990s.[5]

The flow of temporary return visits by Cubans residing abroad has also been studied in the case of individuals living in the United States and Puerto Rico. The results show a sustained growth of interest in trips back to Cuba to visit and also to send remittances to relatives in Cuba. Similarly, these emigrants wanted travel restrictions lifted and travel costs lowered, more mechanisms to encourage family relations, and broader options to enjoy with their families during their stay in Cuba.[6]

Illegal departures by sea to the United States remained a component of Cuban emigration. One study shows that this phenomenon increased after 1998, especially in 1999, 2001, 2004, and during the first nine months of 2005. These figures are based on successful departures (as indicated by arrival in and admission to the United States) and on would-be emigrants returned to Cuba by the U.S. Coast Guard or by the services of third countries where those attempting to reach U.S. territory had landed. The total of such participants between 1995 and 2004 exceeded 21,900, not counting those who may have reached other shores without being sent back.[7]

The increase in those successfully reaching U.S. soil after 1999 was due in part to the growth of human smuggling operations. Moreover, given the difficulty in reaching U.S. shores without interception by the U.S. Coast Guard, new southern routes have been used for illegal departures, e.g., to Honduras, directly or by way of the Cayman Islands, so as to then cross through Mexico into the United States.[8]

Those opting to leave Cuba by sea are primarily young men (68 percent of them between 15 and 35 years old), with secondary or higher-secondary education, a notable level of unemployment (50 percent) and criminal records (20 percent), and 8 percent having made repeated attempts to depart illegally. Studies of the causes and motivations of the decision to emigrate point to economic elements, in a context where other social and political factors vary according to individual characteristics.[9]

In sum, in the early years of the twenty-first century, Cuba continued to display the traits that typify it as a country of emigrants, although Cuban emigration does not contribute greatly to overall worldwide migratory flows.

Cuban Migration Policy

Cuban migration policy has passed through varying periods from 1959 (when there were no travel restrictions in place) to the present. A continual influence on Cuban policy has been hostility and permanent aggression on the part of the United States as well as internal situations.[10]

Since 1961, the Cuban government has viewed migration as a matter of Cuba's national security. Thus, Cuban laws and regulations reflect, and are linked to, the intense counter-revolutionary activity and the utilization of U.S.–Cuba migration toward such counter-revolutionary ends. The application of Cuban law has been based on a series of criteria, mostly related to security issues, such as age, professional level, occupation, political affiliation, and conduct as a citizen.

In the late 1970s and early 1980s, the main shifts in Cuba's migratory policies took shape. Since then, there have been several periods of greater flexibility involving significant changes with respect to permanent and temporary departures from the country. The differential relations with Cuban emigrants in many regions of the planet, as compared with those in the United States and especially in Southern Florida, reveal elements of both continuity and change.

In the first decade of the twenty-first century, there has been a process of adjustment in Cuba's policy toward migration and emigrants, in accordance with the characteristics of the country of destination and domestic and international political realities. There are many challenges involved in developing and applying a policy that is modern, objective, and consonant with the demands of both citizens and national security.

U.S. Political Asylum Policy

U.S. immigration policy with respect to Cuba openly declares offers of political asylum. Its effect is to build up critical pressures on the Island, which are then released through periodic escape valves that produce cycles related to internal situations over the past 50 years.

In November 1966, the United States enacted the Cuban Adjustment Act, which more clearly and directly reaffirmed the special treatment of Cuban emigration by offering Cubans practically automatic status as political refugees. This Act affords an opportunity to change one's immigration status to permanent residence after one year and one day on U.S. soil, without having to leave the United States as regulations require all other immigrants to do. The Act was approved without an expiration date; it remains in force.

Beginning in 1991, when Cuba was hard-hit by economic crisis, the rafter phenomenon reappeared. Illegal departures by sea (including frustrated attempts) rose to more than 60,000 between 1991 and 1994, the year of the so-called "rafter crisis."[11] In the months leading up to this event, a new contradictory behavior by the U.S. government could be observed in granting or denying temporary visas for Cuban citizens to visit their families living in the United States. The number of temporary visas granted significantly declined, with allegations that many of those applying were potential immigrants. As many as 80 percent of such applications were denied, which in turn stimulated illegal departures and created an additional conflict associated with the migratory flow.

The rafter crisis generated a new wave of migration (36,900 people in the first nine months of 1994), which represented a continuation of the changes in Cuban migration patterns begun with Mariel.[12] In this new case, the economic crisis and its social effects were among the main detonators of the people explosion. Most of the rafters were young white men, with secondary or post-secondary education, motivated essentially by personal aspirations for fulfillment that they felt could not be met on the Island in the short term, given the situation there.

The pressures generated by the illegal departures culminated in public disorder, which led the Cuban government to decide on August 12 to eliminate the restrictions on this type of departure. Thus the histories of the events at Camarioca[13] in 1965 and Mariel in 1980 were repeated; in those incidents, too, legal migration from Cuba to the United States had been interrupted and illegal migration took on significant dimensions.

Faced with the new situation, the United States changed course in its immigration policy with respect to Cuba, intercepting the rafters before they could enter the United States and sending them temporarily to its naval base near Guantánamo, Cuban territory occupied by the United States, thereby breaking a tradition more than 35 years old. This U.S. naval base and Panamá received nearly 30,000 people who, for the moment, had no defined migratory status.

In this new situation, the dynamic of migratory relations between the United States and Cuba required a new understanding. The migratory accords signed in 1994 referred, in particular, to the control of illegal emigration by sea from Cuba to the United States; they signified a substantive change in U.S. migration policy toward the largest of the Antilles. Both parties committed themselves to preventing the use of violence in the act of emigration. For the first time in more than 36 years, the United States committed itself to return any Cubans intercepted on the high seas with the intention of entering the country, and Cuba declared that it would accept these individuals without taking any action against them.

This could have been a decisive step in discouraging such departures if the United States had treated Cuban migrants the same as it did the thousands of people from all over the globe who tried to enter U.S. territory in illegal or undocumented fashion. However, for this to occur, the United States would have had to end the special immigration policy for Cubans begun in 1959 and, in particular, to rescind the Cuban Adjustment Act. This did not happen.

Still, a key factor in encouraging legal and orderly emigration from the Island to the United States was broached when the figure of 20,000 annual visas, as a minimum, was considered. To fulfill this goal for the year 1994–95, the accords included the application of a set of powers inherent in U.S. immigration laws for the purpose of easing the awarding of such visas. That was exactly the opposite of what had been put in practice after the migration accords of 1984.

In addition, the United States established a special raffle or lottery for Cuba— separate from its annual lottery for the rest of the world—thus providing another avenue through which Cuban citizens could present their immigration requests.[14] This method of granting immigrant visas was oriented toward the population sectors of greatest interest to the United States. The visas were obtained by young emigrants, with education and professional training, the majority of them white, who presumably would not represent a burden to the United States because they could quickly enter the labor market.

Once these accords were put into effect in 1994–95, a legal, orderly, and regular migratory flow began. However, the illegal departures were controlled only to a degree because the Cuban Adjustment Act remained in effect. From 1995 to 2008, by the author's estimation, no more than 190,000 visas were awarded to Cuban emigrants. These were primarily granted through the lottery process, or for family reunification, or to political refugees, or to those "paroled" as household members of those who had obtained visas in one of the three primary ways.

One issue remained pending from the events of August 1994: the situation of the people interned in Guantánamo and Panamá. New talks were carried out, and on May 2, 1995, it was announced that an amendment to the accords had been signed, providing for the gradual admission of those interned Cubans to the United States. The "joint communiqué" of May 1995 underlined the prohibition of illegal migration by sea, with the commitment to return rafters captured on the high seas to the Island.

Nonetheless, the survival of the Cuban Adjustment Act provoked a different outcome. Though the application of the migration accords stopped further avalanches of rafters, it could not completely close this door because any Cuban emigrant who managed to reach U.S. territory by sea retained a high likelihood of not being returned to Cuba. The case of the boy Elián González revealed what the extreme results of such a practice could be.

This problem remains unsolved. Since 1998, the problem has included the thorny and dangerous component of human smuggling, organized and financed by groups of Cuban-Americans in Southern Florida, putting human lives at risk. Between 1997 and 2008, about 8,000 people reached the Florida coast by this means.

One of the myths that has persisted most strongly is that all Cubans migrating to the United States are members of a homogeneous group. The image remains durable largely because members of one part of the emigration define themselves as exiles. Nonetheless, the social class differences and other distinctions stemming from the socio-demographic characteristics of each migratory wave refute this. The political element is still present but the classification of those who migrate should reflect their motivations, social affiliations, life expectations, and ties to the Cuban social system.

U.S. Immigration Measures Enacted in 2006

On August 11, 2006, the U.S. Department of Homeland Security announced changes in its immigration policy with respect to Cuba, with the declared purpose of discouraging human smuggling and avoiding loss of life. The changes involved increasing opportunities for family reunification as well as an announced intention to work closely with the Congress to adopt more severe punishments for smugglers. At first glance, those actions would appear to complement the migration accords of 1994 and 1995. Nonetheless, a closer analysis suggests other interpretations according to the following.

The Bush Administration's Escalation of Aggression

The U.S. government's aspirations to overthrow the revolution took concrete form in plans for a supposed "transition in Cuba," defined in opposition to what was referred to as a "succession of power" (that is, a transfer of power without a change in political regime). The goal was to interfere with the historical continuity of the Cuban revolution by way of a deeper-than-ever alliance between the extreme-right dominating political power in the United States and the most recalcitrant sectors of the Cuban-American counter-revolution. The July 2006 "Report of the Commission for Assistance to a Free Cuba," under the direction of the secretaries of State and Commerce, devoted several paragraphs to migration. In essence, the writers blamed Cuba for events for which the United States bears the brunt of the responsibility. The report also referred to other related subjects, such as visits to Cuba by Cuban-Americans and their sending remittances to relatives. The report states that:

> While the 1994 Joint Communiqué obligates Cuba to take measures to ensure that migration is safe, legal, and orderly, the Cuban government continues to deny U.S. officials permission to monitor returned migrants outside of Havana; facilitates the departure of thousands of Cubans annually over the land borders into the United States via Mexico; deny [sic] exit permits to otherwise qualified Cuban citizens, making some people wait for years to emigrate; and flatly prohibit [sic] others from emigrating, including doctors and family members of government officials.[15]

It accuses Cuba of creating bureaucratic measures that keep the U.S. Interests Section in Havana from carrying out U.S. commitments under the accord and of using such mechanisms to continue manipulating migratory flows to the United States. It attempts to blame Cuba for supposed failures to comply with its obligations under the Accords and also for carrying out repeated and sustained maneuvers to obstruct legal, orderly, and safe emigration and thus to interfere with U.S. immigration policy.

The sections devoted to other forms of U.S. aggression against Cuba, such as the "Denial of Revenue to the Regime" and the "Regulations of the Office of Foreign Assets Control," are also connected in one way or another to aspects of the migration issue.

Such connections can be drawn with OFAC regulations that prohibit sending remittances to Cuba through third country institutions (that is, a requirement that all remittances be channeled through authorized U.S. firms) or those that prevent the transfer of remittances on pre-paid debit cards to Cuba.

These measures fit into a pattern of migratory regulations stemming from the Cuban Adjustment Act, the interpretation of the so-called "wet-foot, dry-foot" policy,[16] the restrictive rules for Cuban-American travel to the Island (which imply a distorted concept of what constitutes "family"), and the selectivity that favors certain segments of Cuban society for immigrant visas under the migration accord.

In evaluating the process of immigration change in the United States, one cannot forget the activities of the Cuban-American extreme right. In its attempts to pressure the U.S. government to harden its aggressive policy toward Cuba, the right questions the very existence of the migration accords of 1994–95 because of the enforcement (unjust, from this point of view) of the "wet-foot, dry-foot" policy.

Perceptions of the Internal Situation in Cuba

Fidel Castro's relinquishing of his responsibilities because of illness also had repercussions for the migration issue. The first reaction by the U.S. Coast Guard was to announce that there would be no special change in its activities. Nonetheless, press reports on that announcement referred to contingency plans for a crisis in Cuba and U.S. government fears of a new exodus, or of hundreds of Florida Cuban-Americans setting off in small boats in search of their families. This impression was confirmed by the governor of Florida in statements affirming the existence of a plan to prevent a massive wave of immigration, which could create a great risk to human life.

In this context, a new element emerged: for the first time, there was a public statement specifying the number of illegal Cuban immigrants that would be considered a threat to the United States. A report on the Florida governor's meeting with Coast Guard Commandant Thad Allen to review the plan for coping with a possible avalanche stated that 30 ships, patrol boats, helicopters, and Coast Guard airplanes would be deployed if the number of emigrants from Cuba were to reach 300 per week. If the figure were to rise to 700, Navy ships would also be deployed. And if an exodus rose to the level of 3,000 people per week, more than 80 airplanes and ships would join the fray. Since the signing of the Helms–Burton Act of 1996, U.S. administrations have stated repeatedly that massive departures from Cuba would be considered a threat to national security. However, until 2006 the precise minimum they would regard as a pretext for an intervention in Cuba had been unknown.

Another interesting event occurred on August 2, 2006, when the Bush administration showed concern about possible departures by sea from Florida to Cuba. White House spokesperson Tony Snow declared an intention to prevent movement in either direction:"It's also important . . . to tell people stay where you are. This is not a time for people to try to be getting in the water and going either way."[17]

Once again it became clear that, when the interests of Cuban-born counter-revolutionaries occasionally fail to coincide with those of the United States, the balance tilts toward the U.S. interests. Allowing uncontrolled migration between Florida and Cuba does not fit with U.S. policy premises. President William Clinton's decision to send Cuban rafters to Guantánamo, instead of permitting them access to Florida in 1994, indicated the same.

Measures Adopted

The first reports of a possible change in U.S. policy on Cuban immigration coincided with President George W. Bush's first public statements, after the news of the Cuban president's illness, at a Texas press conference on August 8, 2008. Although the U.S. government did not refer to possible changes, word filtered out that a "working draft" was circulating among legislators and government officials. This document contained a plan to put a brake on illegal immigration from Cuba and prevent the entrance of "regime officials who have suspicions of human rights abuses hanging over them."[18] The administration's idea, apparently, was to use the 20,000 annual visas pacted with the Cuban government to aid family reunification. In this way, they may have hoped to prevent Cuban-Americans from encouraging illegal entry by way of smugglers. In the award of immigrant visas, there would also be the goal of promoting the entrance of Cuban professionals, particularly doctors working in third countries who would have a right to take advantage of the 20,000 visa quota.

Changes in U.S. immigration policy announced in 2006 included an increase in the proportion of visas for family reunification, a denial of consideration for U.S. entry for those intercepted at sea who had family residents in the United States, the implementation of a system to inform relatives of the latter in the United States, the denial of migratory benefits to Cuban government officials who were "human rights violators," and the use of the power of parole for the benefit of Cuban doctors in third countries.[19]

The first of these policy changes was based on the joint communiqué of September 4, 1994, which permitted the United States to process a minimum quota of immigrants for the purpose of family reunification. Each year, a significant number of the individuals who applied for family reunification visas had failed to obtain them. The new plan sought to reduce this backlog by recognizing those individuals as a fourth category of immigrants. In addition to the lottery winners, the plan proposed to allow discretionary entrance of this category by means of parole. With this new policy, family reunification would account for approximately 60 percent of those receiving visas each year, with the rest going to lottery winners.

If the measure denying family reunification benefits to illegal Cuban migrants intercepted at sea were put into practice, it could discourage illegal departures by sea, although it would not be decisive so long as the Cuban Adjustment Act and its interpretation in the form of the "wet-foot, dry-foot" policy remained in effect. The denials could be seen as a continuation of the initial intent of the existing migration accords, but still partial, fragmentary, and not addressing the heart of the matter, which truly promotes and facilitates the arrival of Cuban rafters. Therefore, this measure seemed more a response to the U.S. immigration context, in which the subject of undocumented immigrants and smugglers occupies a central and controversial place, than a real attempt by the administration to definitively solve the migration problem with Cuba.

With respect to family reunification and the supposed preference offered by the new U.S. immigration measures for Cubans, these actions would not necessarily have a dissuasive effect on the approximately 55 percent of potential illegal emigrants who have no family in the United States, or whose relatives are uncles, aunts, or cousins who cannot request visas for them. A process of family reunification, which would allow petitions from a greater number of relatives and have a truly dissuasive role, should not be limited to the closest kinship relations, as the immigration laws now require.

Moreover, the implementation of procedures to inform U.S. relatives regarding Cubans intercepted at sea will increase the demand for news about those returned to Cuba and thus also for news about U.S. immigration authorities' attempts to visit those people or send representatives to do so.

Chronological Summary of Shifts in U.S. Migration Policy

2004

January. The United States announces its decision to suspend talks on migration and calls on Cuba to demonstrate willingness to discuss the issues put forward by the U.S. government in previous rounds: still-pending departures of individuals granted visas, a new call for applications for the visa lottery, a better-quality port to receive returned Cuban rafters, and the repatriation of additional Cubans deemed excludable by the United States. Cuba holds the U.S. side responsible for the suspension of talks and for obstructing the main mechanism for dialogue and reviewing fulfillment of the accords. Cuba points to the notable reduction in visas issued and the failure to return some rafters intercepted at sea, among other irregularities and violations by the United States.

2005

August. Thirty-one Cuban citizens die while trying to emigrate in a smuggling operation. Cuba holds the Bush administration responsible. The United States announces its issuance of visas has complied with the accords. It accuses Cuba of failing to grant exit permits to a set of people, refusing to facilitate a new round of lottery entrants, and submitting emigrants whom the U.S. Coast Guard has returned to the Island to persecution and alleged torture.

October. The Coast Guard in Miami recognizes that immigrant smuggling has increased, with smugglers using fast boats from South Florida to traffic in Cuban immigrants.

2006

February. Through an intervention by Fidel Castro on the television program Mesa redonda, Cuba denounces the aggressive policy of the United States, particularly its violation of the migration accords. The U.S. Secretary of State says that U.S. immigration policy with respect to Cuba has not changed.

March. In the United States, two residents of Cuban origin are convicted of illegal human trafficking and the death of a minor during the previous year.

April. Through the newspaper *Granma*, Cuba denounces continued human smuggling organized from Florida and it holds U.S. authorities and the Cuban Adjustment Act responsible.

July. As a result of Florida's review of contingency plans for a possible exodus from Cuba, the numbers of immigrants that would trigger a response by that state's government become known.

August. After Fidel Castro's health status became public knowledge on July 31, a White House spokesperson declared that immigration policies directed toward safe, orderly, and legal migration from Cuba will remain in force. The State Department makes mention of Cuba's supposed lack of compliance, repeating charges made in the past.

December. The European press reports the fulfillment of targets for U.S. immigration visas granted to Cubans and an increase in those issued for temporary visits. The Coast Guard announces that it is prepared to deal with a possible mass exodus from Cuba.

2007

January. The New York Times publishes an article on preparations being made at Guantánamo naval base for a possible mass exodus from Cuba.

March. The Department of Homeland Security coordinates military exercises in Florida to practice confronting a flood of Cuban emigrants.

July. Cuba calls attention to an under-fulfillment of the terms of the migration accords in the granting of visas to Cuban migrants and repeats its condemnation of the Cuban Adjustment Act and the "wet-foot, dry-foot" policy. The United States admits to the under-fulfillment but it blames Cuba, repeating past arguments about a need for more staff in its Interests Section in Havana and a delay in issuing Cuban visas to U.S. officials. The U.S. Bureau of Citizenship and Immigration Services (USCIS) announces the extension of benefits under the Cuban Adjustment Act to citizens of third countries who are descendants of Cubans.

August. Cuba denounces the sending of illegal Cuban emigrants intercepted at sea to the U.S. naval base at Guantánamo.

November. USCIS announces the creation of a new program of permits for family reunification.

2008

April. The United States announces that the program of permits for family reunification is now in effect.

May. The United States brings charges of illegal human trafficking against more than 20 South Florida residents.

October. Word spreads of new indictments of Cuban-Americans for smuggling and kidnapping immigrants from Cuba.

2009

The administration of Barack Obama, representing hopes and opportunities for change, inherits the history of 2000–08. The new administration faces a complex agenda in both domestic and foreign policy because U.S. world hegemony has been breached in many areas and even its ideological allies in Europe have disagreed on more than one occasion with the political actions of the United States.

In this context, Cuba is not one of the Democratic administration's main priorities (as has also been the case at other times during the past 50 years). This does not mean an end to the policy of hostility, aggression, and provocation that the northern empire has carried out against the Cuban revolution. The continuation of the blockade is the most palpable evidence.

Migration issues continue to offer one of the main channels of communication, exchange, and even new measures of rapprochement that can reduce tensions and offer new opportunities for relations between the two countries. To analyze the possible future actions of the United States with respect to Cuban migration issues, we must also consider the domestic U.S. context with respect to immigration overall and the influence of the Cuban community in South Florida.

Immigration Policy Context in the United States

The main factors to take into consideration are:

- The tightening of immigration policy during the Bush administration.
- The events of September 11, 2001. Criminalization of immigrants and immigration.
- The problem of the borders and the ineffectiveness of border control measures given the size of migratory flows.
- The tendency to link national security to the historical phenomenon of immigration and the implementation of measures affecting the human rights of migrants. Growing vulnerability among the undocumented.
- Gradual changes in immigration laws and the structure and function of the related agencies. The National Security Law and the split of the Immigration and Naturalization Service (INS) into two agencies charged with controlling immigration. The Border Protection, Anti-terrorism, and Illegal Immigration Control Act: new penalties for smugglers, retroactive employee verification systems for employers, authorization of state police to demand immigration documents, construction of a wall on the Mexican border, and other measures.
- The implications of the growth of the Latino presence in the United States to more than 40 million, and the factors that stimulate such immigration.
- Ongoing debate over immigration in the legislature, courts, executive branch, and society. Possibility of a bipartisan initiative for a federal immigration reform and fulfillment of presidential campaign promises.

Influence of the Cuban Community in South Florida

Main factors:

- Demographic growth resulting from the continuing migration from Cuba made up of different social actors than those comprising the first waves. The emigrants of the 1990s and early 2000s and their positions toward Cuba.
- Issues that mobilize that community: remittances, travel to Cuba, family reunification, return to the country, blockade, resumption of diplomatic relations, and transition toward democracy.
- Questioning of the "wet-foot, dry-foot" policy but not of the Cuban Adjustment Act. Human smuggling operations and the participation of families

who choose this as the fastest and most practical method for those who do not fit the stipulations of the migration accords.

- Growing distance between the positions of the Cuban-American ultra-right, including its three representatives in Congress, the highly belligerent counter-revolutionary organization, the so-called moderates (within the political spectrum of South Florida Cuban-Americans), and the broader sweep of that population.
- Varying abilities of distinct Cuban-American political and social sectors to affect the new administration's agenda in terms of immigration policy either in favor of or in opposition to its current form.
- Judgments about the impact on that community and other Cuban-American settlements in the United States of substantive changes in U.S. immigration policy with respect to Cuba as it has been for the past 50 years. In particular, possible elimination of the preferences and privileges enjoyed by Cuban immigrants and their categorization as political refugees.
- Presence in the United States of more than 1.25 million people of Cuban origin whose economic, socio-demographic, and cultural positions are higher than those of the majority of Latino immigrant groups in the country. The present and future actions of that enclave in South Florida and its relations within the larger society of the United States and with Cuba as well as its role in encouraging migration.

Continuation of Migration Talks

On July 14, 2009, a new round of migration talks between Cuba and the United States got underway, the first since the United States broke off talks in 2004. Previously, in April 2009, the Obama administration had lifted the restrictions on travel to Cuba by Cuban-Americans. Less than 30 days later, the administration proposed to Cuba a resumption of talks, and on May 31, Cuba agreed.

In this twenty-first round of migration talks, Havana re-affirmed its commitment to the existing bilateral agreements and presented a proposal for a new accord with the goals of guaranteeing legal, safe, and orderly emigration and achieving more effective cooperation in confronting human smuggling. A U.S. state department communiqué announced its intention to keep the talks centered on the best way to advance a policy of safe, legal, and orderly migration. Both parties repeated their main demands.

On February 19, 2010 a new round of talks took place in Havana. As in the previous round in New York, other issues besides migration were discussed. Cuba repeated its July proposals for cooperation in confronting drug traffic, terrorism, and human smuggling as well as protecting the environment and confronting natural disasters. According to official statements, Cuba expressed its willingness to sign an anti-drug agreement with the United States.

The basic issues identified by Cuba for a process of dialogue leading toward improved bilateral relations have been:

- Lifting the economic, commercial, and financial blockade.
- Dropping Cuba from the list of terrorist countries.
- Rescinding the Cuban Adjustment Act and the "wet-foot, dry-foot" policy.
- Compensation for economic and personal damage.
- Return of the land occupied by the U.S. naval base near Guantánamo.
- An end to radio and television aggression against Cuba by the United States.
- An end to financing of internal subversion.
- A request for the release of the five Cuban anti-terrorists in U.S. prisons for the past 11 years. [20]

Related to the February migration meeting in Havana, the atmosphere for dialogue grew darker because of a separate meeting that the U.S. delegation held with alleged Cuban dissidents. Nonetheless, through a declaration by the Foreign Relations Minister, Cuba repeated its willingness to "sustain a respectful dialogue on any issue with the United States government as long as it is a dialogue between equals, without prejudice to independence, sovereignty, and self-determination."[21]

As a result, a possible short- and medium-term scenario for migration relations between the United States and Cuba could be characterized by:

- Fulfillment of all parts of the existing migration accords while including further study of other migration-related issues in future talks, especially regarding communications. This would mean a return to the last years of the previous Democratic administration, using the issue of migration as a possible communication channel between the two sides, as has also occurred at other times over the past five decades.
- Fulfillment of electoral promises: elimination of restrictions on the sending of remittances and on travel to Cuba while opening the means to talks about migration issues, among other topics, though the equilibrium of such a process would remain precarious and subject to possible threats.

Although the key measure to change in U.S. immigration policy toward Cuba would be to end the Cuban Adjustment Act, this is unlikely in the short or medium term, that is, in the first or a possible second term of the Obama administration. Nonetheless, this administration is faced with a set of measures and precedents favorable toward making progress in the normalization of migration relations, which would be of value given the pressures swirling from the larger immigration problem facing the Union. At the same time, such progress on migration could allow for channels of communication and dialogue with Cuba, taking advantage of the Cuban side's repeated willingness to discuss any subject on a plane of full equality.

Cuba, for its part, faces significant challenges in the area of migration, in particular toward the United States, which it has to face with objectivity and with regard to its national interests. It needs a strategy to confront an erosion of its population resulting from a combination of temporary and permanent emigration. Such a strategy must take into account profiles of age, gender, and professional-technical training in various regions of the country. There is also a need to foresee a return to previous Cuban migration patterns, including possible emigration over the next 10 to 15 years, taking into consideration (among other factors): migration currents and tendencies in the region of the Caribbean where Cuba is located; the country's traditions in this regard, especially in eastern Cuba; the economic and social situation of the region, especially in labor force terms; and Cuban perspectives on society and labor in the context of the Island's economy and of globalization and interdependence among nations.

Cuba must assess the complex problem of brain drain and loss of talent, a phenomenon now present in almost every society, from a perspective that considers all professional sectors and with an eye toward policies that favor social and personal development. Cuba must perfect its legal and constitutional provisions regarding emigration, which will require new legislation that takes into account the political, economic, and social importance of this issue. The current state of such regulations indicates the need, within the Cuban legal system, for a branch of law dealing with migration rights so as to make the legal system more efficient as a means of social reform. This suggests legislative review of all the current regulations. Each of the above points implies specific effects on Cuba's migration policies and specifically its policy toward emigration, both of which involve important challenges in which national security cannot be relegated to a secondary plane.

Notes

1 Antonio Aja Díaz, *Al cruzar las fronteras* (Havana: CEDEM-UNFPA, 2009), 108–10.
2 This was a period of economic crisis with deep social impact, caused by the collapse of the socialist bloc and the disappearance of the USSR, which had been Cuba's main economic and political partner.
3 Antonio Aja Díaz, "Cuban Emigration in the 1990s," *Cuban Studies*, no. 26 (2000): 1–25.
4 Aja Díaz, Al cruzar, 199–212.
5 Ibid., 201–10.
6 Study by Consuelo Martín and the author, investigating the temporary return of Cubans living in the United States and Puerto Rico. Fondos bibliográficos del Centro de Estudios de la Migración Internacional (CEMI), Universidad de La Habana, 2004.
7 Antonio Aja Díaz, Consuelo Martín, and Magali Martín, "Estudios de las salidas ilegales por vía marítima desde Cuba hacia los Estados Unidos. Continuidad del análisis a partir de los Acuerdos migratorios de 1994–1995." Fondos bibliográficos del CEMI, Universidad de La Habana, 2006.
8 Aja Díaz, Al cruzar, 199–212.
9 Consuelo Martín and Antonio Aja Díaz, op. cit., 24–40.
10 Antonio Aja Díaz, Al cruzar, 129–131.

11   Ibid., 142.
12   The preceding very large-scale rafter crisis had taken place in 1980, leaving from Cuba's Mariel harbor for Florida.
13   The first of the three very large-scale rafter crises took place in 1965, leaving from Cuba's Camarioca harbor; the next two such crises took place in 1980 and 1994.
14   Ruth Ellen Wasem, "Cuban Migration to the United States: Policy and Trends, Congressional Research Service Report R40566" (Washington DC: Congressional Research Service, 2009). According to Wasem, "eligible registrants must be Cuban citizens between 18 and 55 years of age. They also must be able to answer 'yes' to two of the following three questions. Have you completed secondary school or a higher level of education? Do you have at least three years of work experience? Do you have any relatives residing in the United States? Once selected through the lottery, the successful applicants are given parole status with a visa that is good for six months."
15   Commission for Assistance to a Free Cuba (Washington DC: July 2006), www.cubavsbloqueo.cu.
16   This is a policy applied by the Clinton and subsequent administrations to undocumented Cuban immigrants, attempting to reach the United States by sea, who are captured by the U.S. Coast Guard. When captured at sea, they are regarded as "wet foot" and are returned to the Cuban government as stipulated in the U.S.–Cuba migration agreements of 1994 and 1995. If they reach U.S. soil, they are regarded as "dry foot," whereupon they are not returned to Cuba and have the right to regularize their immigration status in the United States under the Cuban Adjustment Act of 1966.
17   Tony Snow, "Press conference," AFP, Washington DC, August 2006.
18   "Con Castro enfermo, los Estados Unidos se preparan ante posible ola migratoria," Reuters, Miami, August 2, 2006.
19   Tony Snow, "Press Conference," August 2006.
20   Antonio Guerrero, Fernando González, Gerardo Hernández, Ramón Labañino and René González were arrested by the FBI in September 1998.
21   "Declaración del Ministerio de Relaciones Exteriores de la República de Cuba," Havana, February 20, 2010, www.cubaminrex.cu.

13

THE SUBJECT(S) OF ACADEMIC AND CULTURAL EXCHANGE

PARADIGMS, POWERS, AND POSSIBILITIES

SHERYL LUTJENS

Academic, educational, and cultural exchanges between Cuba and the United States have created a complex field of relations in which agency, power, and the possibilities of paradigmatic change are at play. The difficulties of academic and cultural exchange in the first three decades of the Cuban Revolution were often obdurate ones, as have been the challenges and problems marking the 1990s and 2000s. U.S. Cuba policy has aimed to control academic and cultural exchanges, though with little understanding of the relations of education, intellectuals, and knowledge production on their own terms. Using economic transactions as the instrument of control and disciplining historical relations through security narratives, past and present policies have sidestepped the realities of globalization and increasingly transnational dynamics in education, the production of knowledge, and informational technologies that facilitate the rapid circulation of data, ideas, and cultural practices.[1] Those engaged in creating and carrying out exchanges—academic professionals, students, intellectuals, performance artists, others and ourselves—have an important place in U.S.–Cuban relations for obvious and less obvious reasons. Locating the cooperation that marks exchange relations within the dynamics of their historical context, this essay uses the well known and the less visible experiences, achievements, and challenges to reread, in particular, academic/intellectual agencies.[2]

Histories, 1959–89 and Beyond

The history of academic relations and cultural exchanges between Cuba and the United States after the 1959 revolution can be explained in terms of bilateral politics, state policies controlling them, and efforts to renegotiate and extend interactions. Elements of this history, or perhaps competing histories, have been described, analyzed, and interpreted by a number of scholars before and after 1989, though the number of overviews is quite small.[3] The development of academic and cultural relations after 1959 is thus in part a story of persistence and expansion;[4] accomplishments, including the creation of the interdisciplinary field called Cuban Studies, are especially striking given the ongoing difficulties confronting old and new connections and collaborations.

After 1959

The conditioning factors of U.S.–Cuban bilaterality, including the breaking of diplomatic relations, hostility, and Cold War ideology, explain in part the impediments to relations that were seeded after 1959.[5] What Stephenson calls the period of "frozen flows" ended with President Jimmy Carter's opening of travel to Cuba. Already, students and academics had acted on their interest in knowing Cuba; U.S. and other foreign academics conducted research in the early years, producing some of the classic studies of the young revolution; the Venceremos Brigade was created in 1969; and the Center for Cuban Studies, launched in New York City in 1972, organized the first institutionally sponsored meeting between U.S. and Cuban scholars in December 1973.[6] With Carter's opening of travel and new quasi-diplomatic relations embodied in the Interests Sections in Havana and Washington DC, interactions grew. Two U.S. senators traveled to Havana in 1977 and in October 1977, Cuban academics traveled to Houston for the Latin American Studies Association (LASA) International Congress. A formal exchange was established with Johns Hopkins School for Advanced Studies and the University of Havana in 1979.[7] The change in regulations under the Carter administration facilitated "musical openings" as well, including U.S. tours by Pablo Milanés, Silvio Rodríguez, Irakere, and the Conjunto Folklórico Nacional, among others.[8]

In the 1980s, the Ronald Reagan administration reasserted official anti-communism and reinstated restrictions on academic exchanges. The general license for researchers was created in 1982, yet Presidential Proclamation 5377, October 1985, restricted travel to the United States by Cubans; it prohibited entry by officers or employees of the government of Cuba or the Cuban Communist Party. Exchanges continued, however.[9] In 1983, the Centro de Estudios sobre América and LASA signed a formal agreement to create topical research groups with members from the United States and Cuba; the project was funded by the Ford Foundation and lasted for more than a decade. The so-called Berman Amendment (1988) limited the President's ability to control (via licensing) the import and export of informational materials from Cuba, and by 1991 it included publications, recorded materials (music), paintings, drawings, and sculpture.

After 1989

The terrain of academic and cultural exchange had many firm points of contact linking individuals, groups, institutions, and nongovernmental organizations, and despite the setbacks of Republican rule under Reagan and the damaging legislation enacted by Congress in the first part of the 1990s, collaboration expanded into the 1990s. The reconstitution of the world order after 1989 undermined in some ways the national security logic of anti-communism, of course, and changes under William Clinton maintained anti-Castroism with a new interventionism expressed in the Cuban Democracy Act of 1992 and the Helms–Burton Act of 1996. Travel to, and exchanges with, Cuba would now be viewed from an "instrumentalist" vantage, seen that is, as an instrument for achieving the collapse of the Cuban regime.[10] More change was seen with the authorization in October 1995 of "travel related to educational activities," permitting specific licenses for undergraduate study and transactions related to sponsoring a Cuban scholar to teach or engage in scholarly activity in a U.S. university. Cultural relations were encouraged; in Spring 1999, for instance, the Baltimore Orioles played an all-star team in Cuba and then in Baltimore. In May 1999, the general license for research travel by full-time professionals was restored, specific licenses (up to two-year licenses) authorized travel for educational activities by students at all levels as well as for non-academic study that encouraged two-way people-to-people exchange between Cuba and the United States. This Track II of people-to-people exchange, though intended to subvert the Cuban regime, did further open cultural doors. In 1996, the popular Cuban group Los Van Van traveled to the United States and "over the next five years, most of the major figures in contemporary Cuban music made U.S. debuts."[11] Global Exchange organized 5,000 people for its trips to Cuba between 1995 and 2005.[12]

The legislation of the 1990s and the subversive intentions of the Clinton administration produced strong responses from the Cuban state, heralded by Armed Forces Minister Raúl Castro's April 1996 public criticism of several research institutions that regularly engaged in international exchanges. As summarized in *Retreat from Reason: U.S.–Cuba Academic Exchange and the Bush Administration*, a study published in 2006, "Research agendas were revised, new approval procedures were put in place for collaborations with U.S. entities, exit permits for scholars—especially for travel to the United States—became more difficult to obtain, and the pace of work on existing collaborative projects slowed."[13]

Problems of entry and access have characterized academic, student, and cultural exchange relations over time. Writing at the end of the 1980s, Linda Fuller explored a range of difficulties with fieldwork in the "forbidden terrain" of Cuba,[14] including those created by U.S. policy and others reflecting Cuban positions: the limits of research funding, problems of communication, restrictions on travel to Cuba, and a "dearth of information on the country available in the United States."[15] All of these contributed to a withering of the professional and institutional relations that are needed in any research context but perhaps especially in Cuba. In turn, the withered relations affect access for fieldwork. Approval of research projects requires institutional support and securing it could be a years-long project. As Fuller wrote, "Against the backdrop of extreme acrimony which has characterized U.S.–Cuba relations for a long while, linkages—both personal and professional—have atrophied in both directions, and as a consequence many Cubans in positions to facilitate the research of a North American social scientist are sometimes understandably reticent to do so."[16]

Four notable developments in exchange relations have resolved many of the problems of research in forbidden terrain identified by Fuller, though not all of them. Foundation funding has been a critical factor in the expansion of individual research and group and institutional collaborations.[17] It has become easier to find funding for dissertation research in Cuba and some Cubans have been funded for work in the United States.

Communication and information capacities have expanded dramatically since the early days of post-revolutionary academic exchanges. Especially in the last decade, the transition from telephone calls and faxes to Internet and electronic transfer of documents has been astoundingly rapid. Professional communication also blossomed with increased Cuban participation in international and U.S.-based scholarly associations. At least two dozen professional associations in the United States had Cuban members or engaged with Cuba by the early 2000s.[18] The Latin American Studies Association is a uniquely good example. Following the 1977 International Congress, Cuban participation was consistent into the 2000s.[19]

The travel of students to Cuba was another sign of the expanding educational collaborations. By 2003, the Office of Foreign Assets Control (OFAC) had granted 760 two-year licenses to U.S. educational institutions. Stephenson reports at least 35 study abroad programs in Cuba in 2002.[20] By 2004, Cuba was 14th on the list of destinations of U.S. college students.

The flourishing academic and educational cooperation described thus far created an array of spaces defined by different sorts of disciplinary and personal commitments, institutional locations, and purposes. Looking for the spaces and relations of cooperation that thrived in the 1990s (and before) requires more, however. New university programs helped reshape the landscape of exchange, often building on the work and efforts of individual scholars. The David Rockefeller Center for Latin American Studies at Harvard, for example, created a Cuban Studies Program with funding from the MacArthur Foundation, the Ford Foundation, and the Christopher Reynolds Foundation. By 2005, it had hosted more than 60 Cuban scholars, sponsored six academic conferences, edited two collections of essays by Cuban and U.S. scholars, and maintained a systematic exchange with the Pedro Kourí Institute in Havana.[21]

Less visible or recognized are other collaborations, including the scholarship program for U.S. students at the Latin American School of Medicine outside of

Havana. The first U.S. students entered in spring 2001 and by spring 2009 there were more than 119 students from 27 different states (and Puerto Rico and Washington DC). Also marked by the distinctive initiative of individuals is the Radical Philosophers Association's Cuba Conference. It started with a trip of six philosophers to Havana in May 1982; the 20th such gathering was held in Havana in 2009.[22] Another academic collaboration similarly sustained over the years by personal effort is the *Seminario Científico sobre la Calidad de la Educación: Intercambio de Experiencias de Profesionales Cubanos y Norteamericanos* (Scientific Seminar on the Quality of Education: Interchange of Experiences of Cuban and North American Professionals). During 15 years of collaboration, there have been more than 400 participants (some of whom return year after year) and the *Seminario* moved from province to province, unlike other collaborations that develop solely within Havana.[23]

The outcomes of the first three decades of post-revolutionary academic cooperation are many. It will be useful to briefly summarize more of them before turning to inspect impediments, challenges, and agencies in the 2000s. Academic, educational, and cultural exchange has fostered published scholarship in many formats. Work by Cuban authors has been translated for publication in edited volumes, journals, and as single-author monographs; in turn, there has been publication of articles, chapters, and books by U.S. scholars in Cuba.[24] By the 2000s new generations of researchers had emerged, both in Cuba and the United States. Cultural estrangement created by bilateral hostilities has been mitigated by access to film, literature, and performance artists, and the freer flow of cultural and scholarly materials across frontiers. Cuban Studies began to construct disciplinary boundaries, noted by debates and reflection.[25] A Section for Scholarly Relations with Cuba was created within the Latin American Studies Association in the second half of the 1990s. There are several centers for the study of Cuba in the United States, including the Bildner Center's Cuba Project which organizes annual symposia to "reflect and advance excellent academic work in Cuban Studies." *Cuban Studies*, the journal founded in 1970, has been joined by *Temas*, published in Havana, and the *International Journal of Cuban Studies*, an electronic journal published by the International Institute for the Study of Cuba in London.

2000–08

The post-9/11 period of academic and cultural relations seems particularly complicated. U.S. policy regarding educational and other exchanges, framed by the War on Terror, is fraught with the contradictory logics of the George W. Bush administration's intentions. The Homeland Security state aimed to tighten borders, affecting entry of international scholars and students, even as the ends of public diplomacy (and the economic benefits of hosting international students) became more pressing. Bush's "retreat from reason" prioritized subversion, strengthened a sanctions program that was criticized roundly by the international community, and successfully closed many doors to collaboration. Generating resistance and revealing other ongoing challenges of academic and cultural collaboration, anti-Castroism prevailed.

The Bush administration's Cuba strategy took shape against the backdrop of Homeland Security and the War on Terror. Delays with issuing visas reflected new rules for all who would enter U.S. territory, including the exclusion of those who disagreed with U.S. policy. The Initiative for a New Cuba was announced in 2003, its principal strategies being increased family travel by Cuban-Americans and an end to the people-to-people cultural programs that were sending some 40,000 U.S. citizens to Cuba annually for non-academic educational experiences. Licenses were not renewed, for example; the request for renewal of licenses by the Metropolitan Museum of Art and the American Museum of Natural History were denied.[26] New regulations identified more clearly which actors in Cuba were likely agents for change and thus U.S. support, targeting support for opposition groups through workshops, performances, and humanitarian activities. More striking still were the changes advocated in 2004 by the Commission for Assistance to a Free Cuba whose 454-page report provided plans for a post-Castro Cuba, a strategy for hastening change, and the basis for reforming the rules of engagement with Cuba. In June 2004, new regulations were promulgated that eliminated fully-hosted travel; abolished the people-to-people category completely; restricted study abroad to programs of 10 or more weeks in duration (among other changes to study abroad); eliminated travel by high school students; reasserted that attending conferences does not constitute research activity; and severely limited family travel by Cuban-Americans.[27]

The effects of the new regulations were swift and dramatic. Short courses, summer courses, and travel by individual undergraduate students were eliminated and stringent new requirements meant that many existing semester programs in Cuba closed. In 2003, approximately 210,000 people from the United States traveled to Cuba (in all categories). By 2006, there had been an 80 percent decline in family travel and a 90 percent decline in all other licensed travel. Just as visas were denied to international scholars, they were also denied to Cuban academics and performers. For example, only 20 percent of the applications from the Ministry of Culture in the January 2004–June 2005 period received visas.[28] Writing in 2006, Robin Moore lamented that "procedures currently required to invite Cuban performers into the United States are so complex, expensive, and time consuming that they have effectively put an end to all such visits … Cuba may be the only country in the world to be treated in this extreme fashion."[29] The extremes of visa politics are seen in the systematic denial of visas for Cuban scholars to participate in LASA congresses.[30] The deeper politics of visas are revealed by the granting of asylum to 50 of the 53 Cubans who were performing in the "Havana Night Show" in Las Vegas at the time of the LASA Congress in 2004.[31]

Other negative effects of the new restrictions were less visible. Foundations were affected, constrained by the larger post-9/11 fears that produced the Patriot Act and its multiple restrictions on freedoms for academic institutions and individuals, but also by OFAC regulations that narrowed the scope of educational and related activities that could be funded. OFAC launched a ban on publishing the work of scholars from embargoed countries, including Cuba, though litigation resulted in the creation of more ample rules that actually benefitted scholarly collaboration. The José Martí National Library in Cuba did a study of the ongoing effects of the sanctions program and its ratcheting up of restrictions on academics and students. The number of books received declined from 3,293 in 1992 to 872 in 2001 (and copies of journals from 4,623 in 1992 to 2,546 in 2001); while in 2003, 35 North American scholars used specialized reading rooms in the national library, only 8 did in 2005.[32] And access to OCLC (Online Computer Library Center) services was denied in 2003. The dwindling of institutional exchanges contrasts starkly with the U.S. Interests Section's activities. From 2000 to 2005, the U.S. Interests Section distributed over 269,000 books and magazines, some of which were resold (supposedly not permitted); the poundage of shipments to the Interests Section grew from 51,000 to 155,000.[33]

OFAC enforcement and episodes of surveillance contributed to the confusion and fear surrounding legal travel to Cuba. Three administrative law judges were recruited to hold hearings about OFAC actions against individuals as the pursuit of violations grew heated. More than 900 individuals received fines or settled informally with OFAC for violations of the regulations between 2004 and 2009, with at least $1.2 million in penalties collected.[34] Academics and educational institutions have also been targeted by OFAC. The Center for Cross-Cultural Study in Amherst, Massachusetts, a study-abroad provider, made a settlement of $15,000 with OFAC regarding alleged problems with subcontracting. Augsburg College (Minnesota) paid a $9,000 fine for unlicensed travel by its students from 2000 to 2004; Pace University paid a $5,600 fine in 2004 for booking a trip with a travel agency without a proper license (the trip was never taken!).[35] Surveillance by the FBI, mentioned by Fuller as a post-research hazard in the 1980s, continues to be both a real and imagined threat to those who travel to Cuba,[36] one that can take its place among the Patriot Act surveillance schemes.

The security climate raised issues of academic freedom, and these issues were taken up by those wishing to defend academic and cultural exchanges with Cuba. LASA formed a Task Force in 2004, for example, and, with the second blanket denial of visas for Cuban scholars to participate in its congresses, more than 1,500 members of LASA signed a letter to U.S. Secretary of State Condoleezza Rice decrying the violation of academic freedom. The leadership decided thereafter to relocate congresses to third countries to avoid direct U.S. restrictions on Cuban participation. The Emergency Coalition to Defend Educational Travel (ECDET) was created in 2004. With 450 individual academics as members of the coalition, the principal strategy of ECDET has been a lawsuit claiming that OFAC actions were arbitrary (an administrative law problem) and a violation of constitutional rights. ECDET did not win its case (or the appeal), although a lawsuit filed by the ACLU against Florida's state-level ban on travel to Cuba by faculty and students was successful. The Venceremos Brigade launched annual travel challenges, highlighting its resistance to the licensing regime. Another example of academic initiative in the crucible of the 2000s is the "Retreat from Reason" project. Funded by a small grant from the Ford Foundation, the project's goal was to analyze the state of academic and educational relations under the Bush administration and make recommendations for change.[37]

Maintaining existing exchanges is surely an achievement, and there was other forward movement in this period. The University of California, for example, created a six-campus consortium called the UC–Cuba Academic Initiative. Sponsored by the UC system as one of its Multicampus Research Units and Programs, the goals of the UC–Cuba Academic Initiative were formalized in January 2006, reflecting research, education, and information activities already underway. The UC–Cuba Academic Initiative organized a website, trips to Cuba for consortium faculty, lectures and workshops for graduate students, and biannual national conferences. Also notable is the joint statement by Sergio Jorge Pastrana and Michael T. Clegg, published as an editorial in *Science* in October 2008. Recognizing the historical status of the national academies of science in both Cuba and the United States and many areas of potential cooperation, their statement stressed that "the value system of science—openness, shared communication, integrity, and a respect for evidence—provides a framework for open engagement and could encourage evidence-based approaches that cross from science into the social, economic, and political arenas. ... scientific contacts could build important cultural and social links among peoples."[38]

The Bush administration's retreat from reason helped to reshape actors and agencies and in that process raised additional questions about the nature of, and need for, academic exchange. While U.S. policy and regulations tend to preoccupy academics, there has also been change on the Cuban side, including the insistence that researchers enter with research rather than tourist visas and the centralization of group educational travel planning in Havanatur.

One nagging question concerns communication and information capacities. While modernization has aided communication flows, trust in technology does not resolve all problems and the internet and the virtual circulation of information has created others. Given the still sparse coverage of the population in Cuba—and considering the island as a whole and not simply Havana, it cannot be assumed that all Cuban academics have access to technology, nor is access always effective. In Cuba, the complications of technology are multiple, ranging from the bandwidth problem to software costs and control, individual versus collective access, and the role of the U.S. Interests Section in Havana. The digital divide is real and more understanding of imperfect conditions is warranted, even as the electronic decade becomes an "open" decade where access through the internet is vastly improved.

The issues of access posed by questions about technology and capacity are important. It is quite possible to conduct research without traveling to "forbidden lands." It depends on the nature of the research project, however, and there are questions of quality that are associated with research projects as such. These include the "anecdotal methodology" (accidental conversations and casual encounters become evidence) and work done in the interstices of academic exchange structures, among others. Problems of entry and access can exacerbate bad habits and sometimes unethical behavior where research bypasses agreements made in Cuba and with the home U.S. university, claiming that the search for "truth" requires ignoring the rules and norms governing research in any setting. The pride with which such behavior is reported is probably related to the ideological tensions that still exist with regard to studies of Cuba. Even more problematic is the autopoetic reproduction of these ideological practices via the cottage industry of USAID funding. Poor research practices damage academic freedom and contribute to the faulty information that surfaces in U.S. policy-making about Cuba.

Finally, the years of restricted access to the United States have affected Cuban academics who specialize in the United States or have research partners who work in the United States. Important as relations with the U.S. academics may be, however, it is also important to recognize that Cuban scholars and scientists have relations with scholars in other countries around the world.

Anticipating the Obama Administration

Forecasts that U.S. President Barack Obama would make significant change in the Cuba sanctions program were exaggerated, likely the result of wishful rather than observant thinking. With a security structure inherited nearly wholesale from the previous administration, one that is deeply involved in controlling research, educational, and cultural exchange with Cuba, what real options are there for change?

There is noticeable improvement in some of the circumstances that contribute to the possibilities of educational and cultural exchange between the United States and Cuba. For example, there has been some opening of the borders that closed after September 11 to international students. There is an apparent change in the Obama administration position on other sorts of visas. Secretary of State Hillary Clinton ended the exclusion of two scholars whose visa denials had previously been challenged in court. Jameel Jaffer, Director of the ACLU National Security Project, stated that "the decision to end the exclusion of Professors Habib and Ramadan is a welcome sign that the Obama administration is committed to facilitating, rather than obstructing, the exchange of ideas across international borders."[39]

Against this backdrop, there are several measurable changes in academic and cultural relations since the inauguration of Obama in January 2009. In April 2009, Obama announced the liberalization of travel and remittances by Cuban-Americans; travel has since increased. Cuban officials reported 250,000 Cuban-American visits in 2009, compared with 170,000 in 2008.[40] U.S. cultural performance groups, both amateur and professional, are traveling to Cuba and Cuban performers are granted visas to enter the United States. Cultural exchanges are thus recuperating, demonstrating not only the willingness of both governments to cooperate but also the high expectations for this area of collaboration and creativity. While in 2007, OFAC approved licenses for only seven public performances in Cuba, in 2008, it approved 21 licenses for performances (most were for athletic events); by late summer 2009 Obama's OFAC had approved 20 licenses.[41] In March 2009, *U.S. News & World Report* posted the pro-cultural exchange views of Fernando Rojas Gutiérrez, Vice-Minister in the Ministry of Culture: "For both our peoples it's helpful to have an intense cultural exchange. There is a willingness from the Cuban side to appreciate American culture."[42]

Revived cultural collaboration includes research visits in July 2009 by actors Robert Duvall, James Caan, and Bill Murray. In August, 12 Cuban performers traveled to Tuscaloosa, Alabama to collaborate on a joint theatrical production of *A Midsummer Night's Dream* for performance in Havana.[43] Students from USA Youth Debates traveled to Cuba, organized by New College (Sarasota, Florida) professor John Tredway (who had been denied permission on three previous requests)[44] and Juanes held a "Paz sin Fronteras" concert in Havana's Plaza de la Revolución with a million in attendance, one of them Bisa Williams, Head of the U.S. Office of Cuban Affairs.[45] Global Exchange, a San Francisco nonprofit organization that sent groups to Cuba under people-to-people licenses, re-started working with CITMA (the Cuban Ministry of Science, Technology and the Environment) and other Cuban associations dedicated to environmental issues to take groups to Cuba. Carlos Varela's December 2009 trip was less highly publicized in the media. Yet Varela met with five members of Congress, lunched with a White House official, and participated in interviews with news people and panel discussions. "Songs," he said, "can feed the souls of men and women, even the ones who create embargos and wars. For if they listen to the music, it will help them make the world a better place."[46]

Academic exchanges have increased in number. Marazul Charters sent 3,000 people to Cuba in non-family travel in 2009, not a large number but an increase over the 2,000 in 2008.[47] Visas are being granted to Cuban scholars.[48] New student exchange programs have been created at the University of Havana and other institutions, while ongoing programs continue.

Despite these signs of progress, there is much evidence that Obama clings to the old logic of his predecessors' policies regarding Cuba. The Obama administration continues to enforce the sanctions program through the collection of fines for violations of the regulations.[49] Licenses are still denied to academics and those hoping to further cultural exchange. Some 30 U.S. doctors were prevented from participating in the International Congress on Orthopedics in Havana in September 2009 and in October, the trip by the New York Philharmonic was cancelled because the orchestra's sponsors did not get licenses. Visas are denied, including a request of the President of the Cuban National Assembly.[50]

Money is still directed to civil society in Cuba with hopes of changing the regime. Obama continues to emphasize selected people-to-people contacts that differ little from what the Bush administration pursued. Technology remains a pivotal element in the traditional vision, including telephones and the internet. The President's response to Cuban blogger Yoani Sanchez's questions is a surprising example (not only for his expressed disinterest in talking with President Raúl Castro but in wondering which U.S. citizens would have such privileged communication). In 2009, the U.S. State Department Bureau of Educational and Cultural Affairs program included Cuban students in the call for scholarships. The process was administered by the U.S. Interests Section in Havana, selecting 28 students for one-year programs in U.S. schools. A State Department official noted disappointment that Cuban students were not, in the end, allowed to participate,[51] a truly puzzling response since U.S. students have little opportunity to travel to Cuba.

The slow-motion changes have been unsatisfactory for many who expected more and more quickly. A letter was sent to President Obama in July 2009 by 18 policy and education groups, insisting that the regulations on travel to Cuba for academic and educational purposes be eased and urging Cuban authorities to grant exit visas to students and scholars accepted by U.S. academic institutions. A national day of lobbying on Capitol Hill was scheduled for September 20, 2009, sponsored by the Washington Office on Latin America and the Latin American Working Group, two DC policy advocacy organizations. In February 2010, another new bill restoring travel was introduced in Congress.

One month later, Wayne Smith of ECDET acted on these concerns, organizing a one-day conference with speakers to address the range of arguments encouraging the Obama administration to eliminate restrictions on academic and educational travel. The report of the conference summarizes the arguments and some of the issues raised, including the tendencies within the State Department, Obama's expectations for Cuba, the granting of the right to travel to Cuban-Americans but not others, the means for making change (executive decision-making), who benefits from opening educational travel, and the costs of doing nothing for regional policy. The nature of educational programs and the possibility of conducting research in Cuba were topics raised in discussion at the conference ("you cannot do real research in Cuba," said the president of the Association for the Study of the Cuba Economy).[52] Nobel Prize winner Peter Agre (Chemistry 2003) referred to his November 2009 American Association for the Advancement of Science (AAAS) trip to look at Cuban research in the sciences. While the AAAS report is forthcoming, Agre commented positively on interest and the reputations of Cuban scientists.[53] The comments of Stanley Katz of Princeton, head of the ACLS/SSRC joint Cuba Program, appeared several days later, agreeing that there are limits in conducting research in Cuba, just as there were in the Soviet Union, China, Vietnam, or Eastern Europe before 1989. "Needless to say, there are comparable limitations on research, especially social science research, in many countries around the world," but there are opportunities as well.[54]

On January 14, 2011, with little advance notice or fanfare and responding to a variety of voices asking for an end to restrictions, the Obama administration announced changes in the regulations for travel to Cuba. Framed in terms of an ongoing commitment to the embargo and "efforts to reach out to the Cuban people in support of their desire to freely determine their country's future," the Presidential Directive creates a new general license authority for travel by students, full and part-time faculty, and staff of accredited universities, eliminating the 10-week length restriction for study in Cuba, reviving the possibility of consortia-organized programs, and permitting U.S. universities to open accounts in Cuban financial institutions. A general license permits sponsoring and remuneration of Cuban scholars for teaching or research activities in a U.S. academic institution, while specific licenses can be requested for university-sponsored seminars, conferences, and workshops, and importantly, by organizations that sponsor people-to-people (non-academic) educational travel.[55] Widely applauded and published quickly in the Federal Register, the roll back of Bush-era restrictions does not eliminate all of the deeply rooted impediments to academic and cultural exchanges.[56] The specific licenses needed for conferencing and people-to-people educational travel must be reviewed and decided by OFAC on a case-by-case basis, the vagaries of the visa process are not resolved, and key congressional Cuban-American foreign policy actors are among those who oppose the changes. The rather sudden expansion of old and new spaces for cooperation is a promising step.

Given Obama realities and the questions they pose, what possibilities exist for further development of academic and cultural cooperation? There are several, each drawing upon arguments raised in this essay and organized in terms of actors and agencies. First is the possibility of more foundation support for individual and institutional collaborations. Already recognized as having been crucial in the development and maintenance of research and the institutional development of Cuban Studies over the years, the major foundations were affected by the prohibitions and restrictions enacted under the Bush administration. Current economic hard times notwithstanding, the commitments already made by the Ford Foundation, Christopher Reynolds Foundation, and others might be expanded. Such expansion depends, of course, on research directions, interests, and needs that come from foundation planning.

Second, professional organizations have been, and will be, important for taking advantage of the new spaces that are growing within the terrain charted by the Obama administration's implementation of the sanctions against Cuba. The granting of visas means that organizations and associations might expect to have Cuban participants in upcoming professional meetings. Continued use of third countries as the site of international meetings will allow Cuban members to maintain their presence in their scholarly and professional organizations until it is clear that visa politics have abated. In this way, collegial relations can be maintained through the exchange of ideas and research results. Relations of cooperation are always much more than an instrumental transfer of information, of course, and face-to-face encounters accomplish what electronic conversations cannot.

Third, the spread and deepening of university-to-university relations in areas of mutual interest and development seems a likely tendency, one that requires initiative and the two-way exchange of high-level institutional officials impeded by exclusionary U.S. visa practices. In some ways, increasing cooperation through institutional relations will allow for decentering of decision-making that has become centralized in the attempt to control researchers and research dynamics. The new general license for U.S. universities promises more autonomy though there is no reason to expect that universities will act outside the boundaries of state policies. Decentering will allow more flexibility and timeliness in making decisions, encouraging collaborations and empirical research. As much as the ECDET lawsuit needed courageous and committed university administrators, institutional collaborations require energy and vision.

Fourth, student travel to Cuba can easily be expanded and study abroad reconceived to include programs for Cuban students in the United States. Current regulatory changes that lift the U.S. restrictions on academic freedom in the design and implementation of study abroad programs in Cuba facilitate recuperation and growth, and study abroad for Cubans in the United States could be organized in the same fashion as programs in Cuba: on the basis of institutions, study abroad offices, and interested faculty. The U.S. Interests Section would not be involved in calling for participants or building new programs (the Cuban Interests Section in Washington does not do such work with regard to programs in Cuba). Existing studies of student learning in study abroad programs would be useful for thinking about how and where to improve study abroad.

Fifth, as in the past, individual research projects should remain on the agenda of all who are interested in serious study of Cuba, the United States, Cuba–U.S. relations, or as the sciences suggest, in themes and projects whose scholarly significance is not moored in the geographies and politics of bilaterality. The wide reach and generational depth of Cuban Studies—both as a paradigmatic community (à la Thomas Kuhn) and a project of knowledge—suggests that strengths and flexibility exist, especially in the humanities, cultural studies, history, and work on social issues; this is probably a more accurate description of scholarship that does not require systematic field work. The uneven development of exchanges in recent years is seen in the younger generation of Cuban scholars who have had little access to research, study, travel, and conversation with U.S. scholars and institutions, while U.S. scholars have not, in general, suffered the same exclusion from Cuba. With an easing of the visa wars it is possible to see a recuperation of conference activities in the United States, short and longer stays at U.S. universities and research centers, and greater access to library and other resources that may not be available digitally. It would also be useful to consider issues of inequality in research collaborations, more broadly.

Research collaborations will also be increasingly feasible if U.S. visa and licensing restrictions are relaxed and Cuban authorizations of projects and travel are easier to achieve. It is hard to imagine a situation worse than the 2003–08 retrenchment with its many costs. Even small changes can render qualitatively better opportunities when efforts at every stage of a collaborative project bear fruit in a timely fashion. Given the stresses and strains of creating and sustaining collaborative projects, the requisite dosage of patience must be mixed with enthusiasm and drive.

Sixth, re-establishing the people-to-people travel transactions authorization restores a fundamental but only informal right to non-institutional learning for the U.S. people, facilitating the encounters that allow culture to be studied, as well as consumed, in exchange. People-to-people resurfaced in the discourse of U.S. Cuba policy before Obama's January 2011 directive reinstated it; the Congressional Notification regarding Economic Support Funds for the Cuba Project's and Obama's intended $20 million obligation for 2010 identifies $2.5 million for "people-to-people" linkages with others in the region. Perhaps academics, performers, students, and all those interested in ending all restrictions on travel and learning will be able to make the case to Obama, Clinton, U.S. Assistant Secretary of State for Western Hemisphere Affairs Arturo Valenzuela, or Congress, that who decides which "people" talk to which others matters tremendously.

Ultimately, with some or all of the forward movements listed above, academic, educational, and cultural relations will lose the patina of suspicion that has motivated excesses of control, politicization of personal, professional, and collegial relations, and the misreading and misuse of knowledge. One U.S. scholar suggests that one goal of ongoing struggles to make change might be state sponsorship of academic exchanges.[57] More prudent in the present context would be imagining how state policy making can become informed about Cuba and about academic and educational realities and needs that reflect the transnational dynamics of modern life.

Alternative Futures

It is useful to think of the terrain of academic and cultural cooperation as a complex and living network of relational spaces created by individuals and groups, institutions and nongovernmental organizations (and commercial interests, too), and the Cuban and U.S. states. The engagements that regulate and animate the exchanges that map this terrain in 2010 are part of a politics of knowledge production—in Cuban Studies, in the study of U.S.–Cuba relations, and in other fields of scientific and cultural activity. In contrast to other areas of U.S.–Cuba cooperation, the agents of academic, educational, and cultural exchange are directly engaged in creating, maintaining, and enriching relations, reflecting seriously about what we have produced, how, and with what lessons for the future would be useful for thinking about alternatives.

An alternative future might thus begin with the cooperation needed to reflect together on what we have constructed, how, and how well. Such reflection would start with the collecting of new histories of academic, educational, and cultural relations. The resilience of relationships developed since 1959 is impressive as are the expansion and accomplishments of collaborations, and it would be useful to place them in a theoretical framework.

An alternative future might find its reflections in the problems, issues, and successes in the various spaces of cooperation. Since collaborations develop differently (according to actors, subject matter, and objectives), problems, issues, and successes are surely different, too. For example, recognizing the importance of professional groups, such as the Latin American Studies Association, and considering its Section for Scholarly Relations with Cuba created in the late 1990s, thinking critically about LASA and the Cuba Section might lead to new initiatives. Along this line, one possible future might be the creation of a new and independent organization for Cuban Studies. Increased autonomy would be a benefit of such a professional association, though practical issues such as funding, focus, and membership suggest that the replacement of one set of politics for another is a possibility. And Cuban Studies is only one of many spaces for cultural and educational exchange.

Given the politicized realities of exchange and collaboration, there is much work to be done. As the *Retreat from Reason* report argued, one area of work is the creation of a clearinghouse that would provide information useful to those interested in research and educational and cultural exchanges. Such a clearinghouse could provide advice and best practices with regard to licensing, creating study abroad programs, facilitating permissions for research, and organizing cultural events. Improving the informational infrastructure is another area where cooperation can move to a new and qualitatively better level. Innovative mechanisms for sharing resources—new books, articles, reports as well as the research collaborations and cultural exchanges underway—might facilitate multiple goals. Efforts to share information and resources have been made in the past. The website of the LASA Section for Scholarly Relations with Cuba could be staked out more formally as a space for cooperation, one that is available to its members and others interested in joining the community of scholars that the Section embraces. In its desire to represent Cuban and U.S. scholars' needs and interests, much more could be done with the existing space.

In the end, the alternative future might be one where the very issues of the production of knowledge are discussed and debated. Such reflection entails locating ourselves in terms of agencies, powers, and paradigmatic constructions of individual and collective scholarly labors. Debate might begin with an assessment of past and present production, move on to discuss how production can be enhanced, and then further engage matters of context, constraints, and conflicts. Much as critical methodologies demand new research relationships, our own collaborations—whether academic, educational, or cultural—might benefit from a better understanding of the power of cooperation.

Notes

1 Sheryl L. Lutjens, "National Security, the State, and the Politics of U.S.–Cuba Educational Exchange," *Latin American Perspectives* 33, no. 5 (September 2006): 58–80.

2 The author would like to thank the participants in the Taller de Autores, Revista Temas, February 11, 2010, for their suggestions and comments. The focus on academics as subjects in U.S–Cuba relations was the argument presented in much briefer format at "The United States and Cuba: Rethinking Reengagement" Conference, University of North Carolina, Chapel Hill, September 26–27, 2008.

3 For example, Sergio Jorge Pastrana, "Las ciencias en Cuba y los Estados Unidos: Encuentros y desencuentros," in *Mirar El Niágara: Huellas culturales entre Cuba y los Estados Unidos,* ed. Rafael Hernández (Havana: Centro de Investigación y Desarrollo de la Cultura Cubana Juan Marinello, 2000), 217–244; Milagros Martínez, "Academic Exchange between Cuba and the United States: A Brief Overview," *Latin American Perspectives* 33, no. 5 (September 2006): 29–42; Kimberly Stanton, ed., *Retreat from Reason: U.S.–Cuba Academic Exchange and the Bush Administration* (Washington DC: Latin America Working Group Education Fund, September 2006); and Skye Stephenson, "International Educational Flows between the United States and Cuba (1959–2005): Policy Winds and Exchange Flows," *Cuban Studies* 37 (2006): 122–155.

4 Relations between the peoples of Cuba and the United States are part of prerevolutionary colonial and neocolonial histories, carried out through movements (travel, exile, migration) and the forging of cultural connections, from the plastic arts to music, dance, and more. Rafael Hernández, ed., *Mirar El Niágara: Huellas culturales entre Cuba y los Estados Unidos* (Havana: Centro de Investigación y Desarrollo de la Cultura Cubana Juan Marinello, 2000) and Louis A. Pérez, Jr., *Cuba and the United States: Ties of Singular Intimacy,* 3rd edn. (University of Georgia Press, 2003). "Scientific collaboration and academic relations" initiated in the 19th century flourished into the 20th century; Cubans studied in the United States, collaborations in medicine, archaeology, and the physical and biological sciences were augmented with those of engineering, business, and agronomy; and U.S. academics did field work in Cuba. Stanton, *Retreat from Reason,* 12.

5 In 1961, the United States ended diplomatic relations, constructed the total embargo of trade with Cuba (already available under the Trading with the Enemy Act of 1917), and prohibited travel to Cuba by U.S. citizens as contrary to the foreign policy and national security interests of the United States.

6 Stephenson, "International Educational Flows," 128–130, and Stanton, *Retreat from Reason,* 17.

7 Martínez, "Academic Exchange" and Stephenson, "International Educational Flows."

8 Ned Sublette, *The Missing Cuban Musicians* (Albuquerque, NM: Cuba Research & Analysis Group, June 24, 2004), 6–11.

9 The activities of the City University of New York (CUNY)–Caribbean Exchange Program began, Boston College Graduate School of Social Work launched its long-lived fieldwork course in Cuba, and many Cuban scholars were supported for research in the United States. Jean Weisman, "LASA and Travel to Cuba: Academic Exchanges, Lobbying and Civil Disobedience," *LASA Forum* (Winter 1996): 17–21 and Stephenson, "International Educational Flows." Presidents have exercised discretion in implementing the exclusion of party members and Cuban government officials and employees, associated with the use of Section 212(f) of the Immigration and Nationalities Act of

1952 that grants the Secretary of State the authority to exclude those whose entry is considered "detrimental to the interests of the United States."

10 Stanton, *Retreat from Reason*.

11 Sublette, "The Missing Cuban Musicians," 12.

12 Malia Everette, "Interview with Malia Everette, Director of Global Exchange's Reality Tours," Adventure Destinations, http://adventures.bootsnall.com/articles/05-02/interview-with-malia-everette-director-of-global-exchanges-reality-tours.html.

13 Stanton, *Retreat from Reason*, 24, and see the report of the 1998 AAAS study, Part IV, Elise Muñoz, *The Right to Travel: The Effect of Travel Restrictions on Scientific Collaboration between American and Cuban Scientists* (Washington DC: American Association for the Advancement of Science (AAAS), 1998).

14 Fuller explained, "By forbidden research terrains I am referring to whole areas of possible investigation, which may be geographically, intellectually or institutionally defined, where social scientists are strongly discouraged from pursuing research." Linda Fuller, "Fieldwork in Forbidden Terrain: The U.S. State and the Case of Cuba," *The American Sociologist* 19 (June 1988): 99–120.

15 Fuller, "Fieldwork in Forbidden Terrain," 101.

16 Fuller, "Fieldwork in Forbidden Terrain," 103.

17 The Ford Foundation has long been an advocate for U.S.–Cuban academic exchange, joined by the John D. and Catherine T. MacArthur Foundation, Arca, General Service, and the Christopher Reynolds Foundation. Reynolds helped establish the ACLS/SSRC Working Group on Cuba in 1996. Stanton, *Retreat from Reason*, 21–22.

18 Stanton, *Retreat from Reason*, 51.

19 With the exception of the 1985 LASA Congress when the denial of visas to part of the Cuban delegation resulted in a collective decision not to attend. In 1998, more than 70 Cubans traveled to the Chicago Congress, there were 99 Cubans in Miami for the 2000 Congress, and in September 2001, 87 Cubans were at the Washington DC Congress.

20 The first semester program in the University of Havana opened in 2000, run by the Institute for Study Abroad (IFSA). In 2004, there were eight semester study abroad programs at the University of Havana. Stephenson, "International Educational Flows," 142.

21 See the David Rockefeller Center for Latin American Studies' website: http://www.drclas.harvard.edu/cuba/program.

22 When two Cubans invited to the American Philosophical Association meetings were denied visas, the plan for continuing the meetings in Havana was born. The conference was organized with the University of Havana, the Institute of Philosophy, and the Cuban Society for Philosophical Research. See the website of the Radical Philosophers Association, http://www.radicalphilosophy.org/.

23 The *Seminarios* germinated from the denial of visas for Cuban academics to attend the Comparative and International Education Society meetings in the United States in the early 1990s. The first *Seminario* was held in 1994 in Havana, hosted by the Association of Cuban Educators and the Ministry of Education.

24 There has also been co-authored work, such as the collaboration of Manuel Moreno Fraginals, Stanley L. Engerman, and Herbert S. Klein in *The American Historical Review* in the early 1980s or, more recently, the study of Havana undertaken by Dick Cluster and Rafael Hernández, and the history of U.S.–Cuba relations by Esteban Morales Domínguez and Gary Prevost. See Louis A. Pérez, Jr., "The Cuban Revolution Twenty-Five Years Later: A Survey of Sources, Scholarship, and State of the Literature," in *Cuba: Twenty-Five Years of Revolution, 1959–1984*, ed. Sandor Halebsky and John M. Kirk (New York: Praeger Publishers, 1985), 393–412; Dick Cluster and Rafael Hernández, *The History of Havana* (New York: Palgrave Macmillan, 2008); and Esteban Morales

Domínguez and Gary Prevost, *United States–Cuba Relations: A Critical History* (Lanham, MD: Lexington Books, 2008).

25 Pérez, Jr., "The Cuban Revolution Twenty-Five Years Later"; Jorge I. Domínguez, "Twenty-Five Years of Cuban Studies," *Cuban Studies* (1995): 3–26; and Damián J. Fernández, *Cuban Studies since the Revolution* (University Press of Florida, 1992).

26 Sublette, "The Missing Cuban Musicians," 14.

27 Stanton, *Retreat from Reason*, 33–39. Called the Powell Commission after its chair, U.S. Secretary of State Colin Powell, the Commission's report recommended $59 million in spending to promote transition in Cuba. A second report was prepared under Secretary of State Condoleezza Rice in 2006.

28 Lorena Barberia, "Cuba Visas Memorandum," David Rockefeller Center for Latin American Studies, Harvard University, December 5, 2005.

29 Robin D. Moore, *Music & Revolution: Cultural Change in Socialist Cuba* (Berkeley: University of California Press, 2006), 252.

30 In March 2003 when chilling first became visible, only 64 of the 103 who requested visas for the Dallas congress received them. None of the 65 applications was approved for participation in Las Vegas in 2004 and the blanket denial was repeated when 58 requests were denied for San Juan, Puerto Rico on the grounds of Section 212(f) (and one for other reasons).

31 John M. Broder, "Cuban Performers are Granted Asylum," *The New York Times*, July 22, 2005, http://www.nytimes.com/2005/07/22/national/22asylum.html.

32 Vilma Ponce Suárez and Nuria Pérez Matos, *Impact of the Blockade of the United States Government on Cuban Libraries: 2001–2005; Final Report* (Havana: José Martí National Library Scientific Council, 2006), 90, 114–115.

33 United States Government Accountability Office, *Foreign Assistance: U.S. Democracy Assistance for Cuba Needs Better Management and Oversight, November 2006* (Washington DC: GAO, 2006).

34 Mark P. Sullivan, *Cuba: U.S. Restrictions on Travel and Remittances* (Washington DC: Congressional Research Service, 7-5700, October 16, 2009), 15.

35 David Epstein, "Usted No Puede Ir," *Inside Higher Education*, July 7, 2006. http://www.insidehighered.com/news/2006/07/07/cuba.

36 Marguerite Rose Jimenez, "'About that Trip to Cuba ...': When the FBI Came Calling," *CounterPunch*, October 24, 2006. http://www.counterpunch.org/jimenez10242006.html.

37 The project began in 2003 as a bi-national working group with three participants from Cuba and three from the United States. The project's report was presented to several publics in Washington DC in September 2006, including academics in a meeting at George Washington University and then in the House and the Senate in the days that followed.

38 Sergio Jorge Pastrana and Michael T. Clegg, "Editorial: U.S.–Cuban Scientific Relations," *Science* 322 (October 17, 2008): 345.

39 New York Civil Liberties Union, "State Department Ends Unconstitutional Exclusion of Blacklisted Scholars from U.S.," January 20, 2010. http://www.nyclu.org/news/state-department-ends-unconstitutional-exclusion-of-blacklisted-scholars-us. Other hints suggesting a new perspective on exchange relations include President Obama's comments to university students in Turkey in September 2009 and Assistant Secretary of State Valenzuela's comments in Spain in early 2010.

40 Esteban Israel, "Cuban Americans Filling Planes to Homeland," Reuters.com, March 24, 2010.

41 David Adams, "Cracks Open in U.S. Wall around Cuba," Tampabay.com, August 13, 2009. http://www.tampabaycom/newsworld/us-allowing-more-people-to-travel-to-cuba/1027528.

42   Thomas Omedstad, "For Cuba, Eased U.S. Travel Ban Could Open the Door to Cultural Exchanges," *U.S. News & World Report*, posted March 30, 2009, http://www.usnews.com/news/world/articles/2009/0330/for-cuba-eased-us-travel-ban-could-open-the-door-to-cultural-exchanges.html.

43   Jay Reeves, "Cuban Actors Do Shakespeare in Alabama," US Cuba Normalization, August 5, 2009. http://uscubanormalization.blogspot.com2009/08cuban-actors-do-shakespeare-in-alabama.html.

44   Adams, "Cracks Open in U.S. Wall around Cuba."

45   Salim Lamrani, "Cuba Faces Obama Administration Contradictions," *ZNet*, October 25, 2009. http://www.zcommunications.org/contents/76457/print.

46   Center for Democracy in the Americas, "While the U.S. and Cuban Governments Squabble, Varela Wows Washington," *Cuba Central*, December 21, 2009. http://cubacentral.wordpresss.com/209/1221/while-the-u-s-and-cuban-governments...+more311.

47   Bob Guild, Marazul Charters, personal communication, February 22, 2010.

48   Guillermo Ferriol Molina attended the Convention of the National Lawyers Guild in Seattle in October 2009, for example; Antón Arrufat, Abelardo Estorino, Eduardo Arocha and others were invited to participate in a University of Miami event on the theater of the 1960s in March 2010; Rafael Hernández was visiting professor at the University of Texas, Austin, in Fall Semester 2009; and Harvard hosted 15 visiting Cuban scholars in 2009–10.

49   Lamrani, "Cuba Faces Obama Administration Contradictions."

50   Lamrani, "Cuba Faces Obama Administration Contradictions."

51   Wilfredo Cancio Isla, "U.S. Scholarships Get Cuban College Students Expelled," *Miami Herald*, September 4, 2009. http://www.miamiherald.com/581/story/1217104.html.

52   Paul Basken, "Push for Student Exchanges with Cuba Hits Obstacles, Both Political and Academic," *The Chronicle of Higher Education*, March 9, 2010, accessed at the ECDET website, http://www.ecdet.org.

53   Basken, "Push for Student Exchanges."

54   Stan Katz, "Travel to Cuba," *Brainstorm, The Chronicle of Higher Education*, March 11, 2010. http://chroniclecareers.com/blogPost/Travel-to-Cuba/21747.

55   Other changes include general licenses for limited non-family remittances to Cuban individuals and organizations and for religious travel. See "Changes for Cuba and America," The White House Blog, January 14, 2011, http://www.whitehouse.gov/blog/2011/01/14/changes-america-cuba and Department of the Treasury, Office of Foreign Assets Control, 31 CFR Part 515, "Cuban Assets Control Regulations," *Federal Register* 76, no. 19, January 28, 2011, pp. 5072–5078. Expectations for significant change in the rules for travel were high in early fall 2010, either through congressional decisions or the executive branch; action on either front was stymied by the November elections.

56   See "Support for 2011 Presidential Directive," Center for Democracy in the Americas, http://democracyinamericas.org/support-2011-presidential-directive and an official Cuban response, David Vázquez Abella, "Johana Tablada, 'Obama podría ir más allá en sus políticas hacia cuba,'" *Cuba Debate*, January 21, 2011, http://www.cubadebate.cu/noticias/2011/01/21/tablada-obama-tiene-prerrogativas-para-ir-mas-alla.

57   Franklin W. Knight, "Academic Exchanges between the U.S. and Cuba," in *9 Ways for US to Talk to Cuba and for Cuba to Talk to US* (Washington DC: Center for Democracy in the Americas, 2009), 77–84.

14

ACADEMIC DIPLOMACY

CULTURAL EXCHANGE BETWEEN CUBA AND THE UNITED STATES

MILAGROS MARTÍNEZ REINOSA

Within the history of conflict between Cuba and the United States, there exist some spaces of collaboration that, while little publicized, are sustained and growing. Cultural exchange between the two countries has overcome disagreements and ruptures. In the face of the tension which has characterized relations between Havana and Washington, the participants in these interchanges have been, to a great extent, the true diplomats representing each nation in the other: the channels for necessary and fertile people-to-people contact.

Although the umbrella term "cultural exchange" has tended to cover many sorts of contact among scholars, scientists, artists, intellectuals, and figures from the worlds of sports and religion in Cuba and the United States, each of these has had its own dynamic. A retrospective look at the entire spectrum yields a favorable balance, but hindsight requires more. There is a need for critical reflection, and for those involved in these activities to contribute to the preservation of what has been achieved and explore options for the future.

It would be impossible to cover the wide range of exchanges in a single article. This essay, therefore, is limited to analyzing academic exchange, predominantly in the area of the social sciences, emphasizing developments since the end of the Cold War. The essay does not attempt to exhaust this subject nor to recount such bilateral academic collaboration in detail, but rather to identify significant periods that are themselves closely linked to the evolution of the conflict between the two nations and, to some degree, linked with the origin and consolidation of the discipline of Cuban Studies in the United States.[1]

Academic exchange has not been able to isolate itself from the various political junctures and contexts through which the Cuba–U.S. conflict has passed. Nonetheless, it has survived and reproduced itself as a sort of "academic diplomacy."[2] It has had its own life and established a network of formal and informal relationships reflecting well upon the institutions involved, which share the desire and goodwill that relations between the two countries should be based on peace and mutual respect.

History of Academic Exchange

The history of cultural contact between Cuba and the United States is an extensive one, stimulated by economic, commercial, and political ties between close geographic neighbors. Formal collaboration between Cuban and North American scientists in the fields of zoology, botany, meteorology, and epidemiology date from the mid-nineteenth century and have continued ever since at varying levels of intensity.

The triumph of the Cuban Revolution on January 1, 1959 was a turning point in the two countries' traditional relations. As has been well-explored elsewhere, Washington's breaking of diplomatic ties on January 3, 1961 severely limited the number and reach of academic exchanges. This sharp drop did not, however, mean a complete disappearance. Some ties were maintained, if in irregular fashion.

The early 1960s saw a gradual increase in research about Cuba in the United States, but not until the next decade were the first contacts between scholars in the two countries established. From then on, such collaboration grew, especially in the humanities and social sciences,[3] which have always occupied a more privileged space.[4] Thus a difficult but constructive process of academic exchange has unfolded, replete with snags, distrust, and prejudices from both sides, but fruitful on balance.[5]

In the 1970s, Cuban Studies in the United States began to constitute a recognized specialty within the larger Latin American Studies field, with systematized research, specialized research centers, and established sources of funds.[6] This critical mass gave momentum and shape to most of the proposals for collaboration and cooperation with Cuba. As formulated by North American and Cuban-American academics, these proposals had, as their common element, an interest in deepening study and research about the Island.

The pioneers in creating academic ties with Cuba were those of U.S. origin. Not until the 1978 dialogue and establishment of travel to Cuba by the Cuban community abroad did Cuban academics resident in the United States play a significant role. In that latter process, special credit is due to the late Lourdes Casal of Rutgers University and to the Institute of Cuban Studies, directed by María Cristina Herrera and involving many Cuban-American scholars.[7]

In that context, the Jimmy Carter administration's initial inclination to reduce tensions between the two countries, and the consequent opening of interest sections in Washington and Havana on September 1, 1977 favored greater *détente* in bilateral relations. This in turn eased the acquisition of visas, books, and information for academic exchange. Only one month later, seven Cuba scholars traveled to the northern shore, the first group to do so since 1959. The trip was organized by Franklin Knight, Riordan Roett, Alfred Stepan, and Margaret Crahan of Johns Hopkins, Yale, and the City University of New York. Among the many meetings and encounters during their trip, the Cubans' participation in the seventh international congress of the Latin American Studies Association (LASA)[8] in Houston stands out—the first LASA congress to include a Cuban group. Thus, 1977 signaled the beginning of more formal exchanges.

Contacts continued to grow, and Carter administration measures to ease travel to the Island made academic interchange easier as well. This period has been called the "fruitful years." The situation changed abruptly with the conservative trend in U.S. society and the triumph of the Republican right that placed Ronald Reagan in the White House. Among the most onerous of Reagan-era measures that made visits to the United States by Cuban academics and intellectuals extremely difficult was an October 4, 1985 presidential proclamation that prohibited the granting of visas to Cuban government officials or employees, or members of the Cuban Communist Party. Bilateral encounters had to move to Mexico, Canada, and Cuba itself.[9]

In spite of the difficulties during Reagan's two terms—the "hard years"—the 1980s also saw intensified interest within North American academia in research on Cuba, as well as in carrying out joint work with Cuban colleagues. The creation of new centers and study programs broke the monopoly established in the 1970s by Cuban émigrés, which was now challenged by North American and European scholars. According to Nelson Valdés, leadership in the field of Cuban Studies, which had until then belonged to the Center for Latin American Studies at the University of Pittsburgh, was contested by the establishment of the Cuba Program at Johns Hopkins University and another at the University of Miami (with close ties to Radio Martí and full support of the Reagan administration) under the direction of Jaime Suchliki. Pittsburgh's professed impartiality now faced the liberal approach of Hopkins and the conservative one of Miami.

A significant development during this decade was the consolidation of relations with and through LASA. In 1988, thanks to the success of initiatives and pressures that the LASA leadership brought to bear on U.S. authorities, a revival of academic exchanges began. From then on, there was something of a commitment on the part of the State Department to approve visas for Cuban academics and intellectuals invited to LASA's annual congress and other activities.

The Post-Cold War Period: "Golden Years" or Years of Consolidation

When the George H. W. Bush administration took possession of the White House in January 1989, the doors to the United States opened once again for Cuban professors and researchers. An additional factor in this change of policy, besides the work done by LASA, was that of a group of U.S. university professors and administrators who petitioned for exchange with the Island. In that context,

Cubans attended LASA's 1989 congress in Miami. Another important event took place in Halifax, Canada, with a conference commemorating the 30th anniversary of the Cuban Revolution, co-sponsored by Canadian universities and Cuban research institutions, with broad participation by specialists from Cuba and from the United States.

During this period, many ties begun in the 1970s and maintained despite increasing difficulties in the 1980s were consolidated. New Cuban Studies institutions emerged, such as the Cuba Program of Georgetown University, as well as new teaching and research programs in a range of colleges and universities which included Cuba as an object of study. Among the latter, the most noteworthy included American University, the University of Chicago, Harvard University, CUNY, Yale, and the University of California system. Groups of scholars associated with think tanks such as the Institute for Policy Studies, Woodrow Wilson International Center for Scholars, Inter-American Dialogue, and Council on Foreign Relations also renewed contacts with their counterparts on the Island.

During the final days of the intense presidential election campaign of 1992— and in a desperate and ultimately unsuccessful move to win re-election—then-President Bush signed the Cuban Democracy Act, better known as the Torricelli Act, in a Miami ceremony on October 23, 1992. Labeled by some as Bush's political testament, this law tightened the embargo but also introduced the controversial "Track II" which sought to make political use of academic exchange as a means for subverting Cuba's domestic order. This was an attempt to extrapolate from what had happened in the former USSR and the socialist bloc to what might be made to happen in Cuba.

When Bill Clinton won the November 1992 election, the Torricelli Act became a key instrument in Washington's policy toward the Island. The situation grew still more difficult when Richard Nuccio, an academic named as the President's advisor on Cuban affairs, threw himself body and soul into the implementation of the Track II policy—a logical occurrence given that he had been the policy's author when he served as a staff member for the Democratic then-Congressman from New Jersey, Robert Torricelli.

The Cuban government response was quick to emerge. In summary, Cuba assumed a defensive stance in the face of the announcement and implementation of such a policy—a position that many U.S. academics could not understand and, as a result, criticized. Although exchanges continued, they grew more difficult.

In this new era, each proposal submitted by U.S. academic colleagues faced tighter control and analysis on the Island. In response, a group of U.S. counterparts declared, in a rather absolute manner, that the exchanges had fallen under control of Cuban administrators.[10] A proliferation of activities and initiatives from universities and think tanks intensified the renewal of academic debate about Cuba in the United States, which obliged the Cuban side to act more cautiously under the premise that exchanges must have an institutional, orderly, and coherent character.

During this period, in 1996, the Fifth Plenary of the Central Committee of the Cuban Communist Party (Spanish initials PCC) took place. One of its results was an examination of the research focus and projects of a number of Cuban research centers that collaborated with U.S. counterparts—including the Center for the Study of the Americas (CEA), the Center for the Study of Political Alternatives (CEAP), and the Center for the Study of the United States (CESEU).

U.S. experts, programs, and groups maintaining their Cuban ties during the 1990s included those in such universities as Johns Hopkins, Indiana University, CUNY, University of Pittsburgh, and American University. Others re-emerged or arose for the first time in institutions such as Florida International University, the Caribbean Studies Association, Depaul University, Indiana State, and several in the California state system. Also, some organizations within the Cuban-American community—whose profiles included cultural, academic, and social activities—contributed to stimulating more interaction; among these was the Institute of Cuban Studies. On the Island, the Cuban Writers' and Artists' Union (UNEAC) and other non-governmental organizations also participated actively and creatively in the increasing dynamic exchange.

Despite the criticisms, it must be recognized that the above-mentioned Cuban authorities worked very efficiently, because a near-majority of the proposed projects did in fact materialize. Only a few were rejected, but the rejections produced a sense of unease in the academic communities of both countries, especially that of the United States, where Cuban reservations about what seemed to be purely academic proposals were hard to comprehend. The U.S. academics did not understand that the distrust engendered in Cuba by these projects was almost never directed at those proposing to carry them out, but rather at the uses to which their results might be put.

In this period, despite tense moments in which Cuba reacted like a country under siege, considerable advances in the realm of exchanges were made. New milestones in academic cooperation included the opening or consolidation of ties between the Island and a new generation of Cuban-American professors and researchers. Among these stand out Lisandro Pérez, then director of the Cuban Research Institute at FIU; Iraida López, of CUNY's Cuba–Caribbean program; and Alejandro Portes, then chair of the sociology department at Johns Hopkins University. Products of this collaboration, both institutional and individual, included growing numbers of articles, books, and events.

It is worth noting that the Cuban government takes a very critical view of the role that the most conservative sectors of the Cuban-American community have historically played in the design and implementation of Washington's policy toward the Island. To a degree, this has tainted relations with Cuban-American academics, because Cuban official circles have seen them as more likely to mix academic affairs with actions that might to some degree affect the internal dynamic of Cuban society. In the long run, this has rendered decisions about entry permits and authorization of events, research projects, and joint publications involving Cuban-born academics more complicated, with long delays in the response times. In some cases authorization has been categorically denied, or denied for prolonged or indefinite periods of time.

In February 1996, the Cuban government shot down two small airplanes belonging to the organization Brothers to the Rescue which had penetrated Cuban airspace without permission. As a result, the already difficult relations between Cuba and the United States grew extremely tense, with negative results for the academic exchange. From March to December 1996, Cuban professors and researchers invited to participate in activities at U.S. institutions were generally denied visas (though some ups and downs were visible over this time).

Nonetheless, in the 1990s considered as a whole—a decade during which a movement in favor of modifying the two countries' relations had grown up within the United States—there was a marked increase in collaboration, both in absolute numbers and in terms of the reach of actions proposed by U.S. academic circles to stimulate intellectual cooperation with Cuba.[11] Also in this period the sources of foundation financing widened, which made it more possible to carry out research projects, book publication, and attendance by Cuban academics and intellectuals at international events, especially in the United States. Alongside the Ford Foundation, which has played a major role in these efforts, the John D. and Catherine T. MacArthur Foundation emerged as an important funder, eventually displacing the former from its traditional leading role, and became the main sponsor of academic projects with institutions on the Island. Also notable were donations by ARCA Foundation, General Services, and the Christopher Reynolds Foundation.

Another consequence of the foregoing was the opening of new exchange programs. Established ones like those of Johns Hopkins (without a doubt, the most important and prestigious for many years) and the University of Pittsburgh continued, now joined by Georgetown's Caribbean Project, Harvard's David Rockefeller Center for Latin American Studies, CUNY's Bildner Center Cuba Project, and programs at FIU and Tulane.

Similarly, the number of programs for U.S. undergraduates to study in Cuba grew markedly,[12] while other structures designed to facilitate exchanges emerged as well, such as the Cuba program of the Social Science Research Council (SSRC). New channels of communication were established with other institutions such as DePaul University, St. Thomas University in Minnesota, the University of North Carolina in Chapel Hill, the University of Iowa, and the cooperative program of the California State Universities in San Bernardino, Los Angeles, and Pomona (Cal State Polytechnic). Other institutions outside of universities, such as the Center of Marine Conservation and the Smithsonian Institution, became involved in academic collaboration between the two countries, while the participation of Cuba in additional conferences of professional organizations grew. Examples include the International Studies Associations, American Studies Association, American Political Science Association, International American Studies Association,

American Sociological Association, American Public Health Association, American Neurological Association, American Library Association, American Physical Society, and the American Chemical Society.

Several associations made special efforts to offer greater space for Cuban and North American scholars to carry out joint research in areas of common interest. LASA has perhaps been the most outstanding example, and the high number of Cuban academics who have systematically participated in its international meetings as a forum for interchange of ideas, discussion, and analysis is most significant. A growing tendency within this sphere has been the emphasis on research related to artistic and literary culture.

In terms of Cuban participation, the 1990s saw a healthy diversification of the institutions on the Island engaging in joint research and teaching projects. Alongside the pioneers—CESEU, CEA, and CEAP—came more active participation by the Faculty of Philosophy and History at the University of Havana, the Center for Study of the International Economy (CIEI), the Center for the Study of the Cuban Economy (CEEC), the Center for Psychology and Sociology Research (CIPS), the Higher Institute of International Relations (ISRI), the Institute of History, the Cuban National Archive, the José Antonio Echeverría Higher Polytechnic Institute (CUJAE)—especially its Faculty of Architecture—and the Pedro Kourí Institute of Tropical Medicine (IPK).

A subsequent Clinton administration initiative also proved very interesting. Within the Track II strategy, a presidential statement of January 5, 1999 announced that licenses would be granted to U.S. universities for undergraduate student visits to Cuba. This move revived a form of exchange which had previously existed only during the Carter years. The change led to short stays, particularly in the University of Havana but also in other Cuban academic and cultural institutions, which meant a notable increase in travel by young U.S. college students to Cuba.[13]

As a result of the experiences acquired through these visits, and given the success of the courses taught, some U.S. academic institutions proposed the creation of longer-term study-in-Cuba programs. These ranged from summer study to full semester programs which granted credits transferable to U.S. institutions. Thus in September 2000 began the program of the then-named Cooperative Programs for the Americas (COPA), later evolving into the Institute for Study Abroad, based at Butler University. A year earlier, in February 1999, the first Cuban visit of the cruise ship Universe Explorer had occurred, as part of the Semester At Sea program administered by the Institute for Shipboard Education, based at that time at the University of Pittsburgh.

A marker of the maturity of U.S.–Cuba exchanges was, without a doubt, the convening of two important conferences on the 40th anniversaries of the Bay of Pigs invasion and the Missile Crisis, in March 2001 and October 2002, respectively, organized by the National Security Archive of George Washington University together with a group of Cuban academic institutions. Fidel Castro Ruz himself attended these conferences, greatly appreciating their internal dynamics as well as making his own specific comments about the historical events being analyzed. As President of the Council of State and Council of Ministers, Castro voiced his approval of this type of forum. These events also made possible the declassification of a not-insignificant number of secret Cuban government documents related to the Bay of Pigs invasion and the Missile Crisis.

Previous conferences on the second subject had taken place in Moscow in 1989, Antigua in 1991, and Havana in 1992. A conference on the Bay of Pigs also occurred in Georgia (United States) in April 1996, although academics resident on the Island were not present.

Another reflection of consolidation was the meeting of the American Association of State Colleges and Universities (AASCU) in September 2003, announced as the first meeting of top university administrators from Cuba and the United States. Nearly 20 university presidents and leaders of this important association attended.

The Bush Years: Frozen Relations

The electoral victory of George W. Bush and his arrival in the White House in 2001 brought about an abrupt shift in academic cooperation between the two countries. Serious new obstacles began to impose evident limits on the development of cultural and scientific-technical exchange. The difficulties sharpened after the events of September 11, a situation which continued until January 2009. The main reflections of the change were stricter application of existing regulations and the implementation of new policies that drastically limited the granting of Treasury Department licenses for various kinds of programs requested by U.S. institutions as well as the State Department's granting of visas to Cuban academics and intellectuals.

Alongside these limits came more obstacles to the search for financing for exchange programs. These difficulties had appeared toward the end of the 1990s, when foundation administrators and specialists became frustrated with the delays in implementation of the projects they were already financing and with barriers inside Cuba that impeded the creation of new projects that were proposed.

This led to the freezing of some of the most prestigious and serious Cuba research programs in U.S. academic institutions, or sometimes to their dissolution. As a result, serious and objective representations of Cuban reality grew scarcer, a tendency exacerbated by the creation in May 1999 of the Institute for Cuban and Cuban-American Studies at the University of Miami, which soon received millions of dollars in financial support from the Bush administration to carry out far-from-orthodox activities in the area of research on Cuba.

The Bush administration's actions also affected the semester study programs. In May 2003, the license of the Council for International Education Exchange was suspended, and the program closed three months later. Contradictorily, President Bush and his then-Secretary of State Colin Powell had often spoken out about the importance of U.S. citizens studying abroad. Bush himself, after September 11, had declared:

> By studying foreign cultures and languages and living abroad, we gain a better understanding of the many similarities that we share and learn to respect our differences. The relationships that are formed between individuals from different countries as part of international education programs and exchanges can also foster goodwill that develops into vibrant, mutually beneficial partnerships among nations.[14]

In May 2004, the report of the Powell Commission (the so-called Commission for Assistance to a Free Cuba)[15] included a group of recommendations that implied serious new limitations for the development of academic, cultural, and scientific-technical exchange. After these measures were publicly announced in June, the semester study programs closed for good, with the exception of those operating on a solely university-to-university basis. Thus, of the nine study programs established at the University of Havana, only three remained when the 2004–05 academic year began, and the mechanisms of such programs (among the most successful experiences in the realm of academic exchange) had to be redesigned so as to continue working with those few institutions still licensed under U.S. rules. It is worth repeating that the programs created in the fall of 2000 were so successful that according to the Institute of International Education—in spite of a complete lack of commercial advertising, except the irresistible lure of exploring the forbidden—Cuba became one of the top 15 study-abroad destinations of U.S. students between 2003 and 2004, and the number of young people involved grew by 45 percent compared with the previous year.

The young people from the United States who have participated in these programs have turned out to be not only excellent students but also sensitive human beings who have connected with the Cuban people in an experience truly classifiable as "people-to-people" diplomacy. Their stay in Cuba has allowed many U.S. citizens to get to know the realities of our country. They see how Cuba, unjustly included by the State Department in all its lists of fearsome countries, receives them in friendly fashion. They are surprised when they encounter neither resentment nor rejection, and even more so to find that young Cubans have much more in common with them than they have imagined. Daily life experience teaches them to see, understand, and accept the distinctness of Cuba and Cuban-ness. They return to the United States with greater, deeper, and more real knowledge of the Island, free of the manipulated media treatment which floods the northern neighbor. These student-explorers, who came in search of answers, found some and left with new questions. Their inquiries—both those completed and those deepened by fresh food for thought—also reflect the passion and the content of the teaching of their professors in the United States, who have introduced them to the subject of Cuba, and of the academic programs designed at the University of Havana.

On September 28, 2004, when it seemed the gamut of imaginable obstacles might have been run, the United States Interests Section officially informed the University of Havana of the denial of 64 visa applications that Cuban academics and intellectuals had submitted since May in order to participate in the 25th international LASA congress scheduled for October 7–9 in Las Vegas, Nevada. The interests section claimed to be applying Section 212(f) of the U.S. Immigration and Naturalization Law. Though some had expected this decision, it caused surprise and indignation among many members of the Cuban and U.S. academic communities. This was one of the most widely publicized measures, perhaps because of its absurdity. During the Las Vegas congress, members of one panel affected by the absence of their Cuban colleagues had the worthy idea of placing 64 chairs facing their table, each bearing the name of a Cuban scholar whose visa had been denied. They devoted their session to discussing this unheard-of violation of rights.

The 2004 meeting stood in sharp contrast to the tendency during the second half of the 1990s, when many Cubans attended LASA, and especially in contrast to the years from 2000 on. In Miami in 2000, 97 attended; in Washington in 2001, 82 did so. Starting with the 2003 congress in Dallas, Cuban participation began to be restricted by visa problems; 67 Cubans attended that year, while more than 15 were barred from entering the United States.

Consistent with these actions, only five University of Havana (UH) professors were able to fulfill invitations from U.S. institutions to teach courses, give talks, or do research. Continuing the hostile policy, from October 2004 to January 2009 only ten visas were granted to professors from the nearly 300-year-old institution, a clear reflection of the impediments facing any normal process of exchange. Before that period, an average of 25 UH professors per month left for visits to the United States.

In this context—responding to, among other things, the January 2006 denial of all 54 visas requested by Cuban academics and intellectuals to attend the 26th annual LASA congress in San Juan, Puerto Rico—LASA decided in June of that year to move its next conference from Boston to Montreal. The organization further expressed its intention that, as long as Cuban attendance at these events could not be guaranteed, they would always be held outside the United States. The LASA visa denials were among the best-known of the lengthening chain of obstacles the Bush administration placed in the way of normal development of academic exchange.

Obama: Between the Unknown and the Mistrusted

On November 4, 2008 Barack Hussein Obama won the U.S. presidential election and became the nation's 45th president and its first African-American one. Largely unknown—his trajectory through the Washington political world was not the typical one of those who gain the Oval Office—he awakened questions and expectations around the world. The young black Democrat was viewed as a breath of fresh air, one who surely deserved the benefit of the doubt.[16]

For the academic communities of Cuba and the United States, the coming of the "Obama era" meant not just a possibility but a certainty that academic, scientific-technical, and cultural exchange would return to normal. This judgment was influenced by the symbolic fact of the president-elect having himself been a university professor,[17] which implied that he would show a certain sensitivity toward the issue and would have the ability to judge it intelligently and creatively. Hopes for a return to ties established since the 1970s rose again, after these had been so battered during the eight years of George W. Bush.[18]

The Bush administration's legacy was pathetic. One of the worst consequences of the lack of contact was the resultant decline of mutual relationships between those working on Cuban topics on either side of the Florida Straits. Between 2001 and 2009, only the LASA congresses in Montreal and Rio de Janeiro and the conference on "The Measure of a Revolution: Cuba, 1959–2009" at Queens University in Canada allowed re-encounters and the chance to meet the new faces entering the field of Cuban Studies.

The worst mark that Bush left on academic exchange (one that began during the Clinton years with the implementation of Track II) was the mistrust in Cuban governmental circles and also in some academic areas, producing refusals to join any effort originating in the United States. It can be said that such sectors see collaboration as a window for political subversion carried out by the U.S. government against Cuba, a focal point for internal subversion, especially in the case of contact with Cuban social scientists.

In official circles on the Island, while McCain's defeat was certainly nothing to regret, Obama's triumph did not produce any euphoria. The political and administrative apparatus was immune to the mass media seduction generated by the young black politician. In Cuba, some officials labeled the phenomenon of enchantment with the new White House tenant as "dizzy over Obama." Cuban government predictions suggested that Obama's policy, though it might well include tactical adjustments, would continue to pursue the strategic objective of all U.S. administrations since 1959: to induce transformations in the Cuban political system and topple the Revolution. The prediction was that Obama would bring a redesign of Track II, new and different, in which the controversial people-to-people contact would be accompanied by greater use of communications media in the forms of e-mail, web pages, and cellular phones—services to which a considerable portion of the Island's academics, intellectuals, artists, scientists, and students have access.

A good share (or perhaps even a majority) of the Cuban academic, scientific-technical, and cultural community thought that with Obama would come changes in the direction of eliminating the restrictions imposed by Bush, or at least a rapid growth in flexibility that would permit a steady flow of contact with U.S. colleagues. This was also the dominant perception among their U.S. counterparts, most of whom not only voted for Obama but were also actively involved in his presidential campaign. This explains why, after the electoral victory, a great number of proposal for interchanges began to arrive in Cuba, a true avalanche rolling out from U.S. institutions. Cuban responses did not come as quickly as might initially have been hoped. Rather, initiatives from the United States have been examined with great prudence, both by the Cuban counterparts and by the various institutions making up the structure that decides whether such proposals will be carried out or not.

One significant event in these new times was a September 20, 2009 meeting between Bisa Williams, acting Deputy Assistant Secretary of State with responsibility for Central America, the Caribbean, and Cuba in the Bureau of Western Hemisphere Affairs, and the University of Havana academic community. Never before had such a high-ranking U.S. government official visited an institution of higher education, except when ex-President Jimmy Carter was received in the UH's Aula Magna during his Cuban visit of May 2002. The Williams meeting delivered nothing very novel to the group that met with her. The central goal of the encounter was to explore the viability of continuing a program of fellowships begun in fall 2008. This system for leadership training, especially designed for the Island's youth, involved direct application (electronically or in person) to the U.S. Interests Section in Cuba, a procedure that irritated official Cuban circles, who characterized it as counter-revolutionary activity. Williams' proposal was for the contact to run by way of direct procedures between the Cuban academic institution and the State Department. This was judged unacceptable because this is not the fashion in which the nearly 300-year-old Cuban institution arranges fellowships in any other country in the world. Obviously, the United States was not going to be an exception.

The controversial fellowship program, along with the meeting with Ms. Williams, chilled the atmosphere. If this was the type of initiative that would come from the Obama administration, nothing good could be expected from his term. There was an expectation of new actions that, whether overtly or covertly, would try to further and further politicize academic exchange.

In analyzing this situation, it cannot be forgotten that Cuba faces a particular historical circumstance within a complex and sometimes unpredictable international environment. Change on the Island—which is going through a political-institutional transformation that, among other things, has meant the naming of quite a number of new ministers and working groups—must balance continuity of political leadership, governability of the system and revival of the economy while, at the same time, attracting and inspiring the new generations born with the Revolution.

In spite of the above-mentioned expectations for a wider opening from the new U.S. administration, little has changed in Obama's first year. U.S. restrictions remain the same as they were in August 2004. Some say that in the academic arena it is just more of the same, or perhaps even worse because of the fellowship program already described. The Cuban government feels that this path taken by the new administration represents an acceptance of the pressures from the influential conservative minority among emigrants from the Island, based primarily in Miami, who make up the Cuban-American lobby in Congress.

Congruently with the Island's foreign policy, Cuban institutions are consolidating relationships with counterparts in other countries within the framework of special programs with Venezuela and China and, to a lesser degree, Bolivia and Ecuador. Russia and some African countries also are entering the scene in force. All of these programs include participation by a significant number of academics and intellectuals, many of whom had previously been actively involved in academic ties with the United States and, to some extent, become discouraged; they prefer the security of this new type of activity to the obstacles, uncertainties, and even suspicions that accompany initiatives with universities, think tanks, and associations in the United States.

Nonetheless, a more objective assessment would surely reveal a slight and slow-moving improvement[19] because almost all the visas requested by Cuban academics are being granted.[20] More licenses are also being awarded to U.S. institutions seeking to carry out exchanges in Cuba, and OFAC's response to requests to continue or open new semester study programs has also been positive, resulting in a notable growth in this form of academic exchange. As of January 2010, 14 such programs are in operation, and 25 agreements between U.S. and Cuban universities have been signed, 21 of these by the University of Havana. In 2009, 12 semester study programs took place, with a total of 97 students. In the spring 2010 semester, groups from 9 universities are present, totaling 73 students.

In scientific-technical and cultural institutions, more concrete results are visible. In 2009, there was a discreet advance in normalization of relations to do with environmental issues. Particularly notable was the signing in October 2009 of a marine sciences project for the study of dolphins and sharks, as well as the development of joint activities in meteorology.[21] According to political scientist Phil Peters, an analyst at the Lexington Institute and expert in the bilateral conflict, maritime affairs are the best starting point, because proximity and ocean currents mean that our two countries effectively live within the same environment. Also, environmental protection is one of the areas identified by the Cuban government as offering greater opportunity for joint work by scholars and scientists of both countries,[22] an opinion shared by the U.S. academic community,[23] which judges that greater scientific exchange would allow Cuba to prepare itself for the potentially devastating arrival of masses of U.S. tourists. The Island tends to be viewed as a kind of ecological sanctuary.

In November 2009, an important delegation of eight U.S. scientists visited Cuba, including Peter Agre, a 2003 Nobel laureate in chemistry and president of the American Association for the Advancement of Science (AAAS). Agre met with leading teams of Cuban scientists at the University of Havana and the Cuban Academy of Sciences, and with Fidel Castro Díaz-Balart, a nuclear physicist and one of the leaders of the Cuban scientific community. The AAAS group issued a statement which stressed that, at the same time the visit occurred, scientists in both Cuba and the United States were pressing for greater bilateral cooperation. The statement concluded with the opinion that, under the Obama administration, there was a favorable opportunity for developing such contacts.

The realm of culture is also going through a revitalization period. We might mention the September 2009 *Concierto por la Paz*, visits to Cuba by leading film actors such as Benicio del Toro and Sean Penn (the latter of whom conducted the first interview with Cuban President Raúl Castro, published in *The Nation* magazine), the presence of Omara Portuondo to collect a prize in the 2009 Latin Grammy award ceremonies, and visits and tours by Cuban singers and bands in the United States: Buena Fe, Charanga Habanera, and Los Van Van. Nonetheless, all is not milk and honey.

What is going on in the realm of visual arts is quite interesting. Since the 1990s, U.S. collectors have felt particularly attracted by Cuban art. The presence of gallery owners, museum directors, and collectors at the May 2009 Havana Biennial was seen as a foretaste of what might be coming soon.[24]

In sports, the outlook is not very promising. Cuba does not offer the conditions for anything similar to the famous ping-pong diplomacy that favored *détente* between the United States and China. The sport propitious to playing this role between Cuba and the United States would be baseball. However, the Cuban government views the constant wooing of the Island's baseball players (and boxers) as a form or provocation and attack, a "talent theft." This has generated and maintained a chilly atmosphere in the sports arena, marked by a high level of political symbolism which makes it difficult for the Cuban side to design and implement joint activities.

To sum up, during the first year of the Obama administration, there has not been much forward movement. Cuban academics now view the situation with more hope than faith, even if their U.S. and Cuban-American colleagues believe that things may change definitively in the course of 2010. It must be remembered that even though most of the Obama administration's actions, including those of the first few months of 2010, point to a new era of intensification of conflict, a year is a short time—only 365 days out of the total 1,461 that make up a presidential term. So, in spite of the realism or pessimism that springs from recent events, we should not ignore the benefit of the doubt.

Now, at the end of the first decade of the twenty-first century, there are almost no important academic exchange projects on the scale of a good many of those carried out in the previous 20 years—with the exception of the semester study programs, the activities carried out with Harvard University and the University of Alabama, the LASA congresses and associated events, and the Social Science Research Council program now being revived. The absence of large-scale initiatives has created a perception of immobility, lethargy, or inertia, with serious negative results on the field of Cuban Studies in the United States, and on that of studies about the United States within Cuba.

A Look Back

What have been the most salient actions in these 33 years of exchange? We will point out some of those that have left their mark along this lengthy road, which could serve us as paradigms for the design of future academic collaboration projects.

One research project worthy of note is that on the Role of the Agriculture Sector in Cuba's Integration into the Global Economy and its Future Economic Structures: Implications for Florida and U.S. Agriculture, coordinated by the CIEI and the International Agricultural Trade and Development Center (IATCD), the Food and Resource Economics Department, and the Institute of Food and Agricultural Sciences (all at the University of Florida, Gainesville), whose results won a research prize in June 1999 from the U.S. Department of Agriculture.

In the area of academic conferences we must recognize the LASA congresses; the working group of the Social Science Research Council and the Cuban Academy of Sciences, established in 1996; the First Conference on Cuban and Cuban-American Studies, organized by Florida International University's Institute for Cuban Studies in October 1997; the above-mentioned conferences on "The Bay of Pigs: 40 Years Later" and "The Missile Crisis: 40 Years Later," held in Havana in March 2001 and October 2002, respectively; the National Association of Cuban Economists (ANEC) events on Globalization, and the above-cited Halifax conference that took place in Canada in 1989.

The program of the Institute for Cuban Studies at FIU, which between 1991 and 2003 sponsored visits and research projects, and its fellowship program with the Rockefeller Foundation, the first to allow Cuban academics and intellectuals to stay for four-month periods in Miami;[25] and the visiting scholars program of the David Rockefeller Center for Latin American Studies (DRCLAS) at Harvard University, initiated in fall 1998, which has brought nearly 60 researchers from various Cuban institutions, also deserve mention. Among the latter's most significant results are the book *The Cuban Economy at the Start of the Twenty-First Century*, co-edited by professors Jorge I. Domínguez and Lorena G. Barberia of Harvard University and Dr Omar Everleny Pérez Villanueva, a professor and researcher at the CEEC.

In addition, the academic exchanges with members of the Center for Defense Information (CDI) which began in June 1993 were important and certainly groundbreaking in that they involved members of the U.S. military forces—including five-star generals, even though they were retired ones. From 1993 to November 2004, this organization organized nine different trips to Cuba.

Recommendations: An Inventory of Cooperation and Specific Proposals

What can be done to change the current situation which, if it continues, would lead to the near-extinction of academic exchange? The academic communities of both countries must become active—as they were in previous years—in rebuilding the space within which exchange has taken place in the first year of the Obama administration, characterized by alternation between mistrust and the unknown. They must relearn how to talk to each other, how to argue in the face of opposing or differing opinions. Dialogue is harder than resorting to pre-established discourses. Receptivity, the credibility of an idea, has a lot to do with the individual who carries it, with their academic reputation, language, individual way of speaking even about minor things, and human communication they manage to achieve. The potential for academic exchange lies in that substrate, that underground current, that historical and cultural interconnection whose psychological dimension connecting the two peoples has survived and works in favor of communication.

The Cuban academy could be more pro-active in creating proposals and taking the initiative. It is important to think about the need to diversify content, spaces, and participants—to allow younger people more room for action. More specifically, it is important to work on designing and proposing projects which may lead to formal events, to return to the old practice of carrying out small workshops between Cuban and U.S. academics on the Island, and to have research trips and publications. This is important especially in the areas in which collaboration is a necessity: the bilateral conflict, analysis from a legal perspective of the case of the Cuban Five, mutual familiarization with the two legal systems, international migration and Cuban communities in the United States, environmental problems and climate change, policies for confronting natural disasters, the historical study of events shared by both countries, collaboration in public health, public policy, social policy, education, urban and social development problems, research in natural and physical sciences, research on the marine world, nanotechnology, biomedicine, natural and traditional medicine, and theoretical approaches to physics and chemistry. Whenever justified, it is important to also consider participation by officials of both governments, which was previously quite common.

Another proposal from the Cuban side—perhaps from the University of Havana with support by other institutions such as the Ministry of Culture, Ministry of Science, Technology & Environment, and Ministry of Public Health—would be the creation of a catalogue of summer courses or short two-to-three-week courses which would offer credit to U.S. undergraduate and graduate students and which would be particularly focused on Cuban history past and present. (Obviously, this would require a change in the U.S. government's current restrictions on academic exchange.) The design of these courses could include attendance at other lectures or conferences and visits to places of interest.

Academics on both shores must work toward achieving meritorious results from such projects, which would lead the Cuban government to view them as more useful. Some projects could even serve as spaces for informal dialogue, for new contacts between non-institutional actors of both governments.[26]

Colleagues in the United States, especially those classified as academic leaders (presidents and ex-presidents of LASA, professors well known for their work on Cuba) could mobilize themselves to organize meetings with high Obama administration officials who have input into the formulation and implementation of policies toward Cuba. Such efforts should have the express goal of pressing for, at the least, the expected changes which would make academic exchange easier.

Toward that end, they could explore the viability of organizing work sessions in the U.S. Congress, along the lines of the Academic Freedom Focus Group session on U.S/Cuba Academic Freedom Restrictions, sponsored by African-American congresswoman Barbara Lee (D-CA), which met on November 19, 2004, or the meetings of LASA's executive committee or its Cuba Section. Another option would be to rethink the viability of organizing a new work trip to Cuba by the American Association of State Colleges and Universities similar to the above-mentioned one of September 7–12, 2003, which included a workshop on academic exchange between the two countries.

To improve the atmosphere, actions soliciting a change in U.S. policy toward Cuba would also be advisable. We can point to the impact in Cuba of the letter to the U.S. president signed by 12 retired high-ranking officers, including Barry McCaffrey (the "anti-drug czar" of the Clinton administration) and Lawrence B. Wilkerson (Colin Powell's ex-chief-of-staff) in April 2009. Also the July 2009 letter of the National Association of Foreign Studies Abroad and 17 other U.S. academic organizations requesting Obama to end the restrictions on academic travel to Cuba, ease the granting of visas to Cubans, and offer more opportunities for U.S. undergraduate and graduate students to travel to the Island; and the declaration by experts, ex-politicians, and university deans who requested the White House to immediately eliminate restrictions on academic, cultural, sports, and scientific exchange with Cuba, in a March 8, 2010 conference organized by the Center for International Politics and the Emergency Coalition to Defend Educational Travel.

The point is to catalyze a movement within the United States—connected to the Cuban academy—that includes well-known academics as well as younger ones and students who have participated in past semester study programs in Cuba and that can reach the levels of government where Washington's policy toward the island is designed and executed. It is also necessary to make creative use of the spaces offered by LASA. One interesting option might be a Workshop on Academic Exchange sponsored by LASA's Cuba Section in the context of the next international congress of that organization in Toronto, Canada from October 6–8, 2010.

All such actions in the United States and Cuba need to be publicized as widely as possible. The goal is to show the lengths the academies of both countries have gone to modify Washington's current policies toward the Island and to eliminate the restrictions of May 2004. If some changes are won, Cuban officials might perceive a positive achievement toward *détente* in bilateral relations. In such a context, academics on both sides could get to know each other better and reduce the climate of mistrust and the unknown that characterizes the current period. It is within the terrain of exchange that social scientists and intellectuals of the two nations can and must make their political contribution, undermine current stereotypes, and contribute to a process of reflection which would favor coexistence, as long as this includes respect for the rights of sovereignty and independence which the Cuban people justly demand.

Notes

1　On the origin and development of academic exchange between Cuba and the United States, see Milagros Martínez Reinosa, "Academic Exchanges between Cuba and the United States. A Brief Overview," *Latin American Perspectives,* 33, no. 5 (September 2006): 29–42.

2　The term "academic diplomacy," which characterizes that nature and evolution of scientific-technical and cultural exchange between Cuba and the United States since its origins in the 1970s, was coined by the author of this work.

3　Despite important and sustained exchange in the cultural realm, especially in music, film, and visual arts, little research has been done in this area. We can point to institutions such as the Cuban Institute of Music, the Cuban Institute of Cinematic Art and Industry, and the Ludwig Foundation. In the field of literary culture, the work of Casa de Las Américas stands out.

4　For a description of the origin and development of academic exchange in the natural sciences, see Sergio Jorge Pastrana, "Las ciencias en Cuba y los Estados Unidos: Encuentros y desencuentros", in *Mirar el Niágara: huellas culturales entre Cuba y los Estados Unidos,* ed. Rafael Hernández, Centro de Investigación y Desarrollo de la Cultura Cubana Juan Marinello, Havana, 2000.

5　"The obstacles come from both countries. In the climate within which relations between the two countries take place, both have found reasons to limit the issuance of visas and exit permits, preventing travel by academics of many countries. Over time, which of the two governments has acted most restrictively has varied." Lisandro Pérez, "Estamos dispuestos al diálogo y a la colaboración intelectual," *Espacio Laical* (March 2009): 55–56.

6　Andrés Zaldívar, "Algunas consideraciones sobre el surgimiento y desarrollo de la cubanología," reseach report, DISEU-UH, Havana, 1984.

7　Lisandro Pérez, "Estamos dispuestos al diálogo."

8　On the role of LASA in academic exchange, see Milagros Martínez Reinosa, "Una pelea cubana contra los demonios," *LASA Forum,* 37, no. 4 (Fall 2006): 6–8.

9　Jane Franklin, *Cuba and the United States. A Chronological History,* New York, Ocean Press, 1997.

10　Skye Stephenson, "Policy Winds and Exchange Flows: Forty Years of US–Cuban Academic and Educational Exchanges," paper presented at the 15th LASA congress, Las Vegas, 2004.

11　Jean Weisman, "The Impact of the U.S. Academic Community on U.S.–Cuba Relations," paper prepared for the conference "Cuba–United States, 40 Years of Confrontation: Perspectives for the 21st Century," Havana, December 16–18, 1999.

12　Rachel Price and Eric Hershberg, "Expanding U.S.–Cuban Scholarly Relations. The ACLS/SSRC Working Group on Cuba," *LASA Forum,* 30, no. 2 (1999): 11–13.

13　Beth McMurtrie, "Study-Abroad Numbers Rise," *The Chronicle of Higher Education,* Washington DC, 2005, available at http://chronicle.com.

14　George W. Bush, *Securing America's Future: Global Education for a Global Age,* Report of the Strategic Task Force on Education Abroad, November 2003.

15　For detailed information on the members and work of the Commission for Assistance to a Free Cuba, also known as the Powell Commission, see Kimberly Stanton, ed.,

Retreat from Reason: U.S.–Cuban Academic Relations and the Bush Administration, Latin America Working Group Education Fund, Washington DC, 2006, based on works by Carlos Alzugaray, Soraya Castro, Sheryl Lutjens, Milagros Martínez, Louis A. Pérez and Kimberly Stanton.

16 Aurelio Alonso, "Para una evaluación de los 100 días del mandato de Obama," *Entorno. Boletín Especial de Cubarte,* Havana, April 2009.

17 After Woodrow Wilson, Obama is the second United States president who previously worked as a university professor. He taught at the Law School of the University of Chicago.

18 On the negative effects seen in academic exchange between Cuba and the United States after George W. Bush's victory, see Kimberly Stanton, *Retreat from Reason*.

19 OFAC's delays in granting licenses and the delays in the Cuban side's response if the U.S. institutions' proposals were accepted made the process of academic exchange so slow that, in some cases, proposed projects have been canceled.

20 In the case of the University of Havana, only eleven visas were requested in 2009, and ten were granted. The eleventh was not classified as denied, because the request was not filed in time to match State Department requirements (three months in advance of the travel). Also, since the final quarter of 2009, the duration of the visas granted has usually been limited to only one month.

21 "Declaraciones de José Rodríguez Chamero, director de relaciones internacionales del Ministerio de Ciencia, Tecnología y Medio Ambiente," ANSA, October 8, 2009.

22 See the speech by Cuba's Minister of Foreign Relations, Bruno Rodríguez, to the United Nations General Assembly in October 2009.

23 David Guggenheim, U.S. marine scientist and president of the NGO 1planet1ocean, in a conference he organized jointly with the University of Havana's Centro de Investigaciones Marinas, said, "We need dialogue in order to talk, at a minimum, about urgent matters. However one looks at it, everything points to need for collaboration and communication, rather than continuing Cold War policies." Israel Esteban, Reuters, October 27, 2009.

24 "Pamela Ruiz, a U.S. curator who maintains an office in Havana, estimated that there were at least a thousand U.S. visitors on the exhibit grounds and 95% of them wanted to buy art, or were curators, or worked for NGOs." Israel Esteban, Reuters, May 16, 2009.

25 See Lisandro Pérez, "Estamos dispuestos al diálogo."

26 Such contacts form part of a broader proposal presented at LASA 2007 by Phillip Brenner about the process of normalization of relations between Cuba and the United States. For a deeper examination see Phillip Brenner, "A Puerta Cerrada: Re-thinking the Impasse in US–Cuban Relations," paper presented at the 28th LASA Congress, Montreal, September 2007.

INDEX